Strategic Brand Management

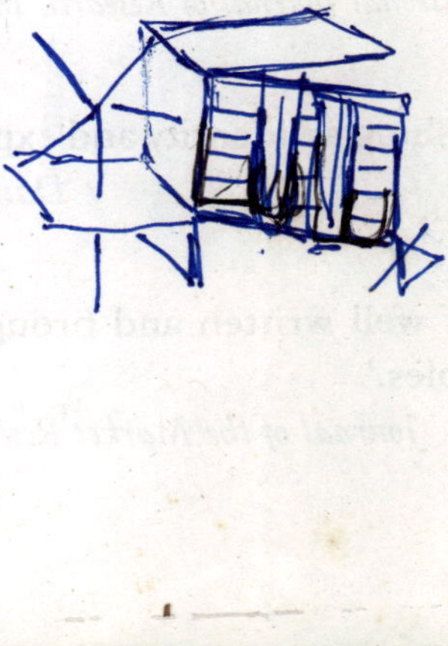

'A real thought provoker for marketing and business people. *Strategic Brand Management* is an essential tool to develop strong marketing strategy.'

P Desaulles, Vice President, Du Pont de Nemours Europe

'In the sports business, branding has become complex. This book is very useful at CEO level.

J F Gautier, President and CEO, Salomon Worldwide

'A solid contribution written with depth and insight. I recommend it to all those who desire a further understanding of the various dimensions of brand management.'

David A. Aaker, University of California at Berkeley, and author of *Managing Brand Equity.*

'After reading Kapferer's book, you'll never again think of a brand as just a name. Several exciting new ideas and perspectives on brand building are offered that have been absent from our literature.'

Philip Kotler, Northwestern University

'The best book on brands yet. It is an invaluable reference for designers, marketing and brand managers.'

Design Magazine

'The treatment of brand-product strategies, brand extensions and financial evaluations are also strengths of the book.'

Journal of Marketing

'A "think book". It deals with the very essence and culture of branding.'

International Journal of Research in Marketing

'An authoritative analysis about establishing an identity and exploiting it.'

Daily Telegraph

'A full and highly informative text ... well written and brought to life through numerous appropriate examples.'

Journal of the Market Research Society

Strategic Brand Management

Creating and Sustaining Brand Equity Long Term

Second Edition

JEAN-NOËL KAPFERER

KOGAN PAGE

First South Asian Edition 2000
Reprinted 2003
Reprinted 2005
Reprinted 2006
Reprinted 2007
Reprinted 2008

Kogan Page India Private Limited
4737/23 Ansari Road
Daryaganj
New Delhi 110 002.

This edition is for sale in India, Bangladesh, Nepal, Pakistan and Sri Lanka only. Not for export elsewhere.

ISBN 81-7554-109-1

Published by Vinod Vasishtha for Kogan Page India Private Limited, 4737/23 Ansari Road, Daryaganj, New Delhi - 110 002 and printed & bound at Raj Press, R-3 Inderpuri, New Delhi - 110 012.

Contents

List of figures

List of tables

Preface to the second edition

COMPETITION IN BRAND HOSTILE ENVIRONMENTS

There is a world of difference separating the first edition of this book and the second. Since the previous edition, an economic crisis has heralded the end for several well-known brand names and undermined quite a few 'certainties' and 'dogmas'. Competition has become tougher, mainly from distributors' own brands, discount stores and 'superstores', also known as – and the term speaks for itself – 'category killers'. Distributors' own brands are no longer confined simply to the mass market, but also exist in the industrial goods sector or intra-industry trade. On top of this, discount products from the same retailers or from neighbouring hard discounters are in competition with the distributor's own brand.

This explains why we have created three new chapters centred on the life span of brands. The first of these chapters reminds us that what is commonly known as brand equity (brand awareness, brand image) is not inevitably adding value in the consumer's mind. The second analyses in depth the factors which dictate the life expectancy of brands and their weaknesses. The third examines the processes which lead us to say that certain brands have grown old: are they beyond remedy? Is it possible to rejuvenate declining brands?

Alongside this, firm concentration on brand management has continued, as has the resulting reorganisation of companies' brand portfolios. This explains why the chapter dedicated to multibrand strategies has been expanded. On the other hand, a chapter concentrating on the problems linked to the transferring and merging of brands, which is becoming more and more frequent, has been added. Certain lessons concerning the factors which make strategic change a success or a failure can be learnt from the numerous concrete examples which exist today.

Furthermore, new sectors of activity such as industrial firms, banks and insurance companies, service industries, retailers selling their own brands and producers of luxury products have discovered, and have had to put into practice, brand management strategies in order to stay competitive. To respond to this we have increased the coverage of these markets. To date the debate about brands has been restricted too narrowly to consumer food products, despite the fact that it is not representative of all markets. Readers interested specifically in other markets may refer to the subject index to verify that a place has been given to those sectors which are economically more important than the traditional food sector.

From now on, the Europeanisation of brands, which started in 1990, will become a regular activity for most companies. This debate has lost its ideological character as those in favour of voluntary globalisation have learnt from their experiences. Today, questions abound about how to put a globalisation strategy into place. How can homogeneity be created where before there was only heterogeneity? Here again the chapter has been expanded and improved. Finally, particular attention has been paid to the problem of accounting principles related to brands. This has become necessary as the debate, arising from the possibility of including brands on the balance sheet, has intensified.

This new edition, which is nearly twice as long as its predecessor, confirms the importance of this area and the transformations which it is undergoing. We have also given more space to the most important advances which have been made in brand research such as the effect of the typicality of the product on brand extensions, the economic analysis of the success factors of distributors' own brands, etc.

To conclude, this new edition owes a great deal to all the companies who, having consulted me on a particular aspect of the management of their brands, have enabled me to reflect more on the subject and to question certain assumptions. I must also thank my doctoral students, as the findings of the research for their theses on the behaviour of brands are included throughout this new edition.

Finally, I must mention the support that I have received from HEC, the leading business school in France, and perhaps tomorrow in the whole of Europe.

Introduction

THE BIG BRAND CHALLENGE

The 1980s marked a turning point in the conception of brands. Management came to realise that the principal asset of a company was in fact its brand names. Several articles in both the American and European press dealt with the discovery of 'brand equity', or the financial value of the brand. In fact, the emergence of brands in activities which previously had resisted or were foreign to such concepts (industry, banking, the service sector, etc) vouched for the new importance of brands. This is confirmed by the importance that so many distributors place on the promotion of their own brands.

For decades the value of a company was measured in terms of its buildings and land, and then its tangible assets (plant and equipment). It is only recently that we have realised that its real value lies outside the business itself, in the minds of potential buyers. In July 1990, the buyer of Adidas summarised his reasons in one sentence: after Coca-Cola and Marlboro, Adidas was the best known brand in the world.

The truth contained in what many observers took simply to be a clever remark has become increasingly apparent since 1985. In a wave of mergers and acquisitions, triggered by attempts to take up advantageous positions in the future single European market, market transactions pushed prices way above what could have been expected. For example, Nestlé bought Rowntree for almost three times its stock market value and 26 times its earnings. The Buitoni group was sold for 35 times its earnings. Until then, prices had been on a scale of eight to ten times the earnings of the bought-out company.

Paradoxically, what justified these prices and these new standards was invisible, appearing nowhere in the companies' balance sheets. The only assets displayed on corporate balance sheets were fixed, tangible ones, such as machinery and inventory. There was no mention of the brands for which buyers offered sums much greater than the net value of the assets. The acquiring companies generally posted this extra value or goodwill in their consolidated accounts. The actual object of these gigantic financial cash flows and the relentless takeovers which preceded them was invisible, intangible and unwritten.

What changed in the course of the 1980s was awareness. Before, in a takeover bid, merger or acquisition, the buyer acquired a pasta manufacturer, a chocolate manufacturer or a producer of microwave ovens or abrasives. Now companies want to buy Buitoni, Rowntree (that is, KitKat, After Eight), Moulinex or Norton. The strength of a company like Heineken is not solely in knowing how to brew beer; it is that people all over the world want to drink Heineken. The same logic applies for IBM, Sony, McDonald's, Barclays Bank or Dior.

By paying very high prices for companies with brands, buyers are actually purchasing positions in the minds of potential consumers. Brand awareness, image, trust and reputation, all painstakingly built up over the years, are the best guarantee of future earnings, thus justifying the prices paid. The value of a brand lies in its capacity to generate such cash flows.

Hardly had this management revolution been born than conflicting arguments arose regarding the reality and the durability of brand equity. With the systematic rise in distributor's own brands it was argued that the capacity of brands had been exaggerated. The fall in the price of Marlboro cigarettes in the USA in April 1993 created panic on Wall Street, with the share prices of all consumer goods firms falling. This mini-Pearl Harbor proved healthy. At the height of recession we realised that it was not the brand – registered trademark – as such which created value, but the policy of brand management conducted by the firm. Consumers don't just buy the brand name, they buy branded products which are an amalgamation of the tangible and intangible benefits created by the efforts of the company. Given time, the brand may contain a certain number of associations, qualities and differences, but these alone do not comprise the whole offer. A map alone is not enough to know the underlying territory.

Just as we had exaggerated the overwhelming power of brands, so the opposition to brands will be short-lived. The value of brands comes from their ability to continuously add value while at the same time remaining at the market price. Another question is: who is best placed to make use of brands? You must be very wary as regards ideological preferences; for example, there are very few manufacturers' brands on the furniture market other than those of Italian designers, yet everybody talks about Habitat or Ikea. They are seen as agents offering strong value added style in the first case and competitive prices and youth appeal in the second. The development of copy-cats and the belief that those who manufacture them can get away with it is not good for the industry, especially when they can be seen on the shelves of large modern retail stores. It has been amply shown in the past (see, for example, Kapferer and Thoenig, 1989) that manufacturers' brands help to bring about economic growth, through both investment and innovation. Many distributors' own brands act as economic parasites, no matter what attempts at justification they may offer, as they follow in the wake of these innovations without bearing any of the costs. The counterfeiting of prestigious brands abroad is seen as unacceptable, yet the imitation of consumer goods or products of little importance on the domestic market is seen as legitimate.

Brand management is still in its early stages even though brands are a business asset. At present, in many cases, the tendency is to manage products which happen to have a name. Yet brand management involves different and specific reasoning and approaches. This will be the main focus of this book. Management books and marketing bibles have not yet assimilated the full implication of the brand revolution. Marketing books focus on the process of launching new products, when marketing the brand is considered merely as a tactical and final decision which is developed through communication such as advertising, packaging and the logo. Yet the reality of the situation is very different. From now on companies will be faced with the strategic issue of whether or not growth should come about through existing brands by developing their sphere of activity or through new brands (either created or bought).

Classic strategic models talk about product portfolios, whereas in reality companies have to manage their brand portfolios. Several companies have product managers but few have brand managers. This may cause problems in so far as more and more brands are being extended to more and more differentiated products, resulting in the delegation of the management of value to several decision centres. In the medium term this may diminish brand equity because decisions are taken without any integration of the decision centres.

The brand is not the product but it gives the product meaning and defines its identity in both time and space. Companies are discovering that this brand equity has to be managed, nourished and controlled. Branding is raising new questions for managers: How many brands do you need? How do you manage your brand portfolio? What extensions can you give the brand and which products and services could and should these encompass? Or, on the other hand, into what areas should you not extend the brand even if you expect it to sell? Going too far may weaken brand equity. How do you manage brands over time and keep them up to date, as technology, products and customers change? How do you change while staying the same? How do you manage coherently and benefit from the synergy of a range of products sold under a single brand? How do you optimise image in the relationship between products and their brand? How far can a brand be extended geographically? Does it have the potential to become a homogeneous global brand in all countries? Or is this impossible or even undesirable? Several companies have the same name as their brand (eg Renault, Nestlé, IBM, BT, etc), so what is the difference between managing a brand image, a corporate image and an institutional image? Finally, given that brands have a value, how can this be measured so as to survey and control it? Should it be included on the balance sheet to indicate its true economic value to shareholders, investors and financial partners?

These are all new questions, each one deserving a chapter to itself. For a long time the answers to these questions were found intuitively and the decisions made on a trial and error basis. The goal of this book is to provide the reader with a framework for comprehensive reflection and analysis and thus a rational means to finding answers. The models of analysis and decision-making presented here have grown out of research and have been tested in consulting situations and confirmed in practice. As demonstrated by the numerous case studies, the models offered concern brands ranging from industry to service, from luxury goods and fashion to consumer goods and distributors' own-brands.

Too often brands are examined through their component parts: the brand name, its logo, design or packaging, advertising or sponsorship, the level of image and brand awareness or, more recently, in terms of financial valuation. Real brand management, however, begins much earlier, with a strategy and a consistent, integrated vision. Its central concept is brand identity, not brand image. This identity must be defined and managed and is at the heart of brand management. It calls for new ways of thinking and methods of investigation; these are presented here.

Part One

UNDERSTANDING BRANDS

1

Brand equity in question

World economic interest in brands is a recent phenomenon. Indeed, some would argue that for a long time now advertising agencies and marketing managers have been doing their best to convince others that brands are a company's most precious asset. However, even though the argument seemed plausible, most people didn't believe it, as is shown by the multiples used to value companies for sale; firms making small profits were worth very little, according to analysts. All of this changed during the 1980s when there was a wave of takeovers, mergers and acquisitions of companies with brands by giants such as Nestlé, Philip Morris, Seagram, Lever or Procter & Gamble. There was an increase in the multiples (or price:earnings ratio) once the target company had well-known brands, even if it was losing money. Helped by the intuition and premonition of a few famous raiders who made customer goodwill a priority, CEOs and financial directors realised that the value of brands was a concept distinct from the net income of the company. The perception of the added value of a brand was seized by several sectors of activity even though accounting standards were not yet allowing companies to include brands on their balance sheets. Financial experts, auditing firms and bankers offered methods of financially valuing brands and intangible assets in general, of which the brand is the principal component for mass market consumer goods. Since 1991 the buzz word has been brand equity. Surveys comparing brand awareness, brand esteem and the perceived quality of hundreds of domestic and international brands are flourishing. Respectable financial institutions publish hit parades of the financial value of brands (Equitrend Index, Financial World Index, etc), allocating billions of dollars to the most well-known names (Table 1.1). Sometimes there are marked differences between one institution and another.

Hardly had the economic world's infatuation with brands begun, helped along by media publicity, than people were questioning the wisdom of this collective frenzy. Several CEOs had become disillusioned at the end of the 1980s

Table 1.1 An estimate of the financial value of brands

Rank	Brand	Value (billion $)
1	Coca-Cola	39.0
2	Marlboro	38.7
3	IBM	17.1
4	Motorola	15.3
5	Hewlett-Packard	13.1
6	Microsoft	11.7
7	Kodak	11.6
8	Budweiser	11.3
9	Kellogg's	11.0
10	Nescafé	10.3
11	Intel	9.7
12	Gillette	9.6
13	Pepsi	7.8
14	General Electric	7.4
15	Levi's	6.9
16	Frito-Lay	6.9
17	Compaq	6.8
18	Bacardi	6.5
19	Campbell's	6.5
20	Pampers	5.9

Source: Interbrand, Financial World, 1995

due to the start of the recession, the aftermath of the Gulf War, and the important socio-cultural changes that were taking place. Was the increase in the number of distributors' own brands and later of hard discounters' products not proof of the weakness of brands (meaning producer brands)? Little more was needed to create a backlash, and the death of brands or, at least, the uncertainty of their future was announced in every economic journal. In reality this only concerned producers' brands, not all brands. One must remember that own brands are also brands, from both a legal and a consumer point of view. A recent survey conducted in the UK asked respondents to name the first ten brands that came to their mind as symbols of quality. The results were the following (in decreasing order): Marks & Spencer, Cadbury, Kellogg's, Heinz, Rolls-Royce, Boots, Nescafé, BBC, Rowntree and Sainsbury. Marks & Spencer, Boots and Sainsbury are distributors. In an identical study carried out in France the author found that Carrefour was one of the best known brands across all sectors of activity. In fact, it is important to clarify the issue: are all brands a threat, or only the manufacturers' ones? And among these brands would it be the leaders or the challengers who would be most at risk, and why?

In order to reply to these questions it is necessary to carry out an in-depth analysis of how brands work and why they can result in growth and profitability. The reason why so many distributors have created their own brands is because they have discovered this source of profitability. At the same time, this model should take into account the opposite situation: that is, the fact that certain brands lose value.

GOODWILL: THE CONVERGENCE OF FINANCE AND MARKETING

The 1980s witnessed a Copernican revolution in the understanding of the workings of brands. Before this, ratios of seven or eight were typical in mergers and acquisitions, meaning that the price paid for a company was seven to eight times its earnings. After 1980 these multiples increased considerably to reach their peak. For example, Groupe Danone paid $2.5 billion for Nabisco Europe, which was equivalent to a price:earnings ratio of 27. Nestlé bought Rowntree Macintosh for three times its stock market value and 26 times its earnings. It was becoming the norm to see multiples of 20 to 25. Even today when, because of the recession, financial valuations have become more prudent, the existence of strong brands still gives a real added value to companies. What happened between the beginning and the end of the 1980s? What explanations can be given for this sudden change in the methods of financial analysts? The prospect of a single European market certainly played a significant role, as can be seen by the fact that large companies were looking for brands which were ready to be European or, even better, global. This explains why Nestlé bought Buitoni, Lever bought Boursin, L'Oréal bought Lanvin, Seagram bought Martell, etc. The increase in the multiples can also be explained in part by the opposing bids of rival companies wishing to take over the few brand leaders which existed in their markets and which were for sale. Apart from the European factor, there was a marked change in the attitude towards the brands of the principal players. Prior to 1980, companies wished to buy a producer of chocolate or pasta: after 1980, they wanted to buy KitKat or Buitoni. This distinction is very important; in the first case firms wish to buy production capacity and in the second they want to buy a place in the mind of the consumer.

The vision has changed from one where only tangible assets had value to one where companies now believe that their most important asset is their brands, which are intangible and immaterial. These intangible assets account for 61 per cent of the value of Kellogg's, 57 per cent of Sara Lee and 52 per cent of General Mills. This explains the paradox that even though a company is making a loss it is bought for a very high price because of its well-known brands. Before 1980, if the value of the brand had been included in the company's earnings, it would have been bought for a penny. Nowadays brand value is determined independently of the firm's net value and thus can sometimes be hidden by the poor financial results of the company. The net income of a company is the sum of all the financial effects, be they positive or negative and thus includes the effect of the brand. The reason why Apple lost money in 1996 was not because its brand was weak, but because its strategy was bad. Therefore it is not simply because a company is making a loss that its brand is not adding value. Just as the managers of Ebel-Jellinek, an American-Swiss group, said when they bought the Look brand: the company is making a loss but the brand hasn't lost its potential. Balance sheets reflect bad management decisions in the past, whereas the brand is a potential source of future profits.

It is important to realise that goodwill is in fact the difference between the price paid and the book value of the company. The difference is brought about by the psychological goodwill of consumers, distributors and all the actors in the channels: that is to say, favourable attitudes and predisposition. Thus, a close relationship exists between financial and marketing analyses of brands. Accounting goodwill is the monetary value of the psychological goodwill which the brand has created over time through communication investment and consistent focus on products, both of which help build the reputation of the name.

The financial value of the goodwill which has been created thanks to brands with millions of consumers and hundreds of distributors is the cause of the increase in the multiples. This goodwill results in a profit over and above the expected profit from the same activity if no brand existed. What exactly are the effects of this goodwill?

- The favourable attitude of distributors choosing the brand because of its expected rotation, even though they will still be demanding in terms of discounts, listing fees and other charges which have become customary. In fact a retailer may lose customers if it does not stock a well-known brand which by definition is present everywhere; that is to say certain consumers will go elsewhere to look for the brand. This goodwill assures the presence of the brand at the point of sale, which is the key to selling for durable as well as consumer goods.
- The support of wholesalers and resellers in the market for slow-moving or industrial goods. This is especially true when they are seen as being an exclusive brand with which they are able to associate themselves in the eyes of their customers.

- The propensity of the consumer or the end user to buy the product. It is this favourable attitude and in certain cases the attachment or even loyalty to the brand which is the key to future sales. Brand loyalty may be reduced to a minimum as the price difference between the brand and its competitors increases but attachment to the brand does not vanish so fast; it resists time.

The brand is a focal point for all the positive and negative impressions created by the buyer over time as he comes into contact with the brand's products, distribution channel, personnel and communication. On top of this, by concentrating all its marketing effort on a single name, the latter acquires an aura of exclusivity. The brand continues to be, at least in the short term, a byword for quality even after the patent has expired. The life of the patent is extended thanks to the brand, thus explaining the importance of branding in the pharmaceutical or the chemical industry.

The brand performs an economic function in the mind of the consumer and thus has a lasting and memorable effect on the company's activities, be it as distributor or owner of the brand. It is also because of this that it is seen as an asset from an accounting point of view: its economic effects extend far beyond the mere consumption of the product.

Legally a brand is simply a symbol which distinguishes a company's product and certifies its origin and thus only obtains its value through registration and conformity. In the financial world, and in this book, the concept of a brand has a much broader meaning. The value of a brand comes from its ability to gain an exclusive, positive and prominent meaning in the minds of a large number of consumers. It is not simply a crocodile sewn onto a shirt: it is all the different things that the buyer thinks of as soon as he sees the Lacoste symbol. These refer to the tangible attributes of the product as well as the more intangible, which may be either psychological or social.

These associations have been acquired over time through continued investment by the company: in production in order to maintain a higher level of quality; in new product research which has been adapted to changes in consumer tastes; in distribution channels; in the sales force both in Europe and worldwide; in communication; in legal defence against counterfeits. Taking the example of Lacoste again, the brand is more than the crocodile logo and the name, it is the significance that they have acquired since 1933 among the wealthy worldwide. The tangible and intangible benefits which are derived from the consumption of a product of the brand are encapsulated in the strong brand. When a brand is created at first it is worth nothing – except the cost of the legal deposition and the fees associated with the creation of the brand. Over time the logo acquires significance by the means outlined above. Advertising is forgotten quickly whereas a brand stays in the memory along with the implications which are attached to it by the public. The brand is 'stocked' in the mind of potential consumers – thus the brand can be considered as an asset of the company. This is known as share of mind. As well as this the brand is an asset in the accounting sense of the word because it has a lasting effect on the company's activity and is not consumed by the first user.

In order to understand in what way a strong brand (having acquired distribution, awareness and image) is a generator of growth and profitability it is first necessary to remind ourselves of the functions that it performs with the consumers themselves, and which are the source of this valuable goodwill. Once these functions are valued, the consumer seeks out the brands and becomes attached, indeed loyal, to them and, in accordance with the valuation, is often prepared to pay more for the branded product. On the other hand, when these functions are either not fulfilled or not valued by the public, the attraction of the branded product decreases and its premium price becomes unacceptable. Thus the market is dominated by the retailers' copy-cat products or the discount versions.

THE BRAND: A SOURCE OF VALUE FOR THE CONSUMER

Although this book deals primarily with brands and their optimisation, it is important to clarify that brands do not necessarily exist in all markets. Even if brands exist in the legal sense they do not always play a role in the buying decision process of consumers. Other factors may be more important. For example, research on 'brand sensitivity' (Kapferer and Laurent, 1988) shows that in several product categories, buyers do not look at the brand when they are making their choice. Who is concerned about the brand when they are buying a writing pad, a rubber, felt tip pens, markers or photocopy paper? Neither private individuals nor companies. There are no strong brands in such markets as sugar and socks. In Germany there is no national brand of flour. Even the beer brands are mostly regional.

Inherently, brands exist as soon as there is perceived risk. Once the risk perceived by the buyer disappears, the brand has no longer any benefit. It is only a name on a product, and it ceases to be a reference mark, a guide or a source of added value. The perceived risk is greater once the unit price is higher or the repercussions of a bad choice are more severe. Thus the purchase of long-lasting goods is a long-term commitment. On top of this, because humans are social animals, we judge ourselves on certain choices that we make and this explains why a large part of our social identity is built around the logos and the brands that we wear. As far as food is concerned, there is a certain amount of intrinsic risk involved whenever we ingest something and allow it to enter our bodies. The brand's function is to overcome this danger which explains the importance of brands in the market for, for example, spirits such as vodka and gin.

The importance of perceived risk as a generator of the legitimacy of a brand is highlighted by the categories within which distributors' own brands (and perhaps tomorrow's discount products) dominate if the same were to happen in Europe as is happening in Germany, for example in the markets for tinned vegetables, milk, orange juice, frozen pizzas, still mineral water, kitchen roll, toilet paper and petrol. At the same time producers' brands still have a dominant position in the following categories: instant coffee, tea, cereals, toothpaste, deodorant, cold sauces, fresh pasta, baby food, beauty products, washing powder, etc. For these products the consumer has high involvement and does not want to take any risks be they physical or psychological.

Nothing is ever acquired permanently, and the degree of perceived risk evolves over time. In certain sectors, as the technology becomes commonplace, all the products comply with standards of quality. Therefore we are moving from a situation where consumers examined products and some 'failed' whereas others 'passed', towards one where there is competition between competitors, all of whom are excellent, but some are 'more excellent' than others. The degree of perceived risk will change depending on the situation. For example, there is less risk involved in buying rum for a punch, or whisky for whisky and coke, than for a rum or a whisky on the rocks. Lastly, all consumers do not have the same level of involvement. Those who have high involvement are those that worry about small differences between products or who wish to optimise their choice: they will talk for hours about the merits of such and such a computer or of a certain brand of coffee. Those who are less involved are satisfied with a basic product which isn't too expensive, such as a pastis or a whisky which may be unknown but which is good value for money and is sold in their local shop. The problem for most buyers who feel a certain risk and fear making a mistake is that most products are opaque: we can only discover their inner qualities once we buy the products and consume them. However, many consumers are reluctant to take this step. Therefore it is imperative that the external indicators highlight the internal qualities of these opaque products. A reputable brand is the most efficient of these external indicators. Examples of other such external indicators are: price, quality labels, the retail outlet where the product is sold and which guarantees it, the style and design of the packaging.

At this stage it is interesting to remind ourselves of the classifications drawn up by Nelson (1970) and by Darby and Karni (1973). These authors make the distinction between three types of product characteristics:

- the qualities which are noticed by contact, before buying;
- the qualities which are noticed uniquely by experience, thus after buying;
- credence qualities which cannot be verified even after consumption and which you have to take on trust.

The first type of quality can be seen in the decision to buy a pair of men's socks. The choice is made according to the visible characteristics: the pattern, the style, the material, the feel, the elasticity and the price. There is hardly a need for brands in this market. In fact those that do exist only have a very small market share and target those people who are looking for proof of durability (difficult to tell before buying) or those who wish to make their identity known. This is how Burlington socks work as a hallmark of chic style. Producers' brands do exist but their differential advantage compared to distributors' brands (Marks & Spencer) is weak, especially if the latter have a good style department and offer a wide variety at a competitive price.

A good example of the second type of quality is the automobile market. Of course, performance, consumption and style can all be assessed before buying, as can the availability of options and the interior space. However, road-holding, the pleasure of driving, reliability and quality cannot be entirely appreciated during a test drive. The response comes from brand image; that is, the collective representation which is shaped over time by the accumulated experiences of close relations, word of mouth and advertising.

Finally, in the market for upmarket cars, the feeling that you have made it, that certain feeling of fulfilment and personal success through buying and owning a BMW are typically the results of pure faith. They cannot be substantiated by any of the post-purchase driving experiences: it is a collective belief which is more or less shared by the buyers and the non-buyers. The same logic applies to the feeling of authenticity and inner masculinity which is supposed to result from smoking Marlboro cigarettes.

The role of brands is made clearer by this classification of sought-after qualities. The brand is a sign (therefore external) whose function is to disclose the hidden qualities of the product which are inaccessible to contact (sight, touch, hearing, smell) and possibly those which are accessible through experience but where the consumer does not want to take the risk of trying the product. Lastly, a brand, when it is well-known, adds an aura of make-believe when it is consumed, for example the authentic America and rebellious youth of Levi's, the rugged masculinity of Marlboro, the English style of Dunhill, the Californian myth of Apple.

The informational role of the brand covers a very specific area which varies according to the product or service, the consumption situation and the individual. Thus, a brand is not always useful. On the other hand, a brand becomes necessary once the consumer loses his traditional reference points. This is why there is an increase in the demand for branded wine. Consumers were put off by too many small chateaux which were rarely the same and had limited production of varying quality and which sometimes sprung some unpleasant surprises. This paved the way for brands such as Mouton Cadet. In Germany there is no national brand for flour, yet in France there is one and only one, Francine. The success of Francine can perhaps be explained by the interest of the French in finding a flour which they are sure will not create lumps. Francine made available a range of specialised flours for chefs which was available all over France and which is now appearing on supermarket shelves thanks to advertising, thus influencing consumers in their purchasing decision.

As we can see, a brand provides not only a source of information (thus revealing its values) but performs certain other functions which justify its attractiveness and its monetary return (higher price) when it is valued by buyers. What are these functions? How does a brand create value in the eyes of the consumer? The eight functions of a brand are presented in Table 1.2. The first two are mechanical and concern the essence of the brand; that is, to function as a recognised symbol in order to facilitate choice and to gain time. The following three functions reduce the perceived risk. The last three have a more pleasurable side to them. Ethics show that buyers are expecting, more and more, responsible behaviour from their brands. Many Swedish consumers still refuse Nestlé's products because of the issue of selling Nestlé's baby milk to poor, uneducated African mothers.

Anglo-Saxons are right to make a distinction between trademarks and trustmarks. A recent survey of the food sector by Groupe Danone showed that brands are not necessarily trustmarks. Evian got a vote of confidence of 82 per cent, Danone 75.8 per cent, Nestlé 73.4 per cent, Kellogg's 44 per cent, Motta 42 per cent and Coca-Cola 30 per cent.

These functions are neither laws nor dues, nor are they automatic; they must be defended at all times. Only a few brands are successful in each market thanks to their supporting investments in quality, R&D, productivity, communication and research in order to better understand foreseeable changes in demand. A priori, nothing confines these functions to producers' brands. Moreover, several producers' brands do not perform these functions. In Great Britain, Marks & Spencer (St Michael) is seen as an important brand and performs these functions, as does Migros in Switzerland.

Table 1.2 The functions of the brand for the consumer

Function	Consumer benefit
Identification	To be clearly seen, to make sense of the offer, to quickly identify the sought-after products.
Practicality	To allow savings of time and energy through identical repurchasing and loyalty.
Guarantee	To be sure of finding the same quality no matter where or when you buy the product or service.
Optimisation	To be sure of buying the best product in its category, the best performer for a particular purpose.
Characterisation	To have confirmation of your self-image or the image that you present to others.
Continuity	Satisfaction brought about through familiarity and intimacy with the brand that you have been consuming for years.
Hedonistic	Satisfaction linked to the attractiveness of the brand, to its logo, to its communication.
Ethical	Satisfaction linked to the responsible behaviour of the brand in its relationship with society (ecology, employment, citizenship, advertising which doesn't shock).

The usefulness of these functions depends on the product category. There is less need for reference points or risk reducers when the product is transparent (ie its inner qualities are accessible through contact). The price premium is at its lowest and experiences cost very little when there is low involvement and the purchase is seen as a chore, eg trying a new, cheaper roll of kitchen paper or aluminium foil. Certain kinds of shops aim primarily at fulfilling certain of these functions, for example hard discounters who have 650 lines with no brands, a product for every need, at the lowest prices and offering excellent quality for the price (thanks to the work on reducing all the costs which do not add value carried out in conjunction with suppliers). This formula offers another alternative to the first five functions: ease of identification on the shelf, practicality, guarantee, optimisation at the chosen price level and characterisation (refusal to be manipulated by marketing). The absence of other functions is compensated for by the very low price.

Functional analysis of brand role can facilitate the understanding of the rise of distributors' own brands. Whenever brands are just trademarks and operate merely as a recognition signal or as a mere guarantee of quality, distributors' brands can fulfil these functions as well and at a cheaper price.

Table 1.3 summarises the relationships between brand role and distributors' own-brands' market share.

THE BRAND: A SOURCE OF VALUE TO THE COMPANY

Why do financial analysts prefer companies with strong brands? Because they are less risky. Therefore, the brand works in the same way for the financial analyst as for the consumer: the brand removes the risk. The certainty, the guarantee and the removal of the risk are included in the price. By paying a high price for a company with brands the financial analyst is acquiring near certain future cashflows.

If the brand is strong it benefits from a high degree of loyalty and thus from stability of future sales. At Volvic 10 per cent of the buyers of this brand of mineral water are regular and loyal and represent 50 per cent of the sales. The reputation of the brand is a source of demand and lasting attractiveness, the image of superior quality and added value justifies a premium price. A dominant brand is an entry barrier to competitors because it acts as a reference in its category. If it is prestigious or a trendsetter in terms of style it can generate substantial royalties by granting licences, for example, Naf-Naf earned over £6 million in net royalties in 1993. The brand can enter other markets when it is well-known, is a symbol of quality and offers a certain promise which is valued by the market. The Palmolive brand name has become symbolic of mildness and has been extended to a number of markets besides that of soap, for example

Table 1.3 Brand functions and distributor/manufacturer breakdown

Function or role of brand	Typical product category or brand	Power of manufacturer's brands
Recognition cue	Milk, salt, flour	Very weak
Practicality of choice	Socks	Weak
Guarantee of quality	Wine, food, staples	Weak
Optimisation of choice, sign of high quality performance	Cars, cosmetics, appliances, paint, services	Strong
Personalising one's choice	Perfumes, clothing	Strong but challenged
Permanence, bonding, familiarity relationship	Trust brands	Strong but challenged
Pleasure	Polysensual brands	Strong
Ethics and social responsibility	Reference brands, corporate brands	Strong but challenged

shampoo, shaving cream and washing-up liquid. This is known as brand extension (see Chapter 8) and saves on the need to create awareness if you had to launch a new product on each of these markets.

In determining the financial value of the brand, the expert must take into account the sources of any additional revenues which are generated by the presence of a strong brand. Additional buyers may be attracted to a product which appears identical to another but which has a brand name with a strong reputation. If such is the company's strategy the brand may command a premium price in addition to providing an added margin due to economies of scale and market domination. Brand extensions into new markets can result in royalties and important gearing effects. To calculate this value, it is necessary to subtract the costs involved in brand management: the costs involved in quality control and in investing in R&D, the costs of a national, indeed international, sales force, advertising costs, the cost of a legal registration, the cost of capital invested, etc. The financial value of the brand is the difference between the extra revenue generated by the brand and the associated costs for the next few years, which are discounted back to today. The number of years is determined by the business plan of the valuer (the potential buyer, the auditors). The discount rate used to weigh these future cashflows is determined by the confidence or the lack of it that the investor has in his forecasts. However, a significant fact is that the stronger the brand, the smaller the risk. Thus, future net cashflows are considered more certain the stronger the brand.

Figure 1.1 shows the three generators of profit of the brand: the acceptable price premium, the differential of attraction and of loyalty, and the differential of the margin. These gearing effects work on the original market for the brand but they can be offered subsequently in a variety of forms on other markets and for other product categories, either through direct brand extension (for example, Tefal moved from frying pans to domestic appliances to telephony and recently to home automation) or through licensing, from which the manufacturer benefits from royalties (for example all the luxury labels).

Once these generators are measured in pounds, yen, dollars or any other currency they may serve as a base for evaluating the marginal profit which is attributable to brand management. They only emerge when the company wishes to strategically differentiate its products on a basis which is tangible or intangible, functional or symbolic. This wish can come about through three types of simultaneous and permanent investment:

- Investment in production, productivity and R&D. Thanks to these, the company can acquire specific know-how, a knack which cannot be imitated and which in accounting terms is also an intangible asset. Sometimes the com-

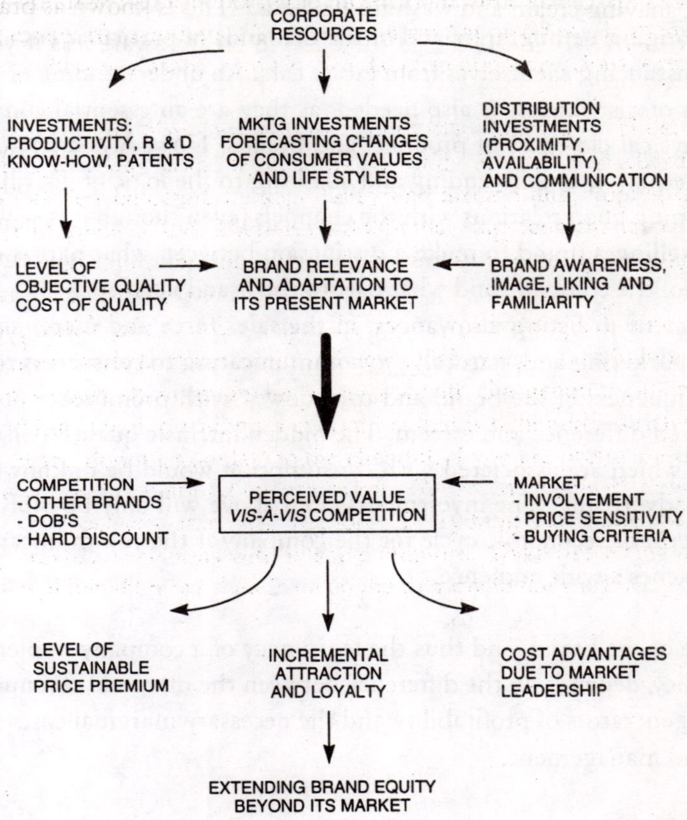

Figure 1.1 The leverages of brand profitability

pany temporarily monopolises the product by registering a patent. This is the basis of marketing in the pharmaceutical industry (a patent and a brand) but also of companies like Ferrero, whose products are not easily imitated despite their success. The Kinder egg is the leading children's candy in Europe: there are hardly any copies or imitations because of the patent linked to the production method. This is also how Polaroid forced Kodak to pull out of the market for instant photography: Kodak had to use the patented processes of its competitor. Patents are on their own an intangible asset: the activity of the company benefits from them in a lasting manner.

- Investment in research and marketing studies in order to detect, to sense and to anticipate the changes of consumers' tastes and lifestyles in order to be able to define any important innovations which will match these evolutions.

Chrysler's Spacewagon is an example of a product created in anticipation of the changing demography and of the demands of particular customers who were distancing themselves from estate cars. An understanding of the expectations of distributors is also needed, as they are an essential component of the physical closeness of products and brands. Nowadays a key element of brand equity is understanding and adapting to the logic of distributors, and developing good relations with the channels (even though it is still necessary when selling a brand to make a distinction between what part is due to the power of the company and what part to the brand itself).

- Investment in listing allowances, in the sales force and merchandising, in trade marketing and, naturally, in communicating to consumers to promote the uniqueness of the brand and to endow it with prominence (awareness), perceived difference and esteem. The hidden intrinsic qualities or intangible values which are associated with consumption would be unknown without brand advertising. The investments cited above will only be profitable over an acceptable economic cycle for the company if the communication is fast and reaches a wide audience.

The value of the brand, and thus the legitimacy of a company implementing a brand policy, depends on the difference between the marginal revenues coming from the generators of profitability and the necessary marginal costs associated with brand management.

FROM BRAND ASSETS TO FINANCIAL VALUE

An interesting survey carried out by the agency DDB asked marketing directors what they considered to be the characteristics of a strong brand, a significant company asset. The following were the answers in order of importance:

- brand awareness (65 per cent);
- the strength of brand positioning, concept, personality, a precise and distinct image (39 per cent);
- the strength of signs of recognition by the consumer (logo, codes, packaging) (36 per cent);
- brand authority with consumers, brand esteem, perceived status of the brand and consumer loyalty (24 per cent).

Numerous types of surveys on the measurement of brand value (brand equity) exist. They usually provide a national or international hit parade based just on one component of brand equity: brand awareness (method may be top of the mind, aided or unaided depending on the research institute), brand preference, quality image, prestige, first and second buying preferences when the favoured brand is not available, or liking. Certain institutions may combine two of the components: for example, Landor published an indicator of the 'power of the brand' which was determined by combining brand-aided awareness and esteem, which is the emotional component of the brand–consumer relationship. The advertising agency, Young & Rubicam, carried out a study called 'Brand Asset Monitor' which positions the brand on two axes: the cognitive axis is a combination of salience and of the degree of perceived difference of the brand among consumers; the emotional axis is the combination of the measures of familiarity and esteem (see page 150). In France, Sofres, in its study Megabrand System, uses six parameters to compare brands: brand awareness, stated use, stated preference, perceived quality, a mark for global opinion and an item measuring the strength of the brand's imagery.

Certain institutions, which believe that the comparison of brands across all markets makes little sense, concentrate on a single market approach and measure, for example, the acceptable price differential for each brand. They proceed in either a global manner (what price difference can exist between an IBM PC and a Toshiba PC or a PC from Tandy?) or by using a method of trade-off which isolates the net added value of the brand name. Marketing directors are perplexed because so many different methods exist.

There is little more consensus among academic research. Sattler (1994) analysed 49 American and European studies on brand equity and listed no fewer than 26 different ways of measuring it. These methods vary according to several dimensions:

- Is the measure monetary or not? A large proportion of measures are classified in non-monetary terms (brand awareness, attitude, preference, etc).
- Does the measurement include the time factor – that is, the future of the brand on the market?
- Does the brand take the competition into account – that is, the perceived value in relation to other products on the market? Most of them do not.
- Does the measurement include the brand's marketing mix? When you measure brand value, do you only include the value attached to the brand name? Most measures do not include the marketing mix (past advertising expenditure, level of distribution, etc).
- When estimating brand value do you include the profits that a user or a buyer could obtain due to the synergies which may exist with its own present brand portfolio (synergies of distribution, production, logistics, etc)? The

majority of them don't include this, even though it is a key factor. Seagram bought Martell for five billion francs in order, among other things, to gain access to its distribution channels in Asia which allowed it to develop its sales of other brands, such as Chivas, in this area.

- Does the measurement of brand equity include the possibility of brand extensions outside the brand's original market? In general, no.
- Finally, does the measure of brand equity take into account the possibility of geographical extension or globalisation? Again, most of the time, the answer is no.

The analysis allows us to identify the most popular measures of brand equity.

a) A short-term, non-monetary measure which does not include the competition, the risk, the marketing mix, synergies nor potential future extensions. In general, this method is used by polling institutes and only gives the information that is provided by surveys of consumers.
b) A short-term, monetary measure which takes into account competition but does not include the marketing mix, uncertainty, risk, synergies nor potential expansion. This typical method tries to attach a premium price to the brand either by a 'dollarmetric' approach or a 'trade-off'.

In order to clarify these questions, it is necessary to make the distinction between brand assets and brand value. The measurement of brand assets is based on the final buyers and the distribution. Brand value or equity poses another problem: what are these assets worth in monetary terms, ie what extra profit does the company make from pursuing a brand policy? Brand assets mean:

- brand awareness (the capacity of the brand to symbolise the category, to be a prototype of it, the best model or representation);
- the level of perceived quality compared to competitors;
- the level of confidence, of significance, of empathy, of liking;
- the richness and attractiveness of the images conjured up by the brand, of the intangible values which are linked to the consumption of the brand.

These factors are combined in the mind of the consumer to determine the perceived value of the brand, compared to that of competitors, which is the source of its attractiveness and brand loyalty.

What are these assets really worth? Let us remind ourselves that in all countries accounting classifies an asset as an element which has a lasting effect on the profitability of a company. This is why the normal brand evaluation method consists of measuring this contribution over a period of five to ten years depending on the business plan and thus including time, risk, competition, the logic of the distributors and their own brands, the probable spreading of technological know-how, the development of the market, and potential expansion into new categories or overseas. If the valuation is carried out by a potential buyer, the resulting benefits of synergy with its own brand portfolio should be included. Chapter 13 deals solely with this subject.

It should be noted that the transition from the non-monetary measurement of brand assets to the monetary one of brand equity includes other intangible assets which play a role in the market share forecasts; these include the patents, the company's exclusive know-how and the quality of the relationship with the different channels. The financial value of the brand contains everything else which is intangible, with the brand being the receptacle of all these contributions.

Figure 1.2 summarises the relationship between the different concepts of brand analysis. It allows us to understand the confusion which exists among several companies who have painted an enticing picture of the strength of brand assets in order to justify the price of expensive acquisitions. However, once acquired, the buyers discovered that these assets didn't have the expected value in the eyes of the consumer. It is no longer enough to be recognised, to

Brand Awareness
+ Image
+ Perceived Quality
+ Evocations →
+ Familiarity, Liking

= Brand Assets → Brand added value, perceived by consumers
- Costs of branding
- Cost of invested capital

Brand financial value (Brand equity)

Figure 1.2 From brand assets to brand equity

have an image, to be liked. Several brands of champagne focused solely on this and saw their sales plummet. The chances of Lanvin and Balmain becoming profitable for their acquirers grows slimmer and slimmer as time goes by. A more mundane question is: will the brand Apple survive despite its awareness and excellent public image? This also goes for several mass market consumer goods. A number of names which were famous and renowned in their day can now be found in brand cemeteries. Their brand assets still exist but they hold no value in the eyes of the consumer, nor of the distributor.

THE CHALLENGE OF DISTRIBUTORS' OWN BRANDS

A key year in the history of Coca-Cola, a paragon of brand culture, was 1994. For the first time, in Sainsbury's retail outlets the sales of own-brand cola surpassed those of Coca-Cola (see Table 1.4), a demonstration of sorts that loyalty at any price no longer exists. An important fall in price, the guarantee of the Canadian company Cott (for the concentrate quality and taste), similarities in packaging bordering on counterfeiting and a product of sufficient quality are dissuading occasional buyers of the brand. What happened to the world's number one brand had already struck many well-known brands. The generators of profitability examined above seem to have been put to bad use in many sectors. The recession has certainly changed consumer behaviour, leading to more price sensitivity, but the lessons learned through the purchase of distributors' brands will not easily be forgotten by consumers and distributors. In fact, the principles explaining the sources of profitability generated by the brand also explain the loss of affection which brands can create in several markets.

Firstly, if it is true that the three principal generators of brand profitability are:

- the price differential allowed compared to a non-branded product
- the differential of attraction and loyalty
- the differential of the margin coming from the economies of scale and the consequences of being market leader when such is the case

Table 1.4 Coca-Cola *vs* Sainsbury's cola (in units)

	March 1994	June 1994
Coca-Cola	60%	33%
Own-label	18%	60%
Other brands	22%	7%
(Index) category volume	100	150

most brands have chosen to benefit only from the price differential. This explains the following acknowledgement of the directors of BSN (now Danone): 'Fuelled by consumption growth and concealed by high inflation, producers tend sometimes to increase the price too much in an attempt to maintain their margins' (IREP, 1994, p. 35). In the US, the consequence of the sudden fall in the price of Marlboro, known as the famous Marlboro Friday, was to bring to an end the continued rise in price of this brand. Once a company is lucky enough to have this differential in price, it is necessary either to have a clearly superior product due to investment in R&D (in the case of computers, cosmetics or washing powders) or to invest heavily in advertising in order to create intangibility. However, the equilibrium between tangible and intangible added value depends on the product category. As we have already seen, little emphasis is placed on intangible value in the men's sock market, so this product does not create psychological involvement. On the other hand, many jeans manufacturers aim to appeal to young people by drawing on a largely mythical idea of the young and rebellious American, using iconic figures such as James Dean, Marlon Brando or Marilyn Monroe. Many managers have placed disproportionate faith in intangible values. Perhaps influenced by their success in the luxury goods market, they have extended the logic of intangibility too far. However, mass market brands are not born from the aristocracy of luxury brands; they democratise technical progress. Strong brands were historically created when the mass-producers could create products in large quantities of similar quality and cheaper than the craft industry. This progress was announced to as many people as possible through advertising. If it is true that the brand is an intangible asset, it is wrong to believe that its image has to concentrate on the intangible. Everyday products with low involvement leave very little to the imagination. If you decide to invest exclusively in advertising for these brands you risk weakening the brand because you will have to sell a product for £1.20 even though it is only worth £1 in the eyes of the consumer, with the extra 20p corresponding to the price of the advertising. This is where the disequilibrium comes from, which the image cannot overcome.

All brands do not build on this price differential: KitKat, Swatch and even Coca-Cola have always seen to it that they are within as many people's reach as possible in terms of price. As the CEO of Coca-Cola, R. Goizetta, said, Coke must be the same price as tea in China. Which, in fact, it is. Swatch, faced with Japanese and Asian competitors, decided deliberately on a low price strategy. Thanks to its design, variety, fashion appeal and Swiss quality, Swatch has succeeded in maximising the price/quality relationship in its favour, thus creating considerable value attraction with its consumers.

The brand crisis started when we tried too hard to be semioticians and forgot industrial logic. Did we not limit the brand to its legal definition: a sign which distinguishes the goods of a company from those of other entrepreneurs while guaranteeing its origin? Many people believed that the sign alone – stimulated through advertising – would, from now on, not only distinguish products but also, miraculously, legitimise a price premium.

This theory was thrown into disarray when products which were functionally as good and cheaper than branded versions appeared on the market. When you find imported Italian spaghetti from an unknown but authentically Italian producer selling for 42p a kilo, whereas the same product by Panzani (the market leader in France) costs 72p a kilo on promotion, the price differential widens – not through the fault of Panzani's management but because of the arrival of external actors on the market who are capable of supplying the same quality at a substantially lower price. The functions of practicality, identification, guarantee and permanence which make up the Panzani brand are perhaps worth a differential of 10p per kilo but not 30p. The difference in price is no longer explained by the added value: it has become an exorbitant sacrifice in the consumer's eyes. In truth due to the fact that distributors are not aiming to create dreams, they have concentrated on the reality, on the products. If the early own-labels were of average quality, own-brand products have constantly improved in quality. Closely focused on the national brands, they have thus followed their price increases, but have maintained a price differential of 20 per cent. The shock came from German hard discounters like Aldi and Lidl. This type of distribution was created in 1948 during the reconstruction of Germany and is, therefore, a form of distribution typical of a rich country. Spreading throughout Europe because of the recession, it should continue to develop even when the economy starts improving. However, the products of German hard discounters are 50 per cent cheaper than those of national brands: but is this at the expense of quality? No. Aldi's instant coffee is made by Nestlé. Long-established partnerships with large producers, the search for maximum economies of scale and the reduction of any costs which fail to add value throughout the value chain have led to the launching of 600 unbeatable products in terms of price/quality relationship. In a recent comparison of the technical characteristics and quality of 50 consumer products, the Nielsen group found that in 25 per cent of the cases the national brands were superior, in 20 per cent of the cases the products of German hard discounters were better and in 36 per cent of the cases the quality was identical. Discount products launched by retail outlets to defend themselves were found, in 55 per cent of the cases, to be of inferior quality. A blind tasting test by Nielsen revealed identical results (see Table 1.5). If products which cost half the price come second in a quality test, the extra price of the national brand is an extra cost rather than extra value. Admittedly there are always intangible aspects to the image of food products because everything that enters our body poses a certain amount of risk, but this can be overcome by buying from a well-known retailer that guarantees its own brand.

Table 1.5 Comparison of quality levels of food products (blind test)

Type of brand or product	Average ranking	Main strength
International brands	First overall, but fourth in 25% of the cases	Flavour and design
Products of German hard discounters	Second overall, but first in 20% of the cases	Colour and texture
Distributors' own brand	Third overall, but second in 45% of the cases	Texture and flavour
Products of local discounters	Fourth overall, but fifth in 25% of the cases	Smell and colour
Discount products of hypermarkets and supermarkets	Fifth overall, but second in 20% of the cases	Smell

Source: Nielsen, Paris

The long-term problem is that hard discounters' products may become tomorrow's references for consumers in terms of both quality and price once this type of shop is present throughout the country and can operate as a nearby shop for everyday products (600 products per outlet). Then you will have to justify paying twice as much for a man's shirt than for a quality Tex, Carrefour's brand of clothes.

In Germany, more than half of the national sales of orange drinks are made by Aldi. Brands will cease to exist unless they are able to offer added value due to an exceptional product or a unique taste and a strong image (like Tango or Orangina, for instance). Certainly, Tropicana thrives: but it is a niche brand. The whole category has become a price-led commodity.

This change in competition will result in the price differential on the shelves noticed by consumers increasing from 20 per cent (compared to a classic brand) to 45 or 50 per cent. Thus, it is inevitable that there will be a fall in demand.

The threat also comes from the fact that less and less shelf space will be given to national brands. These two phenomena will rapidly reduce the gains due to margins which are created by the economies of scale, the experience curve and the leadership advantages which have been lost.

In several markets the future of national brands is precarious (see Table 1.6). But perhaps it is important to take into account the fact that in these product categories, the brand was a necessary but interim phenomenon. Once a product category emerges, it is necessary to explain it, put it into the consumption systems and overcome any prejudices. As the anthropologist Claude Lévi-Strauss said when talking about food products: 'Food must be good to think about before it is good to consume.' Advertising is the driving force behind this cultural role. Over time the perceived risk grows smaller, the levels of quality of the different actors become equivalent and consumers' involvement falls. Of course, the taste could still be improved but the marginal costs associated with a 1 per cent improvement in perceived taste are enormous and would result in the product no longer being in the price range of the mass market and becom-

Table 1.6 Market share of discount products, own-brand products and national brands

	1992	1996
Mineral water	%	%
Discount product	22	36
Own-brand	10	7
Manufacturer's brand	52	44
Others	16	13
UHT milk		
Discount product	40	49
Own-brand	28.5	24
Manufacturer's brand	15	14.5
Others	16.5	12.5
Frozen pizzas		
Discount product	9.5	16
Own-brand	21	14.5
Manufacturer's brand	51	48.5
Others	18.5	21
Cartons of orange juice		
Discount product	14	38
Own-brand	40	36
Manufacturer's brand	13	11
Others	33	15
Margarine (block)		
Discount product	9.5	16
Own-brand	27.5	25
Manufacturer's brand	56.5	54.5
Others	6.5	4.5
Washing powder (5 kg)		
Discount product	4.5	11.5
Own-brand	7	2.5
Manufacturer's brand	86.5	84
Others	2	2

Source: IRI Secondip

ing stuck in the small upscale segment. It would be better to invest in productivity in order to lower the price while maintaining the quality. Desk-top computers are a typical example of this.

The above scenario mainly affects the mature product categories with a functional characteristic and low involvement. It is not by chance that hard discounters concentrate on 600 or 650 products. These are normally products where there is no technological, emotional or social added value. It is in these areas that distributors' own-brands are the strongest and where the legitimacy of the manufacturer's brand is challenged. On the other hand, as can be seen in Table 1.7, big brands continue to dominate certain specific markets due to the barriers to entry created by the rate of innovation, permanent progress brought about by R&D, advertising investment and high consumer involvement.

In order to test the explanatory power of the concept of added value, a comparison of two apparently similar markets should be sufficient: women's tights and men's socks. In the market for the former in 1995, discount products accounted for 5 per cent of the sales and own-brands 14.4 per cent. In the lat-

Table 1.7 Highest share of national brands in volume, 1995

	%
Baby food	100
Eaux de toilette	92
Tea	91
Television, video recorders	90
Beauty products	90
Washing powder	90
Deodorant	90
Toothpaste	89
Soup	89
Shampoo	88
Shaving products	87
Toilet soap	87
Exotic food	83
Cereal bars	82
Bleach	81
Instant coffee	81
Fresh pasta	81
Roasted coffee	80
Whisky	80
Cold sauces	78
Cereals	80
Camembert	56

Source: Nielsen

ter, for the main product of the market (plain cotton socks) discount products account for 57 per cent of sales and own-brands 16.5 per cent, thus leaving only 26.5 per cent to the big brands. This is not by chance. The market for tights is continually changing due to innovations in the fibre, the texture, the comfort, the elasticity, the endurance, the feel and the brightness.

There are only two strategies possible for manufacturers of branded mass market goods:

- either invest in creativity, innovations, quality and R&D in order to give the products a differential advantage, while at the same time communicating to a wide range of people to maximise the exclusiveness and the image of quality associated with the product. This has been the successful strategy of, among others, L'Oréal, Procter & Gamble, Michelin, Gillette, Sony, Ferrero, 3M, Philips;
- or reduce costs through improving productivity in an attempt to maintain the pressure on prices. Pepsi-Cola, Bic and Benetton try to reduce costs by economies of scale. They keep prices low to discourage the entry of own-brands while reinforcing their image thanks to a policy of umbrella marketing and brand extensions.

Throughout this chapter, several conclusions have emerged. From now on it will become more difficult, more costly and more demanding to remain a big brand, a buyer's reference. Only large companies who have the resources to invest in R&D, productivity and total quality control, who are able to foresee the future through market research and who invest in visibility and proximity on distributors' shelves and in communication in order to consolidate the strong product image and the exclusivity of their brands will benefit from the new environment. The strength of a brand will depend directly on the strength of the company who owns it.

On the other hand the price premium is definitely going to fall if the big brands wish to stay at the heart of the market and not be sidelined as upmarket products, as nowadays it is the distributors who set the prices. Everybody is concerned with this, from champagne and mineral water manufacturers to the makers of office equipment, electrical domestic appliances or desk-top computers. This explains why, coming back to the financial valuation of brands, the multiples which had reached their peak (25 or 30) are returning to more acceptable levels. The result of this is that brand assets have no longer the same value as they did in 1990. The gearing effect is less, as can be seen in Figure 1.3. (Chapter 13, which deals with financial evaluation and accounting procedures for brands, will examine this point in detail.)

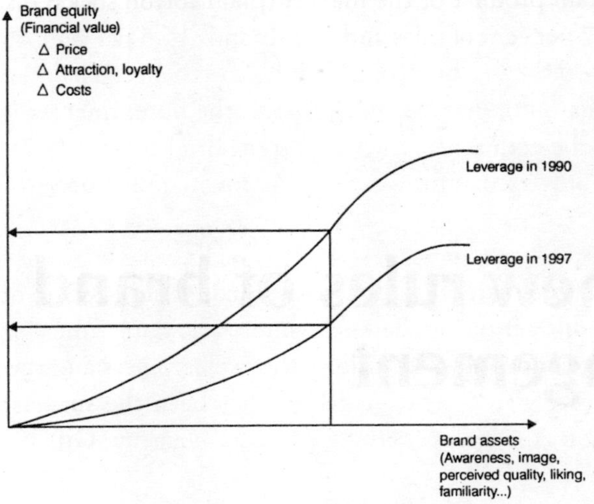

Figure 1.3 How the new economic environment impacts on brand equity

Let us take an example. Yesterday, the third or fourth brand on the market was very proud of its performance. Today, such a brand would have a hard time getting shelf space in a store. This phenomenon is happening in all markets. In the hotel trade the market share premium has increased. General Electric will now only deal with one hotel company when making travel arrangements for its executives. This is why it is vital for the Accor group hotels to buy Meridien so that it is able to, with its Sofitel hotels, obtain the required market share. The well-known brand Apple realised that its market share of 10 per cent was of no longer any interest to software manufacturers. Its alliance with IBM on a common standard was its only means of survival. The marked increase in the leader's advantage is clear from the PIMS (Profit Impact of Market Strategy) database. On average, market leaders generate a profit of 12.1 per cent from their sales, those who are second generate 8.3 per cent and those who are third only 3.5 per cent.

Thus the national brand is under threat in several markets, but for a company a brand is still the best way to become profitable. This explains why distributors are themselves becoming more interested in brand thinking. However, as we have seen, to be a brand is not to be a name on a product: rather it is, through constant investment in know-how, to become and remain the reference of quality at an acceptable price, implying the promise of tangible and intangible benefits. Certain distributors' own-brands are already on the right track and certain manufacturers' brands have deviated from it. For all types of consumer there are only two types of brand: those which justify their price, and those which don't.

2

The new rules of brand management

Many companies have forgotten the fundamental purpose of their brands. A great deal of attention is devoted to the branding activity itself, which involves designers, graphic artists and advertising agencies. This activity thus becomes an end in itself, receiving most of the attention. In so doing, we forget that it is just a means. Branding is seen as the exclusive prerogative of the marketing and communications staff. This undervalues the role played by the other parts of the company in ensuring a successful branding policy.

Yet branding, which we now consider indispensable, is the terminal phase of a process that involves the company's resources and all of its functions, focusing them on one strategic intent: creating a difference. Only by mobilising all of its internal sources of added value can a company set itself apart from its competitors.

WHAT DOES BRANDING REALLY MEAN?

Branding means much more than just giving a brand name and signalling to the outside world that such a product or service has been stamped with the mark and imprint of an organisation.

Branding consists in transforming the product category

Brands are a direct consequence of the strategy of market segmentation and product differentiation. As companies seek to better fulfil the expectations of specific customers, they concentrate on providing the latter, consistently and repeatedly, with the ideal combination of attributes – both tangible and intangible, functional and hedonistic, visible and invisible – under viable economic conditions for their businesses. Companies want to stamp their mark on different sectors and set their imprint on their products. It is no wonder that the word 'brand' also refers to the act of burning a mark into the flesh of an animal as a means to claim ownership of it. The first task in brand analysis is to define precisely all that the brand injects into the product (or service) and how the brand transforms it:

- What attributes materialise?
- What advantages are created?
- What benefits emerge?
- What obsessions does it represent?

This deep meaning of the brand concept is often forgotten or wilfully omitted. That is why certain distributors are often heard saying – as a criticism of many a manufacturer's brand whose added value lies only its name – 'For us, the brand is secondary, there is no need to put something on the product.' Hence, the brand is reduced to package surface and label. Branding, though, is not about being on top of something, but within something. The product or service thus enriched must stand out well if it is to be spotted by the potential buyer and if the company wants to reap the benefits of its strategy before being copied by others.

Furthermore, the fact that a delabelled item is worth more than a generic product confirms this understanding of branding. According to the 'brand is just a superficial label' theory, the delabelled product supposedly becomes worthless when it no longer carries a brand name, unless it continues to bear the brand within. In passing, the brand has intrinsically altered it: hence the value of Lacostes without 'Lacoste', Adidases without 'Adidas'. They are worth more than imitations because the brand, though invisible, still prevails. Conversely, the brand on counterfeits, though visible, is in effect absent. This is why counterfeits are sold so cheaply.

Some brands have succeeded in proving with their slogans that they know and understand what their fundamental task is: to transform the product category. A brand not only acts on the market, it organises the market, driven by a vision, a calling and a clear idea of what the category should become. Too many brands wish only to identify fully with the product category, thereby expecting to control it. In fact they often end up disappearing within it: Frigidaire, Xerox, Caddy, Scotch, Kleenex have thus become generic terms.

According to the objective the brand sets itself, transforming the category implies endowing the product with its own separate identity. In concrete terms, that means that the brand is weak when the product is transparent. Talking about 'Greek olive oil, first cold pressing' for example, makes the product transparent, almost entirely defined and epitomised by those sole attributes, yet there are dozens of brands capable of marketing that type of oil. Going from bulk to packaging is also symptomatic of this phenomenon. The weakness of fresh vacuum-packed food brands is partially due to the fact that their packaging, though designed to lure the buyer – such as with sauerkraut in film-wrapped containers – only recreates transparency. Significantly, Findus and Dim do not just show their products, they *show* them *off*. This is the structural cause of Essilor's brand weakness, as perceived by the customers. They do not perceive how Essilor transforms the product, nor its input, its added value. To them, glass is just glass to which various options can be added (anti-reflecting, unbreakable, etc) as with cars. The added value seems to be created solely by the style of the rims (hence the boom in spectacle frame brands) or the service, both of which are palpable and in the store. What is invisible is not perceived and thus does not exist in their eyes. However, the example of mineral water reminds us that it is always possible to make a transparent product opaque, thereby customising an otherwise standard product and lending it some distinctive characteristic. The major mineral water brands have been able to exist, grow and prosper only because they have made the invisible visible. We can no longer choose our water haphazardly: good health and purity are associated with Evian, fitness with Contrex, vitality with Vittel. These various positionings were justified by the invisible differences in water contents. Generally speaking, anything adding to the complexity of ingredients also contributes to creating distance *vis-à-vis* the product. In this respect, Coca-Cola is doing the right thing by keeping its recipe secret. When Orangina was taken over by Pernod-Ricard, its concentrate was remixed into something even more complex. Antoine Riboud, the former CEO of Danone worldwide, expressed a similar concern when declaring: 'It is not yoghurts that I make, but Danones'.

A brand is a long-term vision

The brand should have its own specific point of view on the product category. Major brands have more than just a specific or dominating position in the market: they hold certain positions within the product category. This position and conception both energise the brand and feed the transformations which are implemented for matching the brand's products with its ideals. It is this conception which justifies the brand's existence, its reason for being on the market, and provides it with a guideline for its life cycle. How many brands are capable today of answering the following crucial question: 'What would the market lack if we did not exist?' The company's ultimate goal is undoubtedly to generate profit and jobs. But brand purpose is something else. Brand strategy is too often mistaken for company strategy. The latter most often results in truisms such as 'increase customer satisfaction'. Specifying brand purpose consists in (re)defining its *raison d'être*, its absolute necessity. The notion of brand purpose is missing in most marketing textbooks. It is a recent idea and conveys the emerging conception of the brand, seen as exerting a creative and powerful influence on a given market. If there is power, there is energy. Naturally, a brand draws its strength from the company's financial and human means, but it derives its energy from the specific niche it occupies in the product category. A brand builds up gradually from this niche. If it does not feel driven by an intense internal necessity, it will not carry the potential for leadership and energy.

The analytical notion of brand image does not clearly capture this dynamic dimension, which is demanded by modern brand management: the features of its image will merely result from the vision, the purpose.

Thus, many banks put forward the following image of themselves: close to their clients, modern, offering high-performing products and customer service. These features are, of course, useful to market researchers in charge of measuring the perceptions sent back by the market. But from which dynamic programme do they emanate, which vision do they embody?

Certain banks have specified what their purpose is: for some it is 'to change people's relationship to money', while for others it is to remind us that money is just a 'means towards personal development'. Several banks have recently worked at redefining their singular reason for existence. All of them will have to do so in the future.

More than most, multi-segment brands need to redetermine their own purpose. Cars are a typical example. A multi-segment brand wants to cover all market segments. Each model spawns multiple versions, thereby theoretically maximising the number of potential buyers: diesel, gas, three or five doors, estate, coupé, cabriolet, etc. The problem is that by having to constantly satisfy the key criteria of each segment (bottom range, lower mid-range, upper mid-range and top range), ie to churn out many different versions and to avoid over-typifying a model in order to please everyone, companies tend to create chameleon brands. Apart from the symbol on the car bonnet or the similarities in the car designs, we no longer perceive an overall plan guiding the creative and productive forces of the company in the conception of these cars. Thus, competitors fight their battles either over the price or the options offered for that price. No longer brands, they become mere names on a bonnet or on a dealer's office walls. The word has thus lost most of its meaning.

Major brands can be compared to a pyramid (see Figure 2.1). The top states the brand's vision and purpose – its conception of automobiles, for instance, its idea of the types of cars it wants, and has always wanted, to create, as well as its very own values which either can or cannot be expressed by a slogan. This level leads to the next one down, which shows the general brand style of communication. Indeed, brand personality and style are conveyed less by words than by a way of being and communicating. These codes should not be exclusively submitted to the fluctuating inspiration of the creative team: they must be defined so as to reflect the brand's unique character. The next level presents the brand's strategic image features: amounting to four or five, they result from the overall vision and materialise in the brand's products, communication and actions. This refers, for example, to the positioning of Volvo as a secure, reliable and robust brand, or of BMW as a dynamic, classy prestigious one. Lastly, the prod-

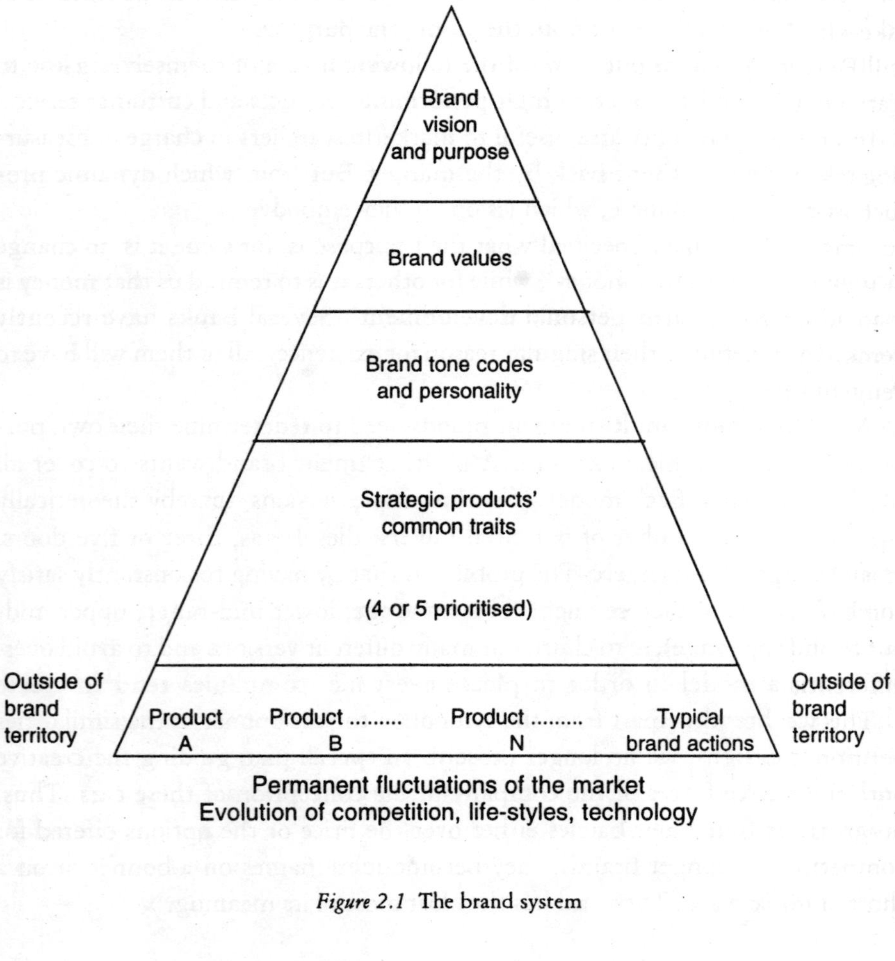

Figure 2.1 The brand system

uct level, at the bottom of the pyramid, consists of each model's positioning in its respective sub-market.

The problem is that consumers look at the pyramid from the bottom up. They start with what is real and tangible. The wider the pyramid base is, the more the customers doubt that all these cars do indeed emanate from the same automobile concept, that they carry the same brand essence and bear the stamp of the same automobile project. Brand management consists, for its part, in starting from the top and defining the way the car is conceived by the brand, in order to determine exactly when a car is deserving of the brand name and when it no longer is – in which case, the car should logically no longer bear the brand name, as it then slips out of its brand territory.

As automobile history is made of great successes followed by bitter failures, major multi-segment brands regularly question their vision. Thus, after its smash hit models, the 205 and 405, Peugeot was somewhat perturbed, both internally and externally, by the series of set-backs with the 605 and the slow take-off of the 106 and 306. A basic question was then asked: 'Are Peugeots still Peugeots?' Answering it implied redefining the long-term meaning of the statement 'It's a Peugeot', ie the brand's long-lasting automobile concept.

Internal hesitation about brand identity is often revealed when searching for slogans. There is no longer a trend toward obvious and meaningless slogans such as 'the automobile spirit', which neither tell us anything about the brand's automobile ideal, nor help to guide inventors, creators, developers or producers in making concrete choices between mutually exclusive features: comfort and road adherence, aerodynamism and feeling of sturdiness, etc. Renault's slogan demonstrates a good understanding of the issues at stake: 'Cars for living'. Peugeot's does too: 'The drive of your life.'

CONSTANTLY RENEWING BRAND DIFFERENCE

It is often argued that certain products within different brands are identical. Some observers thus infer that, under these circumstances, a brand is nothing but a 'bluff', a gimmick used to try to stand out in a market flooded with barely differentiated products.

This view fails to take into account both the time factor and the rules of competition. Brands draw attention through the products they create and bring onto the market. Any brand innovation necessarily generates plagiarism. Any progress made quickly becomes a standard to which buyers grow accustomed: competing brands must then adopt it themselves if they do not want to fall short of market expectations. For a while, the innovative brand will thus be able to enjoy a fragile monopoly, which is bound to be quickly challenged unless the innovation is or can be patented. The role of the brand name is precisely to protect the innovation: it acts as a mental patent, by becoming the prototype of the new segment it creates – advantage of being a pioneer.

If it is true that a snapshot of a given market often shows similar products, a dynamic view of it reveals in turn who innovated first, and who has simply followed the leader: brands protect innovators, granting them momentary exclusiveness and rewarding them for their risk-taking attitude. Thus, the accumulation of these momentary differences over time serves to reveal the meaning and purpose of a brand and to justify its economic function, hence its price premium.

Brands cannot, therefore, be reduced to a mere sign on a product, a mere graphic cosmetic touch: they guide a creative process, which yields the new product A today, the new products B and C tomorrow, and so on. Products come to life, live and disappear, but brands endure. The permanent factors of this creative process are what gives a brand its meaning and purpose, its content and attributes. A brand requires time in order for this accumulation of innovations to yield a meaning and a purpose.

A BRAND IS A LIVING MEMORY

The spirit of a brand can be inferred through its products and its advertising. The content of a brand grows out of the cumulative memory of these acts, provided they are governed by a unifying idea or guidelines. There must be accumulation, not mere juxtaposition. The importance of memory in the making of a brand explains why its image can vary between generations. This is the problem with dual brands such as Citroën: the brand image of those who discovered it through the 2CV is diametrically opposed to that of the discoverers of the DS or XM. And those who knew the famous pre-war Traction Avant model may still remember it vividly. The memory factor also partly explains why individual preferences endure: within a given generation, people continue, even 20 years later, to prefer the brands they liked between the ages of seven and 18 (Guest, 1964; Fry *et al.*, 1973; Jacoby and Chestnut, 1978).

It is precisely because a brand is the memory of the products that it can act as a long-lasting and stable reference. Unlike advertising, in which the last message seen is often the only one that truly registers and is best recalled, the first actions and message of a brand are the ones bound to leave the deepest impression, thereby structuring long-term perception. In this respect, brands create a cognitive filter: dissonant and atypical aspects are declared unrepresentative, thus discounted and forgotten. That is why failures in brand extensions on atypical products do not harm the brand in the end even though they do unsettle the investors' trust in the company (Loken and Roedder-John, 1993). Bic's failure in perfume is a good example. Making perfumes is not typical of the know-how of Bic as perceived by consumers: but sales of ball pens, lighters and razors kept on increasing.

Ridding itself of atypical, dissonant elements, a brand acts as a selective memory, hence endowing people's perceptions with an illusion of permanence and coherence. That is why a brand is less elastic than its products.

A BRAND IS A GENETIC PROGRAMME

A brand is both the memory and the future of its products. The analogy with the genetic memory is central to understanding how brands function and should be managed. Indeed, the brand memory that develops contains the programme for all future evolution, the characteristics of upcoming models and their common traits, as well as the family resemblances transcending their diverse personalities. By understanding a brand's programme, we can not only trace its legitimate territory but also the area in which it will be able to grow beyond the products that initially gave birth to it. The brand's underlying programme indicates the purpose and meaning of both former and future products.

If it exists, this programme can be discovered by analysing the brand's former production, communication and significant actions, since its inception. If a guideline or an implicit permanence exists, then it must show through. Research on brand identity has a double purpose: to analyse the brand's production on the one hand and to analyse the reception, ie the image sent back by the market, on the other. The image is indeed a memory in itself, so stable that it is difficult to modify it in the short run. This stability results from the selective perception described above. It also has a function: to create long-lasting references guiding consumers among the abundant supply of consumer goods. Thus, in men's and women's ready-to-wear, each brand is labelled and catalogued. That is the reason why a company should never turn away from its image, which alone has managed to attract all the latest buyers and all the new ones, ie the most reliable ones for the future. Customer loyalty is created by respecting the brand features that initially seduced the buyers. If the products slacken off, weaken or show a lack of investment and thus no longer meet customer expectations, better try to meet them again than to change expectations. In order to build customer loyalty and capitalise on it, brands must stay true to themselves.

Questioning the past, trying to detect the brand's underlying programme, does not mean ignoring the future: on the contrary, it is a way of better preparing for it by giving it roots, legitimacy and continuity. The mistake is to embalm the brand and to merely repeat in the present what it produced in the past. In fighting competition, a brand's products must always belong intrinsically to their time, but in their very own way. Rejuvenating Lanvin or Balmain means connecting them to modernity, not mummifying them in deference to a past splendour that we might wish to revive.

A brand, therefore, is not a static reality. After all, consumers do not just buy products, they buy branded products. The latter must thus be contemporary as much on the technological, environmental and ergonomic levels as on the pleasure-giving one. They must also conform with the ever-changing standard of the average market price, either at the bottom of the range, in the middle or at the top but never outside it. A car maker incapable of reaching total quality and yet set on remaining competitive pricewise would not stand a chance in today's market. A brand must be able to adapt to its time and to changes both in technology and consumer behaviour so it can remain up to date: through both its material manifestation (as products or services) and its symbolic one (communication). Thus a brand grows a little each day and is not coined once and for all. Of course, its past must not determine its future too narrowly. But when a brand starts developing in all directions, it can very well lose its meaning and substance.

Major brands have a meaning which indicates what they are made of and where they are headed. In the area of household appliances, for example, Siemens means durability, reliability and trust; we can just picture those careful and meticulous German workers. GE stands for practicality, carefree use and the intimacy of a close family friend who has been around long enough to see the children grow up. Philips conveys a sense of innovation to the general public and mass technology for the benefit of all. It thus becomes apparent that in all markets each well-known brand has its own specific meaning. It is very important for hi-tech goods, because it tells buyers in what direction the brand's research, innovation and overall efforts are heading. Here durability, there practicality or innovation. Just as a word cannot bear two meanings at once, since one always dominates the other, no one brand can successfully focus on all possible meanings. Each one maps out its own course, ploughs its own furrow, leaves its own mark.

A given brand will not be jeopardised by competitors offering similar products, unless there are large quantities of the latter. It is indeed inevitable for certain models to be duplicated in the product lines of different brands. Suppose that brand A pursues durability, brand B practicality and brand C innovation: the spirit of each brand will be especially noticeable in certain specific products, those most representative or typical of the brand meaning. Each product range thus contains products demonstrating the brand's guiding value and obsession, they bear the brand's meaning and purpose. Citroën, for instance, is best epitomised by its top-range cars, Nina Ricci by its entrancing evening gowns, Lacoste by its shirts, Sony by its Walkmans and camcorders.

However, there are some products within a given line which do not manage to clearly express the brand's intent and attributes. In the television industry, the cost constraints at the low end of the range are such that trying to manufacture a model radically different from the next-door neighbour's is quite difficult. But, for economic reasons, brands are sometimes forced to take a stake in this very large and overall highly competitive market. Likewise, each bank has had to offer its own savings plan, identical to that of all other banks. All these similar products, though, should only represent a limited aspect of each brand's offer (see Figure 2.2). All in all, each brand stays in focus and progresses in its own direction to make original products. That is why communicating about such products is so important, as they reveal the brand's meaning and purpose.

The problem arises when brands overlap too much, preventing the other from asserting its identity. Using the same motors in Peugeots and Citroëns would harm Peugeot, built on the 'dynamic car' image. It is when several brands sell the same product that a brand can become a caricature of itself. In order to compete against Renault's Espace and Chrysler's Voyager, neither Peugeot or Citroën, Fiat or Lancia could take the economic risk of building a manufacturing plant on their own; neither could Ford or Volkswagen. A single

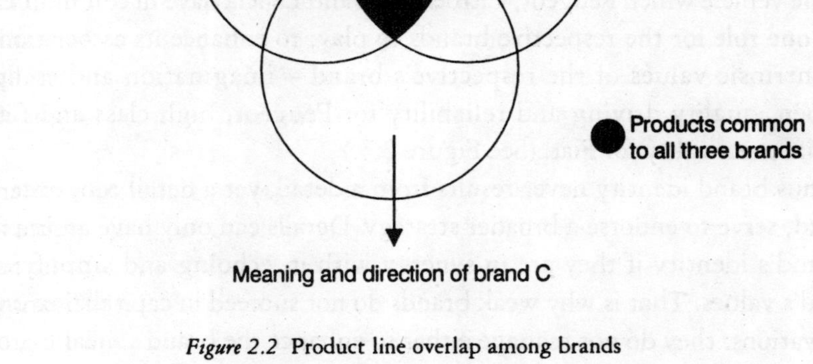

Figure 2.2 Product line overlap among brands

car was made for the first four brands. Similarly, a Ford-Volkswagen plant in Portugal was set to produce a common car. The outcome, however, is that in producing a common vehicle, the brand becomes reduced to a mere external gadget. The identity message was simply relegated to the shell. So each brand has had to exaggerate its outward appearance in order to be easily recognised.

BRANDS ENDOW PRODUCTS WITH MEANING

Products are mute: the brand is what gives them meaning and purpose, telling us how a product should be read. A brand is a both a prism and a magnifying glass through which products can be decoded. Renault invites us to perceive its models as 'cars for living'. On the one hand, brands guide our perception of products. On the other hand, products send back a signal that brands use to underwrite and build their identity. The automobile industry is a case in point, as most technical innovations quickly spread among all brands. Thus the ABS system is offered by Volvo as well as by BMW, yet it cannot be said that they share the same identity. Is this a case of brand inconsistency? Not at all: ABS has simply become a must for all.

However, brands can only develop through long-term consistency, which is both the source and reflection of its identity. Hence the same ABS will not bear the same meaning for two different car-makers. For Volvo, which epitomises total safety, ABS is an utter necessity serving the brand's values and obsessions: it encapsulates the brand's attributes. BMW, which symbolises high-performance, cannot speak of ABS in these terms: it would amount to denying the BMW ideology and value system which has inspired the whole organisation and helped generate the famous models of the Munich brand. BMW introduced ABS as a way to go faster. Likewise, how did the safety-conscious brand, Volvo, justify its participation in the European leisure car championships? By saying 'We *really* test our products so that they last longer.'

The vehicle which Peugeot, Citroën, Fiat and Lancia have in common has left only one role for the respective brands to play: to enhance its association with the intrinsic values of the respective's brand – imagination and escape for Citroën, quality driving and reliability for Peugeot, high class and flair for Lancia, practicality for Fiat. (See Figure 2.3.)

Thus brand identity never results from a detail, yet a detail can, once interpreted, serve to endorse a broader strategy. Details can only have an impact on a brand's identity if they are in synergy with it, echoing and amplifying the brand's values. That is why weak brands do not succeed in capitalizing on their innovations: they do not manage either to enhance the brand's meaning or create that all-important resonance.

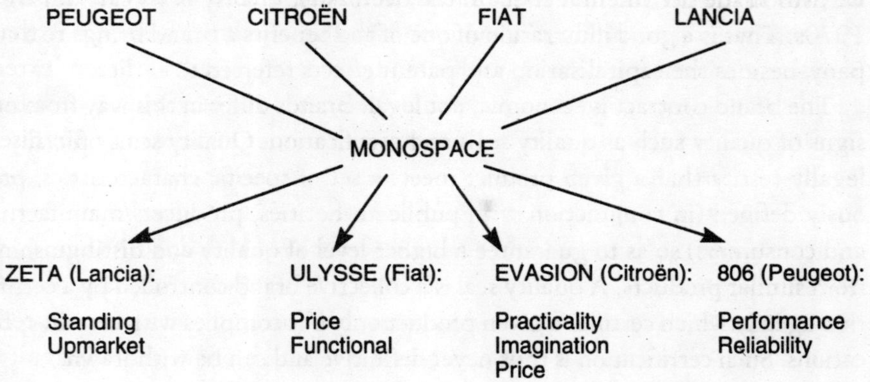

Figure 2.3 **Brands give innovations meaning and purpose**

A brand is thus a prism helping us to decipher products. It defines what and how much to expect from the products bearing its name. An innovation which would be considered very original for a Fiat, for instance, will be considered commonplace for a Ford. However, though insufficient engine power may scarcely have been an issue for many car-makers, for Peugeot it is a major problem. It disavows Peugeot's deeply-rooted identity and frustrates the expectations that have been raised. It would be at odds with what should be called Peugeot's 'brand contract'.

In fact, consumers rarely evaluate innovations in an isolated way, but in relation to a specific brand. Once a brand has engaged in a specific contract, it has to assume all of its implications and fulfil its promises. Brands should respect the contract which has attracted customers and made them successful.

A BRAND IS A CONTRACT

Brands become credible through persistency and repetition. Over time, their programme gradually commits them to the long-term view. By creating satisfaction and loyalty, the programme indeed forces the brand to fulfil the quasi-contract that binds it to the market. In return, the market is likely to view the brand's pending products favourably from the very start. This mutual commitment explains why brands, whose products have temporarily declined in popularity, do not necessarily disappear. A brand is to be judged over the long term: a deficiency can always occur. Brand support gives products a chance to recover. If not, Jaguar would have disappeared long ago: no other brand could have withstood the detrimental effect of the decreasing quality of its cars during the 1970s. That is a good illustration of one of the benefits a brand brings to a company, besides the capitalisation and patent effects referred to earlier.

The brand contract is economic, not legal. Brands differ in this way from other signs of quality such as quality seals and certification. Quality seals officially and legally testify that a given product meets a set of specific characteristics, previously defined (in conjunction with public authorities, producers/manufacturers and consumers) so as to guarantee a higher level of quality and distinguishing it from similar products. A quality seal is a collective brand controlled by a certification agency which certifies a given product only if it complies with certain specifications. Such certification is thus never definitive and can be withdrawn.

Brands do not legally testify that a product meets a set of characteristics. However, through consistent and repeated experience of these characteristics, a brand becomes synonymous with the latter.

BRAND CONTRACT REQUIREMENTS

A contract implies constraints. The brand concept assumes first of all that the various functions in the organization all converge: R&D, production, methods, logistics, marketing, finance. The same is true of service brands: as the R&D and production aspects are obviously irrelevant in this case, the responsibility for ensuring the brand's continuity and cohesion pass to the management and staff, who play an essential role in clientele relationships.

The brand concept requires internal as well as external marketing. Unlike quality seals, brands set their own ever-increasing standards. Therefore, they must not only meet the latter but also continuously try to improve all their products, even the most basic ones, especially if they represent most of their sales and hence act as the major vehicle of brand image: in so doing, they will be able to satisfy the expectations of clients who will demand that the products keep pace with technological change. They must also communicate and make themselves known to the outside world in order to become the prototype of a segment, a value or a benefit. This is a lonely task for brands, yet they must do it to get the air of uniqueness and that of exclusivity they need. The brand will have to support its internal and external costs all on its own. These are generated by the brand requirements, which are to:

- closely monitor the needs and expectations of potential buyers. This is the purpose of market research: both to optimise existing products and to discover needs and expectations which have yet to be fulfilled;

- react to technical and technological progress as soon as it can to create a competitive edge both in terms of cost and performance;
- provide both product (or service) volume and quality at the same time, since those are the only means of ensuring repeat purchases;
- control supply quantity and quality;
- deliver products or services to intermediaries (distributors), both consistently over time and in accordance with their requirements in terms of delivery, packaging and overall conditions;
- give meaning to the brand and communicate its meaning to the target market, thereby using the brand as both a signal and reference for the product's (or service's) identity and exclusivity. That is what advertising budgets are for.

Strong brands thus bring about both internal mobilisation and external federalisation. They create their company's panache and impetus. That is why some companies switch their own name for that of one of their star brands: BSN thus became Danone, CGE became Alcatel-Alsthom. In this respect, the impact of strong brands extends far beyond most corporate strategies. These only last while they are in the making, after which they either vanish or wind up as pompous phrases ('a passion for excellence') posted in hallways. In any case, a brand is the organisation's external facade and, as such, it remains both demanding and determined to constantly outdo itself, to aim ever higher.

Becoming aware that the brand is a contract also means taking up many other responsibilities which are all too often ignored. In the fashion market, even if creators wish to change after a while, they cannot entirely forget about their brand contract, which helped them to get known initially, then recognised and eventually praised. This can indeed cause serious problems for international brand management, as different countries tend to perceive brands in different ways. Thus in Europe, Polo by Ralph Lauren typifies the Bostonian preppie style. Meanwhile, in the US, the Ralph Lauren brand has changed its image significantly by launching the Safari fragrance, which is radically different from the previous style of its products.

In theory, both the brand's slogan and signature are meant to embody the brand contract. A good slogan is therefore often rejected by managing directors because it means too much commitment for the company and may backfire if the products/services do not match the expectations the brand has created so far.

BRANDS AND OTHER SIGNS OF QUALITY

In many sectors, brands coexist with other quality signs. The food industry, for instance, is filled, besides brands, with quality seals, certificates of norm compliance and controlled origin and guarantees. The proliferation of these other signs results from a double objective: to promote and to protect.

Certifications of origin (eg real Scotch whisky) are intended to protect a branch of agriculture and products whose quality is deeply rooted in a specific location and know-how. The controlled origin guarantee capitalises on a subjective and cultural conception of quality, coupled with a touch of mystery and of the area's unique character. It segments the market by refusing the certification of origin to any goods that have not been produced within a certain area nor raised in the traditional way. Thus in France, since 2 July 1990 law was voted, Roquefort has become a name tied to a controlled origin. Even if Danish or American cheese-makers were to produce a 'roquefort' cheese elsewhere that buyers were unable to tell apart from the roquefort cheese made in the Roquefort village itself in the traditional way, their products can no longer lay claim to the name 'Roquefort'. Greek feta cheese did not achieve this: in fact, most so-called Greek feta cheese is made in Holland or France.

Quality seals are promotional tools. They convey a different concept of quality, which is both more industrial and scientific. In this respect, a given type of cheese, for example, involves objective know-how, using a certain kind of milk mixed with selected bacteria, etc. Quality seals create a vertical segmentation, consisting of different levels of objective quality. The issue here is not so much to present typical characteristics as to satisfy a stringent set of objective criteria.

The legal guarantee of typicality brought by a 'certified origin' seal means more than a simple designation of origin, a mere label indicating where a product comes from, in that the latter implies no natural or social specificity – although it may mislead the buyer into thinking that there is one. Moreover, several modern cheese-makers deliberately mix up what is genuine and what is not, inventing names for their new products that are reminiscent of places or villages in an effort to build their own rustic, parochial imagery (the Saint-Moret cheese, for example).

It is interesting to see how European countries tried to reassure consumers during the 'mad cow crisis' in order to redress the 40 per cent drop in beef consumption:

- Although it is not legal under EU regulations, they reinstated designations of origin referring to a country (ie French beef). This did not prove fully reassuring since it was soon heard that French cattle could have eaten not only local grass but also contaminated organic extracts imported from the UK;

- certifications of origin (ie Charollais beef) add typicality but cannot guarantee a 100 per cent safe meat;
- seals of quality did not exist and had to be created but it would take years to promote them: however, unless full control of the entire cattle raising process is guaranteed, the output itself cannot be guaranteed;
- the crisis highlighted the need for meat brands. Since 1989, alerted by early warnings, McDonald's had indeed sought new suppliers in Europe, scrutinising the way in which each and every one raised and fed their cattle.

Whether or not official indications of quality in Europe should still exist in 2001 is a bitter issue that is still being discussed among northern countries (United Kingdom, Denmark etc) who believe that only brands should prevail, and southern countries (France, Spain, Italy) who support the idea of having official collective signs of quality coexist with brands (Feral, 1989).

The northern European countries claim that brands alone should be allowed to segment the market and thus build a reputation for excellence around their names, thanks to their products and to their distribution and marketing efforts. These countries tend to favour an objective concept of quality: it does not matter that the feta cheese that the Greeks prefer is made in Holland or that Smirnoff vodka is neither Russian nor Polish. The southern European countries believe for their part that collective signs enable small companies to use their ranking and/or their typical characteristics as promotional tools, since they do not have their own brands. As their products do not speak for themselves, their market positioning is ensured by quality or certified origin seals. Clearly, behind the European debate on whether or not brands that have built their reputation on their own should coexist with official collective signs of quality lies another more fundamental debate between the proponents of a liberal economy on the one hand, and the partisans of government intervention to regulate it on the other. From the corporate point of view, choosing between brand policy and collective signs is a matter of strategy and of available resource allocation. Brands define their own standards: legally, they guarantee nothing, but empirically they convey clusters of attributes and values. In doing so, they seek to become a reference in themselves, if not the one and only reference (as is the case with Bacardi, the epitome of rum). Thus, in essence, brands differentiate and share very little. Brands distinguish their products. Strong brands are those that diffuse values and manage to segment the market with their own means.

In handling the 'mad cow' crisis, McDonald's wondered whether they should rely on their own brand only or also on the collective labels of origin.

On an operational level, let us once again underline the fact that brands do not boil down to a mere act of advertising. They contain recommendations regarding the long-term specificities of the products bearing their name, such as attractive prices, efficient distribution and merchandising, as well as identity building through advertising. It is easier for a small company to earn a quality seal for one of its products through strict efforts on quality, than it is to undertake the gruelling task of creating a brand, which requires so many financial, human, technical and commercial resources. Even without an identity, the small company's product can thus step out of the ordinary, thanks in part to the legal indicators of quality.

OBSTACLES TO THE BRANDING PRINCIPLES

Within the same company, brand policy often conflicts with other policies. As these are unwritten and implicit, they may seem innocuous, when in fact they are a hindrance to a true brand policy.

Current corporate accounting, as such, is unfavourable towards brands. Accounting is ruled by the prudence principle: consequently, any outlay for which payback is uncertain is counted as an expense rather than valued as an asset. This is the case of investments made in communications in order to inform the general public about the brand's identity. Because it is impossible to measure exactly what share of the annual communications budget generates returns immediately, or within a specified number of years, the whole sum is taken as an operating expense which is subtracted from the financial year's profits. Yet advertising, like investments in machinery, talented staff and R&D, also helps build brand capital. Accounting thus creates a bias that handicaps brand companies because it projects an undervalued image of them. Take the case of company A, which invests heavily to develop the awareness and renown of its brand name. Having to write off this investment as an expense results in low annual profits and a small asset value on the balance sheet. This usually occurs during a critical period in the company's growth, when it could actually use some help from outside investors and bankers. Now compare A to company B, which invests the same amounts in machines and production and nothing whatsoever in either name, image or renown. As it is allowed to value these tangible investments as fixed assets and to depreciate them gradually over several years, B can announce higher profits and its balance sheet, displaying bigger assets, will project a more flattering image. B will thus look better in terms of accounting, when, in fact, A is in a better position to differentiate its products.

The principle of annual accounting valuation of products also hinders brand policy. Every product manager is judged on his yearly results and on the net contribution generated by his product. This leads to 'short-termism' in decision evaluation: those decisions which produce fast, measurable results are favoured over those that build up brand capital, slowly no doubt, but more reliably in the long term. Moreover, product-based accounting discourages product managers from putting out any additional advertising effort that would serve essentially to bolster the brand as a whole, when the latter serves as an umbrella and sign for other products. Managers thus only focus on one thing: any new expenditure in the general interest will be charged to their own account statement. For example, Palmolive is a brand covering several products: liquid detergent, shampoo, shaving cream, etc. The brand could decide to communicate only one of these products singled out as a prominent image leader. But the investment made would certainly be higher than could be justified solely by the sales forecast of that product. This new expenditure will in fact always be on the given product, even though its ultimate purpose is to collectively benefit all products under the umbrella brand.

In order to react against the short-term bias caused by accounting practices and the underestimation of (corporate) value as shown in the balance sheets, some British companies have begun to list their own brands as assets on their balance sheets. This has triggered a discussion on the fundamental validity of accounting practices that emerged in the 'age of commodities', when the essential part of capital consisted of real estate and equipment. Today, on the contrary, intangible assets (know-how, patents, reputation) are what make the difference in the long run. Beyond the need for an open debate in Europe, and worldwide, on how to capitalise brands, it has become just as important to find a way for companies to account for the long-term pros and cons of short-term brand decisions in their books. It is all the more compelling as brand decision-makers themselves rotate often, perhaps too often.

Even the way in which the various types of communication agencies are organised fails to comply with the requirements of sound brand policy. Even if an advertising agency has its own network of partner companies – in charge of name research, packaging, graphic identity, event- or promotion-based corporate communication – and can thus promote itself as an integrated communications group, it remains the crux of the network. Furthermore, advertising agencies think only in terms of campaigns, operating in a short, one-year time frame. Brand policy is different: it develops over a long period and requires that all means be considered at once, in a fully integrated way.

It is clear that a company rarely finds contacts inside so-called communications groups who are actually in charge of strategic thinking and of providing overall recommendations rather than merely focusing on advertising or on the necessity to sell campaigns. Moreover, advertising agencies are not in a position to address strategic issues, such as what should be the optimal number of brands in a portfolio. As these affect the survival of the brands which are under their advertising responsibility, the agencies find themselves in the awkward position of being judge and jury. That is why a new profession has been created: strategic brand management consulting. The time had indeed come for companies to meet professionals with a mid-term vision who are capable of providing consistent, integrated guidelines for the development of brand portfolios without focusing on one single technique.

A high personnel turnover disrupts the continuity a brand needs. Yet companies today actually plan for their personnel to rotate on different brands! Thus, brands are often entrusted to young graduates with impressive degrees but little experience and the promotion they expect often consists of being assigned to yet another brand! Thus product managers must achieve visible results in the short term. This helps to explain why there are so many changes in advertising strategy and implementation as well as in decisions on brand extension, promotion or discounts. These are in fact caused by changes in personnel.

It is significant that brands which have maintained a continuous and homogeneous image belong to companies with stable brand decision-makers. This is the case for luxury brands: the long-lasting presence of the creator or founder allows for sound, long-term management. The same is true of major retailers where senior managers often handle the communication themselves or at least make the final decisions. As a means to alleviate the effects of excessive brand manager rotation, companies aim not only at incorporating brand value into their accounts, but also at creating a long-term brand image charter. The latter represents both a vital safeguard and an instrument of continuity.

Business organisation is sometimes an obstacle to brand management. To be commercially efficient, EDP service companies, for instance, are organised in divisions: each one focuses on the specific problems of a sector or function in particular, thereby offering optimal treatment. In this field, ADS, for example, comprises divisions for travel, transportation, economy and finance, human resource management, marketing and so on. The problem then is that it becomes difficult to invest collectively in the name they all share, ADS. This goes against their organisational principles: every division manager is assessed on his/her own financial results, which he/she naturally seeks to optimise.

Another syndrome pertains to the relationship between production and sales. In the Electrolux group, for instance, production units are specialised according to product. Both mono-product and multi-market, they sell their product to the sales units who are, on the contrary, mono-market and multi-product (grouped under an umbrella brand). The problem is that these autonomous sales divisions, who each have their own brand, all want to benefit from the latest product innovation so as to maximise their division's turnover.

What is missing is a structure for managing and allocating innovations in accordance with a consistent and global vision of the brand portfolio. As we will see later, there is no point in entrusting a strong innovation to a weak brand. Moreover, this undermines the very basis of the brand concept: differentiation.

Lastly, if words mean anything at all, communications managers should have the power to prevent actions that go against the brand's interest. Thus, Philips never succeeded in fully taking advantage of its brand baseline: 'Philips, tomorrow is already here'. In order to do so, they would have needed to ban all advertising on batteries or electric light bulbs that either trivialised the assertion, contradicted it, or reduced it to mere advertising hype. It would also have been possible to communicate only about future bulb types rather than about the best current sales. Unfortunately, nobody in the organisation had the power (or the desire) to impose these kinds of constraints. When the Whirlpool brand appeared, however, the managers from Philips actually created the organisation they needed for implementing a real brand policy: as it was directly linked to general management, the communications department was able to ensure the optimal circumstances for launching the Whirlpool brand, by banning over a three-year period any communication about a commonplace product or even a best-selling product.

Failing to manage innovations has a very negative impact on brand equity. Even though sales people go up in arms when they are not given the responsibility of a strong innovation, it is a mistake to assign the latter to a weak brand, especially in multi-brand groups. When dealing with a weak brand, attractive pricing must indeed be offered to distributors as an incentive to include the latter in their reference listing. But since the brand's consumers do not expect this innovation (each brand defines its type and level of expectations), the product turnover is insufficient. As for the non-buyers, such a brand is not reassuring. If the innovation is launched a few weeks later under a leading brand name, distributors will refuse to pay for the price premium due to a leader because they purchased it at a lower price just a while back from the same company. Thus, even with the strong brand, the sales price eventually has to be cut.

Breeding many strong brands, L'Oréal allocates its inventions to its various businesses according to brand potency. Innovation is thus first entrusted to prestigious brands sold in selective channels as the products' high prices will help cancel out the high research cost incurred. Thus, liposomes were first commercialised by Lancôme, the new sun filter Mexoryl SX by Vichy. Innovation is then diffused to the other channels and eventually to the large retailers. By then, the selective channel brands are already likely to have launched another differentiating novelty.

However, this process is affected by the fact that innovation is not exclusively owned by any one company; it quickly spreads to competitors, which calls for immediate reaction. That is why Plénitude (a brand dedicated to hypermarkets) was quick to market liposomes. When two competing brands within the same group share the same innovation, they must nonetheless capitalise on it in their own specific way. Thus, L'Oréal was not the first company to market AHAs (alpha hydroxy acids), which are cosmetic copies of acid vitamin A, prescribed by dermatologists to smooth out wrinkles. Estée Lauder was the innovator. L'Oréal did not wish to react by using Lancôme because AHAs are aggressive, and so do not express the softness symbolised by the star brand. Instead, L'Oréal marketed in pharmacies and under the Vichy brand name an AHA version called Novactia, focusing the message on the new product's purity, in keeping with Vichy's brand identity. At the same time, L'Oréal did not hesitate to offer an AHA-based cream under the Plénitude brand name in large stores. This weakens Vichy's uniqueness somewhat, but also Lauder's. As we see, the competitive system impacts on the brand equity system.

Along the same lines, when a producer supplies a distributor's brand with the same product it sells under its own brand, it will eventually erode its brand equity and, more generally, the very respectability of the concept of a brand. This simply means that what customers pay more for in a brand is the name and nothing else. When the brand is dissociated from the product it enhances and represents, it becomes merely superficial and artificial, devoid of any rational legitimacy. Ultimately, companies pay a price for this as sales decrease and distributors seize the opportunity to declare in their advertising that national brands alienate consumers, but that consumers can resist by purchasing distributors' own-brands. This also justifies the sluggishness of public authorities regarding the increasing amount of counterfeit products among distributors' own-brands. Finally, such practices foster a false collective understanding of what brands are, even among opinion leaders, which contributes to the rumour that nowadays all products are just the same!

IMPLICATIONS OF THE BRAND EQUITY CONCEPT

The fact that brands are a part of company equity is now well recognised; however, what this awareness implies has not yet been fully analysed. As is often the case, phrases such as 'brands are our equity' become company leitmotivs. The truth is that, when taken at its word, this 'brand equity' awareness has actually revolutionised operational marketing. The most salient aspects of this development are described below.

Implications at the top

The first noticeable change is the fact that top management itself is now in the habit of paying close attention to their brands. In the beginning, brands were considered as a mere communications issue, then as the sole prerogative of the marketing managers; nowadays, CEOs themselves consider brands to be their responsibility. Y. Barbieux, formerly CEO of Nestlé Thailand, France and now of Italy, declared: 'Brands can no longer be entrusted to the marketing people only.' They have thus been disowned in a certain way, as they are no longer the only ones in charge of brand policy. Nowadays, financial, accounting, technical and legal managers, and of course managing directors, are all participating in this task. This new situation has also led multi-brand groups to redefine the position held by their communications managers. No longer serving the marketing departments, they now directly report to general management. This is the case at Whirlpool Europe: thanks to their new position, communications managers are now able to manage fund allocation for the creation of a new brand independently from market share constraints and from the relative power pressure exerted by the group's various brands (Whirlpool, Laden, Bauknecht, Ignis).

In terms of organisation, companies have become aware that their structures are often too ephemeral for efficient brand management. A company must have people who ensure continuity in and respect for the brand's intangible attributes once they have been defined. On the other hand, companies have become aware that a given brand can be linked to several different technologies. Buitoni, for instance, is a brand that sells frozen, canned and vacuum-packed foods, all produced by different companies and marketed by different sales teams. It became necessary to create a new profession: brand management across companies. Finally, the typical pyramid-shaped marketing structures have caused responsibilities to be diluted and managers to specialise more and more in only one particular facet of the brand. That is why the Danone group has flattened its hierarchy down from four to three tiers, thus leaving a brand marketer, a brand marketing manager in charge of the brand's overall management and a marketing director in charge of coordination and, more specifically, of the 'mega-brands'.

The end of dispersal

Apart from the brand's new internal environment, the notion of brand equity means it is essential to manage the value of this equity. In doing so, the key word is 'capitalisation'. Yet it seems impossible to capitalise on several brands at the same time, unless the company is a powerful multinational. Most companies therefore reduce their brand portfolios and focus only on one of several brands. As a matter of fact, brand portfolios are often overloaded, due more to successive acquisitions than to thorough planning of what each brand needs to do, both for its consumers (through their specific positioning) or for its distribution channels (in order to avoid conflicts). This tendency is even stronger in the industrial sector: as many companies pursued their growth through buy-outs, they now have to cope with a stack of local brands, product or product-line brands and company brands, as well as with a set of problems for which they are not prepared.

Reducing the brand portfolios has a corollary effect: fewer brands now encompass more products. Products whose brands no longer exist must be allocated to existing ones. Danone, for instance, covers more than 100 product lines. It has therefore become necessary to create intermediate product-line brands in order to structure Danone's overall product range, such as Taillefine for waist-conscious consumers, Charles Gervais for gourmet adults, Kid for children, Bio for the health-conscious, etc. Each product-line brand has its own target market and its own positioning, and is meant to encompass several sub-brands itself. At Danone, product brands are now history. The full product range is hierarchically organised both within Danone and within the different product-line brands. In order to ensure that the structure benefits Danone and does not represent a mere patchwork, each product-line brand sets its own brand image objective, yet all of them share two features inherent to Danone's identity: proximity and health. In a similar way, the Nestlé company has selected a limited number of master brands (Nescafé, Maggi, Buitoni, Nestlé, and so on), each of them acting as a source brand for a wide range of products and sub-brands.

The end of new brand proliferation

This urge to capitalise has thus put an end to the proliferation of brands and product names which has so far worked against all major groups. It is true that any product manager in charge of launching a new product is tempted to give it a name of its own: its own brand name. This is especially true in industry where the naming process is practically the only way both for the manager and the new product to gain instant recognition from all. That is why companies registered bucket-loads of brand names for their new products, encouraged by the classical Procterian ideology of the product brand. Those times are over. Not only did it prove expensive (Du Pont Agricultural Products has almost 800 brand names to manage, which costs a lot of money) but also inefficient: most of the names remained unknown, legally defined as brands, but meaning nothing whatsoever to buyers. It would have been wiser just to retain the best-known names and to break them down into umbrella brands. That is the only way to capitalise.

Having experienced the same syndrome, Nestlé decided to create a brand management department in their headquarters in Vevey, Switerland, uniquely entitled to create new brands all over the world. The results were radical: in 1991, Nestlé launched nearly 101 new products worldwide, but only created five new brands. Thus 96 innovations were launched either under the umbrella or the endorsement of existing brands! For example, chocolate-flavoured cereals were launched under the Nesquik brand name because they serve the same purpose: to provide mothers with a means of coaxing their children into drinking milk. In order to prevent itself being perceived as a censor and arbitrary ruler, 3M distributed worldwide an internal booklet specifying both the market conditions under which creating new brands would be authorised (eg Post-it) and the most prevalent ones under which innovations must bear one of three name possibilities: the generic one plus the 3M brand name (3M cassettes or overhead projectors); its own surname within an existing product-line brand (Magic Tape by Scotch); a generic name plus the product-line brand (video cassettes by Scotch). This document, entitled '*Brand Asset Management*', made it possible to internalise some basic management principles. This explains why requests for new brands at 3M dropped from 244 in 1981 to 70 in 1991. That year only four were accepted, versus 73 in 1989, and is how 3M managed to reduce its portfolio from 1500 to only 700 brands! At 3M, all brands are intrinsically global and international, hence creating local brands is now strictly forbidden. The only time the creation of a new brand can be envisaged is when a new primary need is discovered: such was the case for Post-it. Creating new sub-brands such as Scotch's 'Magic' can be done only if using the brand name (Scotch in this case) does not allow sufficient differentiation among products (see page 210).

Building brands with innovations

Seen from a distance, these rules may seem to limit and restrict the creative drive. From within, though, they have proven to be the only means of renewing existing brands, enhancing both their value and their worldwide impact. Brands manage to grow only if they constantly renew themselves and if the new products end up accounting for a significant part of their turnover. Brands demonstrate their contemporary relevance by showing their ability to market new products that satisfy new needs and meet modern expectations. Yet most of the time product managers would prefer to launch innovations under their own new brand name. This amounts to depriving existing brands of the aura of modernity conveyed by new products. When naming their new instant mashed potatoes Mousline instead of Maggi, one of the corporation's mega brands, the Nestlé managers tarnished the latter's image by slightly outdating it. Thinking in terms of capitalisation thus requires addressing the issues in the reverse order: choosing a name for a new product no longer matters as much as deciding which new products should be launched under the existing brand name. Brands are rejuvenated by new products matching new needs, not by advertising. That is why Cadbury-Schweppes did not allow a new soft-drink to be launched as 'Wipps': instead, it became 'Dry' by Schweppes. For young people, 'Wipps' would have caused Schweppes to lose contact with youth and to become a brand associated with their parents. 'Dry' by Schweppes at least aimed to connect the new brand with the new consumers, and thus ensured a better future for the Schweppes brand name. Today, Coca-Cola would never have launched its light version as 'Tab' (1964), but immediately as Diet Coke – without waiting until 1981 to do so. Meanwhile, Pepsi-Cola reacted to Tab by launching Diet Pepsi, which gave the brand an upbeat, health-conscious image.

Managing innovation allocation

The capitalisation concept also impacts on the way in which innovations are allocated in a company with a multi-brand portfolio. As already mentioned, when companies do not properly allocate their innovations, they actually undermine the strong brand's premium while failing to increase the weaker brand's sales.

It is, therefore, not up to the brand managers to decide whether their brand needs an innovation or not. The marketing manager, who has a clear vision of each brand's territory and boundaries, must alone determine innovation allocation, according to the respective contract and positionings. This helps clarify both the consumers' and the distributors' perception of each brand's function on the market. It also increases profitability. The problem is that many brands no longer know why they even exist, as they get handed down from one generation to another, often inherited from mergers and acquisitions. They do project a more or less clearly defined image of course, but neither their positioning nor the role they are supposed to play on the market in connection with the other corporate brands have ever been specifically stated. Capitalising on a brand can only be done if we know where we are headed and what we are fighting for. That is why all headquarters elaborate brand charters, which aim at defining once and for all the brand's values and its specific features, its uniqueness and core business (see page 126).

Identity prevails over image

Up to now, brand management has been governed by brand image research. The brand's main concern is to know how it is perceived. Today, marketing considers the notion of identity as the core concept of brand management: before knowing how we are perceived, we must know who we are. Only identity can provide the right framework for ensuring brand consistency and continuity (multi-product, multi-domestic) and for making capitalisation possible. It is not up to the consumer to define the brand and its content, it is up to the company to do so. Certainly it will make use of market facts and data and consumers' opinions. However, the latter have no feelings about long-term interest and coherence within brand portfolios. Today there are too many people, both internally and externally, taking part in brand management. The more participants there are, the more distortions, personal interpretations and variations in style there are. Even though brands act democratically by bringing progress onto the market, they should be managed by an enlightened despot, not by a democrat. Someone has to be both the boss and the guarantor of its continuity and identity. This guardian, as mentioned above, is to be found high up in the hierarchy nowadays. He/she is thus in the perfect position to resist different sorts of daily pressure, which can be tempting in terms of short-term turnover but damaging in the medium term. One must be capable, for instance, of refusing attractive proposals of brand extension under licensing, if these do not fit the brand's intrinsic identity. The latter can only build up with time and continuity. That is why the current turnover of marketing managers goes against brand interests. It is therefore necessary to have a brand charter that serves as a guarantor for brand identity, perpetuity and consistency, and that encompasses all of the countries, managers and products which it endorses. Knowing the brand project intimately is the best way of sharing it both internally and externally and, thus, of leaping into the future.

Exploiting brand equity

Capitalising is a good thing, of course, but it is also legitimate to take advantage of the return yielded by the brand's equity. This is what brand extension is all about. For decades, marketing managers just adopted Procter & Gamble's brand management model. Those days are over. Reducing a brand to only one product means shrinking brand equity. This can jeopardise the brand since all products eventually die out – and often their brands, too. That is what nearly happened to VW: as VW was exclusively associated with the famous 'Beetle' for too long, the destiny of its brand became too dependent on the car's lifecycle. All products enter a downward phase at some time. Likewise, the French cigarette brand, Gauloises, knew when to pull out of the declining market for dark cigarettes and transfer its image to that of light cigarettes. Brand extension is now a must. Nivea is a good example: it would have been a mistake to associate Nivea exclusively with its well-known, yet basic, multi-purpose mono-product (its moisturising cream). Nivea has now created a full range of creams. The values attributed to a brand often help segment markets other than that in which the brand was born. Thus Bic symbolises 'cheap, relaxed lifestyle, simple and practical product'. These values were first embodied in the famous ball-point pen; thereafter, they proved relevant for disposable lighters and razors. This brand extension was legitimate, as it was reinforced by similar distribution channels. However, these values do not segment the market for body perfume. Thus that extension failed, though it would have worked for air fresheners. Hence, brand extension uses awareness and image equity in order to gain significant market share at minimal entry costs. That is why Essilor has now become threatened by two unexpected newcomers to the market for corrective glasses: Seiko and Nikon. The values of precision, detail and high technology conveyed worldwide by Seiko justify its presence on the huge international market hithero dominated by Essilor. As we see, brand values generate brand financial value and price justification.

Brand equity and price war

As the economic crisis has reached a climax, it has become quite common to talk about brand chaos and crash. Such alarming statements pertain above all to consumer goods but also to services and industrial goods. They address the general issue of brand value. In effect, distributors' own brands and low priced goods (hard discount products) now occupy about 40 per cent of large retailers' shelf space. As this trend is bound to last, the survival of many national brands is a matter of concern. Why are brands, or at least certain renowned brands, becoming less attractive?

The main reason for this is the discrepancy between price and value, which is actually caused by the producers themselves. Too many of them have indeed taken equity for a guaranteed source of income. They have thus neglected to work on maintaining the perceived difference and have systematically raised the selling prices since 1980. This remained unnoticed during times of inflation. Neither decreases in VAT nor increases in productivity were passed on to consumers. All in all, prices kept on rising so that even the more classical, quality-focused distributors' own brands had to follow the upward price trend. In doing so, producers actually gave way to a new, hitherto undeveloped, segment of buyers: those wanting to buy the cheapest possible and those who do not care enough about the product class to want to pay more. Unconditional brand loyalty does not exist. Marlboro's repeated price increases were bound to reach a limit some day. Price perception is definitely a relative concept: as new producers entered the market with cigarettes 40 per cent cheaper, the price perception of that brand, and of many other consumer good brands, became totally exaggerated. In fact, lowest price products no longer mean worst quality products. The price difference no longer corresponds to a perceived difference in quality: the brand is no longer in equilibrium. Price increases due to sole intangible values no longer prevail.

After 40 years of economic growth, managers have inherited a false idea about price. During these years, market growth and inflation compensated for most pricing mistakes. For many executives, to lower prices is to give in. This is no longer true: price competitiveness has become the sign of performing companies.

What brand strategies, then, should be implemented? They differ according to two main brand types. Those based on technology (cosmetics, hygiene, beauty, detergents, etc) must invest in R&D in order to recreate a difference in performance which advertising should help feed to the brand. The other type of brand has no better option than to maintain volume levels in order to cover fixed costs. In this case, the only solution is to cut prices 'in order to come back and compete in the mainstream market'.

However, some brands are making risky moves. They think that they should drop their prices to the level of the lowest priced products. But such a decrease in prices is bound to undermine the brand's long-term credibility as far as its loyal customers are concerned, in which case the latter might start wondering about the brand's true value. Moreover, it would not be well-grounded, nor would its purpose be clear. The market mechanism can indeed be compared to a trammel-hook (Degon, 1994). As shown in Table 2.1, there is a hierarchy of segments in every market. Real competition first takes place within the segment itself. Today, it is obvious that the cheapest product of each segment is most attractive. As a matter of fact, they are the only ones with increasing volumes. The strategy thus consists in assessing a realistic price difference, taking into consideration both brand image and awareness.

Brand equity and producing distributors' own brands

The brand equity concept directly impacts on the way in which producers address the following key issue: should we produce for the distributors' own brands?

First of all, both the low price and the DOB segments often represent an important share of the market (40 to 50 per cent), which can no longer be

Table 2.1 An illustration of the trammel-hook model: the price–volume relationship

Product class: Pastas	Brands	% volume change April/May '93	Price (French francs) April/May '93
Made with eggs	Barilla (upscale)	+2.1	23.69
	Other producers	+6.4	18.87
	No. 2 brand	−7.5	15.94
	Distributors' own-brands	+22.3	15.12
	No. 1 brand	+43.1	14.07
Standard quality	Barilla (upscale)	+4.3	14.57
	No. 2 brand	−5.4	11.54
	No. 1 brand	−8.7	10.36
	Distributors' own-brands	−0.9	7.90
	Other producers	+12.9	6.95

Source: Nielsen/Degon (1994).

neglected. These are bound to last and to develop. Thus, it would be unreasonable for many corporations not to produce for those two segments. The brand concept calls for precautions, as mentioned below:

- Brands based on technology have no reason to concede their technology. In this respect, L'Oréal does not supply distributors' own-brands. The competitive advantage of L'Oréal's brands is entirely generated by R&D and advertising. It is thus legitimate to want to preserve it exclusively. L'Oréal actually discourages the entry of DOBs by means of its brand portfolio, which contains a brand for each level of consumer involvement. In fact, for L'Oréal, the equivalent of DOBs in functional terms is Nivea or Oil of Ulay.
- Well-known producers should not invest to produce distributors' own-brands. Indeed, distributors' choice of producers is often changing so quickly that it would be risky to make any specific industrial investment.
- Producers should not concede their best technology but the one which is almost, or entirely, the same as that produced by their competitors.
- DOB activity must be intrinsically profitable. It is thus necessary to stop reasoning in terms of marginal cost, given the increasing volumes such activity generates. Resulting cashflow can then be used to defend the brands and preserve their competitiveness.

These are some aspects of the management revolution resulting from the realisation that companies must create, preserve and use that precious brand equity of theirs. This revolution is just starting. The obsession now is capitalising on the best brands. This is quite contrary to current practice. A majority of companies still spend a lot more time on their weak than on their strong brands, which should be the ones guiding them into the future. In this respect, it is quite revealing that Edwyn Artzt, CEO of Procter & Gamble, was nicknamed 'Terminator' for having terminated many brands incapable of yielding added value: Citrus Hill orange juice, Solo laundry detergent, White Cloud paper. Whenever the price differential barely covers the marketing and advertising costs needed for brand upkeep, there is no good reason for the brand to live on.

SERVICE BRANDS

There is no legal difference between product, trade or service brands. These are economic distinctions, not legal ones. By focusing only on branding *per se*, ie on signs only, the law does not help us much to understand either how brands and the branding process work or what the specific characteristics among the various players are.

Service brands do exist: Europcar, Hertz, Ecco, Manpower, Visa, Club Med, Marriott's, Méridien, HEC, Harvard, BT, etc. Each one represents a specific cluster of attributes embodied in a quite concrete, though intangible, type of service: car rental, temporary work, computer services, leisure activities, hotel business or higher education. However, some service sectors seem to be just entering the brand age. They either do not consider themselves as being a part of it yet or have just started becoming aware that they are. This evolution is fascinating to watch, as it highlights all that the brand approach involves and reveals the specificities of branding an intangible service.

The banking industry is a fine example. If bank customers were asked what bank brands they knew, they probably would not know or understand what to answer. They know the names of banks, but not bank brands. This is significant: for the public, these names are not brands, identifying a specific service, but corporate names or business signs linked to a specific place.

Until recently, bank names designated either the owner of the corporation entrusted with the customers' funds (Morgan, Rothschild) or a specific place (Citibank) or a particular customer group. Name contraction often signals that a brand concept is in formation. Thus, for example, Banque Nationale de Paris has become BNP. Some observers consider this as just a desire to simplify the name, as per the advertising principle 'what's easy to say is easy to remember', as short signatures make it easier to identify the signer. Such abbreviations have definitely had an impact; however, they seem to reduce the whole branding concept to a mere part of the writing and printing process solely within the realm of communication.

As they are contracted, these bank names come to represent some kind of relationship instead of a mere person or place. In order to become visible, this relationship may take the form of specific 'bank products' (or standard policies in the insurance industry). But these visible and easy-to-imitate products are not the explanation and justification for why they have decided to build a true brand. They are merely the brand's external manifestation. Banks and insurance companies have understood the key to what makes them different: the relationships that develop between a customer and a banker under the auspices of the brand.

Finally, one aspect of service brands that contrasts with product brands is that service is invisible. What does a bank have to show, except customers or consultants? Structurally, service brands are handicapped in that they cannot be easily illustrated. That is why service brands use slogans. No wonder: slogans are indeed vocal, they are the brand's *vocatio*, ie the brand's vocation or calling. Slogans are a commandment for both internal and external relations. Through a slogan, the brand defines its behavioural guidelines, and these guidelines give the customer the right to be dissatisfied if they are transgressed. Claiming to be the bank with a smile or the bank who cares is not enough. These attributes must be fully internalised by the people who offer and deliver the service. The fact that humans are intrinsically and unavoidably variable is definitely a challenge for the brand approach in service industries.

THE CASE OF LUXURY BRANDS

Luxury brands are very distinct. And yet, even though France, Italy, Germany, the UK and the USA have created famous luxury brands, there is still some confusion over the concepts of luxury and luxury brand, not to mention the French concept *griffe* which cannot adequately be translated into English (or into any other language – *griffe* literally means 'claw' in French). Naturally, everyone is able to sense the differences and to quote a typical example for each of those concepts. However, when pressed for an exact definition, most people hesitate to give a straightforward answer.

This issue is much more than just a search for some definitions and for the minimum requirements to be met in order for a product to qualify as luxury brand. In reality, this nebulous definition of luxury hints at the fact that some essential differences between the management of a luxury brand and that of, say, a mass market brand are gradually disappearing. At a time when most luxury goods manufacturers are losing their independence as they get absorbed by big industrial groups with high-performing marketing techniques, it is important to recall the meaning of concepts and categories. This, indeed, helps people to become aware of the limitations and dangers of simply applying classical marketing methods to luxury brand management. Yet it also reminds them that luxury has become a real industry, demanding a high level of profitability.

What is luxury?

The problem with the word 'luxury' is that it is at once a concept (a category), a subjective impression and a polemical term, often subjected to moral criticism. Thus, what is luxury for some is just ordinary for others: while some brands are qualified as 'luxury brands' by one half of public opinion, others are simply considered as 'major brands' by the other half. Likewise, given the economic crisis, it has become ethically more dubious 'to like luxury' or 'to pursue luxury'. Real luxury brands remain attractive, but the word itself has lost its clout and sparkle because of the economic downturn in industrialised countries. The word 'luxury' has fallen out of favour a little: a hindrance to market researchers, who wish to measure their customers' sensitivity to luxury.

In economic terms, luxury objects are those whose price/quality relationship is the highest on the market. By 'quality', economists mean 'what they know how to measure', ie tangible functions. Thus, a McKinsey report defines luxury brands as those which 'have constantly been able to justify a high price, ie significantly higher than the price of products with comparable tangible functions'. This strictly economic definition of the luxury brand does not include the notion of an absolute minimum threshold. What counts, indeed, is not the absolute price, but the price differential between 'luxury' products and products with comparable functions. This price differential can vary from £10 for a cologne brand to hundreds of thousands of pounds (see Figure 2.4).

As we see, this strictly economic perspective does not help differentiate the upper-range brand from the luxury brand and *a fortiori* from the *griffe*. Furthermore, even though a Jaguar has always been cheaper than a Porsche, in terms of comparable tangible functions Jaguar still has a stronger luxury image than Porsche, which is most often perceived as a very sporty brand with technical features. Finally, the economic approach does not help clarify the confusion because it is based on the following dichotomy: a brand either is or is not a luxury brand. Yet, as we shall see further on, it is time for us to recognise that Dior is a *griffe* for one part of its activities, a luxury brand for the second part and an

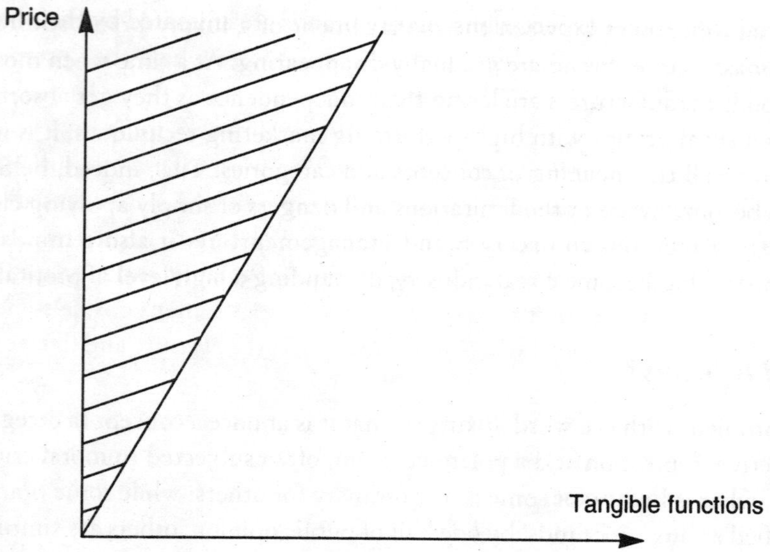

Figure 2.4 The luxury industry according to McKinsey

upper-range brand for the third part. By wanting to classify the brand once and for all, we often forget to make the appropriate distinctions according to its various functions and processes. It may help to define upper-range products as tangibles associated with a specific product category, while luxury products are intangibles associated with values and ethics. Simultaneously managing the three types of action of a given brand is precisely the challenge that luxury brand managers face today.

What does the luxury concept actually encompass? What are the essential attributes of this category of so-called 'luxury' items? Once again, etymology will help us clarify the concepts. Luxury comes from 'lux', which means light in Latin. This explains the typical characteristics of so-called luxury items. Luxury glitters. The fact that luxury is visible is also essential: luxury must be seen, by the consumer and by others. That is why luxury brands externalise all of their signs: the brand signature must be seen and recognised on the person wearing the brand, and it must be recognisable worldwide. Made to perfection, luxury items stand out and embody certain ideals. Luxury defines beauty; it is art applied to functional items.

Like light, luxury is enlightening (critics would rather say 'blinding'). Luxury brands are the tangible references to the most sophisticated fashions of a given time. As such, these brands implicitly convey their own culture and way of life: hence Saint Laurent is not Chanel. They offer more than mere objects: they provide references of good taste. That is why luxury management should not only depend on customer expectations: luxury brands are animated by their internal programme, their overall vision and the specific taste which they promote, as well as by the pursuit of their own standards.

On a symbolic level, light means life and fertility. Luxury is thus both creation and the vital source of inspiration. In effect, most luxury institutions were founded by a creative genius, whose constantly renewed inspiration attracted the attention of the ruling classes and the elite. Relating to luxury requires two things: the monetary capacity to pay the price of quality and a propensity to appreciate the object's artistic, creative and sensuous dimensions, ie something beyond mere practicality. Luxury items provide extra pleasure and flatter all the senses at once.

Etymology is not the only means of deciphering the mystery of the concept of luxury. Sociology and history can also help. Luxury is the natural accompaniment of the ruling classes. It is indeed widely acknowledged that luxury plays a classifying role according to which a restricted group bonds together and distances itself from the rest of society in terms of price and preferences (ie taste). In this respect, luxury brands are just perpetuating and exemplifying the signs and attitudes of the former aristocracy. Is it not paradoxical that luxury has blossomed in a society which eradicated the aristocracy, yet has preserved the aristocrats' social ideal? Luxury ennobles both the object and its owner. Coats of arms have disappeared, but blazons and brand seals are today's ostentatious adornments. Not many luxury symbols exist, but those that do represent the past privileges of the European aristocracy (according to the definition of T. Veblen): living a life of leisure, free of all working, money, time or space obligations. That is why the horse, Hermès' founding symbol, works so well: anything even remotely connected to a horse conveys elegance. That is also why modern luxury has produced cars such as Jaguars and Rolls-Royces. Everything is made to conceal mere practical utility: the leather, the polished wood, the hushed engine are multiple details which make them more like a drawing room than a car. In this respect, Ferrari and Porsche are regarded as prestigious sport brands rather than typical examples of luxury. Created by a talented engineer, they certainly convey the mythical quest for speed, but they nonetheless embody above all the basic automobile function: mobility.

Likewise, luxury constantly seeks to escape time constraints: by focusing on leisure, or by concealing the effects of time with wigs and face make-up. As for perfume, it also helped to distinguish aristocrats from the common folk. As we can see, it is significant that modern luxury brands have fallen for the cosmetics and perfume industry, not to mention the other essential class attributes: clothing and jewels.

Luxury brands and 'griffes'

A good deal of confusion surrounds the meaning and relationship of these two terms. Many people use the term *griffe* if a prestigious brand is applied to many different products. Others claim that brands can become *griffes*.

In reality, brands and griffes must be distinguished in terms of the ground they cover and the way they work. Confusion has been caused by the fact that some famous names, eg Dior, are *griffes* for one part of their production and brands for another. Hence, a *griffe* can become a brand, but the reverse is not true.

The law scarcely clarifies the differences between brands and *griffes*: in its eyes, a *griffe* is the fixed image of a signature, set down to be used as a trademark. Fortunately, we can understand the '*griffe*' concept by examining the word itself. A *griffe* has something to do with instinct, violence and lightning: it conveys something unpredictable, that leaps out and leaves its mark. The *griffe* is the mark of an inspired and instinctive creator. Last, but not least, *griffe* has the same root as the word 'graphic', thus referring back to the hand. The *griffe*'s specific territory is clearly that of pure creation. Its world of reference is art, it employs hand-made production and its aim is to create a work of unsurpassable, striking, perfection. The term 'work' is crucial: the ideal behind a *griffe* is a unique work of art which can never be reproduced. Yves Saint Laurent is a *griffe* when he signs his haute couture gowns in his boutique on the Rue St Honoré: they are one of a kind, luxury brand items. Nina Ricci, on the contrary, is no longer a *griffe* since her visibility in the small circle of haute couture has faded.

That explains why Dunhill, Dupont, Montblanc or Boss are not *griffes* in this sense, but luxury brands. These products were not born in a workshop but in a factory, and they are not intended to be unique pieces, but products made in series – usually limited series, granted, but not always! Their manufacturing is not based on instinct but on streamlined production. Workshops can become industrialised and move into series, then mass production. But the opposite has never happened.

The fact that the luxury industry comprises three levels must be acknowledged (see Figure 2.5). At the top of the pyramid, there is the *griffe* – the creator's signature engraved on a unique work. This explains what it fears most: copies. Brands, on the other hand, particularly fear fakes/counterfeits. The second level is that of luxury brands produced in small series within a workshop, ie a 'manufacture' in its etymological sense which is seen as the sole warrant of 'good-facture'. Examples include Hermès, Rolls-Royce or Cartier. The third level is that of streamlined mass production: there we find Dior or YSL cosmetics and perfumes and SL Diffusion textiles. At this level of real industrialisation,

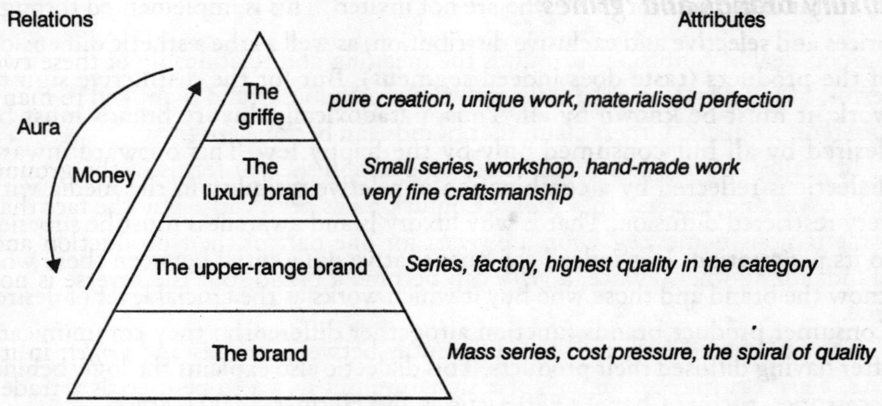

Figure 2.5 The luxury and brand system

the brand's fame generates added value for expensive and prime quality products, which nonetheless gradually tend to look more and more like the rest.

The whole issue of luxury management hinges on the interactions between these three levels. The perpetuity of *griffes* depends on their integration in industrial conglomerates capable of providing the financial and technical means (R&D) to launch new worldwide products on the third level (Sanofi-Elf for cosmetics, L'Oréal for perfumes). Profit accrues at this level and it is the only means to survive, given the huge investments required to preserve the *griffe*'s aura and creativity. If the latter ever disappears, the amount of profit at the bottom of the pyramid will certainly drop, as the brand name will lose its prestige. And yet, the more brand equity is used, the more it needs to be regenerated: that is why the industrial groups, which have invested a lot in luxury brands, would be mistaken if they decided to cut the expenses incurred through financing haute couture and the process of pure creation. These are expenses which help build up new dream and aura capital. What happens is that this capital gradually gets used up by the series process introduced at the third level, ie the upper-range brand. Reality consumes dreams: the more we buy a luxury brand, the less we dream of it. Hence, somewhat paradoxically, the more a luxury brand gets purchased, the more its aura needs protection.

Principles of luxury management

Historians and sociologists have pointed out some of the basic principles of luxury brand management: for instance, the necessity of protecting clients from non-clients, by creating a distance, a no-mix area, or, as economists would put it, entrance barriers for those who are not invited. This is implemented through prices and selective and exclusive distribution, as well as the æsthetic dimension of the products (taste does indeed segment). But for the distinctive sign to work, it must be known by all. Thus, paradoxically, luxury brands must be desired by all but consumed only by the happy few. This outward/inward dialectic is reflected by a combination of relative visibility in the media with very restricted diffusion. That is why luxury brand awareness must be superior to its penetration. It is indeed the quantitative differential between those who know the brand and those who buy it which works as the crucial lever of desire. Consumer product brands function altogether differently: they communicate after having diffused their products. This dialectic also explains the logic behind accessories, such as Chanel's £80 earrings and Hermès' £100 scarves.

Loss of control occurs precisely when luxury brands no longer protect their clients from the non-clients. In our open democratic societies, groups are constantly trying to recreate separations of all kinds. The latter do eventually disappear when, for instance, prestigious brands get distributed in hypermarkets. The infinite multiplication of Vuitton bags (not counting the counterfeits) also hinders the distinctive function of luxury. Likewise, distributed in large quantities, Chanel T-shirts ended up being worn by an excessive number of women, far beyond the initial target.

Chanel thus became associated with too many women. But above all, such an ordinary T-shirt proved that the marketers had forgotten a crucial element: an object must always be up to par with its brand, and not just serve as a mere prop for the brand name. The genuine luxury brand ensures that both frame and picture, the exterior and interior, are worth the same. If the two get disconnected, the luxury brand enters the realm of sham and abdicates in favour of counterfeit. If the luxury brand itself no longer believes in the object itself but only in the fluff around the sign, it encourages people to deliberately buy counterfeits. In doing so, they are purchasing the brand's lasting halo rather than the object itself, as it has been reduced to a mere advertisement prop with no edge to it. In the short term, it is highly profitable to multiply licences and to extend the luxury brand to a great deal of ordinary products, such as underwear and accessories. But in doing so, the luxury brand becomes not only democratised but also commoditised. On the contrary, luxury is always meant to be slightly excessive: excess of detail, excess of care, excess of precaution, all reflecting a traditional way of working which scarcely exists in this age of standardisation and cost minimisation. This does not mean that the past is a shrine, as some luxury brands unfortunately tend to think: in worshipping tradition so, they might end up disappearing along with their ageing clients. The challenge modern luxury now faces is to please and preserve today's consumers. Explicitly reminiscing about the past can be alienating. Having fully understood that, Cartier introduced steel in its watches, but still presented it as a precious metal. Likewise, Hermès' traditional crocodile or leather suitcase is now also available in carbon fibre yet its interior still contains numerous personalising details and is made of soft, sensual leather.

The modern luxury brand must belong to those who rule the world today. Their reference points are no longer land or castle, but mobility. It is true that excessive practicality can harm the luxury product – in that respect, Seiko and Sony are not luxury brands. Conversely, though, if the products are not practical enough, they gradually start to lag and become obsolete. Luxury brands cannot just ignore the threat of basic brands which are strictly focused on practicality: by constantly improving the quality of their products, the latter are indeed continually redefining the ever-increasing standards of 'basic' quality. However prestigious and potentially attractive Jaguar may have been, it was doomed by its deficiencies both in its engine and in its basic components. By relying too heavily on its symbolic added value, Jaguar actually lost some of its global luxury value and attractiveness. Its legend was no longer leading it: it had been left behind.

Basic brands are meant to democratise progress, thanks to a virtually circular mechanism and to competition. Quality standards are rising all the time, even at the cheapest price possible, thanks to mass production. Being partly freed from price constraints, luxury brands, on the contrary, perpetuate an exceptionally high level of quality. For them, a wide variety of sensations counts just as much as a wide variety of functions. That is why they use the finest materials for their products and extensively customise them in order to prove how customer-focused they are. In so doing, they actually condemn mass production as they make service an integral part of their offer. Anything that is considered optional or added on for 'normal' brands is the norm for luxury brands, because for them what is extra is ordinary. Luxury brands would be wrong, however, to think that they are totally safe. Luxury does not always have to be exorbitant. In the car industry, for instance, technological improvements have made production more flexible, and thus capable of providing greater scope for customisation at no extra cost. Therefore, the customisation differential is being jeopardised by the cost differential, due to the deliberate differences in the two production processes. Neither the rarity of the object nor the potency of the brand image can alone continue to justify the price differential. As we see, luxury defines the ideal degree of personalisation and sublimation of a given object against which the more basic brands can measure themselves. In turn, the latter challenge luxury by their continuous technical improvements and very competitive pricing. Luxury watches, for instance, were challenged by quartz technology, developed for the mass market, which soon established new standards of precision and reliability and which no mechanical system could possibly meet – within the limits of realistic production costs. Both the economic cost of this quality differential and the negative impact on brand image were all the greater as the renown of luxury watch brands had long been associated with lifetime guarantees.

Brand awareness and desire

We mentioned above that the necessary inward/outward dialectic of luxury brands had an implication that was often ignored: the need always to preserve a differential between brand awareness and brand diffusion. The dream of luxury has to be constantly regenerated, as it gradually gets eroded by the real world and as consumers buy. Therefore, there need to be more people who know and understand the brand than actually buy it. This was confirmed by RISC (1991) in their recent survey of 12,500 people aged 15 and above, throughout Europe. Presented with a list of major luxury brands, the participants were asked to say which ones they knew (awareness), which ones they dreamed of (attractiveness) and which ones, if any, they had purchased in one form or other (having bought, for example, Cardin cigarettes is enough). As demonstrated in Figure 2.6, there is a strong correlation between the brand's dream potential and the differential – not its awareness *per se* – between the number of people who just know it and those who have actually purchased it. Thus all the brands above the line have a greater dream potential than they should have had, given their awareness and consumption percentages. All the brands below the line suffer from a dream deficiency.

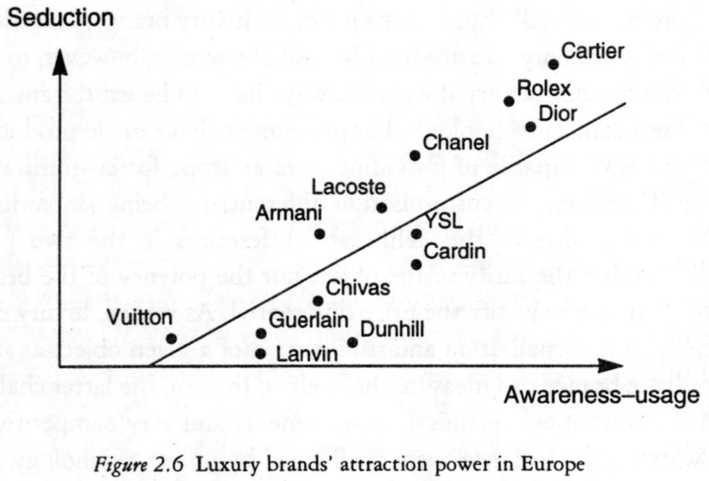

Figure 2.6 Luxury brands' attraction power in Europe

Those who know a given brand are divided, according to the survey, into buyers and dreamers. By analysing each brand, it has thus been possible to identify four different situations; that is, four customer types:

1. The buyers who still dream of the brand are the addicts. They are the brand's proselytes. They must be encouraged and rewarded for their loyalty.
2. The buyers who no longer dream of the brand are 'blasé', saturated. Their desire must be revived.
3. The non-buyers who dream of the brand but do not actually buy, for whatever reason. They must be encouraged either through a more appropriate price/product policy or through wider distribution.
4. Finally, the non-buyers who do not dream of the brand, are indifferent and off target.

If we consider a brand such as Armani, known by 46 per cent of all Europeans, each customer type respectively represents 6, 5, 12 and 23 per cent. Thus, there is an enormous potential market of non-buyers who dream of the brand. The Emporio Armani line and its specific stores have been created so that the latter can make their dream come true. However, in Givenchy's case, the figures are respectively 2, 6, 3 and 30 per cent. The small number of proselytes and the large number of indifferent people show that this brand name is no longer on target.

From creator to brand

Established for the sake of creation, most luxury institutions quite naturally bear the name of their creator. This is the case for Cardin, Saint Laurent, Ricci, Armani, Chanel, Calvin Klein, etc. Paradoxically a luxury brand starts its real existence (life) when its creator disappears. As long as the latter is alive and actively managing the institution, the brand name's destiny is synonymous with the personal achievements or interests of its creator. Thus, many people criticise the licensing policy adopted by Cardin, ie the way in which this name has been over-extended to a wide variety of product categories. This policy actually conveys Pierre Cardin's personal intellectual curiosity and appetite for adventure. A creator cannot be submitted to managerial directives or any other constraints. Creators are in control of two inseparable destinies: that of their brand and their own. Hence, the brand stays hidden in the shadow of its creator until he or she passes away. At this point, there is no need for a brand charter highlighting its positioning. The creator's existence is all that is needed.

Only when the creator disappears can the brand at last take on new identities. It then becomes fully responsible for launching new products, fragrances, events. It rules over those hired to take over the founder's creative function. Previously, the latter was sole commander. Now, however, the new managers must adapt, in part at least, to the characteristics of a brand which already has a powerful identity. It is actually quite significant that renowned couturiers, capitalising on their '*griffe*', often keep a boutique in their own name: there, they can express their personal style, freed from any constraints linked to the necessity of adapting to the '*griffe*'. This was the case for Claude Montana when he worked for Lanvin and for Karl Lagerfeld when he worked for Chanel.

The creator's death generally causes immediate problems either for the inheritors of the name or for the managers taking over. From being a mere patronymic, the name changes into a fully-fledged decision-maker. But what are its specific projects, its set of values, its ethics and its inner essence? In fact, many luxury brands do not know who they are. Having so far been implicitly borne by the creator, the brand's programme may not have been clearly stated but, rather, revealed in the artist's work. Now, it must become explicit if it is to be shared with and accepted by all the players in the world of the brand: staff, new creators, worldwide distribution channels.

When Mr Ricci died, Nina Ricci's new managers launched a research study on their own identity, aimed at revealing the genetic programme of the brand. However, the concept of a brand's intrinsic identity should by no means be limited to the results of research on brand image, as this only reflects the way in which the brand is perceived by different consumers throughout the world. Moreover, each continent generally perceives the brand in a different way. Unlike basic brands, luxury brands are not meant to be managed democratically, for example, by asking the Japanese, the Americans or the Germans what they expect from Nina Ricci and how they expect it to develop in the future. As we well know, an image is only a fragmented, heterogeneous reflection of the brand. Brand identity on the contrary, is unique. There is not one Balmain for the Asian continent and another for the United States: Balmain is Balmain. As we have seen, the identity concept is crucial to luxury brand management: it alone provides the basis for long-term capitalisation, respect for the brand's specific agenda and for worldwide harmonisation. Everyone is aware of the pressure for change, which could result in discontinuity, exerted by the numerous parties involved in the brand's international diffusion. The golden rule, therefore, is never to compromise on the brand's set of values or its deeply-rooted identity traits. The brand is a living memory. Thus, it is necessary to understand the genetic programme of the brand in order to successfully control its future life. The brand's truth lies within itself. The purpose of brand identity research is to try to detect the brand's most striking attributes: those which have had the greatest impact. From past to present, the brand's most typical products should be carefully scanned: from what underlying programme do they seem to emanate?

THE LOGIC OF CO-BRANDING

With increasing frequency, companies today are undertaking joint marketing projects. That is, two different companies pair their respective brands in a collaborative marketing effort:

- New product launches clearly identify the brands that cooperated to create and market them. Thus Danone and Motta introduced 'Yolka', a yogurt ice cream with packaging that uses both brands to endorse it. Similarly, M&Ms and Pilsbury invented a new cookie concept, and Compaq and Mattel combined their respective expertise to bring out a line of hi-tech, interactive toys.
- Many line extensions capitalise on a partner brand's equity. Häagen Dazs, for example, launched a Bailey's-flavoured ice cream. In the same vein, Delicious brand cookies now includes a Chiquita banana taste in its line, Yoplait sells a Côte d'Or chocolate cream, and new Doritos ads tout 'the great taste of Taco Bell' or 'Pizza Hut'.
- To maximise their brand extension success rates, many companies seek help from other companies' brands, whose established reputation in the new market might prove decisive. Hence Kellogg's co-branded its cereals for health-oriented adults with Healthy Choice.
- Co-branding may help usage extension. In Europe, for instance, Bacardi and Coke advertise together. This helps Bacardi's market penetration strategy because the ads demonstrate another way to drink Bacardi. Moreover, Bacardi's status is a powerful endorsement for Coke as the ideal mixer. Thus the pairing also benefits Coke, which wants to remain the number one adult soft drink.
- Ingredient co-branding has now become commonplace. Nutrasweet, for example, wanted to bolster its image, so it encouraged and co-financed advertising campaigns by its client brands. In turn, these client brands endorsed Nutrasweet and endowed it with connotations of pleasure and affective values, until now sugar's exclusive domain. The same holds true for Lycra, Woolmark and Intel: these ingredient brands are eager to promote co-branding, both on the product itself and in advertising and promotion.
- Image reinforcement may also be an objective of co-branding. In the detergent industry, for instance, famous white goods brands endorse particular detergents, and vice versa. Thus, Ariel and Whirlpool recently launched a co-branded advertising campaign, whose claim is 'The art of washing,' illus-

trated by a famous 1914 Renoir painting. By these means, Ariel seeks to reinforce its market leader status and gain a more affective image. As for Whirlpool, the campaign bolsters its European launching strategy, and creates a caring image. Orangina and Renault provide two more examples. To get closer to the youth market, Orangina launched specially designed cans, co-branded with famous youth brands (eg Lee Cooper). For its part, Renault launched limited series of its Twingo car, endowing them with famous designer names – Twingo Kenzo, Twingo Easy (Kickers).

- Co-branding appears in sales promotions too. Whirlpool, for instance, includes Findus or Bird's Eye coupons in its refrigerator owner's manuals. Similarly, companies find that prizes, such as Club Med vacations, work better than cash awards in promotional consumer contests or sweepstakes.
- Loyalty programmes, increasingly, include co-branding arrangements. Although co-branded loyalty programmes are not new (GM initiated the concept, with co-branded credit cards), a new twist has appeared. That is, corporations are sharing the cost of loyalty programmes between their own brands. For example, Nestlé issued a collector's booklet that includes all of its brands (from KitKat to Buitoni, Perrier and Findus).
- Co-branding may signal a trade marketing operation. For instance, the product may be designed specifically for a distributor and signed by both manufacturer and retailer. Thus Danone created a special yogurt for Quick, the European fast-food chain that competes against McDonald's. Yoplait did the same for McDonald's.
- Capitalising on synergies among a number of brands is another co-branding objective. Nestlé is a case in point, and it has a number of brands that could gain from a joint marketing action (eg Nestlé's yoghurts, Nescafé, Nesquik, Herta's pork and bacon). To compete against Kellogg's and increase its market share in the breakfast market, therefore, Nestlé launched joint advertising campaigns, showcasing all these brands around a 'healthy breakfast' theme.

Is co-branding new? No. There are the early classics – detergents endorsed by white goods brands, and oil brands endorsed by car manufacturers. Later, in the 1960s, Kellogg's began making Pop Tarts with Smucker's fruits, and in 1967 General Mills' Betty Crocker added Sunkist lemon cake as a line extension. Finally, Grand Marnier flavoured ice creams are well known.

What *is* new is today's corporate awareness that strategic alliances are essential to acquiring and maintaining a competitive edge. 'Coopetition', a new word coined by Brandenburger and Nalebuff (1996), illustrates this new attitude. The idea: sometimes corporations may have to cooperate with and compete against the same company. From this standpoint, co-branding is an alliance made visible. Furthermore, co-branding involves recognising that the public's knowledge of an alliance is added value.

Even though co-branding has become fashionable, not all alliances should be made visible:

- In the photocopy market, many products sold by, say, Canon are actually made by Ricoh.
- In the car industry, although the Rover company is now owned by BMW, at the product level Rover cars show no BMW insignia. Mercedes and Swatch have created a joint venture to produce and market a revolutionary new car, called Smart, to which each company will add its specific expertise. However, Mercedes is unlikely to put its trademark on the Smart!
- To conquer the iced tea market (despite late entry), Nestlé and Coca-Cola decided to unite against Unilever's Lipton range. Nestlé would create and market the product, and Coca-Cola would distribute it. The product, called Nestea, is not co-branded, though – the Coca-Cola Company gets only a small mention on the back of the packaging.

3

Brand identity

Few brands actually know who they are, what they stand for and what makes them so unique. Classic marketing tools do not help answer such questions. Every advertising campaign is, of course, based on a copy strategy, which varies from one campaign to the other. However, very few brands actually have a brand charter defining the brand's long-term identity and uniqueness. Nor can the answers be found in any graphic guidelines, which often focus only on the brand's outward appearance. Yet understanding what the brand truly represents is not just a graphic exercise. It is an investigation of the brand's innermost substance and of the different facets of its identity. This chapter aims to explore these facets and to suggest the basis for a brand charter.

Defining what a brand is made of helps answer many questions that are asked every day, such as: Can the brand sponsor such and such event or sport? Does the advertising campaign suit the brand? Is the opportunity for launching a new product inside the brand's boundaries or outside? How can the brand change its communication style, yet remain true to itself? How can decision-making in communications be decentralised regionally or internationally, without jeopardising brand congruence? All such decisions pose the problem of brand identity and definition – which are essential prerequisites for efficient brand management.

BRAND IDENTITY: A NECESSARY CONCEPT

Like the ideas of brand vision and purpose, brand identity is a recent concept. In the very fashion-conscious, trendy milieu of communications, is it just a sheer linguistic novelty, or is it really essential to understanding what brands are?

What is identity?

To appreciate the meaning of this significant concept in brand management, we shall begin by considering the many ways in which the word is used today.

For example, we speak of 'identity cards' – a personal, non-transferable document which tells in a few words who we are, what our name is and what distinguishable features we have that can be instantly recognised. We also hear of 'identity of opinion' between several people, meaning that they have an identical point of view. In terms of communication, this second interpretation of the word suggests brand identity is the common element sending a single message amid the wide variety of its products, actions and slogans. This is important since the more the brand expands and diversifies, the more customers are inclined to feel that they are, in fact, dealing with several different brands rather than a single one. If products and communication go their separate ways, how can customers possibly perceive these different routes as converging towards common aim and brand?

Speaking of identical points of view also raises the question of permanence and continuity. As civil status and physical appearance change, identity cards get updated, yet the fingerprint of their holders always remains the same. The identity concept questions how time will affect the unique and permanent quality of the sender, the brand or the retailer. In this respect, psychologists speak of the 'identity crisis' which adolescents often go through. When their identity structure is still weak, teenagers tend to move from one role model to another. These constant shifts create a gap and force the basic question: 'What is the real me?'

Finally, in studies on social groups or minorities, we often speak of 'cultural identity'. In seeking an identity, they are in fact seeking a pivotal basis on which to hinge not only their inherent difference but also their membership of a specific cultural entity.

Brand identity may be a recent notion, but many researchers have already delved into the organisational identity of companies (Reitter and Ramanantsoa, 1985; Schwebig, 1988). There, the simplest verbal expression of identity often consists in saying: 'Oh, yes, I see, but it's not the same in our company!' In other words, corporate identity is what helps an organisation, or a part of it, feel that it truly exists and that it is a coherent and unique being, with a history and a place of its own, different from others.

From these various meanings, we can infer that having an identity means being your true self, driven by a personal goal that is both different from others' and resistant to change. Thus, brand identity will be clearly defined once the following questions are answered:

- What is the brand's particular vision and aim?
- What makes it different?
- What need is the brand fulfilling?
- What is its permanent nature?
- What are its value or values?
- What are the signs which make it recognisable?

These questions could indeed constitute the brand's charter. This type of official document would help better brand management in the medium term, both in terms of form and content, and so better address future communication and extension issues. Communication tools such as the copy strategy are essentially linked to advertising campaigns, and so are only committed to the short term. There must be specific guidelines to ensure that there is indeed only one brand forming a solid and coherent entity.

Brand identity and graphic identity charters

Many readers will make the point that their firms already make use of graphic identity 'bibles', either for corporate or specific brand purposes. We do indeed find many graphic identity charters, books of standards and visual identity guides. Urged on by graphic identity agencies, companies have rightly sought to harmonise the messages conveyed by their brands. Such charters therefore define the norms for visual recognition of the brand, ie the brand's colours, graphic design and type of print.

Although this may be a necessary first step, it isn't the be all and end all. Moreover, it puts the cart before the horse. What really matters is the key message that we want to communicate. Formal aspects, outward appearance and overall looks result from the brand's core substance and intrinsic identity. Choosing symbols requires a clear definition of what the brand means. However, while graphic manuals are quite easy to find nowadays, explicit definitions of brand identity *per se* are still very rare. Yet, the essential questions above (ie the nature of the identity to be conveyed) must be properly answered before we begin discussing and defining what the communication means and what the codes of outward recognition should be. The brand's deepest values must be reflected in the external signs of recognition, and these must be apparent at first glance. The family resemblance between the various models of BMW conveys a strong identity, yet it is not *the* identity. This brand's identity and essence can actually be defined by addressing the issue of its difference, its permanence, its value and its personal view on automobiles.

Many firms have unnecessarily constrained their communication because they formulated a graphic charter before defining their identity. Not knowing who they really are, they merely perpetuate purely formal codes by, for example, using a certain photographic style which may not be the most suitable. Thus Nina Ricci's identity did not necessarily relate to the company's systematic adherence to English photographer David Hamilton's style.

Knowing brand identity paradoxically gives extra freedom of expression, since it emphasises the pre-eminence of substance over strictly formal features. Brand identity defines what must stay and what is free to change.

Identity: a contemporary concept

That a new concept – identity – has emerged in the field of communications, already well-versed in brand image and positioning, is really no great surprise. Today's problems are more complex than those of ten or 20 years ago and so there is now a need for more refined concepts that allow a closer connection with reality.

First of all, we cannot over-emphasise the fact that we are currently living in a society saturated in communications. Everybody wants to communicate these days. If needed, proof is available: there have been huge increases in advertising budgets, not only in the major media but also in the growing number of professional magazines. It has become very difficult to survive in the hurly-burly thus created, let alone to thrive and successfully convey one's identity. For communication means two things: sending out messages and making sure that they are received. Communicating nowadays is no longer just a technique, it is a feat in itself.

The second factor explaining the urgent need to understand brand identity is the pressure constantly put on brands. We have now entered an age of marketing similarities. When a brand innovates, it creates a new standard. The other brands must then catch up if they want to stay in the race, hence the increasing number of 'me-too' products with similar attributes, not to mention the copies produced by distributors. Regulations also cause similarities to spread. Bank operations, for example, have become so much alike that banks are now unable to fully express their individuality and identity. Market research also generates homogeneity within a given sector. As all companies base themselves on the same lifestyle studies, the conclusions they reach are bound to be similar as are the advertising campaigns they launch, in which sometimes even the same words are used.

Finally, technology is responsible for growing similarity. Why do cars increasingly look alike, in spite of their different makes? Because car makers are all equally concerned about fluidity, inner car space constraints, motorisation and economy, and these problems cannot be solved in all that many different ways. Moreover, when two makes of car such as Peugeot and Citroën share many identical parts (eg chassis, engine, gearbox), for either productivity or competitiveness purposes, it is mainly brand identity, along with, to a lesser extent, what's left of each car, which will distinguish the two makes from one another.

Diversification also jeopardises identity. Brands launch new products, penetrate new markets and reach new targets. This causes both fragmented communications and patchwork images. Though we may still be able to discern bits and pieces of the brand here and there, we are certainly unable to perceive any global or coherent identity.

IDENTITY AND IMAGE

What does the notion of identity have to offer that the image of a brand or a retailer doesn't have? After all, firms spend large amounts of money measuring the brand or retailer's image.

Why speak of identity rather than image?

Brand image is on the receiver's side. Image research focuses on the way in which certain groups perceive a product, a brand, a politician, a company or a country. The image refers to the way in which these groups decode all of the signals emanating from the products, services and communication covered by the brand.

Identity is on the sender's side. The purpose, in this case, is to specify the brand's meaning, aim and self-image. Image is both the result and interpretation thereof. In terms of brand management, identity precedes image. Before projecting an image to the public, we must know exactly what we want to project. Before it is received, we must know what to send and how to send it. As shown in Figure 3.1, an image is a synthesis made by the public of all the various brand signals, eg brand name, visual symbols, products, advertisements, sponsoring, patronage, articles. An image results from decoding a message, extracting meaning, interpreting signs.

Where do all these signs come from? There are two possible sources: brand identity of course, but also extraneous factors ('noise') which speak in the brand's name and thus produce meaning, however disconnected they may actually be from it. What are these extraneous factors?

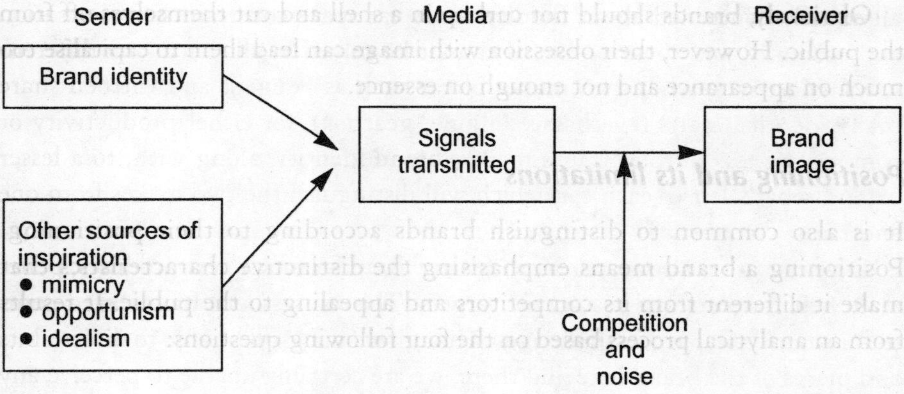

Figure 3.1 Identity and image

Firstly, there are companies which choose to mimic, as they have no clear idea of what their own brand identity is. They focus on their competitors and imitate their marketing communication.

Secondly, there are companies which are obsessed with the need to build an appealing image that will be favourably perceived by all. So they focus on meeting every one of the public's expectations. That is how the brand gets caught in the game of always having to please the consumer and ends up surfing on the changing waves of social and cultural fads. Yesterday, brands were into glamour, today they are into 'cocooning', so what's next? The brand can appear opportunistic and popularity-seeking, and thus devoid of any meaningful substance. It becomes a mere façade, a meaningless cosmetic camouflage.

The third source of 'noise' is that of fantasised identity: the brand as one would ideally like to see it, but not as it actually is. As a result, we notice, albeit too late, that the advertisements do not help people remember the brand because they are either too remotely connected to it or so radically disconnected from it that they cause perplexity or rejection.

Since brand identity has now been recognised as the prevailing concept, these three potential communication glitches can be prevented.

The identity concept thus serves to emphasise the fact that, with time, brands do eventually gain their independence and their own meaning, even though they may start out as mere product names. As living memories of past products and advertisements, brands do not simply fade away: they define their own area of competence, potential and legitimacy. Yet they also know when to stay out of other areas. We cannot expect a brand to be anything other than itself.

Obviously, brands should not curl up in a shell and cut themselves off from the public. However, their obsession with image can lead them to capitalise too much on appearance and not enough on essence.

Positioning and its limitations

It is also common to distinguish brands according to their positioning. Positioning a brand means emphasising the distinctive characteristics that make it different from its competitors and appealing to the public. It results from an analytical process based on the four following questions:

- A brand for what? This refers to the brand promise and consumer benefit aspect: Orangina has real orange pulp, The Body Shop is environment-friendly, Twix gets rid of hunger, Volkswagen is reliable;
- A brand for whom? This refers to the target aspect. For a long time, Schweppes was the drink of the refined, Snapple the soft drink for adults, Tango or Yoohoo the drink for teenagers;
- A brand for when? This refers to the occasion when the product will be consumed. When a brand says 'we try harder', for instance, it caters to customers with pressing requests; J&B whisky caters to night owls;
- A brand against whom? In today's competitive context, this question defines the main competitor(s), ie those whose clientele we think we can partly capture. Tuborg and other expensive imported beers thus also compete against whisky, gin and vodka.

Positioning is a crucial concept (Figure 3.2). It reminds us that all consumer choices are made on the basis of comparison. Thus, a product will only be considered if it is clearly part of a selection process. Hence the four questions which help position the new product or brand and make its contribution immediately obvious to the customer. Positioning is a two-stage process:

- First, indicate to what category the brand should be associated and compared.
- Secondly, indicate what the brand's essential difference and *raison d'être* is in comparison to the other products and brands of that category.

Choosing the category to which the product belongs is essential. While this may be quite easy to do for a new toothpaste, it is not so for very original and unique products. The Gaines burger launched by the Gaines company, for instance, is a new dog food, a semi-dehydrated product presented as red ground meat in a round shape like a hamburger. Unlike normal canned pet foods,

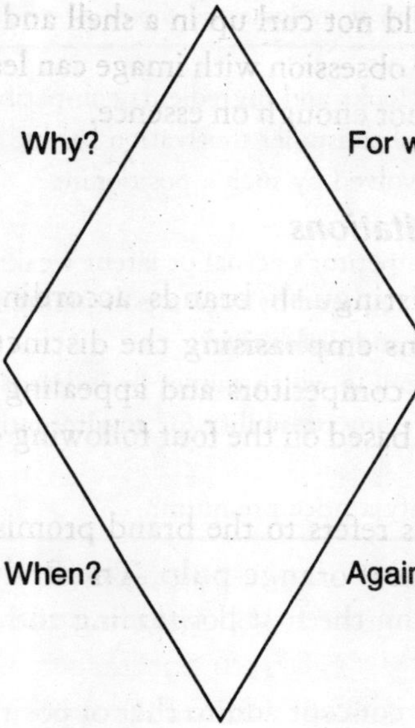

Figure 3.2 Positioning a brand

moreover, it does not need to be refrigerated, nor does it exude that normal open-can smell.

Given these characteristics, the product could be positioned in several different ways, for example by:

- attacking the canned pet food market by appealing to well-to-do dog owners. The gist of the message would then be 'the can without the can', in other words, the benefits of meat without its inconveniences (smell, freshness constraints, etc);
- attacking the dehydrated pet food segment (dried pellets) by offering a product that would help the owner not to feel guilty for not giving meat to the dog on the basis that it is just not practical. The fresh-ground, round look could justify this positioning;
- targeting owners who feed leftovers to their dogs by presenting Gaines as a complete, nutritious supplement (and no longer as a main meal as in the two former strategies);
- targeting all dog owners by presenting this product as a nutritious treat, a kind of doggy Mars bar.

The choice between these four strategies was made by assessing each one against certain measurable criteria (Table 3.1).

Table 3.1 How to evaluate and choose a brand positioning

- Are the product's current looks and ingredients compatible with this positioning?
- How strong is the assumed consumer motivation behind this positioning?
- What size of market is involved by such a positioning?
- Is this positioning credible?
- Does it capitalise on a competitor's actual or latent weakness?
- What financial means are required by such a positioning?
- Is this positioning specific and distinctive?
- Is this a sustainable positioning which cannot be imitated by competitors?
- Does this positioning leave any possibility for an alternative solution in case of failure?
- Does this positioning justify a price premium?

The firm ended up choosing the first positioning and launched this product as the 'Gaines burger'.

What does the identity concept add to that of positioning? Why do we even need another concept?

In the first place, because positioning focuses more on the product itself. What then does positioning mean in the case of a multi-product brand? How can these four questions on positioning be answered if we are not focusing on one particular product category? We know how to position the various Scotch-brite scrubbing pads as well as the Scotch video tapes, but what does the positioning concept mean for the Scotch brand as a whole, not to mention the 3M corporate brand? This is precisely where the concept of brand identity comes in handy.

Secondly, positioning does not reveal all the brand's richness of meaning nor reflect all of its potential. The brand is restricted once reduced to four questions. Positioning does not help fully differentiate Coca-Cola from Pepsi-Cola. The four positioning questions thus fail to encapsulate such nuances. They do not allow us to fully explore the identity and singularity of brand and store names.

Worse still, positioning allows communication to be entirely dictated by creative whims and current fads. Positioning does not say a word about communication style, form or spirit. This is a major deficiency since brands have the gift of speech: they state both the objective and subjective qualities of a given product. The speech they deliver – in these days of multimedia supremacy – is made of words, of course, but even more of pictures, sounds, colours, movement and style. Positioning controls the words only, leaving the rest up to the unpredictable outcome of creative hunches and pre-tests. Yet brand language should never result from creativity only.

Creative hunches are only useful if they are consistent with the brand's legitimate territory. Furthermore, though pre-test evaluations are needed to verify that the brand's message is well-received, the public should not be allowed to dictate brand language: its style needs to be found within itself. Brand uniqueness often tends to get eroded by consumer expectations and thus starts regressing to a level at which it risks losing its identity.

A brand's message is the outward expression of the brand's inner substance. Thus we can longer dissociate brand substance from brand style, ie from its verbal, visual and musical attributes. Brand identity provides the framework for overall brand coherence. It is a concept that serves to offset the limitations of positioning and to monitor the means of expression, the unity and durability of a brand.

THE SIX FACETS OF IDENTITY

A specific set of concepts and tools is needed for tackling the new type of market we are in. When products were rare, the USP (unique selling proposition) was the key concept. As we leave brand image, positioning and personality behind, we enter the modern age of brand identity.

In order to become, or to stay, strong, brands must be true to their identity. The notion of brand image is both volatile and changing: it focuses too much on brand appearance and not enough on brand essence. The notion of brand (or retailer) identity shows that communication managers are now willing to look beyond the surface for the brand's innermost substance. The identity concept is crucial for three reasons: a brand needs to be durable, to send out coherent signs and to be realistic. It is thus a defence against the risks of an idealised, fickle or opportunistic brand image.

The identity prism

Brand identity can be represented by a hexagonal prism (see Figure 3.3):

1. A brand, first of all, has physical qualities – its 'physique'. It is made of a combination of either salient objective features (which immediately come to mind when the brand is quoted in a survey) or emerging ones.

   Physique is both the brand's backbone and its tangible added value. If the brand is a flower, its physique is the stem. Without the stem, the flower dies: it is the flower's objective and tangible basis. This is how communication traditionally works: focusing on know-how and classic positioning, relying on

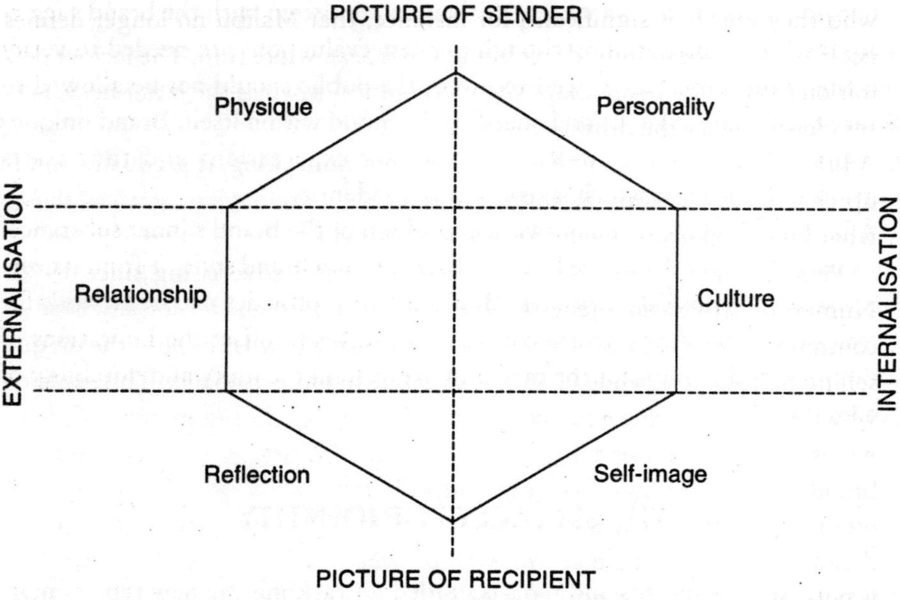

Figure 3.3 Brand identity prism

certain key product and brand attributes. Physical appearance is important but it is not all. Nevertheless, the first step in developing a brand is to define its physical aspect: What is it concretely? What does it do? What does it look like?

That is why the small round bottle is so important each time Orangina is launched in a new country. The bottle used today is the same as it has always been. From the beginning, it has served to position Orangina, thanks to its unique shape and to the orange pulp that we can actually see. Only later was it marketed in standard family-size PET bottles and in cans. In this respect, it is also quite significant that there is now a picture of the famous Coca-Cola bottle on all Coke cans. It is true that modern packaging tends to standardise brands, making them all clones of one another. Thus, in using the image of its traditional bottle, Coca-Cola aims to remind us of its roots.

There are several delicate issues regarding Coke's physical aspect. For example, is the dark liquid part of its identity? If this is the case, then there could never be any such thing as Crystal Coke, even though there is such a thing as Crystal Pepsi. Likewise, would grapefruit Orangina, in the round bottle, be conceivable?

Many brands have problems with their physical facet either because their functional added value is weak or because they cannot manage to determine who they are. It is significant, for instance, that Malibu no longer defines itself as a Caribbean light drink but as Caribbean white rum. The former definition focused more on image than on content, whereas the latter helps better identify what the drink actually is.

2. A brand has a personality of its own. By communicating, it gradually builds up character. The way in which it speaks of its products or services shows what kind of person it would be if it were human.

Personality has been the main focus of brand advertising since 1970. Numerous American agencies have made it a prerequisite for any type of communication. Ted Bates had to come up with a new USP (now, the unique selling personality), while Grey had to define brand personality. This explains why the idea of having a famous character represent the brand has become so widespread. The easiest way of creating instant personality is to give the brand a spokesperson or a figurehead, whether real or symbolic. Pepsi-Cola often uses this method, as do all perfume or ready-to-wear brands.

3. A brand has its own culture, from which every product derives. The product is not only a concrete representation of this culture, but also a means of communication (in the media). Here culture means the set of values feeding the brand's inspiration. The cultural facet refers to the basic principles governing the brand in its outward signs (products and communication). This essential aspect is at the core of the brand. Apple was the product of Californian culture in the sense that this state will forever symbolise the new frontier. Apple was not interested in expanding geographically but in changing society, unlike the brands of Boston and the East Coast. Even in the absence of Apple's founders, everything carried on as if Apple still had some revolutionary plan to offer to companies and to humankind. This fruit symbol is a source of inspiration which is manifested not only in Apple's original products and services, but also in its way of communicating.

Major brands are certainly driven by a culture but, in turn, they also convey this culture (eg Benetton, Coca-Cola, IBM etc). The cultural facet is the key to understanding the difference between Adidas, Nike and Reebok or between American Express and Visa. In focusing too heavily on personality, advertising has neglected this essential facet (we will also notice this with retailers: the leading ones are those who not only have a personality, but also a culture). Mercedes embodies German values: order prevails. Even at 260 km/h, a Mercedes has perfect handling. Even though the surrounding landscape may be whizzing by, the Mercedes remains stable and unperturbed. Symmetry governs this brand: the three-box bodywork is a strong physical characteristic of Mercedes. The brand symbol set at the nose-tip of every Mercedes further epitomises this spirit of order.

Countries of origin are also great cultural reservoirs for brands: Coca-Cola stands for America, as does IBM, Nike or Levi's. In other cases, however, they are ignored: thus, Mars is a worldwide brand. Canon and Technics deny their Japanese origin whereas Mitsubishi, Toyota and Nissan emphasise it. One of the bonuses for Evian or Perrier exports is that they actually represent a part of French culture. However, this is not the only factor adding to their value. When Americans buy Perrier or Evian, they are not just paying for the cultural facet but for all six aspects of these brands, starting with the basic consumer benefit: that they quench thirst or promote health. American style food is McCain's cultural and symbolic reference; for Jack Daniel's, it is the lifestyle of 1950s America.

Culture is what links the brand to the firm, especially when the two bear the same name. Because of its culture, Nestlé has not succeeded in conveying the image of a fun and enjoyable food brand. Indeed, its image cannot be fully dissociated from that of the corporation, which is overall perceived as austere and puritan. The degree of freedom of a brand is often reduced by the corporate culture, of which it becomes the most visible outward sign. It is no wonder that the Renault brand built its identity on values such as inner car space, cosiness and comfort (hence the slogan 'cars for living in'). No market study dictated that these values are those expected by a majority of car-drivers. As a semi-public firm in 1996 and called 'France's social laboratory', Renault has a natural tendency to favour human values over others, such as the urge to constantly challenge one's limits (Porsche) or to always compete and perform (BMW). Renault's successful participation in Formula 1 was meant to counterbalance this tendency, yet Renault's fundamental values are not associated with car races.

Brand culture plays an essential role in launching a new type of alcohol. Like any psychotropic agent, alcohol is indeed risky. Its risks generate pleasure (the nice feeling of tipsiness) but also fear. One must therefore be able to implicitly reassure consumers. A globally renowned brand can spare itself the effort: it can prove, thanks to its renown, that millions of drinkers around the world enjoy the drink. When launching a new brand of spirit, companies need to give it some history and roots. It cannot just look like a pure marketing product, it must look genuine. That partly explains why Malibu's recent advertisement is set in the Caribbean and why Jameson Irish whiskey invested so much money in rebuilding their old distillery, the Jameson Heritage Centre.

This facet is the one which helps differentiate luxury brands the most because it refers to their sources, to their fundamental ideals and to their sets of values. Culture is also the basis for most bank brands: choosing a bank means choosing the kind of relationship with money one wishes to have. Even though their services are identical (physical facet), the Visa Premier and the American Express Gold cards do not belong to the same cultural system. The American Express Gold card symbolises dynamic, triumphant capitalism. Money is shown, or even flashed about. Visa Premier, on the contrary, represents another type of capitalism, such as the German kind, making steady, quiet progress. Money is handled discreetly yet efficiently, neither gingerly nor flamboyantly.

4. A brand is a relationship. Indeed, brands are often at the crux of transactions and exchanges between people. This is particularly true of brands in the service sector and also of retailers, as we shall see later. The Yves Saint Laurent brand functions with charm: the underlying idea of a love affair permeates both its products and its advertising (even when no man is shown). Dior's symbolises another type of relationship: one that is grandiose and ostentatious (not in the negative sense), flaunting the desire to shine like gold.

   Nike bears a Greek name that relates it to specific cultural values, to the Olympic Games and to the glorification of the human body. Nike suggests also a peculiar relationship, based on provocation: it encourages us to let loose ('just do it'). IBM symbolises orderliness, whereas Apple conveys friendliness. The Laughing Cow is at the heart of a mother–child relationship. The relationship aspect is crucial for banks, banking brands and services in general. Service is by definition a relationship.

5. A brand is a reflection. When asked for their views on certain car brands, people immediately answer in terms of the brand's perceived client type: that's a brand for young people! for fathers! for show-offs! for old folks! Because its communication and its most striking products build up over time, a brand will always tend to build a reflection or an image of the buyer or user which it seems to be addressing

   Reflection and target often get mixed up. The target describes the brand's potential purchasers or users. Reflecting the customer as he/she is is not the target; rather, the customer should be reflected as he/she wishes to be seen as a result of using a brand. It provides a model with which to identify. Coca-Cola, for instance, has a much wider clientele than suggested by the narrow segment it reflects (15- to 18-year-olds). How can such a paradox be explained? For the younger segment (8- to 13-year-olds), the Coca-Cola protagonists embody their dream, what they want to become and do later on when they get older (and thus freed from the strong parental relationship), ie an independent life full of fun, sports and friends will then become true. Youth identifies with those heroes. As for adults, they perceive them as representatives of a certain way of life and of certain values rather than of a narrowly defined age group. Thus, the brand also succeeds in bringing 30- or 40-year-old consumers to identify with this special way of life. Many dairy brands positioned on lightness or fitness and based on low fat products project a sporty young female customer reflection: yet they are actually purchased in the main by older people.

The confusion between reflection and target is quite frequent and causes problems. So many managers continue to require advertising to show the targeted buyers as they really are, ignoring the fact that they do not want to be portrayed as such, but rather as they wish to be – as a result of purchasing a given brand (or shopping at a given retailer's). Consumers indeed use brands to build their own identity. In the ready-to-wear industry, the obsession to look younger should concern the brands' reflection, not necessarily their target.

All brands must control their reflection. By constantly reiterating that Porsche is made for show-offs, the brand has weakened. For a long time, Ferguson committed the mistake of showing its buyers as they were; it was thus on the brink of becoming just an average brand. Brands must always project a flattering image of their clients.

6. Finally, a brand speaks to our self-image. If reflection is the target's outward mirror, self-image is the target's own internal mirror. Through our attitude towards certain brands, we indeed develop a certain type of inner relationship with ourselves.

In buying a Porsche, for example, many Porsche owners simply want to prove to themselves that have the ability to buy such a car. In fact, this purchase might be premature in terms of career prospects and to some extent a gamble on their materialisation. In this sense, Porsche is constantly forcing to push beyond one's limits (hence its slogan: 'Try racing against yourself, it's the only race that will never have an end'). As we can see, Porsche's reflection is different from its consumers' self-image: having let the brand develop such a negative reflection is a major problem.

Even if they do not practise any sports, Lacoste clients inwardly picture themselves (so the studies show) as members of a sports club – an open club with no race, sex or age discrimination, but which endows its members with distinction (see Figure 3.4). This works because sport is universal. One of the characteristics of people who eat Gayelord Hauser health and diet products is that they picture themselves not just as consumers, but as proselytes. When two Gayelord Hauser fans meet, they can strike up a conversation immediately as if they were of the same religious obedience. In promoting a brand, one pledges allegiance, demonstrating both a community of thought and of self-image, which facilitates or even stimulates communication.

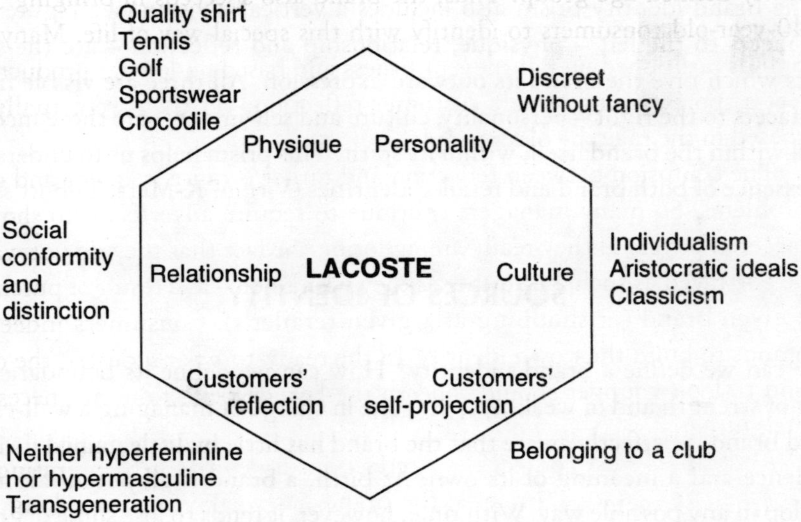

Figure 3.4 Lacoste identity prism

These are the six facets which define the identity of a brand as well as the boundaries within which it is free to change or to develop. The brand identity prism demonstrates that these facets are all interrelated and form a well-structured entity. The content of one facet echoes that of another. The prism concept derives from one basic concept – that brands have the gift of speech. Brands can only exist if they communicate. As a matter of fact, they grow obsolete if they remain silent or unused for too long. Since a brand is a speech in itself (as it speaks of the products it creates and endorses the products which epitomise it), it can thus be analysed like any other speech or form of communication.

Semiologists have taught us that behind any type of communication there is a sender, either real or made up. Even when dealing with products or retailers, communication builds an image of its speaker or sender and conveys it to us. It is truly a building process in the sense that brands have no real, concrete senders (unlike corporate communication). Nevertheless, customers, when asked through projective techniques, do not hesitate to describe the brand's sender, ie the person bearing the brand name. Both the physique and personality help define the sender thus built for that purpose.

Every form of communication also builds a recipient: when we speak, everything seems as if we were addressing a certain type of person or audience. Both the reflection and self-image facets help define this recipient, who, thus built, also belongs to the brand's identity. The last two facets, relationship and culture, bridge the gap between sender and recipient.

The brand identity prism also includes a vertical division (see Figure 3.3). The facets to the left – physique, relationship and reflection – are the social facets which give the brand its outward expression. All three are visible facets. The facets to the right – personality, culture and self-image – are those incorporated within the brand itself, within its spirit. This prism helps us to understand the essence of both brand and retailer identities (Virgin, K-Mart, Talbott's).

SOURCES OF IDENTITY

How can we define a brand's identity? How can we define its boundaries, its areas of strength and of weakness? Anyone in charge of managing a well-established brand is perfectly aware that the brand has little by little gained its independence and a meaning of its own. At birth, a brand is all potential: it can develop in any possible way. With time, however, it tends to lose some degree of freedom; while gaining in conviction, its facets take shape, delineating the brand's legitimate territory. Tests confirm this progression: certain product or communication concepts now seem foreign to the brand. Other concepts, on the contrary, seem to be perfectly in tune with the brand, as it both endorses and empowers them, by giving them greater credibility.

Brand image research does not provide any satisfactory answer to these questions. Neither do the purchasers when asked to say what they expect from the brand. Generally, they haven't a clue. At best, they answer in terms of the brand's current positioning. Thus in the US and the UK, there are only very few purchasers of Saab cars: the brand is not widespread and it is just beginning to expand its market distribution network. That is why English or American owners see their Saab as unusual rather than foreign. When asked what they expect from the brand, they are, indeed, likely to answer that Saab must continue to design unusual, unique cars. In doing so, they expect that the brand will reinforce their own unusuality and uniqueness which they, as the only few marginal Saab buyers, most definitely want to demonstrate. Obviously, however, if Saab focused exclusively on such self-centred expectations, its market share would most certainly remain restricted: the economic future of the Saab automotive division would then be under threat.

Consumers and prospects are often asked what their ideal brand would be and what attributes it would need in order to get universally approved. This approach fails to segment properly the expectations and thus to produce any definition other than the average brand ideal. It is typical for consumers to expect banks to provide expertise and attention, availability and competence, proximity and know-how. These expectations are also ideal in the sense that they are often incompatible. In pursuing them, such brands may lose their identity and regress to the average level. In seeking at all costs to resemble the ideal brand described by the consumers (or industrial buyers), brands thus often begin to downplay their differences and look average.

The mistake is to pursue this market 'ideal': it's up to each brand to pursue an ideal of its own. Commercial pressure naturally requires a firm to stay attuned to the market. Of course no brand envies the destiny of Van Gogh, who lived a life of misery and became famous only after he died. Nonetheless, present brand management policy must be reappraised, because unfortunately it still assumes that consumers are the masters of brand identity and strategy. Consumers are actually quite incapable of carrying out such functions. Firms should, therefore, begin to focus more on the sending side of brand marketing and less on the receiving side.

Trying to define the specifics of a brand's substance and intrinsic values naturally requires an understanding of what a real brand is all about. A brand is a plan, a vision, a project. This plan is hardly ever written down (except for the few brands which have a brand charter). It can therefore only be inferred from the marks left by the brand, ie the products it has chosen to endorse and the symbols by which it is represented. Discovering the essence of brand identity, ie of the brand's specific and unique attributes, is the best way to understand what the brand means overall. That is why research must be done on the typical products (or services) endorsed by the brand as well as on the brand name itself, the brand mascot or figure if there is one, the logo, the country of origin, the advertisements and the packaging. The purpose of all this is to semiologically analyse the sending process by trying to discover the original plan underlying the brand's objectives, products and symbols. Generally, this plan is simply unconscious, neither written anywhere, nor explicitly described. It is simply enacted in daily decisions. Even creators of famous brand names (Christian Lacroix, Yves Saint Laurent, Calvin Klein or Liz Claiborne) are not conscious of it: when asked about the general plan, they are indeed unable to explain it clearly, yet they can easily say what their brand encompasses and what it does not. Brand and creator merge. We have shown (p. 85) that, paradoxically, a brand does not really begin to exist until its creator dies. It then shifts from body and instinct to plan and programme.

In conducting research on brand identity, it may well be that we discover several underlying plans. The history of a brand indeed reflects a certain discontinuity in the decisions made by different brand managers over time. Rather than attempt the impossible task of uniting opposing brand policies, brand managers must choose the one that will best serve the brand in its targeted market and focus only on that one. Finally, when dealing with a weak brand, we might not discover any consistent plan at all: in this case, the brand is more like a name stuck on a product than a real player in the field. This situation is very similar to the initial stage of brand creation: the brand has great latitude and almost infinite possibilities, even though it has already planted the seeds of its potential identity in the memory of the market.

The brand's typical products

The product is the first source of brand identity. A brand indeed reveals its plan and its uniqueness through the products (or services) it chooses to endorse. A genuine brand does not usually remain a mere name printed on a product, ie a mere graphic accessory added on at the end of a production or distribution process. The brand actually injects its values in the production and distribution process as well as in the corollary services offered at the point of sale. The brand's values must therefore be embodied in the brand's most highly symbolic products. This last sentence calls for some attention. Cognitive psychology has taught us that it is easier to define certain categories by simply showing their most typical members than by specifying what product features are required to be considered a member of those categories. As stated in this example, it is difficult to define the 'game' concept, ie to specify the characteristics which could help us identify when we are in a game situation and when we are not. For abstract categories, made of heterogeneous products, the difficulty is even greater. In this case, brands can serve as examples only if they are not exclusively attached to one specific product. What is Danone? When does a product deserve to be named Danone and when does it not? The same holds true for Philips or Whirlpool (see p. 248).

Consumers can easily answer this question: they are indeed able to group products in terms of their capacity to typically represent and perfectly exemplify a large spectrum brand. This is shown in Table 3.2 which ranks Danone's most typical products against Yoplait's, according to the consumers' point of view. The most representative product is called the 'brand prototype', not in the sense of an airplane or car prototype, but rather in that of the best exemplor of the brand's meaning. In this respect, Danone has two prototype products: plain yoghurt (natural) and the refrigerated dessert cream, Danette. The cognitive psychologists around E. Rosch claim that prototypes actually transfer some of their features to the product category (Kleiber, 1990). In other words, if there were no definition of Danone, the public would probably be able to come up with one anyway, by taking a close look at the features of Danone's most representative products. This is what we call prototype semantics. It is true that each brand spontaneously brings to mind certain products – some more than others

Table 3.2 The most typical products of two mega-brands

Products	Danone	Yoplait
Danette – dessert cream	9.33(1)	4.04
Plain yoghurt (natural)	9.16(2)	8.93(1)
Fruit yoghurt	8.64(3)	8.39(5)
Whole milk yoghurt	8.55(4)	8.88(2)
Liquid yoghurt	8.54(4)	8.51(4)
Whipped yoghurt	8.44(6)	6.76
Petit fromage frais	8.13(7)	7.98
Fromage frais	8.11(8)	8.66(3)
Chocolate/coffee delight with whipped cream	8.07(9)	7.6

Key: grading from 0 to 10 (rank in parentheses if grade >8)

Source: Kapferer and Laurent (1996).

– and actions as well as a certain style of communication. These prototype products are representative of the various facets of brand identity. According to some cognitive psychologists, such products may convey brand identity, but above all they generate it. In fact, when questioned on Danone's brand image, consumers are more likely to answer in terms of Danone's prototype products.

Historically, it is quite significant that Danone became famous with its plain yoghurt, a product which had previously been sold in pharmacies as natural medication. That is where Danone's health image originated. And it is now revived by the creation of the Danone Foundation. But the duality of prototypes has also contributed to soften Danone's image: Danette cream dessert signifies hedonism, pleasure and opulence. Danone's brand identity is thus dual: both health and pleasure (Table 3.2).

If this theory holds, another question comes to mind: just what is it, in a typical product, that conveys meaning? A brand's values only convey meaning if they are at the core of the product. Brand intangible and tangible realities go hand in hand: values drive reality, and reality manifests these values.

For example, the essence of Benetton's brand identity is colour. Colour is not just an advertising theme. It is both the symbolic and industrial basis of the brand. It has, in fact, helped Benetton stay ahead of its competitors through its capacity to meet the latest fashion requirements, ie the new colours of the season. Saying it is not enough though: the toughest part is doing it, and they did. Unlike their competitors, Benetton innovated by dyeing pullovers after they were made and not before, which helped save lots of precious time. By delaying their decision on the final colours, they were indeed better prepared for the whims of fashion and last-minute changes. If summer turned out to be magenta, Benetton could immediately react and fulfil expectations. However, although it is the essential pivot of Benetton's brand identity, colour is not just a question of physique (in the identity prism): the colour element also impacts on the other facets of the prism, especially the cultural (which has sometimes made brands look like religions), a key facet when a brand markets to youth.

Colour does not merely serve to position the brand (the colour brand); it is the outward sign of an ideology, a set of values and a brand culture. In its very name 'United Colours of Benetton', as in its posters showing a blond and a black baby, the brand expresses its inspiration and its idealistic vision of a united world in which all colours and races live together in harmony. Colour then ceases to be a mere feature distinguishing the manufacturer. It is a banner, a sign of allegiance. Colour is celebrated by the youth who wears it. Brotherhood and cultural tolerance are the brand's values. That is why the provocative style of Benetton's recent advertising is so disturbing: it is at odds with the brand's past identity.

Orangina is the case of a brand in search of identity, substance and psychological depth. For years Orangina has been represented by both a certain physique and a unique product: a fizzy orange soft drink. What makes it really stand out is that the orange pulp is purposely left in the liquid. This feature was so crucial to the product that an orange-shaped bottle was designed especially for it and its advertising focused on the need to shake the bottle well in order to disperse the pulp and experience the unique and best-tasting flavour of Orangina. The brand further developed its own personality through its TV advertising which was done in a jumpy, video-clip style so popular among young people. The last stage in this process consisted of conveying the full meaning of the brand and, to do this, the brand/product relationship had to be reversed. Until then, Orangina was merely the name of a soft drink containing orange pulp. Thus, adopting a modern style does not change the structure of this relationship. Today, the basic question is asked the other way around: what are the values that a soft drink containing orange pulp could serve to embody? Coca-Cola's leadership among 13- to 18-year-olds cannot be attacked from the basis of physique and personality. Coca-Cola is a brand that vows an allegiance to the all-American cultural model. Pepsi-Cola embodies the values of the new generation, as does Virgin in the UK, hence its ability to challenge Pepsi's second place in terms of cola market share with its own Virgin Cola. Orangina must find its own source of inspiration as well as the set of values which its product will embody. This search for identity is based on a fundamental axiom of brand management: the truth of a brand lies within itself. It is not by interviewing consumers or consulting oracles of socio-cultural trends that the brand will discover itself. Roots last, trends don't.

The values which Orangina has conveyed since the beginning are: spontaneity, humour and friendliness. Orangina is a healthy, natural drink, a mixture of pulp and water. It symbolises sunshine, life, warmth and energy. All combine latently to give a typical taste and feeling of the American South (underlying it all, there is a common model: the Southern model). The word 'model' reminds us that a strong brand is always the product of a certain culture, hence of a set of values which it chooses to represent. In the case of Orangina, Southern values seem to be a potent alternative to the North American values of Coca-Cola. Living in the South means both looking at the world and experiencing it in a different way. Unfortunately, after a while, this Southern concept was perceived as being restrictively Hispanic. Moreover, American South imagery means nothing at all to those living in the southern hemisphere or in Asia, and yet these are the new frontiers around the world that Orangina has to conquer.

The Lacoste shirt now only represents 30 per cent of the company's world sales. It is nonetheless a core product, since it conveys the brand's original values. This shirt was indeed designed at a time when tennis was still being played in long trousers and shirts with rolled-up sleeves. One day, René Lacoste asked his friend André Gilliet to make a 'false' shirt: something that would look like a shirt (so as not to shock the Queen at Wimbledon), yet would be more practical, ie airy (hence the cotton knit), sturdy and with straight sleeves. Thus right from the beginning, and by accident, René Lacoste's shirt came to embody the individualistic and aristocratic ideal of living both courageously and elegantly. Whatever the occasion, a Lacoste is always appropriate: perfectly suited to the person who, overall, cares to respect proper dress codes, but not in very minute detail. Lacoste is neither trendy nor stuffy: it is simply always appropriate.

All major brands thus have a core product in charge of conveying the brand's meaning. Chanel has its gold chain, Chaumet its pearls and Van Cleef a patented technique of setting stones in invisible slots. These features do not merely characterise the products, they actually embody the brands' values. Dupont, on the other hand, does not seem to have much at stake: it certainly endorses superb lighters, but beyond them is there any dynamic brand concept in evidence? In terms of ready-to-wear clothing, 501 jeans are at the heart of the Levi's brand and of the carefree and unconventional ideology it represents. (On this point, it is significant that the product most frequently worn with a Lacoste shirt is a pair of jeans.) Conversely, brands such as Newman suffer from never having created a real core product, one exclusive to the brand which conveys its very identity.

These examples serve to illustrate a key principle for brand credibility and durability: all facets of brand identity must be closely linked. Moreover, the brand's intangible facets must necessarily be reflected in its products' physique. This 'laddering' process is illustrated by the Benetton case (Table 3.3). Likewise, Lacoste's identity prism can neither be dissociated from the story behind its famous shirt nor from the values of its emblematic sport, tennis. Similarly, Salomon's brand identity is a mix of values: those of Alpine skiing, of the prototype product itself (ski bindings) and of George Salomon's personality. Hence the reason the Salomon brand does not in any way have the same identity as Rossignol.

The power of brand names

The brand's name is often revealing of the brand's intentions. This is obviously the case for brand names which, from the start, are specifically chosen to convey certain objective or subjective characteristics of the brand (Steelcase or Pampers). But it is also true of other brand names which get chosen for subjective reasons rather than for any apparent objective or rational ones: they too have the capacity to mark the brand's legitimate territory. Why did Steve Jobs and Steve Wozniak choose Apple as their brand name? Surely, this name neither popped out of any creative research nor of any computer software for brand name creation. It is simply the name that seemed plainly obvious to the two creative geniuses. In one word, the Apple brand name conveyed the exact same values as those which had driven them to revolutionise computer science.

What must be explained is why they did not go for the leading name style of that period, ie International Computers, Micro Computers Corporation or even Iris. The majority of entrepreneurs would have chosen this type of name. In deciding to call it Apple, Jobs and Wozniak wanted to emphasise the unconventional nature of this new brand: in using the name of a fruit (and the visual symbol of a munched apple), was it taking itself seriously? With this choice, the brand demonstrated its values: in refusing to idolise computer science, Apple was in fact preparing to completely overturn the traditional human/machine relationship. The machine had, indeed, to become something to enjoy rather than to revere or to fear. Clearly, the brand name had in itself all the necessary ingredients to produce a major breakthrough and establish a new norm (which

Table 3.3 Brand laddering process: the Benetton case

- Physical attribute: colour and price.
- Objective advantage: the latest fashion.
- Subjective advantage: the brand for young people who want to be 'in'.
- Value: tolerance.

all seems so obvious to us now). What worked for Apple, however, did not work for Apricot. Apple reflected the founders' values, which materialised into user-friendly computers. This is indeed a far cry from just choosing a similar name (Apricot) without prior verification that such values as Apple's could indeed be conveyed by the brand.

The brand name is thus one of the most powerful sources of identity. When a brand questions its identity, the best answer is therefore to thoroughly examine its name and so try to understand the reasoning behind its creation. In so doing, we can discover the brand's intentions and programme. As the Latin saying goes: *nomen est omen* – a name is an omen. Examining the brand name thus amounts to decoding this omen, ie the brand's programme, its area of legitimacy and know-how as well as its scope of competence.

Many brands make every effort to acquire qualities which their brand name fails to reflect or simply excludes altogether. 'Apple' sounds fun, not serious.

Other brands simply proceed by ignoring their name. The temptation for a brand to just forget about its name is caused by a rash interpretation of the principle of brand autonomy. Experience indeed shows that brands become autonomous as they start to give words specific meanings other than those in the dictionary. Thus when hearing of 'Bird's Eye', no one thinks of a bird. The same is true of Nike. Mercedes is a Spanish Christian name, yet the brand has made it a symbol of Germany. This ability is not only characteristic of brands but also of proper nouns: we do not think of roofing when talking of Mrs Thatcher. Thus, strong brands force their own lexical definitions into the glossaries: they give words another meaning. There is no doubt that this process takes place, but the time it requires varies according to its complexity.

A name – like an identity – has to be managed. Certain names may have a double meaning. The purpose of communication then is to select one and drop the other. Thus, Shell naturally chose to emphasise the sea-shell meaning (as represented in its logo) rather than the bomb-shell one! Likewise, the international temporary employment agency, Ecco, has never chosen to exploit the potential link with economy suggested in its name. On the other hand, it does use its name as a natural means to reinforce its positioning in the segment of high quality service: its advertising cleverly plays upon the theme of duplication – those stepping in from Ecco will of course perfectly duplicate and echo those stepping out of the company.

Generally speaking, it is best to follow the brand's overall direction as well as its underlying identity, whenever possible. All Hugo Boss is entirely contained in that one short, yet international, name – Boss: it conveys aggressive success, professional achievement, conformity and city life. Rexona is a harsh name all over the world because of its abrupt R and its sharp X: thus it implicity promises efficiency.

Brand characters

Just as brands are a company's capital, emblems are a brand's capital equity. An emblem serves to symbolise brand identity through a visual figure other than the brand name. It has many functions such as:

- to help identify and recognise the brand. Emblems must identify something before they signify anything. They are particularly useful when marketing to children, since the latter favour pictures over text, or when marketing worldwide (every whisky has its own emblem);
- to guarantee the brand;
- to give the brand durability – since emblems are permanent signs – thereby enabling the company to capitalise on it. Thus Hermès' legendary horse is the common emblem of 'Equipage', 'Amazone' and 'Calèche';
- to help differentiate and personalise: an emblem transfers its personality to the brand. In doing so, it enhances brand value. But it also facilitates the identification process in which consumers are involved.

Animal emblems are often used to perform this last function. Animals symbolise the brand's personality. It is quite significant, in this respect, that both the Chinese and Western horoscopes represent human characters by animals. The Greek veneration of animals reflected their conception of a certain spiritual mystery. The animal is not only allegorical of the brand's personality but also of the psychological characteristics of the targeted public. Clan Campbell's hawk symbolises the independent mind and free spirit of the drinker of this particular whisky. The red grouse, symbol of Scotland and a rare bird, has been chosen as the emblem of Famous Grouse whisky in order to reflect the aesthetic ideal of its consumers.

Emblems epitomise more than one facet of brand identity; that is why they play such a crucial role in building identity capital. The world of whisky is filled with wild, rare, untameable animals that symbolise the natural, pure and authentic character of this alcohol. The associated risk perceived by the customer is thus reduced. They also demonstrate, as we saw above, the brand's personality: the red grouse is known for its noble gait and carriage; the wild turkey is a stubborn and clever bird symbolising independence in the US. These animals also represent the brand's value and culture facet, either because they are geographical symbols (the grouse for Scotland, the wild turkey for the US) or because they refer to the brand's essence itself.

Many other brands have chosen to be represented by a character. A character can, for example, be either the brand's creator and endorser (George Killian for red beer) or an endorser other than the creator (Gerard Depardieu for Barilla pasta). It can also be a direct symbol of the brand's qualities (Nestlé's bunny rabbit, Mr Clean, the Michelin bibendum). Some characters serve to build a certain relationship and an emotional, prescriptive link between the brand and its public (Smack's frog, Esso's tiger). Others, finally, serve as brand ambassadors: though Italian, Isabella Rossellini embodies the type of French beauty that Lancôme promises to all women.

Such characters say a lot about brand identity. They were indeed chosen as brand portraits, ie as the brand's traits, in the etymological sense. They do not make the brand, yet they define the way in which the brand brings to reality its traits and features.

Visual symbols and logotypes

Everybody knows Mercedes' emblem, Renault's diamond, Nike's dash, Adidas' three stripes, Nestlé's nest, Yoplait's little flower and Bull's tree. These symbols help us to understand the brand's culture and personality. They are actually chosen as such: the corporate specifications handed over to graphic identity and design agencies mainly pertain to the brand's personality traits and values.

What is important about these symbols and logos is not so much that they help identify the brand but that the brand identifies with them. When companies change logos, it usually means that either they or their brands are about to be transformed: as soon as they no longer identify with their past style, they want to start modifying it. Some companies proceed otherwise: to revitalise their brands and recover their identity, they milk their forlorn brand emblems for the energy and aggressiveness they need in order to be able to change. Just as human personality can be reflected in a signature, brand essence and self-image can be reflected in symbols.

Geographical and historical roots

The identity of Swissair is intimately associated with that of Switzerland. The same is true of Air France abroad or of Barclay's Bank. Outside of the US, the Chrysler brand represents the cars of the New World. Certain brands naturally convey the identity of their country of origin. Others are totally international (Ford, Opel, Mars, Nuts). Others still have made every possible effort to hide their national identity: Canon never refers to Japan, while Technics has adopted an Anglo-Saxon identity though the company is Japanese.

Some brands draw their identity and uniqueness from their geographical roots. It is a deliberate choice on their part. What advantage did Nokia expect to gain, for example, by launching a Finnish television brand called Salora? As its name suggests, Finland is the country where the earth ends – a cold, austere, remote land, where the sun scrapes the ground. This spontaneous vision both feeds and supports the creation of a high-tech futuristic brand such as Salora which is associated with outer space, telecommunications, satellites, stark design and structure. If this is really the case with regard to Salora products, the brand definitely has strong potential, as its identity and symbolism both take root within the products themselves. If, on the contrary, these products come to lose their uniqueness, Salora's implicit brand contract will default and its name will go to waste.

Brands can benefit from the values of their native soil. Apple has thus adopted the Californian values of both social and technological progress and innovation. There is a touch of alternative culture in this Californian brand (which is not true of all Silicon valley brands, such as Atari). IBM epitomises East coast order, power and conservatism. Evian's symbolism is linked to the Alps, or rather to the image of the Alps, as projected by the company. Roots are crucial for alcoholic drinks too: Glenfiddich means Deer Valley, Grouse is the fetish bird of Scotland. The Malibu drink, on the contrary, has never defined its origin: only recently has its advertising specified that its home was the Caribbean. As for banks, Suez, for instance, has linked its identity to a mythical place reminiscent of industrial grandeur: the times of rising capitalism, of growing colonialism and of public works financed by brand new banks especially set up for that purpose. In addressing the public for the first time when it was privatised, this bank reminded us that only those with such a glorious past as theirs could look upon the future with total confidence.

The brand's creator

Brand identity cannot be dissociated from the creator's identity. There is still some Georges Salomon in Salomon's brand identity, even though the man and the family no longer manage the company. Inspired by its creator, Yves Saint Laurent's brand identity is that of a feminine, self-assured and strong-minded 30-year-old woman. The YSL brand celebrates the beauty of body, of charm, of surrender to romance, and is flavoured with a hint of ostentatious indecency. Paloma Picasso's flaming Mediterranean looks permeate her perfume products and explain why she is so successful in South America, in the US Sun Belt (Florida, Texas, California) and in Europe (Spain, France, Germany). The relationship between a brand and its creator can last far beyond the death of the creator: Chanel is a good example of this: Karl Lagerfeld does not try to imitate the Chanel style, but to interpret it in a modern way. The world is changing: the brand's values must be respected, yet adapted to modern times.

When its creator passes away, the brand becomes autonomous: it forsakes its patronymic, which it comes to dominate. The brand is the creator's name woven into a set of values and a pattern of inspiration. Thus, it cannot be used by another member of the creator's family. This was confirmed in court in 1984 when Olivier Lapidus, son of the founder of the Ted Lapidus French ready-to-wear clothing brand, was refused the right to use the word 'Lapidus'. Even blood kinship thus does not entitle one to use brand name equity in the same sector, so Olivier left for Japan where he launched the Olivier Montagu brand name. Upon his return to France, he only became entitled to use his name by buying back his father's company and brand. This in turn caused an intricate problem: that of managing two identities, Ted Lapidus and Olivier Lapidus.

Advertising: content and form

Let us not forget that it is advertising which writes the history of a brand, retailer or company. Volkswagen can no longer be dissociated from the advertising saga that helped it develop. The same is true of Dim and Marlboro. This is only logical: brands have the gift of speech and they can only exist by communicating. Since they are responsible for announcing their products or services, they need to speak up at all times.

When communicating, we always end up saying a lot more than we think we do. Any type of communication implicitly says something about the sender (who is speaking?), about the recipient we are apparently addressing and the relationship we are trying to build between the two. The brand identity prism is based on this hard fact.

How is this implicit message slipped between the lines and conveyed to us? Simply through style. In these times of audio-visual media, a 30-second TV ad says just as much about the style of the brand sending the message and of the recipient apparently being targeted as about the attributes and assets of the product being announced. Whether or not they are managed, planned or wanted, all brands acquire a history, a culture, a personality and a reflection through their cumulative communications. To manage a brand is to proactively channel this gradual accumulation of attributes towards a given objective rather than just to sit and wait to inherit a given brand image.

Yet what is inherited can also be a boon. Volkswagen tightly controls its marketing, but entirely delegates its communications to its agency. Thus all Volkswagen cars are launched under the same name, no matter what the country. Even though the Passat name was ill-perceived in France because of the old Passat's negative image, despite VAG France's recommendations the new Passat model was still marketed under the same name. However, the

Volkswagen style is definitely a legacy of the advertising genius, Bernbach: indeed, he succeeded in making the entire DDB network follow the stylistic guidelines which he had defined. It is thus through the memorable VW Beetle campaigns that both the brand's specific style and scope of communication began to take shape.

Both in its advertising films and spots, the VW brand has always freely played with the motifs of both the cars and the logo. The brand's style of expression is one of humour and humour only, as shown in its attitude of self-derision, false modesty and impertinence towards competitors as well as in the use of paradox. Volkswagen's advertisements have thus built a powerfully intimate relationship with the public. They appeal to consumers' intelligence, reflecting the image of the pragmatic people who prefer functional features to fancy ones.

The paradox of Volkswagen is that it has always managed to speak of a quite prosaic product in an almost elitist, yet friendly and humorous style. This has enabled Volkswagen to introduce minor modifications as major developments. The selling points put across in the adverts are based on facts and on certain values which the brand has always conveyed, such as product quality, durability, weather-resistance, reliability, reasonable prices and good trade-in value.

But this advertising style, though created outside the Volkswagen company, was not just artificially added to the brand. Who could possibly have created such a monstrous car with an insect-name (the Beetle) which so completely defied the trends in the US automobile world at the time? It could only have been an extremely genuine, honest creator, with a long-term vision. To encourage its own customers to buy, the brand had not only to flatter their ego and intelligence but also to acknowledge them for breaking away – if only this one time – from the stylistic clichés of North American cars. In a tongue-in-cheek style, the brand manages to convey its values and its culture. The Volkswagen style *is* Volkswagen, even though it was created by Bernbach. On the contrary, Citroën's extravagant advertising in the 1980s was not like Citroën at all; rather, it was just arbitrarily associated with this visionary brand, without any concern for the brand's intrinsic identity. The screen ads thus produced were certainly noticed, yet they were off target, as shown by the studies on this issue. The brand's mode of expression derives from its very substance (see also p. 50). In Citroën's case, the advertising style that was invented was totally disconnected from the brand's substance and values.

The David Hamilton–Nina Ricci partnership produced a homogeneous advertising style between 1970 and 1990. Does this mean that the English photographer imposed his style on Nina Ricci? Actually, if we examine the Nina Ricci advertising campaigns from the beginning (1932), we notice that

Hamilton's approach seems to perfectly match the kind of style which the brand had unconsciously been seeking. From the start, Nina Ricci has used the veil motif (over head or face), which is the basic symbol of marriage and purity. Likewise, Hamilton's entire work depicts a hazy world, as seen through a veiled lens. The photographer's focus on adolescents on the brink of womanhood contributed to reinforce the spiritual communion between his own style and Nina Ricci's. Interestingly enough, a closely-related brand, Cacharel, also entered a symbiotic relationship with the photographer Sarah Moon. To a certain extent, the veil has thus become an integral part of both brands' current identities.

ANALYSING A BRAND'S POTENTIAL

In analysing the identity of a brand – which must precede any credible repositioning or revitalisation of a brand – we find that the facets of its identity are not all equally patent. Some indeed are at the tops of our minds, while others are latent, concealed in certain underlying signs of the brand. Rich brands, which have many sources of identity, do not necessarily choose to tap them all. Typically, the latent brand capital is that which is not tapped, but which can be if the company decides to make it an asset. Patent and latent capital alike can be either positive, ie an asset, or negative, ie a liability. The cross-combination of these two dimensions (patent/latent; positive/negative) serves to represent the brand's potential (see Figure 3.5). Revitalising a brand consists of revealing what is currently latent yet positive and concealing what is currently patent yet negative (by simply ignoring it or shifting people's focus). Revitalising a brand (which will be further discussed in Chapter 11) also consists of searching the brand's latent potential for those identity sources that will best revive its messages and actions. Identity is the essence of a brand. It is the vital basis for positioning a new brand or repositioning an old one.

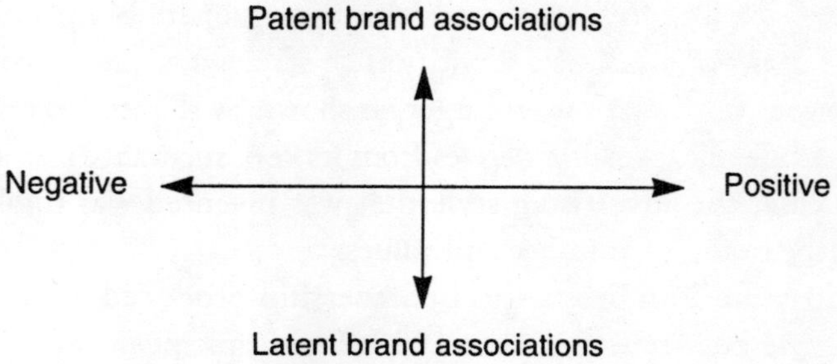

Figure 3.5 Analysis of brand potential

Part Two

BRAND MANAGEMENT

4

Launching new brands

When they came into being, all the major brands examined so far – Nike, Lacoste, Apple, Manpower, L'Oréal, Dash – were of course also new brands. Over the years, and often by intuition, chance or accident, they became major brands, leading brands, powerful brands.

Since at one point they were all necessarily new, we might ask ourselves what the established brands have or have done that the others don't have or have not done. In the previous chapters, we carried out an in-depth examination of major brands and large retailers. Each had a strong identity: a well-identified core activity, a genuine added value, a defined brand personality and a set of values, ie an authentic brand culture, etc. Every one of these established brands seemed both to have a specific meaning – ie to be driven by a specific source of inspiration – and to know where they were heading in terms of products and services which they would not hesitate to endorse.

Here we have all the key requirements for launching a new brand. To paraphrase S King (1973), the best way for a new brand to succeed is to act like an old brand! In other words, instead of worrying about how to launch new brands, we had better think about how we might invent an established brand. Looking at things in this way, though, is not at all common practice at present: launching a new product is still confused with launching a new brand.

LAUNCHING A BRAND AND LAUNCHING A PRODUCT ARE NOT THE SAME

Marketing books devote chapters to the definition of new products, but none to the launching of new brands, except for an occasional word or two on how to choose the name of a new product. This confusion between product and brand is an enduring problem. Most famous brands, rich in meaning and values, started out as the ordinary names of new and better products than those of competitors. These names were generally randomly chosen, without any prior study or analysis: Coca-Cola reflected the contents of the new product; Mercedes was the name of Mr Daimler's daughter; Citroën was a family name; Adidas is a spin-off of Adolphe Dassler; likewise Lip of Lippman and Harpic of Harry Picman. The new product had to be given a new name so that it could be advertised. Advertising was then put in charge of presenting the advantages of the new product as well as the benefits which consumers could expect from it.

After some time, new products usually get copied by competitors. They then get replaced by new, higher quality products, which often benefit from the fame of the existing product name. However, although products change, brands stay. In the beginning then, advertisements will boast the merits of the new, initial product, say X. But, since all products naturally become obsolete over time, X will soon come to announce that it's about to update and upgrade itself by lending its name to a higher quality product. And that's how a new brand comes to life. From then on, it is no longer advertising that will sell the products, but the brand itself.

Over time, the brand will gain greater autonomy and part with its original meaning (often the name of the company founder or of a specific feature of the product) by developing its own way of communicating (about the products), of addressing the public and of behaving. Few British people think of 'clean' when saying 'Kleenex' and few French think of the lotus leaf when saying 'Lotus'. The product name has become a proper noun, meaningless in itself, yet loaded with associations which have built up through experience (of the products and services), word-of-mouth and advertising. Advertising gives us hints of who the X who is now communicating really is: what is its core activity, its project, its cultural reference, its set of values, its personality, and whom is it addressing? Over time, the meaning of X has changed: it is no longer the mere name of a product, it is the very meaning of all products X, present and yet to come. The famous brand, X, is now the purveyor of values, from which its own endorsed products can benefit (as soon as they enter production).

In terms of brand creation, there is only one simple lesson to be learned from this: if the new brand does not convey its values from the very start, ie as soon as it is created and launched, it is quite unlikely that it will manage to become a major brand.

On an operational level, this means that in launching a new brand, choosing the symbolic reference is just as important as deciding on the product reference. Why was Atari not ranked as a major brand when Apple was? It is not due to their products or software. The 520 ST, the 1040, the Portfolio, the Mega and the Transputer were very good products. They concretely represented a manufacturing philosophy that was literally the company leitmotiv. Jack Tramiel, who took over Atari, and the affiliate managers would indeed often say: 'Technology is increasing, prices are decreasing.' And it is true that an Atari 1040 with a laser printer was worth a lot less than even a lower-range Apple Macintosh. What Atari lacked, though, was the meaning and latitude it would have taken to become more than just the name of the manufacturer of the 1040, Mega and Transputer. Nobody, in fact, knew what Atari's project, vision and source of inspiration were, nor what objective and subjective values it was trying to instil into the microcomputer industry by means of its products.

A successful launch requires that the new brand be treated as a real brand, right from the very start – not as a mere product name presented in advertising. Launching a new brand means acting before the product name becomes a brand symbol, with a much broader and deeper meaning than previously. Modern management must show results a lot sooner. From the very beginning, the new brand must be considered in full, ie endowing it with both functional and non-functional values. Creating a brand means acting straightaway as if it is a well-established brand, rich in meaning. This entails a few fundamental principles.

DEFINING THE BRAND'S PLATFORM

Unlike the product launch, the brand launch is, from the very start, a long-term project. Such an approach thus upsets the existing order, values and market shares of the category. It aims both at establishing a new order and different values and at impacting on the market for a long period of time. This can only be achieved if people are convinced of the brand's absolute necessity and are ready to give it all they have. In order to keep staff, management, bankers, clients, opinion leaders and salespeople mobilised for the long term, the company must be driven by a real brand project and a true vision. The latter will indeed serve to justify, internally and externally, why the brand is being launched and what its essential purpose is.

Creating a brand consists first of all in drafting the brand's platform, which is the invisible basis of its long-term identity and its main source of energy. This platform is based on the principal categories analysed in Chapter 2. Table 4.1 provides an example of this.

Many brands no longer know why they exist, so they would be quite unable to answer questions such as those in Table 4.1 defining the brand platform. Such questions reflect a philosophy at the opposite of niche tactics. Only those who are driven by a grand project within can actually set out on the long journey of brand making.

Table 4.1 Brand identity platform: defining a brand's programme

1. Why must this brand exist?
   What would consumers be missing if the brand did not exist?
2. Standpoint.
   From where does the brand speak?
3. Vision.
   What is the brand's vision of the product category?
4. What are our values?
5. Mission.
   What specific mission does the brand want to carry out in its market?
6. Know-how.
   What is the brand's specific know-how?
7. Territory.
   Where can the brand legitimately carry out its mission, in which product category?
8. Typical products or actions.
   Which products and actions best embody, best exemplify the brand's values and vision?
9. Style and language.
   What are the brand's stylistic idiosyncrasies?
10. Reflection.
    Whom are we addressing? What image do we want to render of the clients themselves?

Of course, the brand project will have to be distilled into 'strategic image traits'. In the car industry, we realise that Peugeot cannot be defined by simply a few of its features, such as performance, reliability and pleasure. These image traits do help differentiate Peugeot from Renault, which is rather positioned in terms of comfort, peace and quality (hence its slogan: 'Cars for living'). However, each brand reflects its own fundamental automobile project and its own philosophy. As a result, Renault speaks of cars, Peugeot of automobiles. Finally, without any industrial, marketing or commercial expertise nor any financial means, a project is just a wish.

The preliminary definition of brand identity is not the same for company-named brands as for brands that have their own name. Many companies nowadays act as brands. Alcatel is both company and brand, as are Siemens, Schneider, Du Pont, Philips and IBM. On the other hand, Audi is one of VAG's brands, as Mir is one of Henkel's and Dash one of Procter & Gamble's. Companies become aware that their name is actually a brand when they notice that the purchaser and user are just as important as the financial analyst in the markets in which they operate.

On an operational level, creating a brand with no direct reference to the firm offers a greater degree of freedom: everything is possible, which does not automatically mean that everything is relevant or easy. What it does mean is that we can create the brand's identity entirely from scratch.

In the case of company-named brands, the brand becomes the major spokesperson for the company. There must therefore be a relationship between brand identity and corporate identity. Brand identity has less freedom than in the previous case. The company-named brand is indeed the company's external showpiece: it is the messenger telling the company story to a larger audience. It is therefore vital for the company to identify with this brand as well as fully support this new spokesperson (which is different from the institutional spokesperson, the CEO). That is why we observe that company-named brands have the same culture as the companies from which they emanate (see Figure 4.1).

Renault's brand concept, 'Cars for living', did not just come out of the blue. Renault has been called the social laboratory of France, and its corporate values are, indeed, both humanistic and social: man has greater value than machines. Renault's ideology is therefore entirely focused on improving the quality of life (Renault was the first company in France to have closed down in August in order to give its workers holidays). This value has shifted to the brand itself. Renault's past involvement in Formula 1 in no way contradicted this: such action simply served to reinforce the image of a dynamic car with a high-performance engine system. Renault's true brand identity, though, has its source in the ideal of making 'Cars for living'.

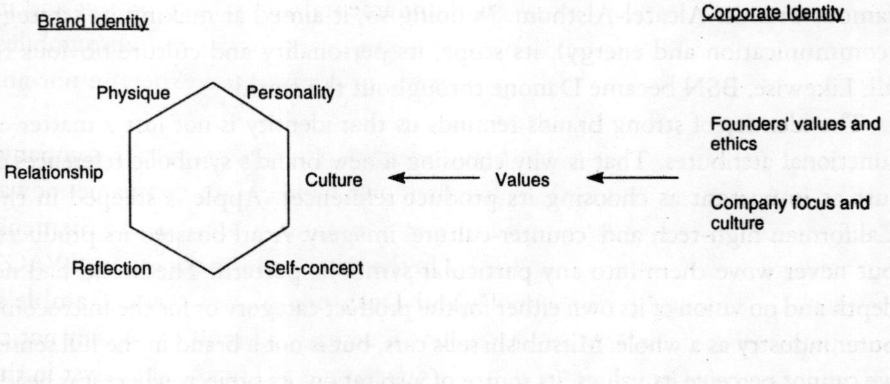

Figure 4.1 Transfer of company identity to brand identity when company and brand names coincide

Nestlé as a brand could never assume a fun and exuberant or greedy and permissive identity. This is because it bears the same name as the company, whose identity is none of these. Even though the public does not know this company, the Nestlé brand is nevertheless strongly influenced by the overall Nestlé corporate identity. Final acceptance of a new brand's identity is a company prerogative. And if the latter cannot identify with the new brand, the brand identity will be modified in order to be in tune with that of the company. This does not mean that the two perfectly coincide, but that there is a bridge between them.

Such a bridge is usually easier to build by means of the cultural facet (see Figure 4.1). There is a theoretical reason for this: a company coins its identity by focusing on one or two key values (Schwebig, 1985). These are the values which feed the brand, give it the company's outlook on the world and the impetus to transform the product category. This 'source-value' gives meaning to the brand. Underlying Peugeot's rigour and quality, there has always been the corporate determination to offer more than a strictly functional product: a car which drivers could truly enjoy.

Over time, this relationship between brand and company is switched around. The company's outward image is reflected inside and becomes far more effective in mobilising the workforce than all of the other here-today-gone-tomorrow 'company projects'. In order to take advantage of this positive feedback, many companies have traded in their old name for one of their leading brand names. Tokyo Tsuhin Kogyo, for instance, has thus become Sony Inc; Tokyo Denki Kagaku adopted the name of its famous brand TDK. Tired of seeing its brand nowhere when it was present everywhere, CGE widely publicised on Tuesday, 10 April 1990, that it was going to adopt the name of its two famous brands: Alcatel-Alsthom. In doing so, it aimed at making its strategy (communication and energy), its scope, its personality and culture obvious to all. Likewise, BSN became Danone throughout the world.

The identity of strong brands reminds us that identity is not just a matter of functional attributes. That is why choosing a new brand's symbolic references is just as important as choosing its product references. Apple is steeped in the Californian high-tech and 'counter-culture' imagery. Atari boasted its products, but never wove them into any particular symbolic pattern. The brand had no depth and no vision of its own either for the product category or for the microcomputer industry as a whole. Mitsubishi sells cars, but is not a brand in the full sense: we cannot perceive its values, its source of inspiration, its project, where it is heading and where it is taking us. It is just a name on a product, to which is attached the reassurance provided by the size of the industrial super-group, Mitsubishi. For non-Japanese people, Mitsubishi means little beyond Japan and a giant conglomerate. Imported Japanese cars have only their price and quality to rely on.

Concretely, how can such a brand project be identified? In keeping with the belief that a brand's truth lies within itself, the crucial sources of information must be the internal ones: opinion surveys should not dictate any brand identity whatsoever. They can be used, however, to evaluate how this identity is given shape in terms of product value and quality of service and communication, and how its added value is perceived against competing brands.

DETERMINING WHICH PRODUCTS ARE MOST TYPICAL

In launching a new brand, companies have to be extremely careful in choosing which product or service to present in their first campaign and how to speak about it, even more so if the overall brand is particularly ambitious. The product to choose should be the one which best represents the brand's intentions, ie the one which best conveys the brand's potential to bring about change in the market. Likewise, in terms of name, only those products which best support the overall project should prominently bear the brand name. On the less typical products, the brand name should intervene far less, serving only to endorse the product.

Not all products of a brand equally represent it. Only those which truly epitomise the brand's identity should be used as support in a launch campaign. Ideally, this identity must be visible. The major car manufacturers are well aware of this. Car design must be the outward expression of the brand's long-term design – no wonder then that the larger Citroën cars (DS, CX, XM) have such a streamlined design, half-way between car and rocket. Thus product design is one way of conveying brand identity – the fact that many cars have come to look more and more alike shows how some brands have lost their identity.

Product features also support the brand's ideology. When speaking of Toshiba, lap-top computers fully express its identity, while the tiny Portfolio has been the best support of Atari's ideology. But what about the service sector? It is true that service brands endorse something intangible: the purchaser has nothing to see other than the service-provider, and there is a fine line between what is not on show and what simply does not exist. Yet the reasoning is the same as for products: choose the services which best exemplify the brand. The tone communicated and the benefits conveyed by that product/service should not be chosen in isolation, but precisely because they are the strategic traits of the brand you are building.

BRAND CAMPAIGN OR PRODUCT CAMPAIGN?

Volkswagen has never produced communications about anything other than its products. Since the beginning, its press ads have consistently reflected a deliberate choice of graphic style – that of purity: hence, the motif of a car on a white background. So, even if the brand treats the rational arguments aloofly, humorously, impertinently or paradoxically, the car remains the 'hero' of the ad. Renault occasionally launches so-called 'brand campaigns', which aim to emphasise the brand's slogan. Whenever a brand is created, there are two alternative strategies: to communicate the brand's meaning either directly, or by focusing on a particular product. Which path is followed depends on the company's ability to select one product which will fully convey the brand's meaning. It is no wonder that Volkswagen took the second option. The Beetle plainly demonstrated the genius of an original artist, an outsider, and obviously represented a different car culture.

In launching its brand in Europe, the photocopier maker, Nashua, took out full-page portraits (rare at the time) of an Indian chief in the most serious newspapers. The caption was terse: 'The most popular photocopiers have an Indian name. Nashua, USA'. This ad was the beginning of a brand campaign. More full-page ads of other tribe members followed, each warrior portraying a different product of the line. This campaign is what actually founded the brand, allowing it to fully convey its key value – reliability (of men and machines alike) – and its symbolic reference – the virtues and universal philosophy associated with American Indians. Through this founding coup, Nashua wanted to clearly announce its identity: not Japanese, but American, yet not the same American as either IBM or Rank Xerox (Manhattan style), two other US photocopier makers. Nashua's America is that of the mythical prairie, the pre-eminence of mankind, long-lasting fraternal bonds. The core value, reliability, meant not only respect for the customer and firm commitment, but also product durability, ie photocopiers that are more dependable (thanks to its exclusive liquid toner system, the LTT). Nashua's identity and core value thus met the five universal brand identity conditions:

- it was specific: no brand other than Nashua could lay claim to it. It was sealed within its name;
- it was well-founded: both the current and future products of the line as well as the LTT gave it shape and form;
- it was motivating: security and carefree use were the main expectations of the segments targeted by the brand;

- it capitalised on the competitors' weaknesses: the technological leader, Rank Xerox, was often criticised for its domineering attitude towards its clients, caused by its market monopoly.
- it was supported internally by all: both the staff and the salespeople identified with the image of this young brand. It was in tune with the company's internal identity.

Nashua deliberately chose not to launch its brand with a campaign boasting either the reliability of one of its models or the exclusive liquid toner process. Clearly, though durability is one of the product features, brand identity does not boil down to durability alone, but rather includes it in an overall, long-term project. The fact is that none of the products could serve to illustrate this project: a Nashua photocopier looks much like a Canon, Minolta, Toshiba or Rank Xerox photocopier. Moreover, the product only represents one part of the brand's identity, that of functional durability. Thus, there was no other choice but to launch a brand campaign: this alone could indeed provide a strong enough basis for ensuring the effectiveness of all the ancillary marketing tools (mailing campaigns launched by dealers, telephone calls, etc). This same approach was followed by Whirlpool when in 1990 it launched its brand in Europe: they also chose to capitalise on the brand values rather than on a specific product (see also page 301) by means of a pan-European TV commercial and print ad campaign.

The reason why banks prefer brand campaigns is quite logical. As service companies, they have nothing tangible to show the potential customer. They can only symbolise their values and their identity. They also encapsulate the essence of their identity in slogans, in this way hoping to make up for their lack of visible products.

BRAND LANGUAGE AND TERRITORY OF COMMUNICATION

Today's vocabulary is no longer just verbal, it may be said to be even predominantly visual. In this multimedia era, in which only a few split-seconds' attention are spent on advertisements in magazines, pictures are far more important than words. The computer company, Bull, has chosen to speak in a metaphorical language focused on the tree symbol. Therefore, any advertisement in the world that now shows a tree reminds us of Bull. Bull has thus marked its very own territory of communication, by appropriating a cluster of words and images. These have become Bull's style of expression; when seeing them, we know who is speaking: Bull. The brand's symbols are also the brand's lair.

A territory of communication does not appear from nowhere, nor can it be arbitrarily assigned to the brand. Brand language allows brands to freely express their ideology. Not knowing which language to speak, we merely repeat the same groups of words or pictures over and over again, so that the whole brand message eventually becomes clogged. There is such a great urge to create unity, resemblance and a common spirit among the different campaigns that in the end they all seem merely to repeat one another. Each specific campaign message thus gets obliterated by an excessive concern to find the missing code!

The code is always rather artificial whereas language is natural: it conveys the personality, culture and values of the sender, helping the latter either to announce products and services or to charm customers. Clearly, each Dim campaign focuses on a specific product. Nevertheless, each one is typically Dim: the brand's jingle partly accounts for that, yet Dim's overall visual identity is much more than that. Dim's image is that of the Parisian woman, just like Marlboro's is that of the solitary, mythical maverick. Dim follows the changes in female expectations – anticipated by Parisian women – by adapting both its products (its liberating tights) and its values.

Brand language finally serves as a means of decentralising decisions. Thanks to the use of a common glossary of terms, different subsidiaries worldwide can adapt the theme of their messages to local market and product requirements and yet preserve the brand's overall unity and indivisible nature. Brand identity must reconcile freedom with coherence, a task which expression guides (also called brand charters) are meant to facilitate. These should not merely address issues such as the position of the brand name on the page and so on. They must also specify the following:

- dominant features of style: Bull has chosen a metaphorical style; Renault has a quiet style, not unlike that of home-made videos;
- the audio-visual characteristics such as a gesture, a close-up of a customer's face, a jingle;
- the graphic layout or narrative structure codes, and the brand's colour codes;
- the principles determining if and how the brand – and its signature, if it has one – can be used in some circumstances. Such cases must indeed be anticipated and defined in the expression guide.

CHOOSING A NAME FOR A STRONG BRAND

Manufacturers make products; consumers buy brands. Pharmaceutical laboratories produce chemical compounds, but doctors prescribe brands. In an economic system where demand and prescription focus on brands, brand names naturally take on a pre-eminent role. For if the brand concept encompasses all of the brand's distinctive signs (name, logo, symbol, colours, endorsing characteristics and even its slogan), it is the brand name that is talked about, asked for or prescribed. It is therefore natural that we should devote particular attention to this facet of the brand creation process: choosing a name for the brand.

What is the best name to choose to build a strong brand? Is there anywhere a particular type of name that can thus guarantee brand success? Looking at some so-called strong brands will help us answer these usual questions: Coca-Cola, IBM, Marlboro, Perrier, Dim, Kodak, Schweppes ... What do these brand names have in common? Coca-Cola referred to the product's ingredients when it was first created; the original meaning of IBM (International Business Machines) has disappeared; Schweppes is hard to pronounce; Marlboro is a place; Kodak, an onomatopoeia. The conclusion of this quick overview is reassuring: to make a strong brand, any name can be used (or almost any), provided that there is a consistent effort over time to give meaning to this name, ie to give the brand a meaning of its own.

Does this mean that there is no need to give much thought to the brand name, apart from the mere problem of ensuring that the brand can be registered? Not at all, because following some basic selection rules and trying to choose the right name will save you time, perhaps several years, when it comes to making the baby brand a big brand. The question of time is crucial: the brand has to conquer a territory of its own. From the very start, therefore, it must anticipate all of its potential changes. The brand name must be chosen with a view to the brand's future and destiny, not in relation to the specific market and product situation at the time of its birth. As companies generally function the other way around, it seems more than appropriate to provide some immediate information on the usual pitfalls to avoid when choosing a brand name, and also to give a reminder of certain principles.

Brand name or product name?

Choosing a name depends on the destiny that is assigned to the brand. One must therefore distinguish the type of research related to creating a full-fledged brand name – destined to expand internationally, to cover a large product line, and to last – from the opposite related to creating a product name with a more limited scope in space and time. Emphasis, process time and financial investments will certainly be different in both cases.

The danger of descriptive names

Ninety per cent of the time, manufacturers want the brand name to describe the product which the brand is going to endorse. They like the name to describe what the product does (an aspirin that would be called Headache) or is (a biscuit brand that would be called Biscuito; a direct banking service called Bank Direct). This preference for denotative names shows that companies do not understand what brands are all about and what their purpose really is. Remember: brands do not describe products – brands distinguish products.

Choosing a descriptive name also amounts to missing out on all the potential of global communication. The product's characteristics and qualities will be presented to the target-audience thanks to the advertisements, the sales people, direct marketing, articles in specialised periodicals and the comparative studies done by consumer associations. It would thus be a waste to have the brand name merely repeat the same message that all these communication means will convey in a much more efficient and complete way. The name, on the contrary, must serve to add extra meaning, to convey the spirit of the brand. For products do not live forever: their lifecycle is indeed limited. The meaning of the brand name should not get mixed up with the product characteristics that a brand presents when it is first created. The founders of Apple were well aware of this: within a few weeks the market would know that Apple made microcomputers. It was therefore unnecessary to fall into the trap of names such as Micro-Computers International or Computer Research Systems. In calling themselves Apple, on the contrary, they could straightaway convey the brand's durable uniqueness (and not just the characteristics of the temporary Apple-1): this uniqueness has to do more with the other facets of brand identity than with its physique (ie its culture, its relationship, its personality, etc).

The brand is not the product. The brand name therefore should not describe what the product does but reveal or suggest a difference.

Taking the copy phenomenon into account

Any strong brand has its copy or even its counterfeit. There is no way out of this. First of all, manufacturing patents end up being public one day. So what is left to preserve the firm's competitive advantage and provide legitimate recompense for investing in research and development and innovating? Well, the brand name. The pharmaceutical industry is the perfect example: today, as soon as patents become public, all laboratories can produce the given compound at no R&D cost and generic products start flooding the market. A brand name that simply describes the product and the product's function will be unable to differentiate the brand from copies and generic products entering the market. Choosing a descriptive name boils down to making the brand a generic product in the long run. That is exactly how the first antibiotics got trapped: they were given names indicating that they were made from penicillin – Vibramycine, Terramycine, etc.

Today, however, the drug industry has become aware that the name is in itself a patent which protects the brand from copies. This name must therefore be different from that of the generic product: in becoming distinctive and unique, it also becomes inimitable. The Glaxo-Roche laboratory, for instance, discovered an anti-ulcer agent which it called 'ranitidine'. Yet the brand name is 'Zantac'. Their competitor, Smith, Kline and French, also identified an anti-ulcer agent called 'cimetidine', but sold it under the Tagamet brand name. This naming policy is a good hedge against copies and counterfeits. Doctors are under the impression that Vibramycine and Terramycine are the same thing. Tagamet, though, seems unique, as does Zantac. The inevitable generic products that will eventually take advantage of the cimetidine or ranitidine patents will not initate the Tagamet or Zantac names.

An original name can protect the brand since it reinforces the latter's defence against all imitations, whether they be fraudulent or not. The perfume name Kerius, for example, was considered as a counterfeit of Kouros: in litigation, legal experts do not judge counterfeit in terms of nominal or perfect similarity but in terms of overall resemblance. Thus Kerius became Xerius, while another company had to pull out all the products it had just launched under the new cosmetic brand name, Mieva. Descriptive names fail to act as patents. A brand called Biscuito would be very little protected: only the 'o' could be protected so as to prevent someone from naming a product 'Biscuita'! Even Coca-Cola was unable to prevent the Pepsi-Cola name! Quickburger, Love Burger and Burger King have similar names, whereas McDonald's name is inimitable.

Distributors' own brands have greatly taken advantage of descriptive brands' scarce protection. Planning to win over some of the leading brands' customers, distributors have chosen names for their own copy-cat brands that are very similar to those of the strong brands to which they refer: this way, consumers are likely to easily mistake one for the other. Ricoré by Nestlé has thus been copied by Incoré, L'Oréal's Studio Line by Microline, etc. Because the packages look alike (Incoré is in a yellow can like Ricoré's, with a picture of a cup and table setting also like Ricoré's ...), consumers get all the more confused as they only rely on visual signs to find their way through the store aisles. As a matter of fact, recent research has shown that confusion rates are often above 40 per cent (Kapferer, 1995).

The way in which the drug industry has been handling the copy problem is extremely promising in terms of the long-term survival of all brands. By creating at the same time a product name (that of a specific compound) and a brand name, they have avoided the Walkman, Xerox or Scotch syndrome. These proper nouns now tend to become common names, merely used to designate the product. In order to overcome such risk of 'generism', companies must create an adjective-brand (the Walkman pocket music-player), not a noun-brand (a walkman). When creating a brand name, it might therefore also be necessary to coin a new name for the product itself (in this case, the pocket music-player).

Taking time into account

Many names end up preventing the brand from developing naturally over time because they are too restrictive:

- 'Europ Assistance' hinders the geographical extension of this brand and has also facilitated the creation of Mondial Assistance;
- Calor etymologically (meaning 'heat' in Latin) refers to heating appliance technology (irons, hair-dryers), and thus excludes refrigerators, The Radiola brand never managed to impose itself in the field of household appliances: its brand name was much too reminiscent of one specific sector;
- as time goes by, Sport 2000, the French sporting goods distributor, seems less and less modern and futuristic;
- the non-fat yoghurt name, Silhouette, was too restrictive in terms of consumer benefit: slimness for the sake of slimness does not necessarily prevail anymore. This is why Yoplait decided to change the name to Yoplait fat-free, after having invested over 20 million dollars since 1975 in advertising the first brand name.

Thinking internationally

Any brand must be given the potential to become international in case it should want to become so one day. Yet many brands still discover quite late that, if such is their desire, they are limited by their name: Suze, the bitter French aperitif wine, almost literally means sweet in German. Nike cannot be registered in certain Arab countries. The Computer Research Services brand name causes problems in France, as does Toyota's MR2. In the US, the almighty CGE name cannot be protected against the famous GE (General Electric) brand name. Prior to internationalising a brand, one must ensure that the name is easy to pronounce, that it has no adverse connotations and that it can be registered without problems. These new requirements explain why there is so much interest in the 1300 words which all seven major languages of the European Union have in common. It also explains the current tendency to choose abstract names which, having no previous meaning, can thus create their own.

GAINING RECOGNITION AND BRAND AWARENESS

Brand power is partly measured by brand awareness: how many people around the world know the brand, if only by its name? This is nothing unusual: the brand is a sign. Brand awareness measures the number of people who know what the brand stands for and are aware of what promises this sign has given, namely in terms of know-how (which products, which services). A brand with no awareness is just something stuck on a product, meaningless and speechless. The purpose of investing in advertising is to reveal the meaning of the brand and convey it to the largest number of people: they should thus feel tempted to try the product being presented by the brand. Three types of awareness are usually distinguished:

- 'top of mind' awareness measures whether the brand is the first to come to the mind of people who are interviewed on the brands of a given product category;
- 'unaided' awareness measures the brand's impact, ie to what extent it is spontaneously associated with a given product category;
- 'aided' awareness – consists in asking the target-audience if they have already heard of certain brands or if they have at least heard their names.

As we can see, the level of difficulty increases from one type of awareness to the next, from the cheapest – 'aided' awareness – to the most expensive – 'top of mind' awareness. From this hierarchy, it is often inferred that 'top of mind' awareness should be every brand's goal. It is a mistake. Each type of awareness has a different purpose and specific implications. Depending on the market, it might or might not be appropriate to invest in order to reach a high rate of 'top of mind awareness'.

The purpose of aided awareness is to reassure – the brand has already been heard of. The brand is not totally unknown so that salespeople can allude to it when selling something to a hesitating client. Unaided awareness refers to the few brands which immediately come to mind: this will benefit them if the buyer, unwilling to spend too much time choosing among them, rather relies out of convenience on immediate memory. In industrial marketing, this awareness rate provides a list of names which will be quickly scanned in a first phase and among which some might later be more thoroughly analysed. 'Top of mind' awareness benefits the brand any time buyers have to make a quick decision (as when ordering a drink in a café, for instance) or want to decide without too much effort (because they are not very involved in the task), as is the case with many household products (Kapferer and Laurent, 1992).

As a result of these differences, it is clear that the pursuit of a particular type of awareness really depends on the way in which buyers of a product make their decisions and on their level of involvement. The financial investment which is needed by a brand eager to gain a strong unaided awareness is not always justified: the market share of a household appliance brand does not simply double if its unaided awareness doubles. However, if it has a satisfactory level of aided awareness, a white goods brand should invest to increase the number of its points of sale. Indeed, with regard to durable products, which are only purchased infrequently, clients do not always know beforehand either what is available on the market or what criteria they should use to decide. They usually decide on the spot, after lengthy comparisons with the other products on sale in the store. Even if the brand only brings back a vague memory, customers are bound to evaluate its products. Thus, in France, Hoover has a low unaided awareness rate, but a very high aided one. Before deleting the Philips brand name, Whirlpool aimed at reaching two-thirds of Philips' aided awareness rate (see also p. 301).

As for products which require less involvement by the purchaser, the unaided awareness rate has more impact on choice since customers neither perceive any great risk nor want to spend any great amount of time in choosing. Yet experience has shown that under certain market conditions, gaining any unaided awareness at all is almost impossible. The brand's aided awareness rate increases but not its unaided awareness? Why is that?

Unaided awareness is not a cold, merely cognitive measure: it has an emotional dimension. This is shown by the correlation that exists between awareness and preferences or global evaluations (see Table 4.2). Awareness, therefore, does not come simply from high pressure advertising. It comes from making people feel attracted and interested. It will thus be more difficult for an unfriendly brand to stand out because of the well-known mechanisms of selective exposure, attention and memory.

Unaided awareness is always acquired at the expense of another brand. If one brand's awareness increases, another's necessarily decreases. This is demonstrated by a fact that is commonly observed in most markets: people who are interviewed

Table 4.2 How liking stimulates brand awareness

Brands	Variation of unaided awareness between 1989 and 1993	Variation of global image between 1989 and 1993
Nissan	+6	+0.4
Toyota	+5	+0.5
Citroën	+4	+0.1
Renault	+3	+0.2
Mercedes	+2	=
Audi	+2	+0.2
VW	+1	+0.2
Peugeot	+1	+0.1
Mazda	+1	+0.2
Opel	=	+0.1
BMW	−1	=
Ford	−1	+0.2
Alfa	−2	−0.3
Fiat	−2	−0.2
Volvo	−3	−0.2

Source: Europanel, PSA

usually quote an average of three or four brands. Given such a limited number, accepting a new brand in such a selective club necessarily means that in turn some other brand will no longer be quoted. This results in the following: when three brands on the market are strongly rated in unaided awareness, scarcely any other brand has a chance of even getting quoted (Laurent, Kapferer *et al* 1995). Access to such markets is said to be 'blocked'. The relationship between aided and unaided awareness is graphically represented by the curve in Figure 4.2(a).

In new markets, where no brands have strong unaided awareness, this selective memory phenomenon does not exist. Unaided awareness can be pursued by investing in advertising and thus gaining a share of voice. In a competitive environment, it *must* be pursued: not only to escape the blocking mechanism described above, but also to benefit from the first mover's, or pioneer, advantage (Carpenter and Nakamoto, 1990; Nedungadi and Hutchinson, 1985).

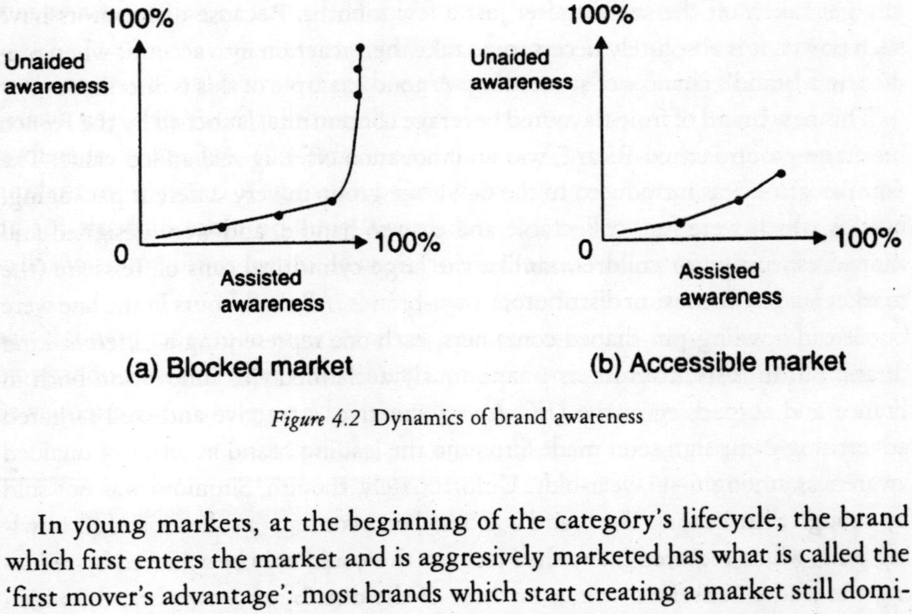

Figure 4.2 Dynamics of brand awareness

In young markets, at the beginning of the category's lifecycle, the brand which first enters the market and is aggresively marketed has what is called the 'first mover's advantage': most brands which start creating a market still dominate it several decades later, even in markets in which competitive advantage does not consist of technological know-how, learning curves or gains in productivity. The psychological explanation of this is that when a market first opens, buyers neither have a set of preferences nor any stabilised decision criteria. Thus the first brand to get known in a new market becomes its prototype and main reference. In other words, this brand is the one to initially define the ideal brand, ie the cluster of attributes that will generate customer satisfaction. This brand is the one which defines the values. That is why later entrants have a handicap. Since they generally adopt a 'me-too' strategy and want to look like the first mover, they lose some of their distinctiveness and become less conspicuous.

TAKING DISTRIBUTORS INTO ACCOUNT

In the field of consumer goods that do not require much consumer involvement, it is no longer the consumer who is solely responsible for the success or failure of new brands, but the distributors. In deciding whether or not to give room to a new brand, they are the ones who can cause it to fail. They are also the ones who can cause the premature decline of a new brand if they judge its turnover to be too slow. Because of this, many projects based on excellent concepts and good products have not survived. New brands now have to fight distributors' own-brands which are pushed forward because of their higher margins, one reason why new brands are no longer easily admitted by distributors. The problem is that when the weighted distribution percentage increases too slowly, investments in advertising have little or no impact. If these are spread out over time or delayed, the new product on the market will not rotate quickly enough and thus will eventually get taken off the shelves after just a few months. Because distributors have such power, it is absolutely necessary to take their reaction into account when predicting a brand's chances of succeeding. A good example of this is Sironimo.

This new brand of fruit-flavoured beverage concentrate, launched by the French beverage group Pernod-Ricard, was an innovation offering real added value. The popular drink was introduced to the 6–11 age group in very different packaging: bottles which were fun, collectable and easy to handle, and were designed and shaped especially for children, unlike the large cylindrical cans of Teisseire (the market leader) or those of distributors' own-brands. All six flavours in the line were bottled in bowling-pin-shaped containers, each one representing a different kind of animal. In tests, consumers unanimously acclaimed this innovation both in France and abroad, eg in the UK. A very creative, attractive and well targeted advertising campaign soon made Sironimo the leading brand in terms of unaided awareness among 6–11-year-olds. Unfortunately, though, Sironimo was not sold by enough distributors. The brand was based on a concept (a collection of six bowling pins) which required many shelf facings: this could only be achieved by reducing the leader Teisseire's facings or those of the distributors' own-brands, which were a major source of profit for the distributor. Without these crucial facings, the launch of the Sironimo product line concept could not be pulled off. Moreover, of the six flavours, some rotated faster than others and so were more likely to be out of stock if the sales reps did not pay attention quickly enough. All these factors were a serious handicap to the launch of Sironimo. In the end, the Pernod-Ricard Group decided to sell the brand to the market leader instead.

5

Sustaining a brand long term

Many apparently modern and up-to-date brands have actually been with us for a long time: Coca-Cola was born on 29 May 1887, the Michelin bibendum appeared in 1898, Gitanes and Gauloises in 1910, Camel in 1913, Danone in 1919, Orangina in 1936 and Marlboro in 1937 to name a few. These are the brands which have survived – others have disappeared from the market even if their names do ring a bell.

The perennial appeal of some brands reminds us that, although products are mortal and governed by a more or less long lifecycle which can be delayed but not avoided, brands can escape the effects of time. It is this resistance to the course of time that leads certain countries to consider in terms of accounting that when a brand is entered as an asset in the balance sheet, it should not be depreciated. Nevertheless, brands can also disappear. If badly managed, any brand is doomed. This phenomenon existed long before the economic crisis; the latter only accentuated the factors leading to decline.

Moreover, in all developed countries, since markets as well as customers come to maturity, fierce competition from DOBs (Distributor Own Brands) can be seen. They not only arise in the food and consumer goods industries, but are developing in sectors such as sporting goods, kitchen appliances, TVs and VCRs, clothing and banking services. DOBs can now even be found selling to companies themselves. Office stationery, for example, is dominated by DOBs and it is ironic to see big food-brand manufacturers buy from the Guilbert company, one of the biggest distributors of office furniture in France, whose products, bought from 3M for instance, are sold under its own store name. There are DOBs in all distribution channels: wholesalers in car equipment and spare parts develop their own DOB. They have surfaced in electrical equipment and are impacting on the market leadership of the Legrand company. This new form of competition which acquires *de facto* a share of shelf space makes the struggle for the remaining space even fiercer, putting, of course, brands on short allowance. Many great and well-known brands have disappeared, others are struggling. Why do some brands last throughout time and seem forever young, whereas others do not?

Time is but a proxy variable, a convenient indicator of the changes that affect society as well as markets, subjecting the brand to the risk of obsolescence on a double front – technological and cultural. With time, technological advances become more widely available and new cheaper entrants arrive that destabilize the balance of added-value of established brands, forcing them into a never-ending cycle of constant improvement. For instance, the sudden growth of Daewoo in the car market is due to the fact that this conglomerate had access to GM assembly lines which were already 'obsolete' although they were just a few years old and were sold by GM at a low price. With the passing of time, consumers either become more sophisticated and expect customised offers, or become blasé and prefer a simplified and cheaper offer. Time also marks the cultural evolution of values, mores and consumer habits. As time goes by, current clients grow older and a new generation emerges which has to be won over from scratch all over again. Finally, time also wears down the signs, the words, the symbols and the advertising campaigns of brands.

Is there a common feature of the seemingly everlasting nature of some brands? For convenience, one could say that an understanding of the brand logic, addressed in a previous chapter, offers the best bulwark against a brand slipping into decline and disappearing. A general definition also sums it up: 'to defend an added-value that is constantly undermined by competition'. The following sentence epitomising the problem is attributed to Antoine Riboud (former CEO of Danone worldwide): 'I do not believe in the overpowering might of brands, but I believe in work.' A brand is not a once-and-for-all construction, but the aim of a constant effort to reconstruct the added value. The current product has to be continuously adapted to meet changing demand while at the same time the new concepts of the future have to be invented that will sustain the growth of the brand.

An analysis of the numerous brands that have survived the crises and lasted down the years may point to the key success factors of this virtuous spiral and is the purpose of the present chapter.

THE EQUILIBRIUM OF ADDED VALUE

Fundamentally linked to product differentiation, is brands bring added values to the market. This can have a tangible basis (ie provides a superior 'augmented' product) and an intangible or immaterial basis. It is the latter that makes us go to McDonald's even if the Big Mac is no better than a Quick's

Giant (its competitor in Europe), or that makes us naturally buy a pair of Levi's even though the item is fairly uncomfortable. It is the added-value which justifies the difference in price to the customer. Either you want a yoghurt or you want a Danone! There is a natural equilibrium between material and intangible added-value on the one hand and price on the other.

The approach of the cheese-manufacturing company Bongrain is a typical example. The company has created more than ten new brands of cheese, in each case systematically taking a generic category and adding a tangible quality edge to it. For example, the cheese 'Caprice des Dieux' provides a never-failing melt-in-your-mouth experience which other camemberts cannot offer as their quality fluctuates too much. Moreover, the company adds on big value in terms of image, through name, packaging and advertising, as a basis for its unique proposition and to maximise its attractiveness. These two elements justify a high price premium, which when multiplied by the sales volume sustains a long-term profit rate partly reinvested in the manufacturing plant and research and development for quality innovations and partly in brand advertising. Figure 5.1(a) sums up the branding approach which is the mark of such a company.

According to sound branding logic, the role of advertising is to accelerate the diffusion of a product that already sells well without it. For cheese, the difference in quality be organoleptic, dietetic, practical or aesthetic. The image stems from what is visible, ie the name of the brand, the visible aspects of the product, the pricing level and the advertising (see Figure 5.2). At Bongrain, the brand should be able to sell without advertising, a sign that the added-value is perceptible on the shelf. At the same time, the advertising communicates that which is not visible – the intangible value-added. That is why an image is made from both tangible and intangible values (see Figure 5.1(a)).

The problem is that the competition does not remain inactive. The basic level of the whole generic category improves at least as far as quality is concerned. This erodes the perceived quality difference of the brand (Figure 5.1b), but it also improves its image, for instance, because of the progress made in terms of presentation by the DOBs (sometimes bordering on slavish imitation). Unfortunately, since the price differential remains the same (when it is not increased by the arrival on the market of good products which are cheaper) the equilibrium of added-value is upset, resulting in a drop in the volume of demand. The company then responds by greatly reducing advertising spend, and so the image differential. The price premium of the brand remains but no longer corresponds to the added value. This is what happened to Bongrain during the recession and forced it to stop advertising support for some of its many product-brands, leading to a downward spiral.

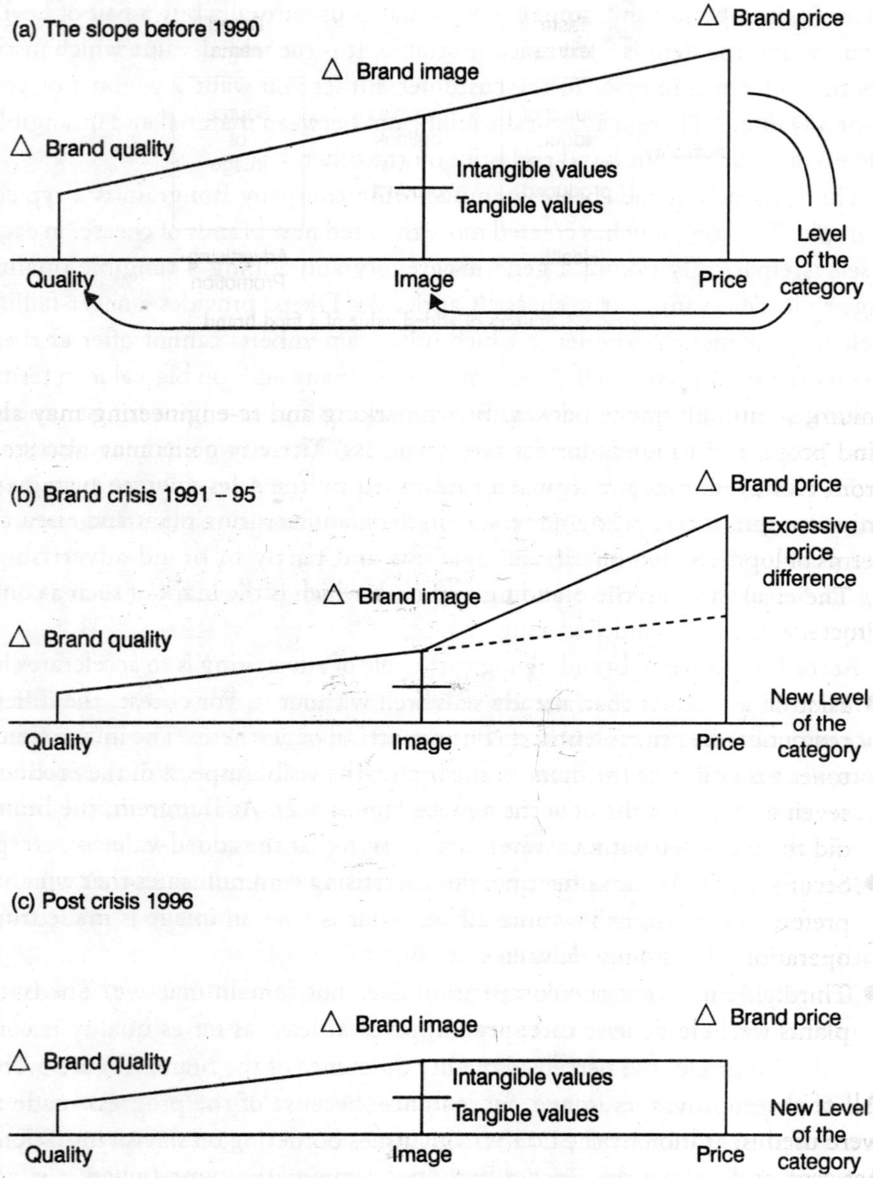

Figure 5.1 Brand and added value

Which strategies can stop that spiral? First of all, one should consider returning to one's original vocation. The manufacturer's brand should excel in manufacturing. This means completely rethinking production, manufacturing plant and value analysis. All sources of cost which do not translate into value for the customer, all the squandering of resources which increases the brand pre-

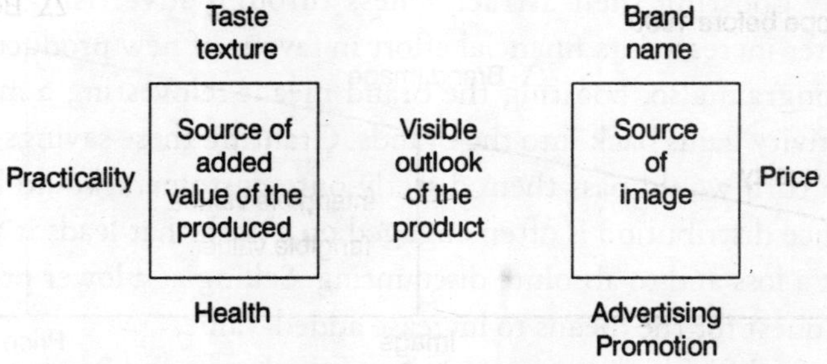

Figure 5.2 Sources of added value of a food brand

mium, should be tracked down. Benchmarking and re-engineering may also find propitious grounds for consideration. Productivity gains may also stem from eliminating any marginal products in extended lines which have been mismanaged, thus cutting out the costs incurred by too many promotions (in terms of logistics, complexity and management costs).

The example of Procter and Gamble is quite revealing. In 1992 and 1993 Procter & Gamble launched a gigantic productivity programme:

- First of all, it withdrew some weak brands (Citrus Hill fruit juices, Clarion cosmetics) and merged others (Puritan oil merged with Crisco, White Cloud toilet paper merged with its stronger cousin, the Charmin brand). Moreover, seven of the 17 varieties of the famous Luvs diapers disappeared, and Camay did the same, letting go of one-third of its products in the line.
- Secondly, the firm adopted a policy called EDLP (Every Day Low Price), thus preferring a constant low price all year round to a multitude of promotional operations which only induced costs and made managing more complex.
- Thirdly, Procter undertook staff reductions and closed some of its plants (30 plants were closed over three years).

All of these economies, which amounted to several hundred million dollars, were used to reduce retail prices spectacularly: 33 per cent on Camay soap, 26 per cent on Luvs diapers, 16 per cent on Pampers, and so on. In doing so, the brands came back into the core of the market, from which they had gradually been pushed out by an increasing price difference. Kellogg's also cut its prices in May 1996. However, it would be a mistake to believe that all the savings in productivity were passed on to distribution. One does not build a long-term brand loyalty by lowering prices; this is achieved by creating and injecting added value into the brand. The main part of the productivity gains should be reinvested in research, in the launching of new products or in renewing existing products by boosting their attractiveness through advertising. In 1992 to 1995, Procter increased its financial effort in favour of new products by 30 per cent. At Bongrain also, boosting the brand meant reinvesting a major part of the productivity gains back into the brands. Granting these savings to distributors who in turn would pass them directly onto customers would have been a mistake, since distribution is often engaged on a path that leads it to the point of selling at a loss and to absolute discounting. Selling at a lower price does not resolve the quest for the means to increase added-value.

The specific difficulty linked to the cheese market and to Bongrain's strategy (to create specialities) is that improving the quality differential of a specific product may end up with the creation of another product. Following improvements to Caprice des Dieux, will we still have Caprice des Dieux? Loyal consumers, who are the basis of 'brand equity', realise this and complain when they do not move on from the old brand. Recall the stir created by the withdrawal of the classic formula of Coke and its replacement by a new taste, that of New Coke. The aim was to get closer to the taste of Pepsi, since blind taste-tests had revealed that the latter was preferred to Coke in the United States. Faced with an outcry of indignation from the customers that was relayed by the media, the Coca-Cola Company had to go into reverse and end its experiment by putting back into stores the classic Coke, the essence of America.

RENOVATIONS AND INNOVATIONS

A brand is the name that progress takes to gain access to the market. The progress marked by the inclusion of enzymes in detergents is called Ariel or Skip or Tide. The progress in convenience coffee is called Nescafé. But progress does not stop. The latest level of quality or performance is quickly integrated by the market and becomes a standard. Before long it can be found in DOBs. Continuous, but from now on selective, innovation is the brand's fate. This also applies to products with a strong intangible added-value: the cologne brand Eau Jeune (literally Young Water) can only survive if it launches new versions capable on each occasion of moving with the times. This applies just as much to stylish brands and to fashion designers as to luxury brands that have to renew constantly not their art but their products. Luxury must move with the times lest it become embalmed.

The exceptional longevity and leadership of Nescafé on the market can only thus be explained. Created in 1945, the brand has never stopped innovating, either by little imperceptible touches which when put together have produced an instant coffee whose taste is ever improving, or by major technological breakthroughs. The product has never stopped developing either in taste or in convenience (glass packaging replaced iron in 1962), or in its ecological considerations (the introduction of refills), or by its look. To signal the technical breakthrough and the progress made by lyophilisation in 1966, Nescafé took on the aspect of small grains under the name 'Special Filter'. In 1981, the aromas of the different coffees were recaptured, which was signalled by the creation of a real product range (Alta Rica, Cap Colombie), and new advertising focusing on South America. In 1992, a new manufacturing process called 'full aroma' was able to capture even better the aroma of freshly-roasted coffee. Innovation and advertising are the two pillars of the long-lasting success of this brand.

The leadership of Gillette follows the same pattern. In 1993, 37 per cent of the sales of this multinational were accounted for by products which had been launched in the five previous years. In launching new innovations when the previous ones are barely established, Gillette keeps ahead of the pack, justifying a comfortable price premium and putting DOBs on short allowance (18 per cent volume on the disposables segment). Figure 5.3 demonstrates this well: there is a strong linear relationship between the innovation rate in a product category and the penetration of DOBs. When brands get lazy, cheaper copies can take a corner of the market, as in the case in the market for cordials and for cheese, for example. It is significant that each year in the Lego catalogue out of 250 product references, 80 are new. In many sectors, the minute the innovation

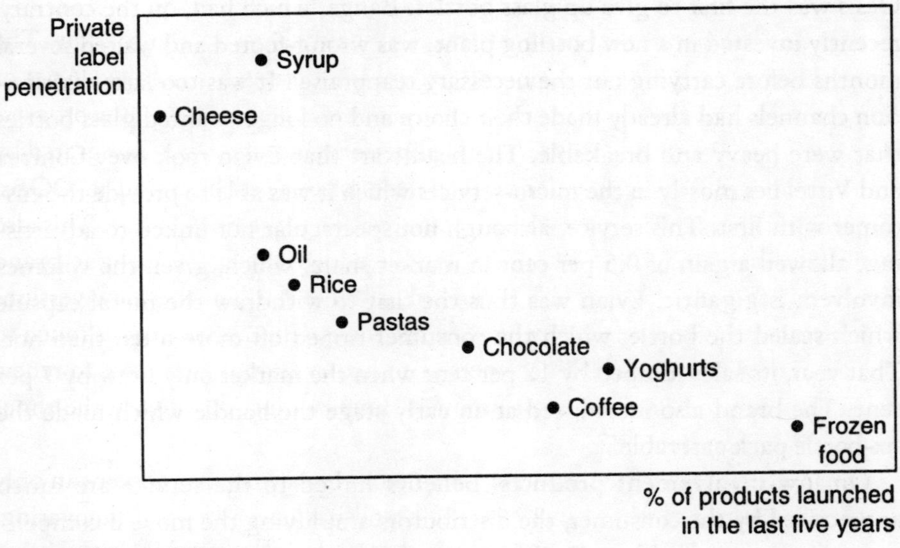

Source: McKinsey, UK

Figure 5.3 Innovation: the key to competitiveness

rate of a company goes down, it starts losing ground. This is why in 1995 when Moulinex was asked why its results were bad, executives answered that the company had only offered 10 per cent innovation when the average in the industry was 26 per cent.

Innovation, source of growth and competitiveness, does not come easy. Here too, there are no miracles. The firms which innovate most, such as Procter and Gamble, L'Oréal and Gillette, devote on average 3.2 per cent of their sales to research and development. Is there a lesson here for the food companies competing against DOBs and price leaders? The giants in the food industry spend much less in comparison on R&D: Unilever devotes 1.8 per cent of its sales to R&D, Nestlé 1.2 per cent, Kraft General Foods 0.8 per cent and Cadbury-Schweppes 0.4 per cent (Ramsay, 1992).

As a consequence, in 1996, own label products accounted for 62 per cent of the 4600 new product launches in the British food and drink market. In the chilled sector, own label product launches represented 79 per cent of the 2188 introductions! Retailers' brands do act as real brands.

Innovation does not have to mean a technological breakthrough. Gillette is an extreme case: the Sensor required ten years in research and led to 22 patents, the Sensor Excel five years and 29 patents, Sensor Plus Pour Elle five years and 25 patents. Many innovations can be linked to the service brought by the brand, in its packaging for example.

The one common explanation for Oasis' leadership over Banga in the fruit drink market is in their advertising strategy. The truth is nothing of the kind. Oasis was the first to give up glass bottles. Banga, which had, on the contrary, recently invested in a new bottling plant, was wrong-footed and waited several months before carrying out the necessary reappraisal. It was too late: distribution channels had already made their choice and no longer wanted glass bottles that were heavy and breakable. The head start that Evian took over Contrex and Vittel lies mostly in the micro-services which it was able to provide the customer with first. This service, although not spectacular nor linked to advertising, allowed a gain of 0.5 per cent in market share, which, given the volumes involved, is gigantic. Evian was thus the first to withdraw the metal capsule which sealed the bottle, which the consumer ripped off more often than not. That year, its sales jumped by 12 per cent when the market only grew by 7 per cent. The brand also introduced at an early stage the handle which made the six-bottle pack carryable.

On low-involvement products, benefits linked to the service are much appreciated by the consumer, the distributors amplifying the move if competitors do not react quickly – distributors prefer novelty.

In order to make milk a less ordinary product and to curb the surge of price leaders, the milk brand Candia multiplied its innovations, giving each its own specific name to accentuate the differentiation and allow for strong advertising support: Viva (milk with vitamins), Grand Lait (enriched milk), Grand Vivre, Croissance (for children), Future Maman (ie for pregnant women). These daughter-brands of Candia stemmed the advance of price-leader brands and enabled distributors to work with high-margin and high-turnover products. These were not major innovations like the Polaroid system, Post-it or the discovery of Teflon, of Nylon or of ABS, but were add-ons of vitamins, minerals and so on to respond to the expectations of demanding customers. In doing so, Candia made the whole category advance forward. Actually, nowadays Viva is rarely bought for its vitamins but for the brand and for what it stands for (a dynamic lifestyle, full of life, of youth). This product which at first was advanced or premium becomes the basis of milk, the reference. Candia was thus instrumental in enhancing the reference level for milk. The premium becomes a standard.

As a conclusion, one often hears Coca-Cola cited as a brand with an opposite strategy which succeeds without innovation, the product apparently being the same since its creation more than a century ago. Actually, far from narrow-mindedly imposing on everyone a single product, Coca-Cola has never stopped segmenting to better address the demands of new markets: caffeine-free Coke, sugar-free Coke, Diet Coke. Moreover, Coke is developing new uses or points of consumption through new formats (cans for vending machines, premix, post-mix, bottles in PVC, then in PET). In the soft drink industry, introducing new formats has a strong impact on customers. They are considered by these companies as real new-product launchings.

NOURISH THE PERCEIVED DIFFERENCE

In our empirical study of the factors that explain brand sensitivity (Kapferer and Laurent, 1992) conducted with G. Laurent in 20 contrasted markets, the main key factor is by far the perception of a difference between brands. Forty years ago BSN transformed the market for water from the status of a bulk supply market to that of a brand market: by revealing the invisible, everything that makes Evian bring a benefit for the customer which is different from other brands. Advertising investments really deserve that name even if, from an accounting point of view, they are often treated as expenses. Such investments confer first a reputation then a positioning to brands, defining their territory and revealing their differences. With their massive presence in distribution and daily presence on the table or in commercials, brands have become familiar, friendly and close, a source of empathy, even of loyalty and attachment. To maintain the strength of brands, it is vital to nourish the two pillars which make the relationship with the brand: one cognitive, the other emotional. Innovation serves precisely this purpose. It enables the brand to differentiate itself objectively and to draw once again the market's attention.

With time, it is noticeable that perceived differences erode faster than the emotional relationship. The liking persists even though we can see that the brand no longer has a monopoly over performance. The study conducted by the American agency, Young & Rubicam (1994), is a reminder of this psychological fact. The survey, called Brand Asset Monitor and conducted on 2000 brands worldwide, situates them against two facets of their relationship: cognitive and emotional (bearing in mind the fact that during the growth of the brand, the first facet precedes the second). The customer learns through communication and distribution the existence of a brand before grasping its difference, which then leads to its pertinence. In the meantime, the seeds of familiarity and esteem have been sewn, reminding us that prompted brand awareness precedes spontaneous awareness and that the latter is correlated with the emotional evaluation. The brands that come to mind spontaneously, as they belong to this group, also happen to be our favourite brands (see also p. 139).

As shown by Figure 5.4, the decline of a brand, however, begins with a slide in the level of perceived difference between it and the competition and, in par-

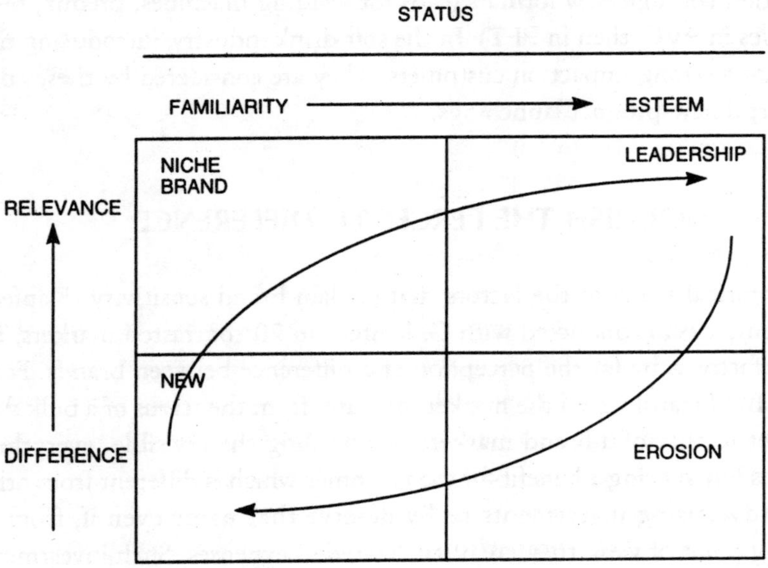

Source: Young & Rubicam

Figure 5.4 Paths of brand growth and decline

ticular, with the opinion leaders of the product category. The esteem and the emotional ties are still alive and well, but the consumer realises that the quality gap has been bridged between the brand and its competition. He still likes it but may now become disloyal!

The benefit of this study is to underscore that the drop in differentiation signals the beginning of the decline, however strong the liking score may be. Unfortunately, many leaders are no longer considered as the qualitative reference of their branch. We like Lotus, Kleenex, brands that we have known since childhood, but we no longer think that they are the sign of superior product quality. They will have to refocus on the product to regain their leadership. The Coke vs Pepsi duel in the United States is a good example of this. One often reduces the struggle between the two giants to a battle of advertising budget size. Actually, Coca-Cola's philosophy lies in the so-called 3A principle: Availability, Affordability and Awareness. Coca-Cola must be within reach everywhere, cheap and on one's mind. Another phrase sums up Coca-Cola's ambitions: 'To be the best, cheapest soft drink in the world' (Pendergrast, 1993). What is exactly the strategy deployed by Pepsi-Cola? As it could not compete in the communication, sponsoring, animation and promotion race it focused on product and price. Pepsi-Cola has always tried to improve its taste to fit as best it could the evolution in the taste of the American public. This is what founded the very aggressive advertising campaigns from 1975 onwards, such as the 'Take the Pepsi challenge', where surprised customers found they preferred the taste of Pepsi in a blind test. Moreover, Pepsi has always sought to be a couple of cents cheaper than Coca-Cola. The strategy proved effective: we know it forced Coca-Cola to change its formula in 1985 so as not to take the risk of being surpassed in taste. This was the famous episode concerning New Coke.

How do you preserve the superior image of a brand, this capital of perceived difference?

- One way is to renew the product regularly, to upgrade it to the current level of expectation. This is why Volkswagen introduced the Golf, then Golf 2, 3 and 4. Detergent manufacturers make minor adjustments every two years or so, and make major changes in their formula every five years. This is how Ariel and Skip maintain their qualitative leadership, making them both the two most expensive brands and the leaders on the market. Moreover, for want of financial means, DOBs cannot keep up in the R&D race, a race which can become an obsession. Some companies get carried away in the effort to surpass the competitors, as happened to Unilever with its new 'Power' formula which proved to be damaging to clothes in usage tests.

- A second way is to integrate new and emerging needs while holding onto the same positioning. In doing so, any car brand, even if it is not specifically positioned on safety as is Volvo, must from now on show that it is equally concerned with security and even the environment.
- A third way is to constantly confirm one's superiority on one particular axis. For example, a brand of shampoo treating hair loss should rapidly propose line extensions covering the different needs of people suffering from this problem – creams, lotions and so on. These extensions demonstrate the concern of the brand to address as best it can the different aspects of the problem on which it focuses and to affirm its leadership by becoming the reference linked to the need.
- The fourth way lies in constantly strengthening the brand's reputation. Even though it appears that persuading the client to purchase can only be achieved by advertising or through experience of the product or service, public opinion is actually always collective, hence the importance of positive word-of-mouth reports from experts and opinion leaders. Every brand should be concerned about how it is perceived by these leaders. This goes without saying for high-tech products where, as McKenna (1991) has said, 'Ten per cent of the people control what the other 90 per cent think.' It also is the case for 'hi-style' products in fashion or creation. This is why in the long term, even if in the L'Oréal culture a key factor is advertising to the public, Vichy should be careful of its standing among the experts in dermo-cosmetology. In the food industry, the fact that French restaurants looked down on Ricard (the national spirit) was influential in limiting its distribution to foreign markets. On the contrary, Italian wines benefited from the support of all pizzerias.
- Finally, perceived difference can only be maintained if the innovations are allocated according to the strength of the brand. More often than not, in multi-brand companies, each brand wants to be the one accorded the latest innovation. But, as we have seen previously, a strong innovation will not sell under a weak brand. It is better to reinforce the price premium of each brand by giving to the stronger brand either the most innovations or the priority, however temporary it may be. *A fortiori*, this argument applies to DOBs: neither L'Oréal, nor Gillette, nor Kellogg's, nor Procter, supply DOBs. Such companies keep their exclusive added-value for themselves. The other companies manufacturing DOBs must be cautious to keep a differentiation: the name of the brand supported by advertising is not sufficient to justify on its own, in the long term, a price differential, unless the marketing costs correspond exactly to the price premium. This differentiation is possible for Nestlé in the food industry because instant coffee is a very technical product and different levels of quality are possible.

There is another requirement for maintaining perceived difference: investment in advertising. Indeed, many products are silent: consumers cannot appraise their qualities just by looking at them. If the quality of the product is the prime factor inspiring loyalty, it is advertising that makes it stand out of the pack in the shopping aisle by drawing attention to it. This requirement deserves separate analysis.

INVEST IN COMMUNICATION

Communication is the brand's weapon. It alone can unveil what is invisible, reveal the basic differences hidden by the packaging which often looks the same among competitors, especially when this similarity is precisely the impression sought by DOBs to create confusion. It alone can sustain the attachment to the brand, even if this loyalty is eroded by many in-store promotions. Advertising is a result of the rise of self-service distribution and reductions in the numbers of salespeople. It is the necessary consequence of investments in R&D that have to pay off ever faster and therefore need an ever bigger public. That this has to be repeated over and over is the proof that there is a confusion in people's minds about the legitimacy of advertising, even within marketing teams, and is why we will use numbers to back our statements.

As Figure 5.5 demonstrates, there is a strong relationship between the penetration of DOBs and the extent of advertising expenditure in a market, measured in percentage of sales spent on advertising. This effort is a barrier to entry. However, upon examining the product categories, it becomes clear that the categories with a high investment in advertising are also those that invest in innovations and renovations, which are perfect opportunities for re-establishing the brand in the public consciousness. It is the conjunction of these two factors (innovation and advertising) that produces added-value.

The role of advertising in defending and sustaining the brand capital is shown by Table 5.1. With the exception of jam, where there is much consumption by children and the idealised reference to home-made jam favours small brands specific to distributors and discount products, advertising is quite efficient. Once more, we may notice that the categories which invest heavily in advertising are also those that regularly innovate and strongly differentiate their products.

REMAIN WITHIN THE MAINSTREAM PRICE

Even if innovation and advertising do increase added-value, loyalty at all costs does not exist. Customers can be both sensitive to the brand but disloyal to it,

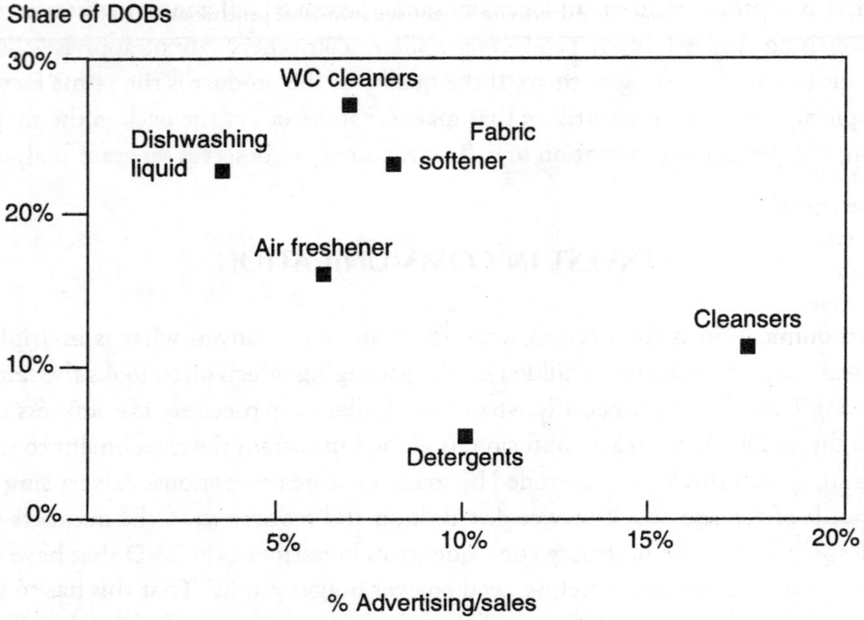

Source: McKinsey, UK

Figure 5.5 Penetration of distributors' brands and advertising intensity

estimating that the price of the brand goes beyond the price span that they are willing to pay for the product category, and beyond the brand premium that seems reasonable to them given the added satisfaction which is expected. Distributors also have the same attitude.

During 40 years of economic growth, the biggest brands were tempted to regularly increase their prices to maximise the overall profit accruing from a strong price premium and a large batch of loyal clients. For financial directors concerned about showing ever-increasing profits, what does a price increase of a few pence or cents per unit represent? For the market, however, it now has the utmost importance. In April 1993, one of the most famous brands, Marlboro, noting a slump in sales, was the first to put into reverse this inclination by unilaterally lowering its prices in the United States. Wall Street reacted badly, thinking the bell was tolling for brands: on that day the stocks of all consumer goods companies dropped significantly. More than a year later, in August 1994, Marlboro's market share reached unprecedented heights (29.1 per cent), seven points more than in March of 1993 just before the famous 'Marlboro Friday'. In France in December 1992, Philip Morris decided to bring down the price of Chesterfields from 11.60F to 10F at at time when competitors were preparing

Table 5.1 Advertising weight and own-label penetration

	Advertising sales ratio %	**Own-label market share** %
Cereals	10	15
Detergents	8	11
Coffee	8	13
Jam	7	47
Butter	5	6
Soft drinks	5	20
Tea	5	26
Yoghurts	2	39
Cider	2	36
Fish	0.7	26
Wine	0.5	61

Source: McKinsey, UK.

to pass on to customers the 15 per cent tax increase imposed by the government. Within two months the sales of Chesterfields jumped by 300 per cent. The market share of the brand went from less than 1 per cent in 1991 to 12.2 per cent in 1994. It became, in a year, the favourite cigarette for young people (71 per cent of buyers were under 25).

One may recall that Procter and Gamble significantly reduced the price of its brands in the United States in accordance with its brand-boosting programme, thanks to the allocation of part of the savings accruing from an impressive programme to increase industrial productivity, marketing and sales. These price reductions were part of the EDLP (Every Day Low Price) policy which put an end to the myriad of micro-promotions. In France, most big brands had to look over their prices again and reduce them: 18 per cent for Wasa, 8 per cent for Unisabi, 2 per cent on average for Danone, 10 per cent for McCain. Findus decided to offer products at the low end of the market for 10F (which, given the production cost, still left room for a comfortable margin).

These price reductions show that the brand has to stay within the core of the market if it wants to continue. This was discovered by European car manufacturers after first the Japanese and now the Korean invasion: they forced all car OEM (original equipment manufacturers) suppliers to reduce their prices by 20 per cent. Portable computer manufacturers also know that they must both innovate and reduce their prices. Indeed, the price premium which pays for the superior added-value is a differential concept. It says nothing of the standard, the reference level of the brand with which it is to compare. But nowadays in many markets this standard is falling in absolute value. If hard discounters spread through the UK, France, Belgium and Italy as they have in Germany, they can impose in certain sectors their own levels of price and quality as the standard that the branded products have to reckon with when setting their price levels. If brands leave their price premiums unchanged, they will not be able to hold their ground. This is the problem faced by Heineken Breweries in France. There are no strong intermediary brands: Heineken is the only strong brand in the portfolio but it belongs to the special beers segment and its price therefore seems totally out of touch with the prices of unknown 6- or 12-packs of German beer which benefit from the quality seal 'Made in Germany' and are 10 to 15 francs cheaper per pack. The same pressure rests on the shoulders of Ricard, the third biggest alcoholic beverage in the world (after Bacardi and Smirnoff), which is sold for twice the price of other aniseed drinks!

The preceding argument is *a fortiori* valid if the price premium is higher than the perceived added-value of the brand. The brand then gets into a niche at a high-end segment of the market and watches its volume drop. The OC & C consulting firm gives an interesting example of certain unsustainable price gaps in the long-run if the price-leader becomes the reference in terms of price comparison (see Figure 5.6). According to OC & C, the latent savings unexploited by industrialists could represent up to 30 per cent of costs. It is true that part of the benefits linked to the product are sometimes not valued by customers or

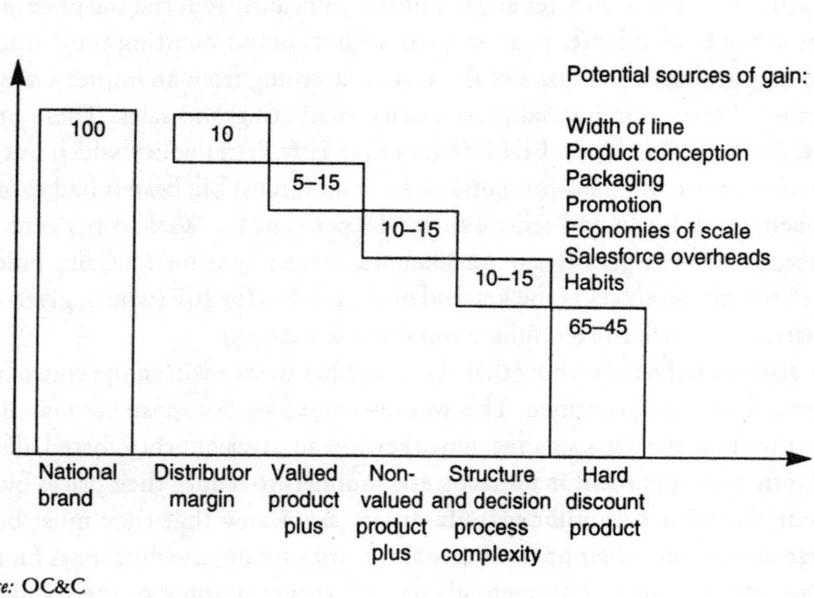

Source: OC&C

Figure 5.6 Sources of price differences

that the upgrade in production costs is not worth it in the customers' eyes. There is more to be gained by suppressing these costs and finding a new price-competitiveness again. Besides, trade-off analyses demonstrate that the logic of 'bigger and better' can be counter-productive if it entails an increase in price. Beyond a certain performance threshold, utility slumps. There are also acceptable price thresholds: the rule for home computers is to always give the client more as long as the retail price does not go beyond the $2000 barrier.

The analysis carried out by OC & C has, however, two limits. First, it neglects, as do most economic analyses, the perceived value of the reputation and image of the brand: a brand does not only bring a product benefit. Secondly, it is not obvious that price-leaders set the standard price which will be the reference for customers when they compare prices. It all depends on the level of involvement of the customer and of the perceived difference! For years, low-priced colas existed but attracted no consumers. Only recently have the Sainsbury's and Virgin colas been able to challenge Coca-Cola. Creating a large shelf space for price-leader detergents will not in itself create a significant sales volume: the quality reference is set by Skip and Ariel. Customers know they are not getting the same quality when, for want of buying power, they fall back onto secondary brands and *a fortiori* on unknown brands. At the other end, the Viva milk created by Candia, far from being perceived as a premium product, has become the milk that all milks should be like, the standard for milk, both modern and advanced. There are indeed other price-leader milks, but they are considered ordinary and lacking in character.

Any price decrease, if it does occur, should not therefore be conducted in comparison with the cheapest product of the category but with the products in the same segment aiming at the same need (see p. 74). The House of Campbell whisky should be careful not to get too far from its real competitors: William Lawson, Black & White, Grants. Even if, in terms of image, the market reference remains J&B, the customer actually hesitates only between products fighting in the same segment. The so-called 'trammel-hook analysis' (Degon, 1994) demonstrates empirically that the brands which are successful are most of the time those that have the lowest price within their own segment. To return to the Chesterfield case, the brand was withdrawn as early as 1988 from the declining segment of upmarket Virginia cigarettes (Marlboro, Stuyvesant, Rothmans) to be positioned in the segment just under it, that of 'popular Virginia cigarettes' (Lucky Strike, Gauloises Blondes). By pricing its pack at 10F, it became the cheapest alternative within this segment and quickly became the leader. Since then, the brand has had to increase its price due to budgetary constraints from the government, but has kept this price positioning.

Finally, if the brand itself is the dominant reference within its category, tests often reveal that its demand does not increase if its price goes down. This is, for example, the case with Orangina in France. There will be a greater chance of a significant increase in sales following a trial or sampling campaign if the company starts working again on having the product discovered by generations that do not know it yet.

As a conclusion, a decrease in price has never in itself solved the problem of making sure a brand lasts. It does not increase added-value but reduces costs. Moreover, a decrease in price on the part of the leader has important consequences in the long term: it will jeopardise the profitability of the whole sector for 20 years to come. The leader should instead aim either to get back to the standard of quality that the customer knows he is leaving behind if he chooses a cheaper product, or to enlarge the market. But to do this the company must invest: lowering prices too much will make financing this effort impossible.

DOMINATE TO INVEST

In 1980 in France, the cider market was falling by the wayside. A multitude of cider breweries, each with their own brands, were fighting for access to the supermarkets by slashing prices. Cooperatives for the most part, they therefore had less profitability constraints and were driven only by selling inventory, hence the staggering drop in retail prices which did not improve the profitability of the industry. Cider breweries went bankrupt one after the other. Any added-value policy conducted on its own by a brewery was bound to fail as the distributors penalised the accrued price discrepancy. As long as a single operator was not of sufficient size in the market to bring it under control, the market would be collectively and irremediably pulled into a downward spiral. This is what the Pernod-Ricard group acted to avoid. By buying up many cider breweries, it was able to reach the size threshold which enabled it to take back control over its prices and not yield to the pressures of concentrated mass-distribution. With the margin which it was once again able to reassert, it was able to finance the investments needed to make the category more exclusive, to create added-value, to innovate by launching new brands (eg La Cidraie blond cider, and Flagger, a fashionable cider).

The case of the cheese-manufacturer Besnier deserves to be addressed separately. With its cheese brand Président, Besnier follows the logic of market domination in both cost and market share, which are, of course, closely intertwined. The Président camembert is the reference for pasteurised camemberts, of which it represented 20 per cent of the market at the end of 1996. Of the market for all camemberts, Président takes up 16.5 per cent and DOBs have 19.9 per cent. Président is therefore a must on a supermarket shelf. Moreover, as a result of radical rationalisation of production, Président is manufactured in one single plant, and came to dominate very quickly, in terms of production costs, the market for pasteurised cheeses. This enabled it also to become the prime supplier for DOB camemberts in France, as the company producing it just needs to change the packaging. Thanks to an umbrella-brand policy (see Chapter 7), the Président brand now covers eight different cheeses, upscale butter not included, and is a symbolic product in the highest sense of the word. The Président brand ranges from Brie to Coulomniers including Emmenthal, Carré de l'Est, Saint Paulain and so on. The advantage in terms of economies of scale is enormous. Besides this, Besnier also owns four other strong brands on the camembert market: Bridel (5.5 per cent of the market), Le Chatelin (1.8 per cent), Lanquetôt (3.9 per cent) and Le Petit (4.5 per cent). On the whole, Besnier controls 32.2 per cent of the market through its brands and close to 45 per cent if the volume sold through DOBs is included. As it keeps a tight grip on the market price, Besnier can keep reinvesting to strengthen its brands. The sign of a strong brand, Président was one of the very few milk-product brands that did not lower its prices during the recession (along with Candia and La Vache-Qui-Rit). Behind every strong brand there is a strong company.

The second possible strategy is that of Ferrero, the unchallenged leader of niche markets. The Kinder egg has no competitor: it is, however, one of the most frequently sold chocolate candies in Europe. Mon Chéri (another Ferrero brand) also has no competitor. Nutella, too, dominates its segment, just like Roche d'Or. Ferrero, which started off as a small-sized company just like Besnier, is managed by engineers who follow through the industrial logic to the end, constantly tracking down economies of scale. For instance, there is Nutella in Ferrero Roche d'Or, while Kinder Bueno is Nutella without the chocolate. The company is constantly wondering if a new product positioned differently can be manufactured on an assembly line used for another product. Moreover, and most importantly, all these products are in niches: this deters competition, suppresses price comparison and yields high margins for the distributor. The economies of scale are reinvested in advertising the effect of which on demand speeds up turnover and enables the Ferrero Group to face negotiation with concentrated mass distributors more confidently.

CONTROL THE DISTRIBUTION SYSTEM

Where marketing is concerned, he who is in contact with the end-user often has a decisive edge. This is a major handicap for manufacturers who are not in control of their distribution network. It may be an illusion to consider that you can bypass supermarkets to sell significant food brands, but this is not the case for many other outlets. Selective distribution is such an example. The evolution of European Union law on selective distribution networks has substituted qualitative criteria for the old quantitative criteria linked to minimum volume quotas.

In the case of Levi's, the unchallenged leader in the blue jeans market, the brand is quite selective in its distribution. While not permitting the sale of its products to supermarkets, Levi's expects its retailers to respect five criteria:

- the first one has to do with the offer range: the latter must comprise quality clothing and only brands that are recognised by the customer where jeans are concerned (therefore no price-leader or anonymous jeans);
- the environment must be as high-quality as the offer;
- product ranges that could alter the image of Levi's must not be found close by;
- the service must be in tune with the brand and the staff must be adequate and competent in the field of clothing;
- last of all, the shop must be part of a fixed construction (not a market stall) with adequate space reserved for jeans and capable of attracting youths aged 15 to 25.

Through this mastery of the channel, Levi's is, in fact, controlling its image and preserving its brand capital. A brand cannot be narrowed down to its advertising and to its products, it involves the customer in the purchasing act and even thereafter. This is also the strength of Benetton, Coca-Cola and Häagen Dazs. Coca-Cola does indeed have to contend with competitors in supermarkets and even with copies from distributors. But the reputation of a soft drink is enhanced by its distribution in cafés, hotels, restaurants and night-clubs. Moreover, the Coca-Cola company offers a wide range of non-colas that make it an exclusive distributor at the sales outlet. Hence, where there is Coca-Cola there usually is no Pepsi-Cola or Orangina.

CREATE ENTRY BARRIERS

This last example draws attention to the importance of entry barriers in sound brand management. By focusing exclusively on the customer's psychology, brand analysis has overlooked the crucial role of the management of the offer itself, which can make it impossible for competitors to enter on the market. This is one of the key questions in the analysis of the financial value of a brand, of the present value of its future profits. The impenetrability of the market is the best warranty for the latter, and the example of Black & Decker is quite revealing.

Why are there hardly any DOBs in the drilling machine market? Because Black & Decker makes it economically impossible for them to enter the market. DOBs sprout up when one or more of the following conditions are fulfilled:

- there is a high volume in the market;
- the offer hardly changes;
- brands are expensive;
- customers perceive little risk;
- customers make their choice essentially according to the visible characteristics of the product;
- technology is accessible at low cost.

Much to the contrary, the market for drills is small, and moreover is cut up into many segments. Black & Decker drives the market and makes it develop at a fast technological pace. In addition, Black & Decker has globalised its production: each plant produces one single product for the worldwide market. The production cost level thus becomes unbeatable, and as Black & Decker is not over keen to increase its retail price, it does not leave much room for copycats to manoeuvre. Lastly, the customer feels safe when buying such a well-known and ubiquitous brand.

What are the main sources of entry barriers?

- The cost of the factors of production is the most important which leads to a long-lasting competitive advantage. This is the strategy of Président, of Black & Decker and also of Decathlon, a sports goods mass retailer. With a view to replicating in Europe its domination of the French market, Decathlon may become for some sports the European number one manufacturer far ahead of any others because of the economies of scale accruing from its products developed at a European level. Moreover, since Decathlon is pursuing a corporate brand strategy capitalising on the fame of its own name, and heavily invests in advertising, the brand could in the long term become a sports authority just as other famous brands on the market.
- Mastering technology and quality is a key success factor for Procter and Gamble, Gillette, L'Oréal and 3M. Turning down any offer to yield an iota of

their know-how to DOBs, these companies keep for themselves their main added-value leverage. This is what enables them to constantly innovate and to remain the reference of the market in terms of quality. Kellogg's even goes to the extent of indicating on its boxes that it does not supply DOBs.

- Domination through image and communication is Coca-Cola's mainstay, although it does not hinder a K-Mart or a Sainsbury brand cola from borrowing as much as possible the distinctive signs of Coke and selling at a lower price. In hard times, sensitivity to price is exacerbated. But as a worldwide brand, Coca-Cola had access to the sponsoring of the Olympic Games in Atlanta and was able to pass on the benefits to bottlers worldwide. This is also the weapon of Nike, Reebok and Adidas. Domination as a result of their fame and image is not solely a result of the titanic size of these companies' budgets. Focusing all their communications on the name itself and applying a brand extension logic beyond the initial segment, Dim and Président were able to dominate in brand awareness. In its field, Decathlon does the same thing: it gives its own products the store name.
- Quickly using up all the aspects of a promising concept through range extension is a method which hinders the entry of competitors. In the United States, and soon in Europe, the Snapple brand is surfing on the wave of so-called 'New Age' drinks and offers a wide variety of tea-based soft drinks. Dim, as we have seen, was quick to offer under one brand name a wide range of products covering different needs and satisfying distributors' and customers' expectations. In the agricultural market, it is possible to count the different kinds of Decis (the leader in insecticides) according to the type of plant, thus reinforcing the worldwide leader status of this brand.
- Putting a name on a product in itself yields a uniqueness of offer and an added-value that competitors will lack. All the giants of the chemical industry produce elastane, a fibre which makes stockings and foundation garments soft and shiny. On the other hand, only Du Pont de Nemours has Lycra, a fibre whose name in itself is used as a sales ploy by Du Pont and by all lingerie brands. Actually, Lycra is the trade mark used by Du Pont to sell elastane. It is not the name in itself which adds value to the fibre: it is ten years of worldwide communication about the glamour linked to the Lycra name which gave the brand its exclusive attractiveness.
- Controlling the relationship with opinion leaders is one of the key success factors for a brand looking to the future. Canson, a school-supplies brand which is part of the Arjomari-Wiggins group, provides an illustration. What is more natural than a sheet of tracing paper or drawing paper for a schoolchild? However, despite the share of supermarket shelf space given to DOBs' drawing and tracing paper, only that of Canson sells. For more than 20 years

the brand has developed a closely monitored relationship with the teaching profession, organising for instance drawing competitions between classes on a national level. The long-lasting presence of Canson on a child's shopping list for school supplies is due to the excellence of what is now called relationship marketing. The main asset of Canson is its loyal teachers within the national education system.

- Controlling distribution is also a major handicap for new entrants. McDonald's will soon have 1000 restaurants in France, and Quick, the second largest burger chain in Europe, will have 500. This sheer number closes the hamburger market off to competition. Mass-distribution brands also freely use this barrier to entry: by imposing their own brand on the shelf, they thus exclude manufacturer's brands. The ice-cream maker Häagen Dazs does indeed control the market of upmarket ice creams through the provision of a high-quality ice cream and through a well-managed word-of-mouth campaign from opinion leaders, but most of all through its own exclusive refrigerator present in all supermarkets and hypermarkets. In Germany, the brand Nur Die is the leader in hosiery: this is due to the uniqueness of its distribution. Nur Die sets up its own shelves in supermarkets and manages on its own the delivery, the variety and the inventory of its products, paying the store in a percentage of sales. The display unit, which is a few metres long, belongs to the brand. If a competitor wanted to enter the market, beyond the advertising expenses required to make itself known, it would have to invest several million marks to create thousands of display units from scratch. The quality of the relationship with distributors is also an efficient barrier. The sales force of Ricard through its size (500 people) and its quality nurtures a matchless relationship with cafés, hotels and restaurants. And since the image of an alcoholic beverage comes from its consumption in these places, the strong image of Ricard lies in the control it has over distribution. Even without advertising, Ricard can thus justify a strong price premium in supermarkets.
- The last barrier to entry is based on legality. The brand must defend its exclusive image against counterfeit products, models or signs. It should not hesitate to defend the exclusive character of its distinctive signs against imitations and distributors' copycat brands. The latter, under the pretence that these are signs of the category, actually try to make their brands benefit from the value of signs developed by the leading brand. The imitations of Coca-Cola try to get as close as possible to the red that Coca-Cola has with time associated with its quality. Beyond the deliberate sought-after confusion, which leads the customer, if he is not careful, to mistake the copy for the original, the similarity between the signs induces a perception of equivalence

(Kapferer, 1995). Just as Dior, Chanel and Cartier invest heavily in law suits against counterfeiter networks, the brands must sue imitators or, at least, state to them that they will tolerate no imitations or copying. From this point of view, the brands which from the start chose non-descriptive signs withstand the test of time and imitation better. The Orangina label is blue: it is not a generic colour and protects this orange-flavoured soft drink brand well.

REINFORCE BRAND LOYALTY

The financial value of a brand is a function of the amount of its future expected return and of the degree of risk on these returns. A brand can only be strong if it has a strong supply of loyal customers. This established fact led to a revolution in the practice of marketing, underway since the beginning of the 1980s: the major concern is loyalty and its related factor, client satisfaction. Leaving behind an approach which implicitly concentrated on conquering clients away from the competition, firms now do all they can to keep their own clients. This is to be expected at a time when, as a result of the abundance of offers, buyers tend to jump from one brand to the next, from one manufacturer to the next. Rather than zero defaults, the aim is zero defections.

A lifetime client at British Airways brings on average £48,000 to the company in revenues. Thus under no circumstance should one customer be lost. It is the same for Carrefour where a loyal client brings £3550 in annual sales. Besides, loyal clients are more profitable. According to a study from the Bain company, a household spends 2162 francs per month in the supermarket to which it goes most often, 553 in the second most frequent and 145 for the one where it only goes occasionally. And not only do loyal clients spend more, but their expenditure grows with time, they become less sensitive to price and they are the source of positive word-of-mouth reports concerning their favoured supermarket or brand. Moreover, they are five times less costly to contact than non-clients. That is why, also according to Bain, by lowering the defection rate of clients by 5 per cent, benefits go up 25 to 85 per cent. The example of Canal Plus is significant: this pay-TV channel benefits from an unprecedented loyalty rate: 97 per cent of its 6 million clients are loyal to it. Bearing in mind that a yearly subscription costs 2028 francs, if the loyalty drops by as little as 1 per cent, it would mean 75 million francs less in annual revenues!

All strong brands are currently establishing loyalty programmes. Nevertheless, a cautionary remark is necessary: no programme of this kind will make up for a service that is not adapted or sufficient. The actions required to keep loyal customers have two aims: the first is defensive, to give the customer no reason for leaving the brand or the company; the other is offensive, to create a personalised relationship with the client, the basis of a more intimate and therefore more involving bond, what Americans call 'Customer bonding' (Cross and Smith, 1994).

The essential part of the defensive side is the identification of the causes of disloyalty and dissatisfied clients. Thus, dissatisfaction linked to the food provided induces, because of disloyalty, a loss in revenue amounting to £5 million pounds at British Airways. The dissatisfaction linked to bad seating costs close to £20 million! Paradoxically enough, the company seeks to get as many voiced dissatisfactions as possible. Indeed, the worst thing is a silent dissatisfied client who, saying nothing to the company representatives, spreads negative rumours among his relatives, colleagues and friends. And there are statistics to prove that a dissatisfied client who is well treated becomes a real proselyte, and even more loyal into the bargain. When asked if they will fly with British Airways again, the rate is 64 per cent 'yes' among those that have never contacted the complaints office. It is, however, 84 per cent among those who have. The treatment of complaints with diligence, care and respect becomes a key lever in customer loyalty.

Seeking client satisfaction implies adding a touch of management spirit where spirit of conquest reigns exclusively. This is why L'Oréal Coiffure is nowadays a company with a conquering as well as an innovative and entrepreneurial spirit. It launches new products one after the other. Hairdressers like the L'Oréal products and L'Oréal knows their product needs well. Unfortunately, this led the firm to somewhat overlook the management spirit: some deliveries were wrong, stockouts occurred, discounts were unevenly granted, etc. The firm responded well to sophisticated needs but somewhat forgot some of the more down-to-earth needs. The hairdresser who put in an order on Tuesday for a tube of light golden brown colouring for a client coming on Friday could not be sure it would be there on time. He could not always count on the company. That is why even when its product launchings were successful, and even if customers were attracted, the sales of L'Oréal Coiffure stagnated for a while. When focusing on client satisfaction, the product alone is not sufficient if the basic service is deficient.

When going over to the offensive, a brand must become a landmark of personal attention. More emphatically, Rapp and Collins (1994) talk of becoming a 'loving company', interested not in the client but in the person. This marks the end of anonymous marketing: attention has to be customised if it is to be efficient. But it has to be acknowledged that even if the terminology of market studies distinguishes between big, medium and small customers, up until recently few companies had developed programmes designed specifically for big customers, who as a rule are also the most loyal. But the loyal client wants to be recognised. He therefore has to be identified, a direct bond has to be established with him and he should be the focus of special attention. This is why what is commonly called relationship marketing (McKenna, 1991; Marconi, 1994) uses databases, customers' clubs and collective events which unite the best customers of the brand. Moreover, realising that a brand which does not have direct contact with customers becomes further and further out of reach – literally as well as figuratively – many brands have stepped out of mere television advertising and off the shelves to establish a direct relationship with customers. Nestlé offers to its customers a dietician, reachable by phone. Six days a week, Nintendo helps out 10,000 children who are stuck in a video game. As long ago as 1992, IBM France created an assistance hotline working around the clock seven days a week all-year-round. Treating clients as friends instead of accounts is the basis to a long-lasting relationship.

FROM BRAND EQUITY TO CUSTOMER EQUITY

In their efforts to increase brand loyalty, brand companies have realised that they have to care about their customer equity or market share. In other words, these companies should focus not only on augmenting brand preference as a mental attitude, but also on increasing brand usage, especially among the best customer prospects: the heavy buyers. Recent findings, for example, recognise that mass-market brand profits come not from the mass-market, but from the top third of category buyers. Furthermore, a brand's greatest potential for additional profit rests on its ability to increase share in this high-profit, heavy-buyer category (G Hallberg, 1995).

Unfortunately, advertising misses the mark with these prime prospects. Instead, it reaches mostly non-buyers or small-quantity buyers. On the other hand, promotions *do* touch the high-profit segment. That is, frequent buyers are more likely to encounter price promotions, coupons, rebates, etc. However, promotions over-sensitise consumers to price and tend to decrease brand loyalty in the high-potential, high-profit segment.

As a consequence, most mega-brands are now experimenting with database marketing on a grand scale. The database marketing concept is twofold:

- All marketing actions should target the prime segment more effectively. The goal is to increase this segment's rate of brand use.

- Effective targeting requires companies to identify each of these customers or households, almost nominally. As a consequence, a by-product of all promotional activities should be a database, ultimately comprising 100 per cent of the high-profit customers.

At this time Procter & Gamble's database in the USA holds more than 48 million names. Danone's database in France holds 2 million names. Nestlé is building its own in each major country, as is Unilever. And this ignores all the broker-created databases for rental to smaller companies.

The function of these selective databases is to deliver customised offers to specific targets, to bring the store shelf to the home (thus decreasing impulse buying and distributors' power), and to promote a 'private image' among loyal and heavy-user customers. Generally, these customers are more involved in the brand, so they deserve recognition and special treatment. They also merit specific information to nourish brand image and equity. These activities constitute the nurturing of a 'private image', as opposed to a broader, general public image.

The recent concern about managing customer equity is illustrated in Figure 5.7. Many consumers hold very favourable attitudes *vis-à-vis* particular brands. Nevertheless, their loyalty is insufficient to inhibit switching within a repertoire of brands. These customers are potential loyals only if a tailor-made pro-

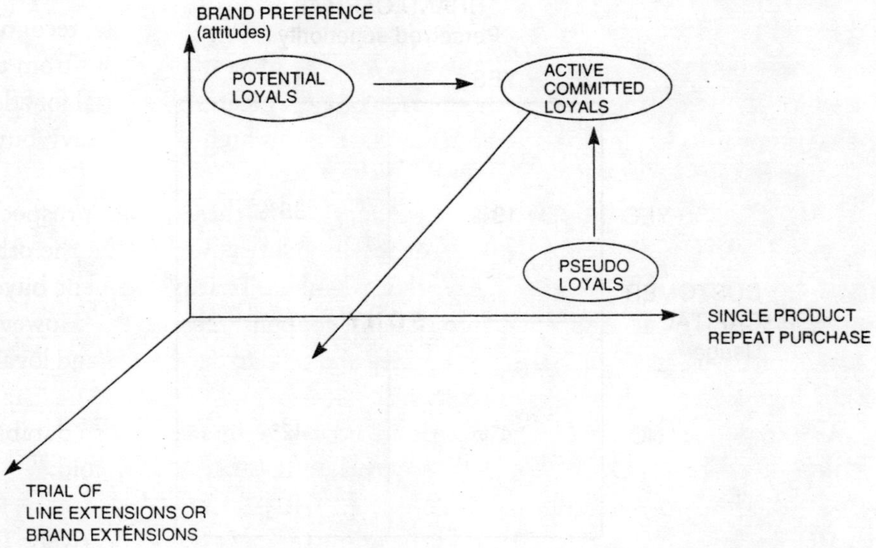

Figure 5.7 The three facets of brand loyalty

gramme is devised to increase the rate of purchase of a particular brand. On the other hand, some repeat-buyers are actually pseudo-loyals: they do not hold strong attitudes regarding the brand. Perhaps, for instance, they buy the brand because of its price or availability. To increase their brand preference, these buyers require a reinforcement of their choice and an increased perception of the brand's superiority. Finally, active and committed loyals should be induced to try more and more new products, whether line or brand extensions. Figure 5.8 illustrates Sony's situation, where committed loyals comprise 19 per cent of Sony's entire customer franchise. The potential loyals represent 4 per cent, and the pseudo loyals 35 per cent. Each group deserves a specific marketing proposition.

There is a final factor that contributes to the longevity of a brand: staying true to itself. Since a brand is a benchmark, it must accept the constraints that go with it. Since it has to adapt at the same time to the evolution of the market and of the competition, attracting new clients by renewed offers, the key issue becomes how to strike a balance between identity and change. This subject is addressed in the following chapter.

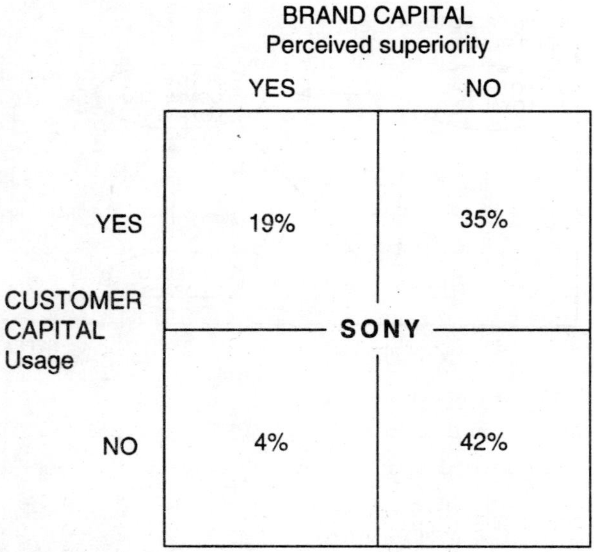

Source: Sofres, Megabrand System.

Figure 5.8 Brand capital and customer capital: matching preferences and purchase behaviour

6

Adapting to the market: identity versus change

It is known that a brand only grows over a long period by remaining consistent. The concept of identity implies that some facets of the brand remain identical through time: continuity is essential to the brand's formation and longevity.

Nevertheless, a brand which does not change with the times fossilises and loses its relevance. Time is merely the indicator of changes in lifestyles, consumer expectations, technology and competitive position. The question of management of the time factor therefore becomes: how do we adapt to these new conditions while keeping our identity? What should we change and what should we leave untouched? Since a brand only exists by means of its products (or services) and its communication strategy, managing the time factor will necessarily involve these two vectors of evolution and continuity. On the communication side, we have the rare example of Marlboro, who initiated the image of the lone cowboy in 1964. Few brands have, in fact, been steeped in such a myth rooted in a specific time and space. Jack Daniel's is another example. Coca-Cola, Volkswagen, Nestlé, Philips and Adidas have updated their advertising and products to adapt to social changes. Brands must therefore learn to change their style and products in order to keep up with the times. It is by staying up to date that a brand survives the test of time.

Technological progress and research ensure a permanent flow of innovations which the brand should incorporate to safeguard against obsolescence or downgrading. Whenever the product does not change, the brand becomes mortal: Volkswagen almost disappeared with the end of the Beetle. Linking a brand's destiny to one single product is a major risk for any company whose product is at the end of its life cycle. Without an ongoing renewal of its products and services, and without non-stop attention to its task, the brand falls by the wayside.

Innovation and new products give the brand the opportunity to demonstrate its mission and direction, and to construct a coherent and specific image. This concerns just as much IBM or Compaq in the crowded computer market, as it does Coca-Cola. Certainly, the basic Coca-Cola formula has remained unchanged throughout the world, but its format and ingredients have evolved in response to changes in lifestyle – e.g. family packs for the weekly shopping in supermarkets, aluminium cans for more convenience when taking home and taking out, derivatives without caffeine or sugar, etc. Recognition of the purchaser's basic needs should be a brand's primary occupation, and requires constant vigilance.

Values, customs and behaviour patterns are constantly changing with time. What seemed revolutionary in 1977 is insignificant in 1997. A brand which anchors its survival on one particular feature is threatened with extinction. Findus is the brand which gave credence to frozen foods by legitimizing a new social behaviour. At the time, the advent of frozen foods helped shatter the traditional concept of the role of women – that their place was in the kitchen. The Findus reputation and its public voice on TV gave authority to the changes which women had long been seeking. Times certainly have changed – the housewife has been replaced by the working wife. The basis of Findus's original argument is now as outdated as Women's Lib. If Findus had not developed, had not broken from its original point of view, the brand would have become dated.

Time also brings about a natural drift away from original symbols. After the Second World War and its deprivations, the cow came to signify the abundance of nature. This suited La Vache-Qui-Rit (the Laughing Cow), the oldest of modern cheeses. Today, the cow is no longer such an omnipresent symbol of nature – even milk cartons do not show cows anymore. It has even become 'mad'. The loveable old cow has gone back to being a stupid animal. This causes a problem for the brand, since it now carries a rather infantile connotation in that it symbolises a cheese which a child stops eating just to show that he is no longer a child. Generally speaking, such effigies can bog down the brand, wrapping it in a symbolism which is prone to change as society evolves. This is why Exxon ceased for a while to communicate through its tiger, deemed too agressive, although it has since been revived. Bibendum does not run this risk – it is an original symbol with no prior connotations. Only Michelin gives it meaning, and vice versa. The bank, Crédit Mutuel, carries in its name a concept which has lost its glamour and which thrived in a particular historic period. Mutuality, accruing from a solidarity movement at a time when savage capitalism ruled, must today prove its value: indeed, the public is still willing to share the losses – hence the success of mutual insurance companies – but is less willing to share the profits. A new significance for the word mutual in the world of banking has still to be found if the brand wants to withstand the test of time: close attention on the part of the benevolent banker seems to fit just that definition. Such a bank should be a model in relationship marketing.

Brands created around a living personality also need to face up to changes in meaning. The personality has his or her own life and acquires a dimension and symbolism which may not always coincide with the brand's strategic interests. Pepsi-Cola discovered that with Michael Jackson. Lancôme abandoned Isabella Rossellini, judging her 'too old', and switched to Juliette Binoche.

Over a period of time, a brand's clientele moves on and becomes older. Those who followed in the footsteps of G.Blitz and Gilbert Trigano and took holidays in the first Club Med village in the Balearic Islands or in Corsica are now well over 60. The brand's success lies in its ability to respond to the needs of those who are today between 20 and 30. In the failure to renew their customer base, Johnny Walker has become the whisky of the parents, not of the new generation. The same goes for Martini, Ballantines and Courvoisier.

Finally, success encourages competitors to offer copies of superior products. The promise of risk-free sales (since the national brand has already done all the market creation work) is also tempting for DOBs and counterfeiters. Once Findus had legitimised the social use of frozen foods through ten years of advertising its products, it was easy for some mass retailers to replace the brand on its shelves with their own products. Nothing is more tempting than to copy or imitate the packaging and the messages of the successful brand. Sainsbury's Classic Cola is a copy of Coke, as is Virgin's. This is the usual way many DOBs operate. Because of the shortcomings in the law on this practice and the apathy of the authorities, the brand is forced to make its difference more marked by innovating and maintaining its leadership in terms of product performance, but also by including new benefits on its packaging. The brand has no other choice but to surpass even itself: it is a never-ending race. To avoid being copied, it must become an ever-moving target.

THE POWER OF CONSISTENCY

Brand advertising messages and slogans are also bound to evolve. In this sense, Evian was, initially, the water of babies, then of the Alps, then the water of balance and now the water of balanced strength. These changes in positioning occurred over a long time period: they demonstrate the evolution of the consumer's attitude towards water, the maturation of the market and the evolution of competitive position. The functions and representations of water are not fixed: they depend on external factors linked to urbanisation, industrialisation, rediscovering nature, discovering pollution, new representations of the body, health and food hygiene. Positioning is the act of relating one brand facet to a set of consumer expectations, needs and desires. As these needs change through time, the brand is obliged to follow suit.

But within a brand's lifetime these changes in positioning should not happen too often, about every four or five years. However, the brand's means of expression can move faster to integrate with the evolution of fashion: new speech modes, new signs of modernity and new looks. It is essential that the brand is perceived as up-to-date although such necessary adjustments and changes make the brand run the risk of a loss of identity.

To retain their identity while changing, brands stick to their communication codes, that is their fixed visual and audio symbols. This is undeniably a factor that contributes to a brand and what it represents being recognised. Even when not named, Dim commercials can be picked out: their music and their style are unique. This also goes for Cacharel, which is often associated with the photographer Sarah Moon, as Nina Ricci was with David Hamilton. But the style itself is subject to obsolescence. The photographer David Hamilton's 'fuzzy' photographic style had its time of glory, but now it looks outdated. Continuing with it could prove fatal to the brand.

Unfortunately, it has to be acknowledged that brands have a hard time parting with their communication codes, even when they feel it is necessary. This is to be expected: they are afraid of losing their identity. But this reluctance is largely due to the fact that brand management concepts are essentially static. Time is not taken into account when it is a key parameter in markets. In that sense, the concept of 'communication territory' is a vision that clings to the ground: it has to do with all the visible signals that the brand uses to communicate its definition and what it represents. However, an identity that defines itself only through signs is subject to an alteration of their meaning. The brand is indeed recognised, but no longer in control of its meaning.

The Volkswagen case illustrates the dialectics of change and continuity. In 1970, the brand only sold one product, the famous 'Beetle'. The brand owed its birth to this car, which was created before the war. Its designers were briefed that they were to create the 'car of the people' (Volks-Wagen literally signifying just that): the founding decision of the brand was part of a wave of solidarity (Ein Reich, ein Volk, ein Wagen). How was the brand to adapt to sociological change, to improved automobile technology and to the growing expectations of car drivers, if it remained a single-product brand and, moreover, a product which remained the same? By adapting its identity to reflect the new context and by insisting on offering a range of different advantages. This was how the concept of rational buying was developed, through economic usage, longevity, strength and security features. ('The Beetle has two doors, one per person, so the children are safe in the back'.) These sales propositions were aimed at the market of the first car buyer and the women's market for the second car in the household. The only common element in these different campaigns: they are slightly tongue-in-cheek, they take a step back from the object in contrast to the seriousness of most advertisements for cars.

The uniqueness of the brand comes from the core value 'solidarity' without explicitly spelling out this concept in its advertising (Cabat, 1989). The identity of the brand did not suffer from the altering of advertising themes from economy, longevity or security to end up as the car of a slightly snob owner of a vehicle that is not affected by time.

The Volkswagen example enables us to introduce the model of time management for a brand (Figure 6.1).

THE THREE LAYERS OF A BRAND: KERNEL, CODES AND PROMISES

The evolution of a brand needs a common stream of thought. Considering the brand as a vision about its product category, it is important to know in which direction it is looking. The brand being a genetic memory to help us manage the future, we must know what drives it, what is its prime reason for existing.

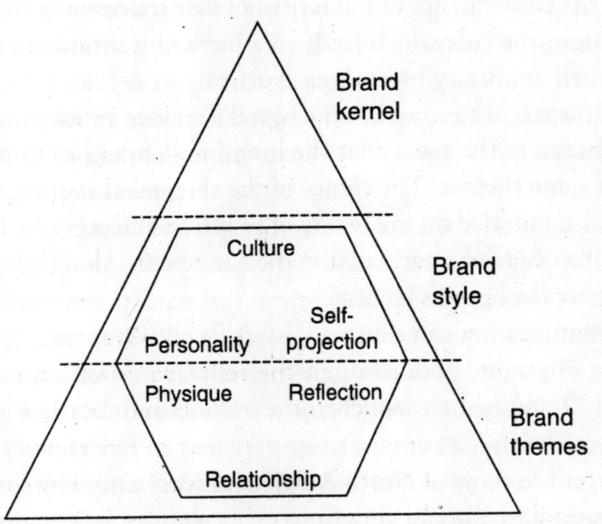

Figure 6.1 Identity and pyramid models

All these concepts (source of inspiration, statement, codes and communication themes) work together in a three-tier pyramid:

- At the top of the pyramid is the kernel of the brand, the source of its identity. Invisible, it must nevertheless be known because it imparts coherence and consistency;
- The base of the pyramid are the themes: it is the tier of communication concepts and the product's positioning, of the promises linked to the latter;
- The middle level relates to the stylistic code, how the brand talks and which images it uses. It is through his style that an author (the brand) writes the theme and describes him or herself as a brand. It is the style that leaves a mark.

Of course, there is a close relationship between the facets of the identity of a brand and the three tiers of its pyramid. An examination of advertising themes reveals that they refer to the physical nature of products or to customer attitudes or finally to the relationship between the two (particularly in service brands). They are the outward facets of identity, those that are visible and that lead to something tangible. The style, as with one's handwriting, reveals the brand's interior facets, its personality, its culture, the self concept it offers. Finally, the genetic code, the roots of a brand, inspires its whole structure and nurtures its culture. It is the driving mechanism. There is, therefore, a strong relationship between stylistic codes and identity. In Volkswagen's case, a sense of humour is the consequence of solidarity because it demonstrates the rejection of car idolisation, the cult which leads to a hierarchical ranking of drivers and therefore to their animosity towards each other.

This idea of levels or tiers within the brand provides a tool which allows freedom for the brand in the sense that the brand no longer has to define itself by repeating the same themes. The choice of the theme has to integrate the needs of the times. It is founded on the reality of products and services. It corresponds to a concern or a desire of a particular market segment. Alongside these criteria, one must respect the brand's identity.

Brand communication can thus vary in its facets. Over time it seems first to start with the physique, goes through the reflected image and ends with the cultural facet. Orangina first launched the orange-pulp bottle which had to be shaken, then modernised to appear more dynamic, before identifying with a set of values different to those of North America as represented by Coca-Cola. This evolution is normal: the brand goes from explicit to implicit communication. It starts as the name of a new product, an innovation and later acquires other meanings and autonomy. In its advertising campaigns, Benetton first emphasized the colour of its sweaters, then included young adults from all over the world. It is now a cultural brand and addresses a range of moral issues. Nike moved from product communications to behaviorial values (just do it!).

The pyramid model leads to a differentiated management of change. The brand's themes must evolve if they no longer motivate: it is obvious that Evian should move from balance to the strength of balance. All themes tend to wear off and competitors do not stand still. The stylistic code, the expression of the personality and culture of the brand, has to be more stable: it enables the brand to gently pass without disruption from one theme to another. Finally, the genetic code is not tangible. Changing it means building another brand, a homonym of the first, but different. This is how, even if the positioning of Evian has changed with time, from being the water of babies, to that of the Alps and that of the strength of balance, there is a strong sense that the basic identity has been preserved. Evian never was a water against something, but a water for something, natural and loving, a source of life. It is not for nothing that its label has always been pink: this colour is linked to the brand's kernel, its essential identity.

Finally, the idea of different tiers within the brand gives particular flexibility to those brands which embrace many products. In managing these products one must respect their individual position in their sub-markets where they carry different promises for each product, provided they appear to emanate from a common source of inspiration. In this respect, such brands work as a superstructure. This is how the communication methods of banks and insurance companies work like so-called source-brands.

Taking into account the importance of this genetic code, how do we recognise it? All brands do not always have this identity basis. Some of them have only communication codes, or a style. When one says that Cacharel is romantic, one talks about a common style and source of coherence between Anaïs-Anaïs, Loulou, Eden, the perfume Cacharel pour l'Homme and the shirt stores. Its products carry within them a very precise and hidden driving principle. The strong brands are in fact Anaïs-Anaïs and Loulou. Cacharel in itself still lacks autonomous substance.

Consumers, clients and even managers are rarely aware of the brand's pivotal guiding force. They readily talk of its visible facets and of its codes, but without penetrating the brand's programme. Nor is the brand's creator aware of it, but carries it subconsciously. He transmits it through his actions and his choices. Thus when Mr Robert Ricci died in the summer of 1988, his successor commissioned an analysis of the identity of the Nina Ricci mother house alongside its worldwide best-selling perfume L'Air du Temps. The death of a creator signals the birth of a brand: respect for it demands understanding. An analysis of identity lies more in the history of the brand than in opinion surveys. The most typical products of the brand are closely examined throughout time: from what unconscious programme do they seem to emanate? Why does Nina Ricci haute-couture sparkle with its dazzling evening dresses? Why did Mr Robert Ricci find in the photographer David Hamilton's 'fuzzy' style a sort of revelation, to the point of signing a long-term and exclusive contract with him? What is the link between the dresses, L'Air du Temps and Hamilton? Once the highest point of the Ricci pyramid is known, the problem of the necessary replacement of David Hamilton's style becomes less acute. We know what he was expressing. Other means of expression will achieve this without using fake Hamiltons. Long-established brands seeking such an overhaul should undergo an inner search before projecting themselves into the future.

A classic error is often made when managing brands through time: thinking you are just touching up the surface of the brand when actually you are interfering with its essence. The Fidji case is revealing. This perfume, launched in 1966, became one of the top five perfumes around the world along with Anaïs-Anaïs by Cacharel and L'Air du Temps by Nina Ricci. After years of communicating the theme 'A woman is an island, Fidji is her perfume', L'Oréal thought they should modernise the message, bring it up to date and relate it to the women of the times, active and liberated. The new creative brief was supposed to transform the brand's association 'from escapism to the instinctiveness of nature'. Throughout the world there appeared posters of a woman with a snake, supported by the new slogan: 'the perfume of rediscovered paradise'. Sales dropped from 7,280,000 units in 1980 to 6,730,000 in 1981, 6,052,000 in 1982 and 5,216,000 in 1984. Luckily the drop in volume was compensated for by an increase in price. In allowing the image of the snake to supersede that of nature, they thought they had preserved the exotic element of the brand, which had been paramount since the perfume's conception.

At the same time, in 1965, the Club Méditerranée was becoming fashionable, as was the idea of escape to tropical happiness. This is what led to the choice of the Fidji name. In so doing, they had selected exoticism as the brand's pivotal identity. Yet it was only a style, a mode of expression. The kernel of the brand's identity, on which its success was founded, had probably escaped even the notice of the creators themselves. By introducing a snake and an orchid, their successors were unwittingly creating another brand. Having failed to appreciate Fidji's motivating force, they had shattered its very substance. The mythical symbolism of the desert island is universal and well-appreciated – hence the perfume's original worldwide success. Unfortunately, they focused on Fidji island itself and on the exotic factor – which proved to be of secondary importance. As for the serpent and the orchid – obvious symbols of seduction – they had no place on this desert island.

RESPECTING THE BRAND CONTRACT

Each brand should be seen as a contract. It binds, promises and engages each side: the company and its clients. The brand expects loyalty from consumers but it must in turn be loyal to them. With time, it is normal that the brand should seek to widen its client base by offering other products and services. In doing so, it communicates more and more on its margins and less and less on its core, on the basic contract.

The source of the current problems of Club Med, which feels it has lost its identity, may also find their source in the forsaking of the founding principles of the brand. However, it was not without reason that the products were differentiated to fit a particular market segmentation who, as they were growing older, expected more comfort in the rooms and sometimes wanted to withdraw from the group and not sit down at mealtimes at the famous eight-people tables. What aged in Club Med's offer is the value system portrayed in its advertising, and which a part of the population no longer identifies with, in particular its opinion leaders. The concept of 'happiness' is a cliché and no longer corresponds to the intense need for meaning expressed by our society. What made the inspired strength of Club Méditerranée was forgotten when the brand was restructured to make it international and renamed Club Med. Indeed, the Mediterranean Sea is not, as one would think, just a reference to the original location of the vacation villages or to some water sports. It is, on a symbolic level, a source of life. The intense need for Club Méditerranée lies in its brand kernel: to replenish, to find one's self again. This drive, remarkably transposed in its time by the famous advertising campaign coined by the FCA agency (love, live, play, talk…), has disappeared and does not seem to inspire the current brand any more, as Club Med has become a vacation club and no longer promotes a particular lifestyle.

The pressures that lead a brand astray from the initial contract by little nudges are numerous and create the risk of identity loss. The management of the Paloma Picasso perfume brand is a good example of this. Through the roots of the brand and the creator whose name it bears, this brand symbolises a violent Latin character, the South, a haughty, self-asserting pride. Its codes of red and black are Latin codes, signs of a strong character, but such an identity creates territorial boundaries for the brand. It is strong in South America, in the Sunbelt in the United States (Florida, Texas, California), and in Europe in all the countries where Spain exerts an attraction (Germany, Great Britain, France). On the other hand, it has not been able to penetrate the Asian market (where the preference is for pastels, tenderness, softness), nor in Oceania, Australia and Scandinavian countries. Hence the question which arose at the launching of the third perfume: should one respect the brand contract – what it has stood for up until now, the basis of its success – or put on the market a softer version?

Revitalising brands also implies the rediscovery of one's roots. With time, we tend to forget the founding principles accumulating compromise after compromise. The Novotel management called the programme which redefined the orientation of the brand 'return to the future'. The aim was not to reconstruct the Novotels from the good old days but to take up again the historic mission of the brand, updated to meet the needs of its clients in the year 2000. In the car industry, it is also symptomatic that the success of the Xantia car signalled the awakening of Citroën after many years in the wilderness. It reactivated the latent positive imagery of Citroën and brought it up to date with the 1990s.

MANAGING TWO LEVELS OF BRANDING

How does one consistently manage a brand such as Laboratoires Garnier, Cacharel, Volkswagen or Renault? These brands are called source-brands in the sense that they include products that have their own individual identity and brand image. In this sense we talk of mother brands and daughter brands, or first-name brands. Thus there is Renault but there are also the personalities of Clio, Twingo, Laguna, Safrane and Espace, each having its own identity. As we will see in Chapter 7, the brand is not content just with endorsing, it adds its values and creates a coherent environment. It is no longer an umbrella brand because there are two levels to the brand (the family name and the first name), whereas an umbrella brand includes products without first names (such as a Philips TV, a Philips razor, a Philips coffee machine ...). The problem which surfaces is that of the balance which has to be struck between coherence and freedom, family resemblance and individuality. This concerns, beyond the examples just cited, all industrial groups that maintain the strong identities of corporate brands, and that do not want to be considered as merely a holding company. The key lies in a systematic approach to the source brand, analysing what each daughter brand brings to or borrows from the whole.

The Laboratoires Garnier brand management may be seen first of all in an understanding of its roots, of its genetic code. The initial and founding product of the brand (before it was bought out by L'Oréal as soon as it got too threatening) was the herbal shampoo created by Mr Garnier. One could already find in it certain key attributes of the brand: naturalness, beauty through care (thus a certain medical benefit), no narrow USP (unique selling proposition) but a large promise and a distribution through pharmacies. Later, after the war, Moelle Garnier was to be the second successful shampoo: it nurtured the hair and still offered beauty and shine through care. Mr Garnier innovated by distributing it not only in pharmacies but in hair salons and finally in what at the time stood for mass distribution. L'Oréal then bought Garnier along with Roja, creating Roja-Garnier, an idea which completely diluted the brand-capital and led it to sink into oblivion from 1976 to 1986.

In 1986, the coherent relaunching of Laboratoires Garnier was decided. A European study was conducted to apprehend what was left in consumers' memories as buried, semi-buried or conscious traces of the old Garnier brand. This analysis revealed that there still existed a rich and lively basis and that beyond the differences in advertising for each of the product lines of the brand, there still stood out a Laboratoires Garnier brand that was coherent, structured, deliberate and sustained by a real aim. The constituent features of the brand were close to the roots of the Garnier mother house, a taste for a wide range of benefits could still be found (beauty through care, not mere dermatology) aimed at active women (but not hyperactive). The brand would not be limited to shampoos, but would extend to 11 product lines. To manage the products and the daughter brands to come, it was paramount to define a philosophy of production. After all, if the brand defines itself as a laboratory, it should hold firm all the underlying principles and apply them to the creation of the products themselves.

The research process resulted from the key principle of brand management: the truth of a brand lies within itself. Taking the 11 products considered the most typical of the Garnier brand and which represented best the brand manufacturer, one searched for what the scientific principle was, the common stream defining the know-how of the brand. Everything was thus brought together to establish the charter of the brand. In this way, it came to be much more than just an umbrella brand endorsing other brands, but a real source-brand, carried by its own set of values, entrusted with a mission and having scientific principles, a philosophy which precisely reflected the woman who uses it. The charter was communicated by audio-visual means in a deliberate fashion to the subsidiaries (by area and country), to the networks and to the reporters, thus putting an end to all the remaining connotations associated with Roja-Garnier. Being more than an endorsing brand, it had now established the basis for a real corporate culture which could be decentralised. This would have to be found in all the lines, current and to come, even a line like Graphic, whose aim was to open the brand to a younger clientele, girls and boys concerned about their looks. Bearing this in mind, it is significant that Graphic was the first line of Laboratoires Garnier to be launched in Great Britain. Conscious that it was doing much more than just launching Graphic but that it was actually launching the source-brand Laboratoires Garnier, the communication emphasised the philosophy of the brand and portrayed Graphic as being inspired by it. It is a known fact that the first steps in creating a brand model its long-term image: its first product acts as a prototype of the brand meaning.

In 1995, the Cacharel brand seemed to be losing ground, no longer supported by the legitimacy of a fashion designer and torn apart because of its different activities: shirt shops in shopping malls and lingerie products with no link to the feminine perfumes Anaïs-Anaïs and Loulou. The visible facet of the brand was the two perfumes, worldwide hits, but for want of a successor seemingly to be going in circles. Anaïs-Anaïs, a floral perfume, symbolises the universal history of femininity, the woman as a flower, essentially innocent. The second perfume, Loulou, which refers to the famous feminine character, symbolised a young woman still introverted. Mrs A. Louite – who has safeguarded the consistency of the brand at L'Oréal since 1976 – came to the conclusion that the brand was too static in its codes of expression, which indeed suggested a series of images, but their purpose was not clear. At the same time, the shirt shops and licensed lingerie sold in supermarkets were exploiting the brand's capital. It became urgent to revitalise the mother-brand Cacharel, give it an outlook on the future, renew it while respecting its basis. The strategy employed consisted of conducting two parallel basic approaches: launching the new Eden perfume and modernising the two previous perfumes.

The interesting aspect in this approach was that Eden was not thought of as a continuation of Anaïs-Anaïs or Loulou, but as an opening for Cacharel, allowing a more modern outlook to the two other products. To replenish the capital of the Cacharel brand, Eden's advertising gave a place to the brand, instead of simply adding another portrait. The place was to be anchored to innocence and to the flower and nature aspect of Anaïs-Anaïs, but would allow for the introduction of a man. The garden of Eden is just the place for innocence and transgression. Eden no longer refers to a woman but to eternal history. This perfume was supposed to allow men into the Cacharel universe, laying the basis for future product launches aimed at them. Moreover, as a world of colour and life, Eden gives another outlook on the two previous perfumes.

Thus, the Anaïs-Anaïs commercial was made livelier with colour, and with a complicity between the two young women, fresher and more up to date. On the other hand, the essence of the brand (duality) and the floral code were respected. As for Loulou, she too was awakened. The evolution and future of the brand meant extending the line to men. But he could not arrive without reason in the Cacharel universe, only through a woman, and Eden provided that opportunity. Finally, new products were launched under both Loulou and Eden names to match new expectations for lighter fragrances: Loulou Blue and Eau d'Eden are range extensions.

RANGE EXTENSION: NECESSITY AND LIMITS

Extending the range is a necessary step in the evolution of a brand through time. Just as living species only survive if they adapt through evolution to their environment and seek to extend their ecological realm, the brand, which historically is designated by a single product (like Coca-Cola or McCain French fries) breaks up into sub-species. The extension of the line or range (we will address the difference between the two concepts later) typically takes on the following shapes:

- multiplication of formats and sizes (typical in cars but also in soft drinks);
- multiplication of the variety of tastes and flavours;
- multiplication of the type of ingredients (for example Coca-Cola with or without sugar, with or without caffeine, types of motors in the Ford Escort);
- multiplication of generic forms for medicine;
- multiplication of physical forms such as Ariel in powder, liquid or micro formula;
- multiplication of product add-ons under the same name, corresponding to a same consumer need in what is called line extension. Thus, Basic Homme by Vichy comprises a line of toiletries including shaving foam, soothing and energising balm, deodorant, and shower gel;
- multiplication of versions having a specific application. For example, the Johnson company transformed its successful spray polish, Pliz, which was a mono-product brand for a long time, into a range called Pliz 'Classic' which offered products specialised for the type of surface. In doing so it also seized the opportunity to reduce its brand portfolio. Favor, a weak brand, became Pliz with beeswax especially for wood. Shampoo brands multiply endlessly, with varieties suited to different types of hair and scalp condition.

Line or range extension must be distinguished from brand extension, which is a real diversification towards different product categories and different clients. It is a highly sensitive and strategic choice that will be addressed in a separate chapter. How can Lu & Belin brand salted products when they have always been associated with sweet biscuits? Should Dim have created products for men under its name? Why does Yamaha brand both motorcycles and pianos? Range extensions represent 75 per cent of new product lines in consumer goods. It is the most common form of innovation in these markets.

Range extension naturally follows the logic of marketing and of even finer segmentation to better adapt the offer to the specific needs of consumers, needs that never stop evolving. At its beginning, we may recall, each brand was a unique product, in both meanings of the word: it is different and there is only one form of it. This was, for example, the case with the famous Ford: everyone could have it in the colour of their choice, as long as it was black. It was the same with the Coca-Cola and the Orangina bottle. With time, the brand becomes less narrow-minded, and acknowledging differentiated expectations, decides to respond to them. As the American advertising for Burger King, the competitor of McDonald's in the United States, says, 'Have it your way' (whatever way you like it, with or without sauce, onions, etc). Again, taking the example of Coca-Cola, while retaining its identity (the dark colour, cola taste, and other physical and symbolic attributes of the brand), the company was able to extend the power of attraction of its brand by allowing people who up until then were reluctant to try the product to indulge in Coke. The multiplication of versions (with or without sugar, with or without caffeine) increased the number of potential consumers. We therefore see that range extension can reinforce the brand by widening its market and its customer base. A variety of formats has the same effect. In the world of soft drinks, the launch of a new format may be considered the same as launching a new soft drink. Indeed, each new format allows the brand to enter a new usage mode. The original Coca-Cola bottle corresponded to use in cafes, hotels and restaurants; the aluminium can allowed for an increase in the number of vending machines sites, at the office for example. The litre glass bottle and the litre and a half in a PET bottle enabled the brand to penetrate the home for family use, and multiplied sales of those formats by ten. As we have seen, extensions push further the boundaries of the market and strengthen the brand's domination of the market.

In so doing, the brand proves itself to be full of energy and sensitivity. It recognises the different expectations of the public and responds to them. It follows the evolution of consumers and changes with them. Club Med was thus able to widen its offer beyond the simple Robinson Crusoe lodge to keep or attract families, then people in their forties seeking more comfort, and finally older people, children of the baby-boom. The range extension is a token of the brand's attentive and caring character. Extending the brand range thus makes the brand interesting and friendly and maintains through these successive mini-launchings a strong visibility. From this point of view, instead of trying to force New Coke on Americans and make them give up the original flavour, the

Coca-Cola Company would have done better to have launched the New Coke as an extension alongside the classic Coke!

Range extension is a way of revitalising many failing brands, by making sure they move closely to meet the expectations of today's customers. What saved Campari was the launching onto the market of a 'flanker' product: Campari Soda. Martini would have fallen by the wayside if it had not been for the launching of Martini Bianco, more in touch with the new modes of alcohol consumption. Pernod made a step towards customers who were not used to the strong taste of liquorice or anise by launching Pernod-Hex in small individual bottles.

Faced with the changes in eating habits especially where cheese is concerned, Babybel would have been threatened with ageing if it had not been boosted by mini-Babybel, the only product that sells in Europe (to the point where the international brand is called mini Babybel and not Babybel). Created 40 years ago and recognisable because of its red coating, the physical facet of its identity, the big Babybel (4000 tons sold currently) is certainly less modern now than when it was created. The market for family-size cheeses coated in wax is not that revolutionary any more, in France, or in Europe. The mini Babybel (6000 tons sold in France), now 25 years 'old', brought a lot of fun, modernity and youth to the image and to the customers (by introducing the brand to children and teenagers because it easily slips into backpacks etc). Moreover it opens a variety of eating occasions, whereas the classic Babybel was linked to the table, and therefore to more adult consumption. This complementarity is used in France in two commercials: one for the mini, showing the friendly, practical and easy-to-carry aspects (used in European commercials as well), the other showing the reason for the red protective coating on Babybel.

These motives may be worthy of praise, but the current proliferation of range extensions to be observed in all consumer goods markets results from frantic competition and from the new psychology of organisations.

In these markets there is a strong relationship between market share and the number of facings, ie the share of shelf space taken up. This is not surprising: the customer involvement in these products is average if not low and the number of impulse buyers (when the choice of brand is done on-site) never stops growing. It is, therefore, in the brand manager's interest to take up the most shelf space possible because it will attract even more attention from the customer, especially if a shelf is not extendible and competitors get pushed out. In many markets, demand is no longer growing and DOBs also occupy a share of the shelf, so the brand manager tries to position his product as 'captain of the category' by presenting a unique offer and so dominating the shelf reserved for national brands.

Distributors have an ambivalent attitude towards range extensions. On the one hand they oppose what is now considered hypersegmentation, the proliferation of range extension. But as each brand tends to offer the same extensions, this creates bottle-necks because of the obsession each brand has to gain access to maximum distribution. This fight for ever-reducing shelf space strengthens the power of the distributor and puts him in a position to ask for increasing amounts of money as a listing fee (Chinardet, 1994).

The problem is that the turnover of extensions, because of their novelty and their price premium, is often lower than that of the original product. When the distributor realises this (if he ever does), he withdraws the extension and awaits the offer of other brands, along with any kind of listing fee that might come with it.

Criticised by, but at the same time popular with distributors, range extensions are appreciated by product and brand managers. First of all, the amount of time needed for development is shorter than that needed for the launching of a new brand. The costs are less than those for the launching of a new brand (they are estimated to be one-fifth), and sales forecasts are more reliable. In the short term at least, it seems an almost automatic way of gaining market share and thus creating observable results that can be attributed to the actions of the manager in a relatively short timespan. This counts for quick promotion within the company, or on another brand in another country. Few managers are willing to take the risk of launching a new brand, but would rather extend the range.

The proliferation of product extensions produces insidious negative effects that are not immediately measurable or measured. First of all, because of small production runs and the increased complexity of production, logistics and management, extensions are more expensive to produce, the cost of which puts up the higher wholesale and retail price. According to Quelch and Kenny (1994), compared to an index of 100 for the cost of production of a mono-product, the corresponding production cost index of differentiated products in a range is, for example, 145 in the car industry, 135 for hosiery and 132 in the food industry. Moreover, in companies which do not take into account direct costs (eg. raw materials, advertising), many costs are considered as common to the entire range and are allocated to different products within it according to sales. The best-sellers therefore attract more of the costs than range extensions, which makes the profitability of the latter rather illusory.

Secondly, non-controlled extension weakens the range logic. The first to find problems with this are the sales people: the salesforce of Ariel or Dash, used to promoting the brand against Skip, had to undertake within a few months a complete cultural revolution. They had to promote Ariel in powder, in liquid and in micro formula formats all together and without ever explaining that one was superior to the other, or what advantages one format has in comparison to the others. The more extensions multiply, the more the specific positioning of each extension becomes subtle. This is accentuated by the fact that extensions are added without withdrawing the existing versions. Organisations always have a good reason for not cancelling this or that version. The thought of losing the odd customer here and there rules the notion out. This thinking overlooks the fact that product withdrawals should also be managed to gently propel customers towards newer, better versions.

The range logic is also lost on the shelf: indeed, the distributor is reluctant to take on the whole range. He will shop around and take only part of a range, which undermines the consistency of the range on the shelf.

Finally, brand loyalty might be undermined by a proliferation of extensions. The hypersegmentation of shampoos according to new hair needs, leads the customer to take into account more needs in his/her choosing process. The brand is but a feature in an ever longer list of criteria. This result was verified empirically by Rubinson (1992).

In reaction to the proliferation of extensions, starting in 1992, Procter & Gamble eliminated within 18 months 15 to 25 per cent of the product extensions that were not achieving a sufficient turnover. In the sector for cleaning products, the growth of new multi-usage products (all-in-one) is on the same principle of simplification. In the car industry, without going back to the Ford, a desegmentation or counter-segmentation logic (Resnik, Turney and Mason, 1979) is emerging. It means a much smaller offer, ie. a reduction in the varieties to choose from, just like the Renault Twingo. On the other hand, this allows for lower retail prices. It also leads companies such as Honda and Mitsubishi to offer from the outset cars where just about everything is added on on the assembly line. Economies of scale apply all the more since the product is designed for the worldwide market. The extreme strategy of counter-segmentation is applied by hard discounters: there is absolutely no choice and products are generally only available in a single version with no variety. Thus, there will only be one type of diaper, whatever the weight or the gender of the baby, in contrast to Phases (boy or girl) by Pampers. On the other hand, because of this it will be 40 per cent cheaper than, say, Pampers.

Quelch and Kennedy (1994) recommend four immediate actions for better management of range extensions:

- Improve the cost accounting system to be able to catch the additional costs incurred by a new variety all along the value chain. This enables the real profitability of each one to be assessed.

- Allocate resources more to high-margin products than to extensions that only appeal to occasional buyers.
- Make sure that each salesperson can sum up in a few words the role of each product within the range.
- Implement a new philosophy where product withdrawals are not only accepted but encouraged. Some companies only launch an extension after having cancelled another with a low turnover. This withdrawal does not have to be brutal, but can be done gradually so that clients turn to other products within the range.

7

Brand architecture: handling a large product portfolio

Why does L'Oréal use the name 'Plenitude from L'Oréal' for its cosmetic line sold in supermarkets while it avoids doing the same for Lancôme? Why do Japanese companies market their products under the same brand name which happens to be the same as that of the company? Why do such retailers as Dominick's, Carrefour or Sainsbury use their store name as a brand name for their own-label products whereas Kroger's used to carry completely different store labels (before moving recently to one single name)?

All these issues refer to brand–product relationship. All companies have to deal with this once they stop producing only one product.

The difficulty of the decision is linked to the dual function of brands. The World Organization for Industrial Property defines a brand in legal terms as 'a symbol serving to distinguish the products or the services of one company from those of another'. Thus, globally, a brand has two functions:

- to distinguish different products from each other;
- to indicate a product's origin.

But as the company starts growing over a period of time, the simultaneous realisation of these two objectives becomes difficult. Philips puts its own name on its televisions (what is usually called corporate branding): but what then are televisions called which are also made by Philips, but are of a lower standard and price than the former? To differentiate between them, they named the latter Radiola and, in doing so, they concealed any clues to the origin of the product. On the other hand, Holiday Inn preferred, initially, to emphasise the origin of their hotels of a higher grade by calling them Holiday Inn Crowne Plaza.

As one would suspect, the multiplication of products in a company first calls for some thought to be given to how the system of names and symbols (emblems, colour etc) given to products will be organised. This system should clarify the overall offer and structure it in such a way that it is easily understood by prospective buyers. It should be logical and follow rules that can be understood and applied by the various divisions of the company. The system should also help sales and product promotions in the short term and the establishment of brand-capital in the medium term. Lastly, it should be able to anticipate the future and possible evolutions in product-lines and ranges in order to last and be applicable to all new products.

There are already many models of the brand–product relationship. We will examine some of them and discuss their advantages and disadvantages presently. Secondly, armed with concepts and models, we will study why many companies have chosen one or the other or a mixed model in order to formulate their decision-making criteria. Thirdly, we will identify the principal failures and dysfunctions appearing in brand–product relationships and in the development of brands. In the following chapter we will also tackle the problem of the number of brands to keep for a certain market or a certain company.

BRANDING STRATEGIES

An analysis of company strategies reveals six models in the managment of brand–product (or service) relationships. Each model denotes a certain role for the brand, its status as well as its relationship (nominal and/or visual) with the products which the brand encompasses:

- the product brand;
- the line brand;
- the range brand;
- the umbrella brand;
- the source brand;
- the endorsing brand.

To each of these six forms of brand–product relationship we can ask another question: should the brand name be that of the company or distinct from it? These six models allow us to structure the brand problem in all sectors: whether it is services, industry, consumer goods or luxury products.

These branding strategies facilitate product distinction or serve as indicators of product origin in varying degrees as shown in Figure 7.1.

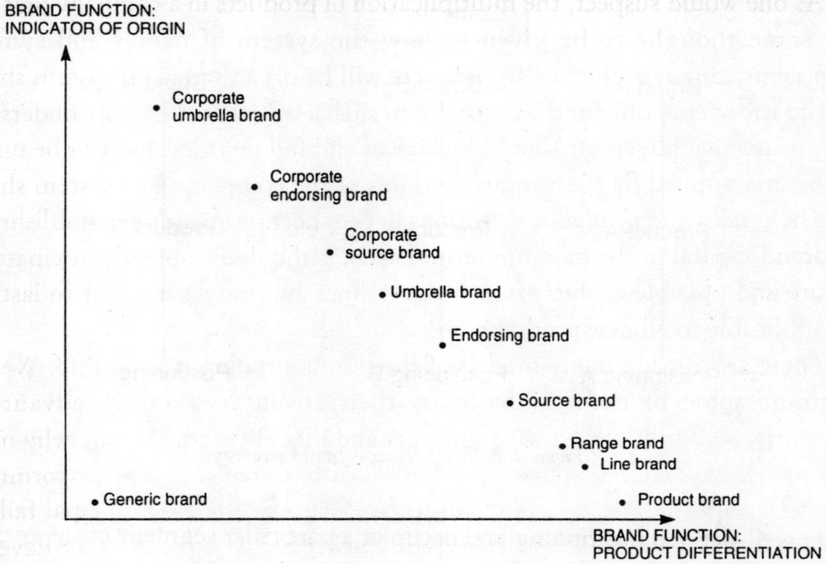

Figure 7.1 Positioning alternative branding strategies

The Product Brand Strategy

It is widely known that a brand is at the same time a symbol, a word, an object and a concept: a symbol, since it has numerous facets and it incorporates figurative symbols such as logos, emblems, colours, forms, packaging and design; a word, because it is the brand name which serves as support for oral or written information on the product; an object, because the brand distinguishes each of the products from the other products or services; and finally, a concept in the sense that the brand, like any other symbol, imparts its own significance – in other words, its meaning.

The product brand strategy involves the assignment of a particular name to one, and only one, product as well as one exclusive positioning. The result of such a strategy is that each new product receives its own brand name that belongs only to it. Companies then have a brand portfolio which corresponds to their product portfolio as illustrated in Figure 7.2.

This brand strategy can be found in the hotel industry where the Accor Group has developed multiple brands for precise and exclusive positions: eg Sofitel, Novotel, Ibis, Formula 1, etc. The company Procter & Gamble has also adopted this strategy as its brand management philosophy. The company is represented in the European detergent market by the brands Ariel, Vizir, Dash and in the soaps market by Camay, Zest, etc. Each of these products has a pre-

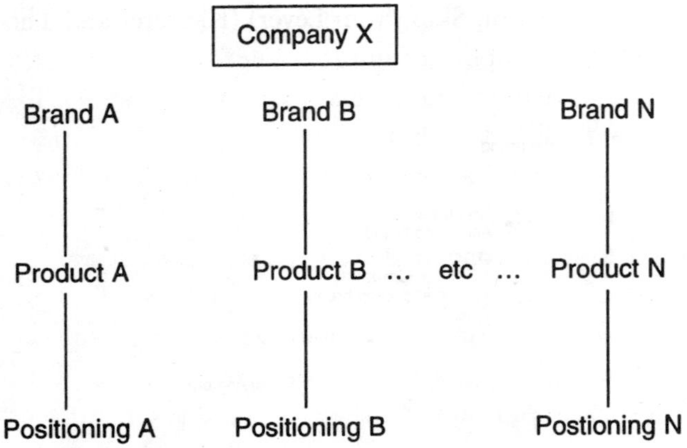

Figure 7.2 The product – brand strategy

cise, well-defined positioning and occupies a particular segment of the market: Camay is a seductive soap, Zest a soap for energy and Monsavon (in France) a natural family soap. Ariel projects itself as the best detergent in the market and Dash as the best value for money in the intermediate price range.

Innovative companies in the food sector create new speciality products which are then distinguished through individual names and therefore these companies have a large brand product portfolio. The cheese company Bongrain markets more than ten brands, such as St Moret, Caprice des Dieux and Chaumes. The mineral water market is composed of only product brands: one asks for Vittel, Evian or Contrex, knowing very well that there will be no ambiguity and one will get the product asked for. Here, the brand, the name of a product, becomes a strict indication of identity.

In an extreme case, the product is so specific that there is no equivalent, and the product is not only a product, but an entire product category of which it is the sole representative. This phenomenon has been explained by some through the neologism 'branduct' (Swiners, 1979), an abbreviation of brand product. In reality, we cannot really indicate products of such a specific nature other than through their brand names. We see this in 'Post-it', Bailey's Irish Cream, Malibu liqueur, Mars, Bounty, Nuts, etc. The product brand concept accounts for this reality.

How is the narrow relationship between name, product and positioning maintained over a period of time? Firstly, the only way to achieve brand extension is by renewing the product. To keep the product at its height and original positioning, the Ariel formula has often been improved since it was launched in 1969. Ariel receives the best technological and chemical inputs from Procter &

Gamble (like its competitor, Skip, from Lever) (Kapferer and Thoenig, 1989). Often, to emphasise an important improvement to the product, the company adds a number after the brand name (Dash 1, Dash 2, Dash 3). To keep up with changing consumer habits, the brand name is applied to various formats (for example, in packaging: packets, drums, in powder or liquid form).

What, then, are the advantages of the product brand strategy for companies? For firms focusing on one market, it is an offensive strategy to occupy the whole market. By indulging in the practice of multiple brand entries in the same market (Procter & Gamble has four detergent brands), the company occupies many functional segments with different needs and expectations and therefore has a greater consolidated share of the market: it becomes category leader.

When the segments are closely related, choosing one name per product helps customers to perceive better the differences between the various products. This may also be necessary when the products resemble each other externally. Thus, one sees that although all detergents are composed of the same basic ingredients, the proportion of these may vary according to the factor that is being optimised: stain removal properties, care for synthetic materials, colour-fast control or suitability for hand washing. The association of a specific name for a type of need underlines the physical difference between the products.

The product brand strategy is one that is adapted to the needs of innovative companies who want to pre-empt a positioning. In fact, the first brand to appear in a new segment, if it proves to be effective, has the advantage of the first player in the market. It becomes the nominal reference for the thus innovative product and maybe even the absolute reference. The name patents the innovation. This is particularly important in markets where the success is likely to induce copying. In the pharmaceutical world where generic copies are a certainty, every new product is registered under two names: one for the product, the formula, and another for the brand. Even if they have the same formula, future generic products appear different because of the originality of the brand name (Zantac, Tagamet) giving a wide cloak of legal protection. On the other hand, where the law cannot provide protection, forgeries and copies attempt to exploit the potential of the product brand by imitating the name as closely as possible. That is why large mass retailers often use product brands or, to be more precise, counter–product brands. Thus, Fortini copies Martini, Whip copies Skip, etc. Scared of having their other brands cast out of favour manufacturers have, until now, hesitated to legally challenge the distributors for forgery or illegal imitation.

Product brand policies allow firms to take risks in new markets. At a time when the future of the liquid detergent was still uncertain, Procter & Gamble preferred to launch a product brand: Vizir. Launching it under the name Ariel liquid would have threatened Ariel's brand image asset and launching it under the name Dash would have incurred the risk of associating a potentially powerful concept with a weak brand and thereby overshadowing it.

Product brand policy implies that the name of the company behind it remains unknown to the public and is therefore different from the brand names. This practice allows the firm considerable freedom to move whenever and wherever it wishes, especially into new markets. Procter & Gamble moved from the creation of the soap, Ivory, in 1882, to the culinary aid, Crisco, in 1911, Chipso in 1926 and the machine detergent, Dreft, in 1933, Tide in 1946, Joy, the dishwashing agent in 1950 and then Dash in 1955, the toothpaste, Crest, in 1955, the peanut-butter, Jif, in 1956, Pampers in 1961, the coffee, Folgers, in 1963, the antiseptic mouthwash, Scope, as well as household paper rolls, Bounce, in 1965, Pringle chips in 1968, sanitary napkins, Rely, in 1974, etc.

Since each brand is independent of the others, the failure of one of them has no risk of rebounding on the others nor on the company name (in cases where the company name remains relatively unknown to the public and different from that of any of the brands).

Finally, the distribution parameter also favours this strategy heavily: the shelf space accorded by a retailer to a company depends on the number of (strong) brands that it has. When a brand covers many products, the retailer stocks certain products and not others. In the case of product brands, there is only one product per brand.

The drawbacks arising from product brands are essentially economic. Thus multi-brand strategy is not for the faint-hearted.

In fact, every new product launch is also a new brand launch. Considering the media costs in various sectors, this involves considerable investments in advertising and promotions. Furthermore, retailers, unwilling to take risks with untested products whose future is uncertain, stock them only when tempted by heavy premiums.

Multiplication of product brands in a market due to the increasingly narrow segmentation weighs heavily on the chances of a rapid return on investment. The volumes required to justify such investment (in R&D, equipment, and sales and marketing expenses) make the product brand strategy an ideal one for growing markets where a small market share could nevertheless mean high volumes. When the market is saturated, this possibility disappears. On the other hand, in a stable market it is sometimes more advantageous to perk up an existing brand with the innovation in question rather than attempt to give it product brand status by launching it under its own name.

The role of impenetrable divisions between product brands is certainly important in times of crises, but in other times it prevents the brand from benefiting from the association created with an already existing brand. The success of brand A will not help other products because their names, B, C, D, etc are different and do not bear any relation to A. As we can see, in this strategy, the firm gives the brand a completely distinct and exclusive function and almost no hints about its origin. New products do not benefit from the renown of one of the existing brands nor from the economies that one could derive from it. On the other hand, this advantage has no role among distributors who are well aware of the company name behind the brand and its reputation for success or failure.

The case of 'branducts' is even more marked. Since they represent an entire category of products on their own, they have to invest twice as much in advertising. While a brand of whisky only has to associate itself with the whisky category for the customer to recall the brand when he wants to buy a whisky, other products such as Sheridan, Malibu or Bailey's cannot fall back on the cushion of a product category. They therefore need a permanent spontaneous awareness: either one thinks of Bailey's or one does not (in which case the probability of a sale is zero). Furthermore, isolated due to the lack of a category shelf, branducts suffer from a lack of prominence and visibility on the shelves. This makes their fame their only strong point. In times of recession, they are the first to undergo budget reductions.

The line brand strategy

In 1981, the Deglaude Laboratories launched a product brand, Foltene: a single product associated with a single pitch, the regrowth of hair. A strong TV advertising campaign made the market explode and Foltene became the leader with a single product and a 55 per cent market share. They should have remained thus, but consumer logic prevailed. Bald people were not looking for a single product. They wanted an all-encompassing service, a total care routine. They wrote asking that shampooing be combined with the Foltene treatment. In 1982 Deglaude launched a mild shampoo (which was later subdivided according to hair type) followed by a daily-use lotion. All this was by way of response to customer demands.

In 1986, Christian Dior launched Capture, an anti-ageing liposome complex for the skin. Following its success, a first spin-off was launched in February, 1989: 'Capture, eye shaper', followed by lip shapers and then other products for the body. The Capture line was born.

Thus, to take up Botton and Cegarra's definition (1990), the line responds to the concern of offering one coherent product under a single name by proposing many complementary products. This moves from extensions of the offer, as in the case of Capture or with the fragrances of an aftershave, to the inclusion of various products within one specific offer, as in the case of Foltene. This is also the case with Studio Line hair products from L'Oréal which offers structuring gel, lacquer, a spray, etc. Calgon (a Benckiser brand) markets a dishwasher powder together with a rinsing agent and lime-scale inhibitor. That these products are completely different for the producer makes no difference to the consumer, who perceives them as related.

It should be clear that the line involves the exploitation of a successful concept by extending it but by staying very close to the initial product (eg Capture liposomes or the Foltene principle). In other cases, the line is launched as a complete ensemble, with many complementary products linked by a single central concept (for Studio Line it was allowing youngsters to do their own hair and give themselves a 'look'). The eventual extension of the line will involve only the marginal costs linked to retailers' discounts and to the packaging. It does not need advertising. It should be compared to the marginal number of consumers that could be won. As one can see, the line brand strategy offers multiple advantages:

- it reinforces the selling power of the brand and creates a strong brand image;
- it leads to the ease of distribution for line extensions;
- it reduces launch costs.

The disadvantages of the line strategy lie in the tendency to forget that a line has limits. One should only include product innovations that are very closely linked to the existing ones. On the other hand, the inclusion of a powerful innovation could slow its development. Thus, even though Capture was the result of seven years' research in collaboration with the Pasteur Institute, received three diplomas and brought with it a revolutionary anti-ageing principle, Dior decided to attach it to a currently existing anti-ageing line. This did not prevent the success of Capture, but unnecessarily delayed it initially.

The range brand strategy

Findus, Bird's Eye and Igloo all propose more than 100 frozen food products. But not all range brands are this extensive. Wild Turkey bourbon covers five products: the eight-year-old, the 12-year-old, the 'Tradition', the '1855' and the 'Legend'. The Tylenol range now covers a number of different products.

Range brands bestow a single brand name and promote through a single promise a range of products belonging to the same area of competence. In range brand architecture, products guard their common name (fish à la provençale, mushroom pizza, pancakes with ham and cheese in the case of Bird's Eye). In the Clarins cosmetic range, products are named 'purifying plant mask', extracts of 'fresh cells', multi-tensor toning solution, day or night soothing cream, etc.

Range brand structure is found in the food sector (Green Giant, Campbell, Heinz, etc), in cosmetics, textiles (Benetton, Lacoste, Rodier, etc), equipment (Moulinex, Seb, Rowenta, Delsey, Samsonite, Vuitton) or in industry (Steelcase, Facom). These brands combine all their products through a unique principle, a brand concept, as is shown in Figure 7.3. The advantages and disadvantages of the structure are as follows:

- It avoids the random spread of external communications by focusing on a single name – the brand name – and thereby creating brand capital for itself which can even be shared by other products. Furthermore, in such a structure the brand communicates in a generic manner by developing its unique brand concept. Thus, the range brand of pet food, Fido, covers many products but in its advertisement it only has a taster dog who marks his approval on a product with a paw print. This commercial transfers the brand focalisation and its pre-eminence to the animal. Another approach consists of communicating the brand concept by concentrating only on certain of the most representative products through which the brand can best express its meaning and convey consumer benefit. This can then be shared by other products of the range which are not directly mentioned.

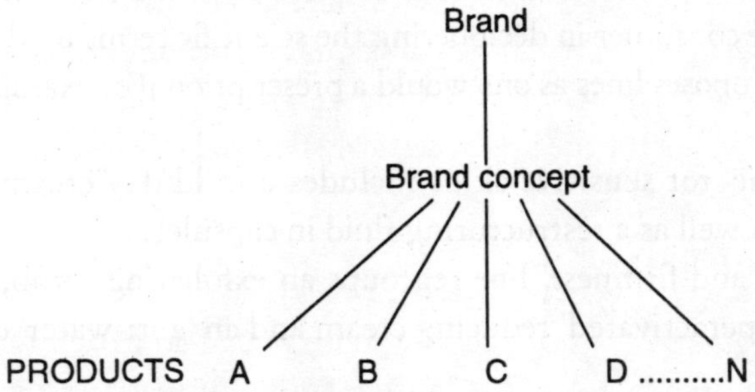

Figure 7.3 Range brand formation

- The brand can easily distribute new products that are consistent with its mission and fall within the same category. Furthermore, the cost of such new launches is very low.

Among the problems that are most frequently encountered is one of brand opacity as it expands. The brand name Findus (from Nestlé) covers all savoury frozen products. It is a good brand – high quality, modern, a specialist in frozen products and a generalist as well because it makes all kinds of dishes. For years, product names were the names of the recipes. But these names are banal. Any brand can claim that it has the same recipe. To enrich the brand and to express its personality on one hand, and on the other hand to help the consumer choose from the mass of products that are on offer, the one product which possesses all the qualities being sought, an intermediate stage must be created between the brand name and each actual product name. This is the role of specific lines such as:

- 'Lean cuisine' that regrouped 18 dishes all recognisable by their white packaging;
- 'Traditional' covering nine dishes with maroon outers;
- 'Seafoods' comprising nine kinds of dishes and assorted products (previously simply called hake cutlets, whiting fillets, etc) in blue packaging.

Such names for a line throw light on the products and also help to structure the range in the same way as shopkeepers organise their shelves. The criteria for segmentation and for the creation of families of products depend on the brand. Thus, should we make the distinctions according to the content (poultry, beef, pork etc, as in a butcher's shop) or according to consumer benefits (light, traditional, exotic, family orientated ...)?

The line structures the offer, by putting together products which are undoubtedly heterogeneous, but all of which have the same function. Thus, in the Clarins cosmetic range brand, the offer is also made more clear and structured by way of lines. To assist the consumer in deciphering the scientific terms used on the products, the brand proposes lines as one would a prescription. For example:

- the 'gentle line' for sensitive skins includes a mild day cream and a mild night cream as well as a restructuring fluid in capsules;
- the 'slimming and firmness' line regroups an exfoliating scrub, a slimming bath, a 'bio-superactivated' reducing cream and an 'anti-water' oil.

The Clarins offer ceases to be a long list of creams, serums, lotions, balms and gels and now forms structured and coherent groups as seen in Figure 7.4.

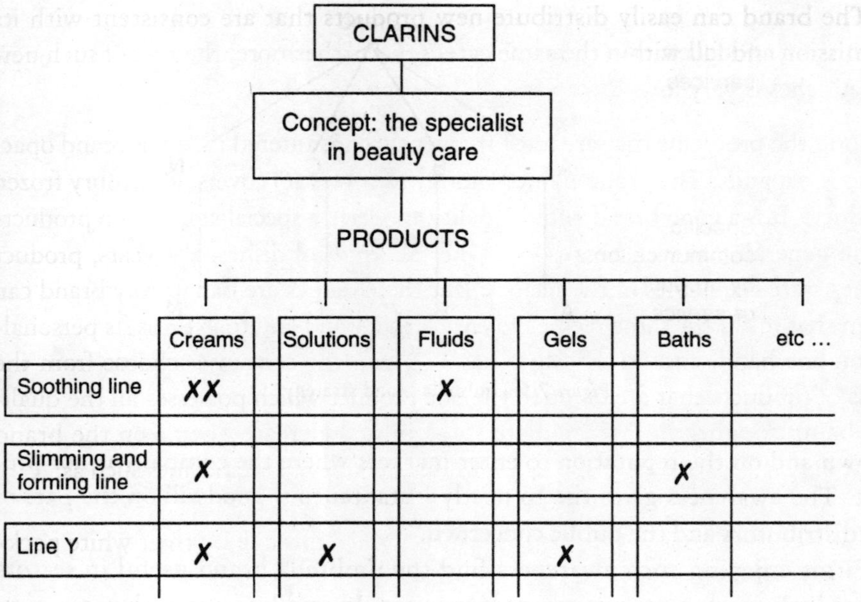

Figure 7.4 Range brand structured in lines

Umbrella brand strategy

Canon markets cameras, photocopying machines and office equipment all under its own name. Yamaha sells motorbikes, but also pianos and guitars. Mitsubishi regroups banks, cars and domestic appliances. Palmolive is a brand name for household products (dishwashing liquid) and hygiene products (soaps and shampoos for the entire family, but also shaving cream for men). These are all umbrella brands: the same brand supports several products in different markets. Each of them has its own advertising tools and develops its own communications (sometimes even has its own advertising agency). Yet, each product retains its own generic name. Thus, we speak of Canon cameras, Canon fax machines, Canon printers. Figure 7.5 illustrates this structure. (Chapter 8 is devoted to the crucial question of brand extension beyond its original domain of activity. Is Philips right in using the same name to cover hi-fi, television, bulbs, computers, electric shavers and small electric appliances?)

The main advantage of the umbrella strategy is the capitalisation on one single name and economies of scale on an international level. Not even one of their undertakings, products or communications fails to contribute to Philips' reputation. Even the occasional setback can add to public awareness of the brand. As a result, this allows one to capitalise on the brand which is already well

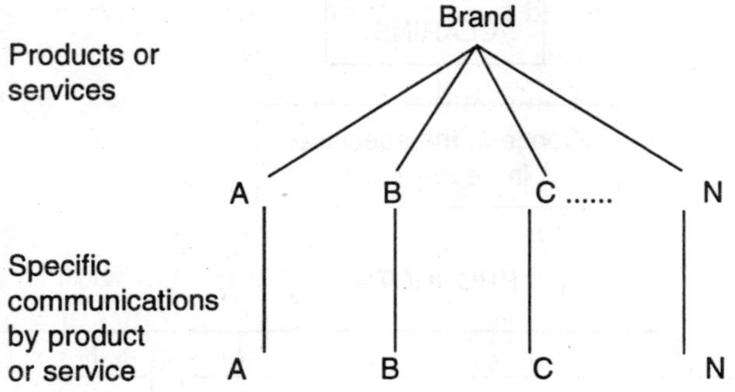

Figure 7.5 Umbrella brand strategy

known and on the reputation to enter markets where the company is not present. The awareness gives rise to nearly instantaneous goodwill on the part of the distributors and the public concerned.

Firms enjoying such awareness find the umbrella brand useful in sectors where little marketing investment is required. In smaller sectors, they can even succeed without any specific communications. It also permits considerable savings when they enter new strategic markets.

The importance of this last point should not be underestimated, especially in the present era of over-communication. Today, in many markets the quest for brand awareness is nearly out of reach given the advertising expenditures of the players already in the market. This is what led Jack Tramiel, former boss of Commodore microcomputers, to buy Atari in 1984 – a very well-known brand, albeit primarily for its video games at the time. This was done so as to be able to penetrate once again the market for home and office computers. Tramiel chose to buy a brand with an established reputation, even if it was associated with other products, rather than create another brand. The same reason explains why one revives ancient brands (like Commodore, Sunsilk, Talbot) to serve as supports for new products that may or may not be close to the original product that people have certainly forgotten, even though they still remember the name. It is better to take advantage from a glimmer in the public mind rather than start from scratch. Research on memorisation and the impact of advertising campaigns shows that their main determinant is brand awareness: one remembers it better if one already knows it.

An umbrella brand strategy allows the core brand to be nurtured by association with products with which it was not previously associated. Thus Schweppes – until then a product brand – became an umbrella brand by entering into the fizzy fruit drinks market occupied by Orangina, Sunkist, Fanta and Tango. Their Schweppes Dry advertising brought modernity and youth to the brand, something that had been very difficult to achieve with their classic Indian Tonic Water without destabilising the giant.

Finally, the umbrella brand imposes very few constraints. Each division has its own communications to increase its market share and to emphasise the specific qualities of its own brand: Toshiba hi-fi and low-fi targets the younger generation while the microcomputer division aims its outstanding, practical, portable computers at modern executives, and its television sets at families. However, in each of these markets the general brand comes up against a multitude of specialist brands, forcing it to demonstrate the relevance of its products in each of the segments where it wants to acquire a dominant position. Brand awareness does not automatically signify a legitimate product – even less so an excellent one – in the eyes of the purchaser. Only companies able to launch superior new products can use the umbrella brand strategy. In each new market, the product will have to succeed on its own merits, despite its brand name. This is typical of Japanese companies.

The problems encountered in umbrella brand administration stem from the failure to appreciate its demands. It sometimes happens that in wishing to save money by diversifying under an umbrella brand, the firm forgets that the purpose of the brand is, above all, to gain money. Awareness is not sufficient in this respect. Every division must use its financial and human resources to show that its products and services are as good as those of specialist brands and even superior, something that is not usually evident. The core of the brand is always stronger than its extensions.

The umbrella brand must not cast a shadow. Bic's image undermined the attractiveness of its perfumes. Furthermore, an accident occurring with one of the products can affect other products under the same umbrella (Sullivan, 1988).

An over-stretched rubber band weakens. Similarly, the result of putting a large number of heterogeneous products and services under the same brand is called the 'rubber effect' by Americans (Ries and Trout, 1987). The more a brand covers different categories, the more it stretches and weakens, losing its force like a rubber band. It then becomes a simple name on the products, a mere indicator of their origin, thereby a guarantee of quality. Distributors do favour umbrella brands for that reason: the large umbrella distributor's brand indicates that all its products are acceptable because they have been selected by this distributor. Strong brands with a precise meaning can also be passed on to embrace heterogeneous products, because they impose their meaning on the products. Sony, for example, is a refined technological innovator and groundbreaker. The brand can cover many categories since the factors contained in the Sony image are attractive and relevant to these product categories even if they are unrelated. Palmolive seems to add softness to everything that it touches: this factor is important every time a product is in contact with the skin. The brand can also cast its net over hygiene as well as beauty, and be relevant for both men and women.

Horizontal extension of the brand is less of a handicap than vertical extension by which brands try to cover all levels of quality and status. The automobile market is a segmented one – lower range, mid-range, upper mid-range and high range, not to mention luxury and sports cars. But it would be wrong to think that the brand programme can have the same influence on all segments. The creative strength of Mercedes is prominent in the high range but loses its edge when faced with the constraints of producing cheaper cars such as Class A. This factor signalled the death of Flaminaire lighters when they tried to compete with both Bic and Du pont. They forgot that the same name cannot be associated at the same time with both convenience and distinction.

The freedom allowed by the umbrella brand sometimes leads to a patchwork brand. It is one thing to allow each divisional manager to take care of his own product communication and another to accept too many variations in brand positioning from one division to another or from one product to the next. The manager may be free to make detailed promises in line with their particular market; however, even though each product has its individual identity, the codes of expression should be homogeneous for them all. Customers do not have just an isolated view of the brand, they come across all the products, each with its own particular message. To them, the brand should appear as an indivisible whole even though it is organised in commercial and industrial divisions. This is why companies adopting the umbrella brand strategy try to enforce the use of a brand identity charter, a minimal and formal tool for communications.

Source brand strategy

This is identical to the umbrella brand strategy except for one key point – the products are now directly named. They are no longer called by one generic name such as eau de toilette or eau de parfum, but each has own name, eg Jazz, Poison, Opium, Nina, Loulou etc. This two-tier brand structure, known as double-branding, is shown in Figure 7.6.

Since this strategy is often confused with the endorsing brand strategy, it is important to specify the differences at the beginning. When Nestlé puts its name on the chocolate Crunch and Galak, on the bars Yes, Nuts and Kit Kat and on Nescafé, Nesquik, etc, the corporate brand is endorsing the quality of the merchandise and acts as a guarantor. The Nestlé name dispels the incertitude that certain products can create. Nestlé takes a back seat position. The product itself is

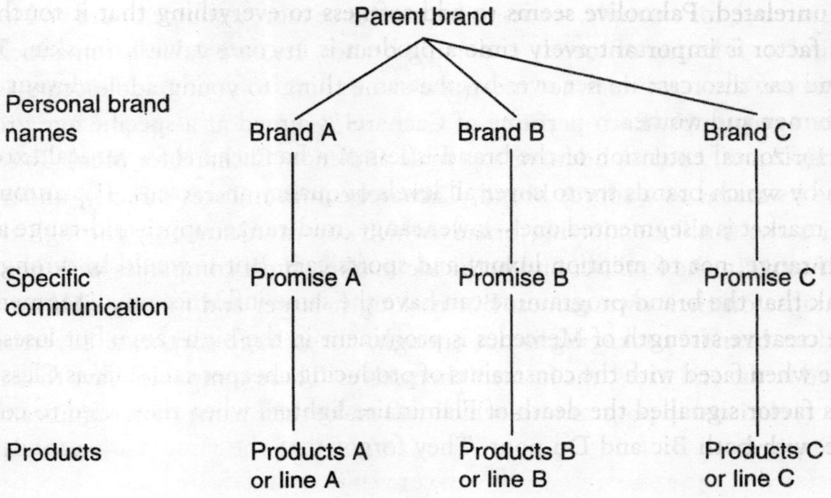

Figure 7.6 Source brand or parent brand strategy

the hero to the extent that few customers of Crunch attribute it to Nestlé. On the contrary, when we see the Yves Saint Laurent name on a perfume such as Jazz, this name is more than a simple endorsement. Here, it is the brand name which holds sway and which accords Jazz the seal of approval and the distinction which it would not otherwise enjoy. Jazz is another key to the door of the Yves Saint Laurent cultural universe. The problem with many brands is that they have converted from source brands to endorsing brands. Within the source brand concept, the family spirit dominates even if the offspring all have their own individual names. With the endorsing brand, however, the products are autonomous and have only the endorsing brand in common. Today, where do Danone or Kellogg's stand? What about Du Pont or Bayer, Glaxo or Merck?

The benefit from the source brand strategy lies in its ability to provide a two-tiered sense of difference and depth. It is difficult to personalise an offer or a proposition to a client without any personalised vocabulary. The parent brand offers its significance and identity, modified and enriched by the daughter brand in order to attract a specific customer segment. Ranges having 'Christian names' allow a brand which needs to maintain its own brand image to win over newer consumer categories and new territory.

The limits of the source brand lie in the necessity to respect the core, the spirit and the identity of the parent brand. This defines the strict boundaries not to be infringed as far as brand extension is concerned. Only the names that are related to the parent brand's field of activity should be associated with it. If greater freedom is sought, then the endorsing brand strategy is more suitable.

Cacharel, for example, wants to become once more a source brand and leave behind its function of merely endorsing brands. Its core value is romanticism. However, the term does not mean the same thing to young adolescents as to other age groups. Each perfume of Cacharel is aimed at a specific age group (Anaïs-Anaïs, Loulou, Eden) or to a male audience (Cacharel for Men). To reinforce its status as a source brand, Cacharel communicates directly, under its own name (unlike endorsing brands which communicate only through their products). In the fertiliser and herbicide market, most companies wish now to capitalise on their own names. But making it larger and more visible on the product brands' packaging is not enough, nor is huge corporate advertising aimed at the end users, the farmers themselves. These companies have to create direct relationship programmes which will make their name more significant to these users.

Endorsing brand strategy

Everyone recognises famous car brands such as Pontiac, Buick, Oldsmobile and Chevrolet in the US or Opel in Europe. Next to their logos and to the signs of the dealers of these brands we always see the two letters: GM. It is obviously General Motors, the endorsing brand. Again, what is the link between the cleaner Pledge, Wizard Air Freshener and Toilet Duck? They are all Johnson products. Greek style Sirtaki biscuits, English-style Pim's, Japanese-style Mikado and Prince chocolate biscuits are all endorsed by Lu. The endorsing brand gives its approval to a wide diversity of products grouped under product brands, line brands or range brands. At Lu, product brands are the norm. Golden Straws, Prince, Sirtaki and Figolu are all brand names. What is Sirtaki? One can describe it in a phrase as a new and unique concept in biscuits. Sirtaki is Sirtaki. In spite of the differences, Lu is the guarantor of their high quality and their finesse. This having been said, each product is then free to manifest its originality: that is what gives rise to the different names seen in the range.

Figure 7.7 symbolises endorsing brand strategy. As one can see, the endorsing brand is placed lower down because it acts as a base guarantor. Furthermore what the consumers buy is Pontiac, Opel, Pim's or Sirtaki. General Motors and Lu are supports and assume a secondary position.

The brand endorsement can be indicated in a graphic manner by placing the emblem of the endorser next to the brand name or in a nominal way by simply signing the endorser's name. Thus, the multiple retailer Casino utilises its brand as an umbrella for all its products except those over which they do not have any legitimacy (eg champagne and perfume). On these, one can read in fine print, 'selected by Casino'. In such a case, it implies the use of an endorsing

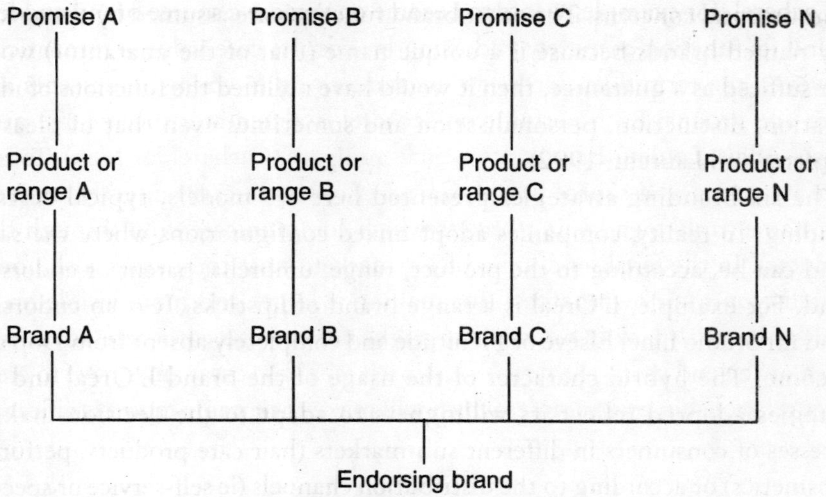

Figure 7.7 Endorsing brand strategy

brand as a quality seal. The manufacturer's identity remains and is endorsed by the quality seal of the retailer that has selected it.

The advantage of the endorsing brand is the greater freedom of movement that it allows. Like the source brand, the endorsing brand also profits from specifically named products. Each particular name evokes a forceful image and has a power of recall for the consumer which in turn enriches and nurtures the endorsing brand (at least in theory, as we shall see later in the analysis of brand dysfunctions).

The endorsing brand strategy is one of the least expensive ways of giving substance to a company name and allowing it to achieve a minimal brand status. Thus, we can see the initials ICI (Imperial Chemical Industries) on Valentine or Dulux paint pots, the name Bayer on packets of garden products and Monsanto on Round Up. The high quality of these brands is guaranteed by the names of these major organisations. On the other hand, through their presence in everyday life these companies become more familiar and close to the people, as in the case of ICI in France. Since the scientific and technical guarantees are assured by the endorsing brand, product brands can devote more time to expressing other facets of their personality.

Therefore, as one can see, there is a division of roles at each stage of the branding hierarchy. The endorsing brand becomes responsible for the guarantee which is essential for all brands and, today, these guarantees not only cover areas such as quality and scientific expertise, but also civic responsibility and environmental concerns. The other brand functions are assumed by the specifically named brands because if a unique name (that of the guarantor) would have sufficed as a guarantee, then it would have nullified the functions of identification, distinction, personalisation and sometimes even that of pleasure (Kapferer and Laurent, 1992).

The six branding strategies presented here are models, typical cases of branding. In reality, companies adopt mixed configurations where the same brand can be, according to the product, range, umbrella, parent or endorsing brand. For example, L'Oréal is a range brand of lipsticks. It is an endorsing brand for Studio Line, Elsève or Plénitude and completely absent from Dop and Lancôme. The hybrid character of the usage of the brand L'Oréal and the strategies adopted reflect its willingness to adapt to the decision-making processes of consumers in different sub-markets (hair care products, perfumes or cosmetics) or according to the distribution channels (ie self-service or specialist stores). In certain cases, L'Oréal guarantees reliability and technical capacity. In others, it wants to achieve recognition (ie in cosmetics) and therefore needs to place itself to the forefront. And finally, in still other cases, L'Oréal has to be invisible – either to avoid being associated with a low-price segment (Dop) or to avoid hurting one of its prestige products (Lancôme). Nevertheless, many hybrid situations result out of the series of small decisions that are taken as and when a new product is launched. Due to the lack of an overall plan for a brand's relationship with its products, a number of non-coherent branding strategies often exist side by side.

3M provides an interesting example of the accumulation of separate branding policies, with as many as five denominational stages (quintuple branding). This is shown in Figure 7.8. 3M is a company focused on high-tech research into industrial and domestic applications of adhesives. This covers a vast area which includes glues, obviously, but also films, cassettes, medical plasters, transparencies and overhead projector products, etc. The 3M name is synonymous with seriousness, power and heavy R&D. But this also leaves an image of coldness. Thus, to humanise the contact with the general buyer, the umbrella brand Scotch was created. Video cassettes, glue sticks and sellotape are all branded Scotch directly. But for the scouring pads, on the other hand, a line brand called Scotch-Brite was created. To counter the challenge of a rival product from Spontex (who simply call them scouring pads) Scotch replaced the generic name by a particular name, the 'Raccoon' (just like the Volkswagen Beetle). This differentiated its product and explained its advantages in a unique manner and gave it a closer and more friendly image.

The 'Raccoon' itself has been expanded into many versions – green, blue, red ... – depending on its shape and use. For its general consumer products, such as

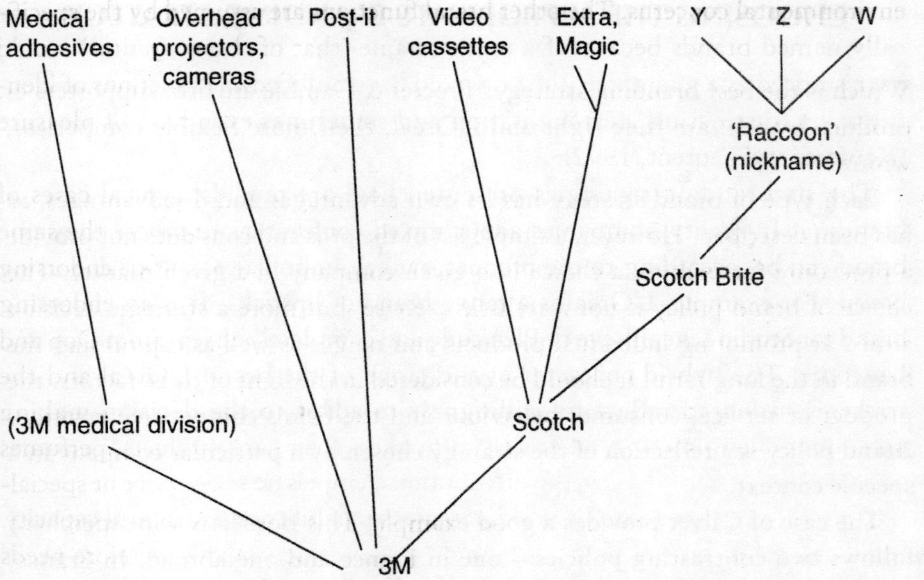

Figure 7.8 A case of brand proliferation and dilution of identity

sponges and glues, 3M was used as an endorsing brand with a signature in small print. Curiously enough, 3M is scarcely in evidence on Scotch cassettes. Is this to distinguish better from the video cassettes marked clearly and exclusively 3M and targeted at professional use? In fact, while 3M provides a guarantee of good performance and an endorsing brand for general consumer products, it serves as an umbrella brand for professional products: all the power and significance of the 3M name is reflected in products such as cameras, overhead projectors and dental cement (coming from the 3M health division). Post-it, the famous 'adhesive notes that serve as a memory tool or a message carrier', is also signed 3M. In order to patent this invention in a better way and to define it in a better manner than the long description used above, that it be given a proper name was to be expected.

Thus, depending on the level of professional end-use that a product has, or the need for an up-to-date image of excellence and performance, it is either signed 3M in a prominent manner or even perhaps exclusively. If not, 3M is present through the brand Scotch. Perhaps this is why the sellotape, Scotch Magic, used the name 3M only as a recall tool. On the other hand, aerosol glue for communication professionals bears the Scotch name in small print and 3M in large letters. There are also differentiated product advertisements for the 'Raccoon', general-use sellotape, Scotch cassettes and Post-it. Beyond the endorsing brand, there are no common codes of expression which appear independent in form and intent.

CHOOSING THE APPROPRIATE BRANDING STRATEGY

Which is the best branding strategy? Procter & Gamble are firm supporters of product brands: are they right and L'Oréal, their more flexible competitor, wrong?

Each type of brand strategy has its own advantages and disadvantages, as has been described. However, a simple list of the pros and cons does not provide a procedure for making a choice in a given company in a given market. The choice of brand policy is not a stylistic exercise, but more a strategic decision aimed at promoting individual products and ranges as well as capitalising the brand in the long term. It should be considered in the light of three factors: the product or service, consumer behaviour and the firm's competitive position. Brand policy is a reflection of the strategy chosen by a particular company in a specific context.

The case of Calvet provides a good example. This Bordeaux wine merchant follows two contrasting policies – one in France and one abroad. In France, Calvet is a product brand that refers to a specific type of Bordeaux wine. Abroad, however, it becomes a multi-product name – an umbrella brand covering not only Bordeaux wine but also burgundy and other regional reds, whites and rosés. This is to be expected. The French customer is more used to interpreting the various specifications on the wine label: region, vintage, type of vine, year, in some cases even the name of the retailer if he has created a reputation for choosing the best wine on a price–quality basis. In such a context, what can the name Calvet convey to the customer? The name only has a function if it can offer something that other Bordeaux cannot. This obviously implies a brand strategy with a specific differentiation in mind. Calvet is therefore a product name. In other countries, however, particularly where there is no substantial wine industry, the consumer may not be used to reading wine labels and may not understand the meaning of region, vintage, vines and 'appellation'. In Japan, they buy wine by the country and the colour. The Japanese consumer needs a name which will identify the wine and help reassure the customer, thus the umbrella brand is the best choice. Calvet can therefore cover many generic regional French wines and serve as an endorsing brand.

Why does the Wagons-Lits Hotel Division use the brand PLM Azur as an endorser, a simple signature in small print after the specific name of the hotel (New Cataract in Egypt, Sahara Palace in Tunisia, Saint-Tropez Beach in Saint Martin)? On the other hand, why does Pullman sign 'Pullman' in bold followed by the specific name of a hotel for its new four-star international hotel chain (The Pullman Konigshof in Bonn, the Pullman Part-Dieu in Lyon, the Pullman Rotary in Geneva)? PLM Azur is the brand for holiday hotels. When choosing their holidays, customers are given a catalogue six months in advance. The catalogue, now on CD-Rom and the Internet, gives a complete description of the hotel, its characteristics, special features and even the cost. What then is the function of the brand in such a context? There is nothing that the customer cannot see for himself. The offer is already very explicit. However, for distant locations, there may be a big difference between the promise and the reality and the customer needs to be reassured that there is little risk. This becomes the function of the endorsing brand PLM Azur. It becomes the final guarantor while the holidaymaker builds his dreams around the actual hotel itself.

But the senior executive sent to Ankara in Turkey for three days to negotiate a deal has no time to dream. He knows the difficulties of the task ahead and therefore wants to avoid all stress. This class of customer is looking for a flawless level of service as far as the hotel is concerned. For him, the brand is an indicator of a specific level of quality of service which does not change from one city to another, nor from one country to another. The brand is a product brand and it matches specific demands. Nevertheless, Pullman does not want to be inflexibly uniform, reproducing room plans and even the furniture in one city after another (as with Novotel). The local suffix also indicates that it is open to influence from the host country where the hotel is located.

Club Med follows a third path – a range brand policy. Although the range has come to be split into segments – from the economy hut villages to the luxury golf hotels – both in summer and winter around the world, the brand name remains unique as does the advertising campaign. Customers only have to specify the chosen geographic destination. This denominative policy is their strategy in a nutshell: Club Med's principles, values and methods cover, transform and group together all these different products. Their common factors are stronger than their differences. The only notable development in their policy has been the progression to the brand name, Club Med – the reference to the Mediterranean having become obsolete as a result of geographical extension, bearing no significance for Americans, Japanese or South Africans.

As we can see, the decision to adopt a denominative policy is not prompted by any aesthetic or formal desire. It stems from the recognition of the brand's role as expected by the customer, compared with the function and meaning of possible product, range and line specific names, and that of other quality indicators such as packaging, catalogue, advertising and the retailer's own recommendations and advice. Nevertheless, given the same data about customers, no two companies will follow the same policy of nominal identities since their precise strategies will differ. Their individual desires will infiltrate the branding process. A comparison between the two cosmetic brands Lancôme and Clarins is illustrative of this factor.

In the cosmetic market there are thousands of products and many scientific terms, and innovations are essential. This is what leads to an opacity in the market. Brands serve as milestones and a question that is frequently asked is which alternative strategy should be used: line products or mono-products? There is no single answer to such a general question: it depends a lot on the brand's conception of itself.

Lancôme prefers a mono-product policy with only a small range derived from the leading product (Progress for the face, eye-liner, anti-wrinkle cream, etc). Thus, in 1990, the brand chose to launch mono-products for body care, each with its own brand instead of a line under one name. There was Cadence for the body (moisturiser), Exfoliance (scrub) and Sculptural (slimmer). Lancôme is not an endorsing brand. It wants to be a source brand and therefore the creator of a precise vision, that of French elegance. The brand wants to serve as a vehicle to express:

- the product's technological level and its performance;
- luxury as perceived in a French manner, that is to say natural sophistication. Lancôme makes laboratories appear charming.

Lancôme expresses itself through its products and the services that surround them (the dialogue and the advice of salespeople). They want a brand policy that is coherent and easily understandable on two levels: the consumer and the seller. But, consumers actually respond badly to brand policy in this sector: they do not usually memorise brand names and may simply ask for the 'moisturising cream from Lancôme' when they enter the shop. The sales assistant then explains that there are two: Hydrix and Transhydrix. The existence of two names helps the assistant explain the existence of multiple products. Through these different product names, the customer understands the different products and the assistant can subsequently promote each one by stressing their individual functions, use and specific characteristics. Thus, at Lancôme, they try to give each product a different name to reflect a function (Nutrix nurtures the skin, Hydrix moisturises it and Forte-Vital makes it firmer) or the main ingredient if it is something new or revolutionary (eg Niosome contains niosomes, Oligo-Majors has oligo elements). This naming policy makes the sales pitch clearer because it explains the differences between the products and other closely positioned products and therefore avoids the confusion that could have occurred had they been in the same line and under a single common name.

This would appear to close the argument clearly between product brands and line brands in favour of the former as far as cosmetics are concerned. But, at Clarins, as a general rule, there are no mono-products and their 70 products are all grouped into lines. Since Clarins is not Lancôme, it does not have the same image, the same identity or the same conception of itself. It projects itself as a Beauty Institute and the profession of beautician is very important to them. This concept implies the use of many products belonging to the same line, just as in a prescription. A mono-product cannot do everything and from this arises the preference for product lines that act in synergy. Clarins wants to create stable lines that can last for years and are in conformity with its identity, personality and brand culture. Finally, it prefers objective product promises rather than a plethora of slogans for mono-products that all play on one factor, presently 'victory over ageing'. From this arises the names for their products, which are always in the beauty sector. The names are always descriptive of the product's actions and do not play upon dreams and fantasies as did Christian Dior when he launched 'Capture'. At Clarins, names are constituted of two or three words, for example, 'Multi-Repair Restructuring Lotion'.

In the past, the creation of any new product was usually also accompanied by the creation of a new brand. In christening the new brand, the product manager gave it life. Without a name, the product had no real existence. Once branded, it had a life. In 1981, at 3M, 244 new brands were created and registered. In 1991, only four new brands were created. The same thing happened at Nestlé: in 1991, the company created 101 new products but only five new brands. The age of brand multiplication is over. What has led to this change in practice?

The realisation that brands are the true capital of the company has led to this revolution. By capitalising on a few brands, companies had to sustain their equity by nurturing them through constant innovations and line or range extensions. Therefore, the question 'what name do we choose?' becomes 'which new product should we put under which already existing brand?'

Companies with decentralised management are particularly susceptible to brand proliferation. Thus, 3M, in spite of its 29th rank in the Fortune 500 companies and its 60,000 products, remains relatively unknown. One part of the explanation for this is the excessive number of trademarks with which it is burdened: over 1500. In order to solve this problem, 3M decided to take the cat by the tail and created a branding committee at the highest level (Corporate Branding Policy Committee) whose mission was to establish a precise doctrine regarding brand policy. Its approval was necessary before the creation of any new brand. Reflecting on the logic of brand capital, it was decided that from then on 3M would be used to sign or guarantee all products (except the cosmetic line). The second decision was the banning of the use of more than two names on one product (as was the case with Scotch Magic) in order to abolish brand pile-ups, as was shown in Figure 7.8. In order to facilitate the integration of the new brand policy that capitalised on a few key brands (also called primary or power brands), 3M distributed, to all its subsidiaries, a guide explaining the policy to be followed in case of branding when faced with a new product. The creation of this guide led to a drastic fall in the requests for new brand creation: be it parent brands (like Scotch) or daughter brand (like Magic).

The decision tree shown in Figure 7.9 puts each innovation through four questions which serve as filters to limit the creation of a new brand to certain very specific circumstances (like Post-it). The first filter question asks if the innovation satisfies one of the following four criteria: Is it a top priority innovation? Does it create a new kind of price/quality relationship? Does it create a new product category that did not exist until then? Is it the outcome of an acquisition? The second filter question asks whether the brand could not be used to nurture an already existing parent brand in 3M's primary brands portfolio. The third filter question seeks to discover whether the new product can provide the occasion for the creation of a new parent brand. The last filter question evaluates the capacity of the new product to justify the creation of a new secondary brand (daughter brand). From the decision tree emerge six exhaustive branding possibilities that are based on measurable market parameters. They go from the extremely simple (slides for overhead projectors from 3M) to multiple level branding (Scotch Magic, the sellotape from 3M). As expected,

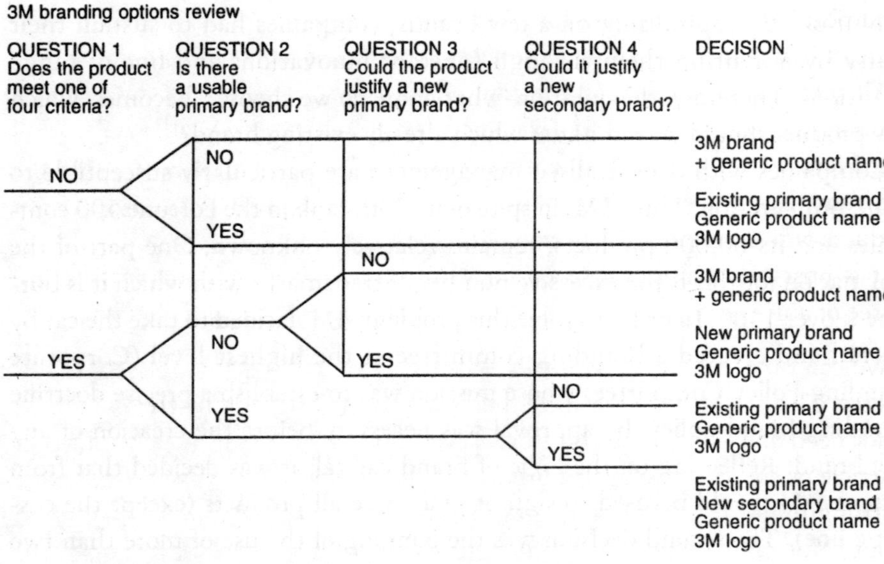

Figure 7.9 3M branding options review

the creation of a new brand (primary or secondary) became the exception rather than the rule. A number of restrictive conditions had to be fulfilled first: mainly, that the innovation creates new primary demand and that none of the existing primary brands are suited.

PRODUCT NAMES: AUTONOMY OR AFFILIATION?

Fiat distinguish their cars by giving each one of them a proper name: eg Panda, Uno, Tipo, Regatta. For years Renault chose to number their models: eg R4, R5, R19, R21, R25, but started a revolution in 1990 with the Clio, followed by the Safrane, the Laguna and the Twingo. BMW grades its brand on a numbered scale: the 3, 5, 7 series. As for Citroën, they coded their range with letters such as AX, BX, CX until the voluntary revolution through the appellation Xantia.

Dior launched its perfumes under the names Diorella, Diorissimo, Miss Dior, and then Poison and Fahrenheit. Its cosmetic products are sold under the names Capture and Resultante, but also Hydra-Dior. Taking the same products, Lancôme uses Niosome or Noctosome and Clarins 'Multi-Reducing' or 'Multi-restoring Cream'.

In the information systems industry, the leading American company ADP takes the extreme stance in umbrella branding by not giving any specific name to their human resource management software. We therefore have ADP-Fast Pay, ADP-Interactive Personal Package or the ADP-Benefit System. Sprint uses its corporate name as a prefix for all of its service-names (ie Sprintvoice). ATT creates a family link by calling its services True-X (ie True Voice).

All these examples denote a certain relationship between the brand and its products, a choice between two extremes: complete autonomy and total affiliation. Here we see the basic dilemma brought about by the brand's two concomitant, but scarcely compatible, aims of creating a distinction between products while retaining the notion of their origins.

It is possible to identify seven forms of strategy each with an increasing degree of autonomy:

1 We can buy Lacoste shirts, socks, jackets, sweaters, rackets and eau de toilette. The products do not have their own names and, as a matter of fact, do not need one. The brand transforms everything that it embraces, turning an article of everyday use into a product of distinction. This is the attitude of a strong brand. A sweater only has to bear the Lacoste symbol for it to stand out. Not only is it noticed, but it also stands out due to the aura created around it. The power of the brand releases it from the confines of the com-

mon lot. This is not a characteristic restricted to luxury goods – it can apply to any brand aiming to raise the overall status of its products. It is the case with St Michael at Marks & Spencer and Sony. On the other hand, this policy is unsuited to weaker brands since they are unable to inject a common substance or spirit to the products bearing their name.

2 Before naming their cars Class A, C, E or S, Mercedes called them the 190, 200, etc. The brand name dominates the product. This policy emphasises a single brand whose image is reflected in every model. Whichever model he buys, the customer will discover all the subjective and objective attributes which go to make up the brand identity. The 190 was not an inferior Mercedes – it was simply the first Mercedes. Comparative figures deal with product performance in such matters as engine power, but do not indicate that there is less 'Mercedes' in the 190 model than in the 300 model. Porsche made the mistake of forgetting this reasoning. The 924 not only stood for a front-located motor, but it also bore no relation to Porsche itself. Together with the 944, the 924 was Porsche only in name. The brand had failed to fully express its difference and superiority in this price bracket. The denominative policy was a source of deception and led to boomerang effects on the brand image itself.

3 Everyone knows that Nescafé, Nescore, Nesquik and Nestea are all part of the same brand, as are the chocolate or the condensed milk. In naming their perfumes Diorissimo, Miss Dior or Diorella, Dior provides a forceful reminder of the source brand. Each product is only a variation of the brand's values arising from a common core. Diorissimo is the height of Dior, while Miss Dior is the representation of the young woman in the world of Dior. This close association between the brand and the product allows the rising brand to express its identity and system of values through those little special touches. It has its limits: it should not be applied to too many products at the same time because the source brand then becomes nothing more than a technical prefix – a simple reminder linking together a random assortment of products. Multiplication of Dior-X products would exhaust the meaning of Dior. This is what happened to Nestlé.

4 When Lancôme calls its products Niosome or Noctosome, it is obvious that they wish to show a link between the brand and the product by using the suffix 'ome'. The brand takes them under its wings and helps express their innovating qualities. It does not want to serve the product, rather to serve itself.

5 Clarins calls its products 'Multi-Tensing Gel', 'Multi-Restoring Fluid' and it would be a mistake to see these terms as simply generic. In fact, 'multi' is part and parcel of Clarins' core identity. There are two reasons for this. First,

the prefix appears in all languages. Secondly, Clarins chose to use the term even though it cannot be patented and is widely used in the pharmaceutical field, because 'multi' refers to a complete course of treatment and that corresponds to the Clarins identity and vision: a product line rather than mono-products, many steps rather than just one.

6 The penultimate stage in the advancement of product autonomy (or, if one prefers, loss of affiliation) is seen in the product's own name. Dior's Capture and Poison are an example in luxury products, Johnson's Pledge in household maintenance goods. Clarins would never have chosen the name Capture since it has poetic and symbolic connotations, but it is perfectly acceptable to Dior because its nominal and semantic detachment allows Dior to extend without destabilising the heart of the brand. In this case, the product–brand relationship is a bottom-up one. New meaning rises to the heart of the brand and the brand gladly accepts this new lifeblood. Exhausted or weak brands find this relationship restores life. In the car industry, for example, when a brand is insufficiently strong itself and cannot pass any positive image on to the products which are in no position to help themselves because they have names such as R5, R9, R19, R21 and R25, these products have to be boosted with their own personality since the brand is unable to provide sufficient help. This is probably why Renault turned to an 'own-name' policy in 1990 with the appearance of Clio and Twingo. These names help the customer to adapt to the model, and identify with it even if he is only moderately attracted by the brand. Volkswagen had done the same with the Golf. The product name creates its specific brand equity and is a booster of product personality.

7 The final stage refers to the fully autonomous product brand that exists without any reference to its source or company: Varilux (all-distance vision glasses), Ariel, Dash, Tide, etc.

Thus, each of the above policies has its own message and rationale. The choice of one of them depends greatly on the strength of the brand, its will, the strength of the new products and the commercial strategy.

There is a close relationship between the company's growth policy and its choice of product names. Some companies have an extensive policy to capture market share while others adopt a more intensive approach. In the first case, growth is achieved through the acquisition of new clients and in such circumstances it is not desirable to present products as part of a range. It is better to present them as distinct products with specific names. This is Procter & Gamble's strategy in the detergent market. Ariel, Dash, Bonux and Vizir cover the entire market. If, on the other hand, the company opts for an intensive sales development policy for existing clients, then product names should resemble each other and appear to belong to the same group. The client who buys one product should be tempted into buying the other products of what appears to be a complete range satisfying other needs too. Having tried Mac Write the computer user will wish to move to Mac Paint or any other software with the prefix Mac!

Finally, the choice of the name depends upon the strength of the brand. Twenty years ago Fiat had a very bad image outside of Italy and this handicapped the sales of new models. Would it be possible to raise the image through ad campaigns for the brand? It is not easy to change a stereotype. Also, the strategy consisted of no longer selling the products through the brand, but rather the brand through the products. Since then, Fiat has given its models their own name in order to give them a strong personality: Tipo, Ritmo, Panda, Regatta, Croma. Each one has to find the energy for market penetration within itself and the names are voluntarily unrelated to Fiat. As a rule, most generalist brands follow Fiat's policy. Specialist car makers do not give first names to their cars.

RETAILER BRANDING STRATEGIES

Nothing illustrates the strategic dimension of brand policy better than a comparison between similar companies in competition in the same sector. This is the case with the retail sector. Faced with the same potential clientele, they opt for different branding policies that reflect their individual identities and strategic preferences. Given that in the retail sector brand policies have their own jargon, we will clarify them first before linking them to the concepts and terms presented in this chapter.

The retailer's brand is not a recent phenomenon. Sainsbury started it as far back as 1869. The first retailer to officially register its brand in France was the Coop in 1929, and until 1976 there were very few changes. These were only umbrella brands, exclusive to the retailer and comprising a number of products within the same category (groceries or household-ware or cosmetics). The main function of these brands was to serve as a defence tool for the retailers against suppliers that would not supply to them.

In 1976, with Carrefour, the establishment of a new type of retailer brand known as the banner brand was seen. This brand was named 'free products' at Carrefour, 'orange products' at Euromarche, 'white products' at Genty, 'super confidence products' at Casino ...

Grouping many products under it, the banner brand was also an umbrella brand. It appeared in no-nonsense packaging without artwork or embellishment and in a single colour (white, orange, etc). It bore no signature, only a guarantee in the visual form of its emblem or initials.

As its name suggests, the banner brand represented an offensive strategy, against manufacturers' brands. This was an occasion for an in-depth renewal of the communication strategies of those hypermarket chains that could develop their vision and competitiveness through support from specific products. Carrefour was thus able to present itself as the consumer's champion, hence the choice of the term 'freedom' to name its new product line. Its positioning was simple: 'as good as national brands and cheaper' (20 per cent cheaper). Thus, these banner brands gave the retailers a new visibility and also, for some, the beginning of an identity. They were moving away from the price–choice–quality–service type of communication and were starting to affirm their culture, motivation and focus.

Besides the competitive interest between distributors, banner products were also interesting in the sense that they won over public opinion in their favour, an indispensable factor in the competition that was inevitable between distributors and manufacturers in the future. In fact, while the image of the large retail stores had greatly suffered due to the elimination of smaller neighbourhood grocery stores, Carrefour's 'freedom' banner products advertised, in all kinds of media, that manufacturers' brands were only an instrument of slavery for the customer and that it was time to liberate the consumer from their clutches. And silence meant consent: manufacturers, unused to collective actions, did not react and thereby lost a battle because of their inaction.

Increasing competition led to the appearance of many generic or unbranded products on supermarket shelves. Though admittedly of lower quality than national brands, they were 30 to 40 per cent cheaper. These products came without any frills, usually in simple white packaging and with nothing but a simple description of the product (eg sugar, oil, etc). This led to a confusion in the consumer's mind as to the difference between low-priced generic products and banner brands. The problem was that the latter were supposed to improve the image of the retailer and lend an image of quality. The confusion threatened to have the reverse effect and drag the image of the retailer down. Carrefour therefore stopped selling its 'freedom' line and launched instead a policy of corporate branding. This policy consisted of putting the store's own name on the products. It was not new – Sainsbury's, Migros in Switzerland and Jewel in the US had been doing it for a long time.

The retailer name can be used in many ways:

- on its own on the products concerned. In such a case it is an umbrella brand and covers a number of different products. Thus, there exist not only Carrefour corn flakes, but also frozen fish, yoghurt, fruit beverages, sports bags, car fluids, etc;
- alone, on the products, it serves as a line brand if these different products are united by some common feature, some concept. This is the case with Monoprix Fitness or Monoprix Green Line. Under the retailer brand name we have the family name of the products that fulfil certain criteria (health products or ecology-oriented products);
- as a signature with another name. In such a case it is an endorsing brand. Carrefour signs its name in fine print on the lower right-hand corner of F. Delacour champagne. In the same manner, the name Printemps appears on ready-to-wear brands such as Essentials and the name is marked both on the tags as well as the products.

The third kind of retailer's brand is called 'own-brand' or private label and it has a name different from that of the retailer: eg Brummel is an 'own-brand' for Printemps. Own-brands can be used as:

- a product brand: as is the case with many beers, biscuits and other food products (Sainsbury's Crunch);
- a line brand: Micro Line hair gel at Auchan hypermarkets is a copy of L'Oréal's Studio Line;
- a range brand: Tex for fabric at Carrefour, or Kenmore, the home appliance brand of Sears Roebuck;
- an umbrella brand such as St Michael, President's Choice, World Classics.

Compared to older, pioneer own-brands, the latter are different in that they are often product or line brands and they are meant to attract the clientele of a targeted manufacturer's brand. It is this that led to the name 'counter-brand' or 'copycat brand'. For instance, Asda Puffin was a copycat of the Penguin biscuit.

The basic advantage of copycat brands is the possibility of their multiplying indefinitely: thus Auchan has more than a hundred. Faced with a market that is being segmented more and more, the retailer can put a copycat brand in each segment, which was not possible under a common single label. Auchan has three different counter-brands for the three segments of whisky. This policy allows for a great flexibility to enter into niches. Compared to other retailers who put their name on products and then reject the manufacturers' brands by simply delisting them, own-brands achieve the same results but more discreetly. The consumer here has the impression of having a much larger and varied choice and reacts less to the disappearance of the big brands.

To maximise their sales, the counter-brand strategy consists of choosing a brand name, packaging, an outer design and colours that are as close as possible to those of the target brand. This creates a confusion in the consumer's mind. Realising that a flux of clientele had been created by the manufacturer's brand due to heavy investment in research and development, quality, performance and marketing, the distributor creates a copy and packs it in the same manner as the original. The simplest way of reducing costs and risk is to imitate closely the marketing strategy employed by the manufacturer's brand. There is a fine line between a counter-brand and a counterfeit and several retailers have already crossed it. But the law can do little about it: most manufacturers are reluctant to sue retailers on the grounds of unfair competition for fear of seeing their products thrown off the retailer's shelves. Recently, however, the manufacturers of the Penguin biscuit won such a case against the Asda copy, Puffin.

As we can see, in spite of a difference in terminology, it is possible to establish a link between the manufacturers' branding strategies examined in this chapter and the concepts involved in retailer branding (see Table 7.1). They are, however, separate on two counts: manufacturers are unable to copy each other as much as the copycat brands not only because counterfeiting is illegal but also because manufacturers do not hesitate to sue each other. Secondly, except in rare cases where the retailer has also vertically integrated the production process, the name of the actual producer of the private label is always hidden and cannot be verified. This also poses the problem in giving a quality seal to a retailer's brand, because manufacturers may be changed from time to time.

Table 7.1 Relative functions of retailers' and manufacturers' named brands

	Brand owner	
Brand's main purpose	**Manufacturer**	**Retailer**
To capture clientele of a targeted brand		Counter-brand Copy-cat brand
To personalise the product	Product brand	Own-label
To incorporate the product among others	Line brand Range brand	Own-label
To identify the product source	Umbrella brand Source brand Endorsing brand	(Banner brand) Retailer named brand
To indicate the manufacturer	Corporate branding	

Besides the major functions expected of a brand, the choice of branding strategy by a retailer depends on many parameters:

- The image value of the store name weighs upon the choice. If it uses the store name, the retailer brand assumes the name is a potential guarantor and benefits from close proximity and familiarity;
- The strategy also depends on the product's degree of involvement. All products do not bear the same importance for the consumer: some are more important than others and some may even be totally secondary. The sources of this importance may vary:
  - 'necessary' products are bought out of necessity: we expect functional utility of them and that is all. These range from paper handkerchiefs (less involving) to vacuum-cleaners (more involving);
  - 'pleasure' products have a pleasure function and can vary from caramel custard to a hi-fi system;
  - ego-expressive products have a social function and through them the buyer reveals his/her personality: this concerns cigarettes, soft drinks, beers and also ready-to-wear clothing.

  Naturally, the products can have more than one source of involvement and it is difficult to apply one retailer brand to ego-expressive products: when these products are displayed, one does not want to create a bad impression, unless the store is one of great renown and distinction (eg Hediard, Fauchon, Harrod's, etc). The fact that Carrefour puts its name in really small letters even if it is offering champagne speaks more of the desires of the enterprise than consumer choice. When the source of involvement is strictly functional, a single umbrella brand can cover many different categories. In such a case, the brand signifies an excellent price–quality relationship, and can embrace a range of prices.

- The motivation of the distributor is also a determining factor. Brand management for the retailer is not, as is often wrongly believed, an exercise in graphics and creativity, and is not restricted to finding a name and good packaging. It is a new profession which implies a concentration on the consumer and the application of both human and financial resources to analyse the market and the consumer's demands, to research and development, to the establishment and follow-up of clients, to permanent quality control checks, and, more and more important, to the capacity for new product development.

These three parameters explain why many retailers do not want to have retailer brand policies, while others practise them to a certain extent and yet more follow them with a passion. The choice reflects an evaluation of the constraints and the identity of the retailer. Right from the start, Casino, like the Swiss Migros, saw itself as an alternative solution to the classic channels of distribution. The retailer must follow in his own tracks and according to his image of himself. He has a mission: to offer a quality product at a low price. To achieve this, Casino has integrated a part of the production process and done away with national brands wherever it could. The brand Casino lives through the products that it signs. It wants to be capable of covering all sectors at all levels. That is why the retailer brand is an umbrella brand everywhere. The only exceptions are so-called products of status needing a strong product brand. In such a case, the retailer's name manifests itself only as that of an endorsing brand.

Carrefour wants to be the quality multiple retailer in France. After its 'freedom products' came the 'concerted products', comparative surveys and other manifestations of its consumer orientation. The retailer obviously puts its name to many of the products, but not all of them. Doing so would give an impression of uniformity and the loss of the freedom of choice. Also, Carrefour uses its name primarily in the grocery section which is at the heart of the original function of a supermarket. Carrefour also puts its name to innovative products and thereby nurtures its image through these exclusive products. At the same time, textile products have their own umbrella brand, Tex.

Intersport is, above all, a commercial retailer. Here, there is hardly any philosophy, project or vision. The chain does not really have an identity. But, it does have a concept of positioning: choice. That is why they have own-brands: Etirel for clothes, Techno Pro for tennis, McKinley for winter sports, Nakamura for bikes, etc.

Empirical research has demonstrated that the effectiveness of a branding policy interacts with other variables such as the type of packaging (differentiated or copycat), the reputation of the store name and the objective quality of the distributor's product (compared to that of the market leader). Thus, the Lewi and Kapferer (1996) field experiment showed that:

- if the private label quality matches that of the leading brand (with blind tests as evidence) and if the store name has a strong image, in order to maximise market share the best strategy is to use the store name and a highly differentiated packaging. In brief, the distributor's brand should behave as a real brand. This option is superior to that of using look-alike packaging and trademark infringement;

- the reverse is true, however, if the retailer does not wish to use its own store name as a brand name. Then, although inferior to the two former cases, the best strategy is that of copycat branding.

FAILURES IN BRAND-PRODUCT RELATIONSHIPS: A FEW CLASSIC EXAMPLES

Branding structures aim at optimally managing the image flows. Sometimes, the downward flow from the brand to the product needs to be emphasised when it is thought that sales could be increased by leveraging the brand. Sometimes the brand needs to be regenerated with the help of a bottom-up image flow. Finally, horizontal flows between the products themselves can be a source of added value and may lead consumers to try more products in the range.

Not all brand structures actually succeed in achieving the desired result: building up brand capital, promoting sales. Here we will deal with some classic examples of failure.

The first is where the brand simply disappears behind one of the products and ceases to have an identity of its own. Therefore, instead of the two brand stages as there should be, there is only one step, that of the product. The parent brand lacks meaning. This situation characterised Nina Ricci, Cacharel, Du Pont and many others. The process is classic: for 15 years Nina Ricci was represented only by L'Air du Temps, its world best-selling perfume. In the end, the brand was overshadowed by the product. The images of the two were mixed and Nina Ricci became confused with the image of ethereal young girls, the image of L'Air du Temps. This was not an ideal situation. Obviously, something did remain of the brand, but this needed to be revitalised so that the brand could regain strength over other products.

The second classic problem is that of brand product disconnection. Many will have heard of Varilux, a revolutionary lens for spectacles which has changed the life of many long-sighted persons. But not many will have heard of Essilor even though it is the world's largest manufacturer of contact lenses and Varilux is one of its products. The name has no significance as far as the public is concerned. Since it prefers to remain in the background, it cannot be used as an endorsing brand. Today Essilor feels endangered by the arrival of brands such as Seiko and Nikon. Would you prefer your glasses with Seiko, Nikon or Essilor lenses? The first two names have already accumulated a worldwide brand awareness, founded on the basis of meticulous precision and high technology for Seiko, to which Nikon has added mastery in the field of optics.

Funnily enough, this phenomenon of brand product disconnection also affects Corning. Though the company is barely known, it owns the Pyrex, Vision and Sunsitive brands which have been badly managed and do not function as brands. For the public, Pyrex is not a brand but a generic name, a kind of ware. Also, since they are not formally related to Corning, they do not add to its brand capital and do not help its image or reputation. Thus, Corning does not gain from it and cannot be used as an endorsement brand for other products. The company itself is very strong, but Corning, as a brand, is not.

The final breakdown of brand product relationships can occur due to the ill-effects of certain accounting principles which conflict with brand policy. This is illustrated in the case of Playtex. The Playtex communication strategy consists in theory of constructing the brand's meaning through its products. The brand has many specific product lines such as Cross Your Heart and Super Look bras, Six o'clock girdles, etc. The idea was that by communicating about these product lines, the Playtex brand itself would acquire a specific meaning in the eyes of consumers and individual lines could then be supported without any advertising.

The problem was that reality was not like that. The intended plan was not pursued. Making each product line financially accountable led to the communication being restricted to one or two lines only. The Playtex brand identity no longer enjoyed the rich benefits of an entire product range. It was supported only by the specific characteristics of those lines which were advertised (in this instance, Cross Your Heart). Hence the whole brand acquired a harsh, functional connotation which was Cross Your Heart's positioning. Moreover, since the other product lines were not getting any advertising, they inherited an image which, instead of coming from Playtex, came *de facto* from Cross Your Heart. The practice of individual, financially accountable lines caused the brand meaning to be modified and in the end to be overshadowed by the image of those few products that were capable of generating sufficient financial resources for communication. In order to get itself out of this mess, Playtex Europe overthrew a taboo in company policy by launching a specific brand campaign on Playtex itself, to make it more up-to-date and attractive and add value to all its lines which do not advertise.

CORPORATE BRANDS AND PRODUCT BRANDS

For years, companies have hidden behind their brands. Through prudence and fear of being affected in case of brand failure, company names have been separate from those of the brands. Thus Procter & Gamble remain unknown to the public while their brands are the stars (Ariel, Pampers). In fact, it is this that allowed the company to keep its turnover stable when the rumour of it being linked to a sect raged through the United States. The brands, well-distanced from the company itself, suffered no setback. Nevertheless, such instances are rare and the tendency is more towards transparency due to communication obligations. Also, the public wants to know, in larger numbers than before, who are the actors behind the brands. They want to know who is the 'brand behind the brand'. This also explains why so many companies have taken on the names of their most famous brands (eg Alcatel-Alsthom, Danone). They get more visibility and acknowledgement. This helps the financial investor also, in cases where he is not an expert or very well-informed, to understand better what he is buying. It may also create a beneficial confusion for the brand itself. After it bought Audi, Seat and Skoda, the VAG Corporation (otherwise known as the Volkswagen Group) is now number one in Europe on a cumulative basis. However, many people mistakenly speak of Volkswagen as a brand being the number one in Europe.

The trend towards greater visibility of corporate names also has other causes. Distribution is one of them. Distributors, multiple retailers and hypermarket chains are not very interested in brands. Their fundamental relationship is with corporations, not with brands. It is a business relationship. The name of the powerful corporation is therefore a potent reminder of that relationship.

Only corporate names can endow brands with stature, an extra-dimension calling for respect. Would Audi have succeeded in its remarkable recovery had it not been known that Audi belonged to the Volkswagen Group? The same holds true for Seat and Skoda. Nissan's status will change because it is now part of the Ford group. As long as car makes are only brands and not part of a larger and more dynamic corporation, they arouse perceived risk among consumers and do not guarantee a long-term presence.

Many companies sell in industrial and commercial markets at the same time. Here, there is the problem of having to choose between the use of product brands or the use of the corporate reputation to support the products. This depends on the quality of the company's endorsement and the degree of visibility that it wants to acquire. In practice, the respective weight to be attributed to the product brand and the corporate brand depends on a case-by-case analysis of the returns brought by each of them on the many targets concerned. Table 7.2 presents the outline of such an analysis.

At ICI three kinds of brand policy are used (see Figure 7.10):

- The first policy is the classic umbrella brand where the products keep their generic names and are signed with the corporate name. Most often this concerns raw materials and undifferentiated products where the company guar-

Table 7.2 Shared roles of the corporate and product brand

Targets	Product brand	Corporate brand
Customers	+++++	+
Trade associations	++++	+
Employees	+++	++
Suppliers	+++	+++
Press	+++	+++
Issues groups	++	++++
Local community	++	++++
Academia	++	++++
Regulatory authorities	+	++++
Government commission	+	++++
Financial markets	+	+++++
Stockholders	+	+++++

antees a certain quality and the differentiation is essentially commercial (ie special conditions offered to the client on a case-by-case basis). An example would be ICI Polyurethanes.

- The second policy is that of the endorsing brand. The company puts its name beside the product brand and this confers a status of high technology and reliability to the product. Thus, Dulux paints are accompanied by the ICI logo.

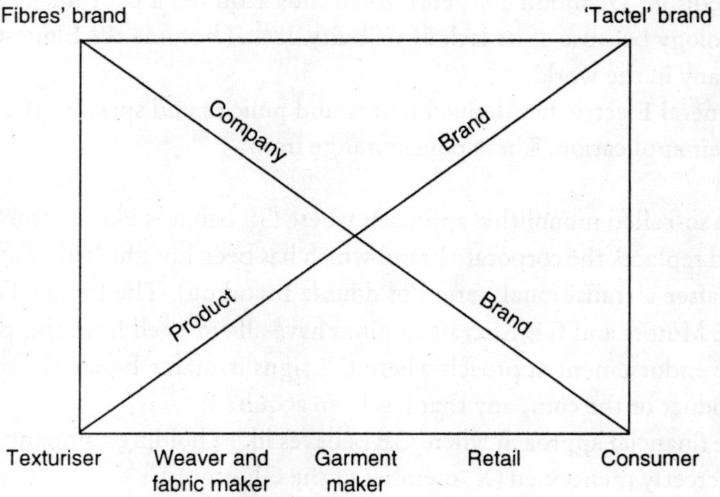

Figure 7.10 Corporate and product branding at ICI

- The third policy makes exclusive use of the product brand. Tactel is one of the most widely sold fibres but it never mentions ICI. The product is sold to the textile industry and to the fashion world, and it is feared that the mention of the ICI name may alter the positive images linked to Tactel. Similarly the insecticide, Karate, which is sold throughout the world, also does not make any mention of ICI. Does this have anything to do with not wanting to step on ecological toes and avoid the possibility of blame regarding the harmful effects of pesticides on ground water? This situation is not only changing through time, but it also changes according to the company. Decis, the world leader in pesticides, makes a reference to Roussel Uclaf (Agrevo division) on its packaging. Similarly, to benefit from its innovations, Du Pont de Nemours mentions clearly 'Lycra by Du Pont' on all its communications for Lycra, the fabric that has revolutionised women's lingerie.

In the industrial sector where external growth is the norm, the question of the status of corporate brands that have been acquired crops up again. Should they be left independent? Should they disappear? Should they be endorsed with a simple visual symbol of the parent company? Or joined to the name of the parent company? If they behave as mere holding companies such firms should not be surprised by their low public recognition. For instance, although it was founded in 1969 and was one of the largest chemical companies in the world, Akzo remained largely unknown. No wonder: all the companies acquired had kept their own company names and brand names (Warner Lambert, Stauffer, Montedison, Diamond Salt, etc). Akzo thus acquired a poor image in terms of technology because of its lack of visibility. It had become the biggest unknown company in the world.

General Electric has defined four brand policies and specifies the conditions for their application. These policies range from:

- the so-called monolithic approach where GE behaves like an umbrella brand and replaces the corporate brand which has been bought (either immediately or after a transitional period of double branding). The brands GE Silicons, GE Motors and GE Aircraft Engines have all emerged from this process;
- the endorsement approach where GE signs its name beside the name of the product or the company that has been acquired;
- the financial approach where GE behaves like a holding company and is only discreetly mentioned (X, member of the GE group);
- the autonomous approach where the acquired company or product makes no reference to GE.

To decide upon a policy, GE uses six selection criteria:

1 Does GE control the company?
2 Does GE have long-term commitments in this company?
3 Does the product category have an image value? Dynamic or not?
4 Is there a strong demand for GE quality in this industry?
5 Is the corporate brand which has been bought strong?
6 What could be the resultant impact on GE?

8

Brand extension

Brand extension is on the increase. When they wish to enter markets from which they have been absent, more and more companies do so using the name of one of their existing brands, rather than using a new brand name created for that purpose. Figures testify to this trend. According to the Nielsen Company, between 1977 and 1984 40 per cent of new product launches in the United States in the supermarket sector were brand extensions. The trend has since become stronger, both there and in Europe. Yet brand extension is not a recent phenomenon (Gamble, 1967). It is inherent in the luxury goods sector: the luxury brands originating in haute couture have extended to accessories, fancy leather goods, jewellery, watch-making, even tableware and cosmetics.

In the same way, the first distributors' brands (Migros in Switzerland, St Michael in Great Britain) covered several differentiated categories of products. Industrial brands themselves were extended beyond their initial product type to cover a range of diversified activities under the same name: Siemens, Philips and Mitsubishi have been using brand extension for a long time. Indeed, brand extension is even used systematically by Japanese conglomerates: Mitsubishi includes shipyards, nuclear plants, cars, high-fidelity systems, banks and even food under the three-diamond brand (the visual symbol of Mitsubishi).

Brand extension has become common practice. What was reserved for luxury goods is becoming a general managerial procedure: Mars is no longer only the famous bar but an ice-cream, a chocolate drink and a slab of chocolate; Tefal gives its brand name to telephones and domestic appliances; McCain covers French fries, pizzas, buns and iced tea; Vittel endorses cosmetics and mineral water. For all those executives brought up on sacrosanct Procterian dogma according to which a brand must correspond to one, and only one, product, the present situation leads to thorough rethinking: even Mars, until now the typical example of a product brand, is becoming an umbrella brand covering very different segments and products. Such development is the direct consequence of the recognition that brands are the real capital of a company.

Indeed, capitalisation can only be carried out for a limited number of brands, hence the shrinking of brand portfolios. Significantly, in November 1991, the Danone Group (then BSN) decided it would no longer have two 'ultra-fresh' brands but only one (Danone), Gervais being relegated to a first-name brand under Danone (and not beside Danone as was the case since the merger between the Gervais and Danone companies). However, if there are fewer brands, there are, still, as many products in ranges. A single brand will have to cover a wider range of products. In November 1995 Nestlé decided to transfer to its own name all Chambourcy products, until then its European brand for dairy products. Chambourcy now designates three products under the Nestlé endorsement. This is brand extension, also called brand diversification. Range extension means introducing different versions of the base product or concept on the same market. Ariel, for instance, can be found in powder, liquid and micro versions. The Vache-Qui-Rit (Laughing Cow) cheese comes in portions, slabs, mini-boxes, small cups and flavoured versions (goat cheese, etc). This way, a brand adds more depth to its offer within a definite market; for example, a brand of soup adding new flavours or using new packaging or technology is considered range extension, but the move by Knorr and Maggi into ready-made dishes (eg couscous, shepherd's pie) is considered brand extension. Of course, there are cases where the differentiation is difficult to make. However, in spite of the imprecise border lines, there are two well differentiated concepts. Brand extension is what will be addressed here. The problem of the proliferation of range extensions has been analysed in Chapter 6.

WHY EXTEND THE BRAND?

What is new is not so much the extension itself but the interest that it generates. This is due to the fact that brand extension has become necessary. Several factors can explain this:

- Companies now understand that being a brand involves something more than just a communication or graphic packaging exercise, it is a real mode of behaviour. The brand only exists and fulfils its mission if it constantly surpasses itself and consumer expectations. Innovation allows the brand to remain up to date and demonstrates an unceasing urge to detect and respond to the profound changes in customer tastes and expectations. Brands which have stuck to a single state-of-the-art product, relying on communication alone to update their image, have not done well. They have become an easy prey for distributors' brands which have access to technology and launch products which are often as good and cheaper. To be modern in today's world, means to be in tune with developments in user habits and practices (eg in the food industry, the offer of simplified meals and individual portions). It also means taking on board new technologies such as deep-freezing, vacuum-packing, chilling, irradiation, etc. If brands do not follow these developments, they run the risk of being left behind.

- A second major factor is the cost of advertising. Brand logic is based on competition and leads to seeking ever increasing gains in productivity and economies of scale. This will only came about by extending market share from the local to the national and to the international level. This is the only way to support both the increasing costs of R&D and industrial investment, and keep the products at a very low price. The only way to achieve this wider market is through advertising. If one adds to this the need to be heard as much as the competitors, at least matching their share of voice, one understands why advertising expenditure is rising so much. This rise stems from the process of constant reinvestment in R&D in the search for difference, quality improvement and higher performance than the competition. The cost of advertising makes it impossible to support too many brands: efforts have to be concentrated on a few brands only. Most firms therefore try to assess their brand portfolio to decide which brands will be advertised. The brands selected will have to be pertinent, innovative and able to bear diversified products.

  Brand extension therefore results from the concentration of efforts on a few brands. New products which previously would have been launched under their own name as a new brand are now introduced under an existing brand name considered as a strategic brand or mega-brand within the company. Firms have thus put an end to the sacrosanct practice of making every new product a new brand. New products are now used to fuel existing brands.

- Brand extension is the only way of defending a brand at risk in a basic market. For example, in the UK, the reference for toilet paper is the Andrex brand, which had a 39 per cent market share in value in 1987. In 1994 this share had dropped to 28 per cent, due to the market becoming a commodity market and also due to the rise of hard-discounters. Thankfully, Andrex had begun by then an intense extension policy, offering kitchen paper, paper tissues, etc. In France, the original market of Oasis, the orange crush market, is now dominated by DOBs and lowest price products. Oasis will disappear if it remains confined to this market. As the brand still enjoys considerable assets such as brand awareness, sympathy and a quality image, the Schweppes group has decided that the brand will offer fruit juices, nectars and even tea-flavoured drinks, so refreshing and natural that they correspond very well to the positioning of Oasis. Furthermore, the brand is also innovating with its first one-litre transparent plastic bottle which is both practical and attractive.

Too many brands have stuck to their original market and disappeared along with it. In 1987, the turnover of the Letraset brand in France was 50 million francs but in 1995 it had gone down to three million. Microcomputers have killed the transfer-letter market. The brand should have reacted earlier and diversified into software. The same goes for Mecanorma. Used to a comfortable position in their markets and to products yielding a 70 per cent margin, these brands underestimated the speed of erosion of those markets. Moreover, the necessary diversification would have forced them to increase their efforts in order to penetrate a new distribution channel – microcomputer retailers – with a lower-margin product and existing and strong competition.

- Brand extension gives access to an accumulated image capital. Part of the high prices reached during takeover bids on companies with a known brand can be explained by the fact that the potential buyer hopes to derive immediate profits from the brand by extending it and earning royalties. It is true that the characteristics of many brands are pertinent in product categories other than the original one. Seiko, due to its fame and its high precision image, is able to compete with Essilor in the spectacle lens market. The Swatch brand now covers small, innovative cars in which its philosophy will be expressed.

  Brand awareness surveys give precious information on the extension potential of a brand. Many brands are spontaneously quoted in product categories to which they do not belong. Kleenex's kitchen paper appears in all the surveys carried out on the brand, and yet it does not exist. This is frequent in the case for home appliances too. Thus, when the French consumer magazine *Que Choisir* asked its readers to give their degree of satisfaction about different brands of home appliances, Miele obtained a good ranking for cookers although it had never marketed any cookers in France! This phenomenon also occurs in the sports goods market. Salomon launched its first pair of skis only in 1990, but it had been thought of as a good ski manufacturer since its creation.

- Extending the brand enables the reinforcement of the image capital of the brand and fuels it. Why did Cadbury-Schweppes name its new soft drink Dry de Schweppes instead of Wipps? The reason was to fuel the Schweppes brand and rejuvenate it, which the ad campaigns on 'Schwepping' had been unable to do. Schweppes, a product brand in France, was ageing and becoming unknown to youngsters. If Wipps had been launched, it would have been fatal to Schweppes. Wipps would have embodied modernity, making Schweppes look even more old-fashioned. With talent and courage, its managers transformed Schweppes into an umbrella brand now resting on several differentiated soft drinks (the traditional Indian tonic, the lemon tonic, the dry ginger, and even a cola).

Indeed, by coming up with new or rejuvenated products, a brand can prove that it is still relevant and up to date. For that reason, brand extension, far from weakening the brand, often makes it healthier. The French popular science magazine *Sciences et Vie* is doing much better now that it has created diversified versions such as *Sciences et Vie Micro*, *Sciences et Vie Economie* and *Sciences et Vie Junior*. In the same way, the Vache-Qui-Rit brand corrected its image as a mono-product brand by launching under its name the modern cheese-bits for parties and the Toastinettes for hamburgers. And the launch of the Camel Shoes product line helped to refuel the Camel brand with values which a communication based on cigarettes could not have demonstrated because of legal constraints. L'Oréal decided to place all dermo-cosmetic products of the brand d'Anglas Laboratories under the Vichy brand in order to strengthen the presence of this brand in pharmacies, a distribution channel more and more threatened as a whole by the supermarkets, thus requiring the strongest of brands.

In order to put Gemey, a forgotten brand, back on tracks, L'Oréal transformed it into a mother-brand covering such diversified products as Eau Jeune, H pour Homme, Ricils, etc. Similarly, Salomon's ski range gave a new dynamism to its image, which had been difficult considering that the company was already number one worldwide for ski shoes and safety bindings, two products which symbolise comfort and technology, but not excitement.

From an operational point of view, this requires distinguishing the products considered to bring in the sales volume from those which carry the image and whose role is to fuel the brand. The criteria used to measure the performance of each are different: for instance, to put down the small sales volumes of cheese-bits is to judge this product according to a different goal. The cheese-bits communication brings modernity to the Vache-Qui-Rit brand by giving it a presence in new lifestyles.

- Brand extension enables the brand to break away from the mono-product. The above example demonstrates that brand extension is necessary in order for the brand to survive, as all products are subject to a lifecycle, and therefore to eventual obsolescence. By being attached to a single product for too long, a brand name becomes a product name, and this name becomes subject to the same obsolescence. Damart Thermowear provides a good example: this brand, specialising in clothing for the elderly, is closely tied to a single product which has been the centre point of its communication for decades: 'thermolactyl', a fibre used in warm underwear. Yet a change in lifestyle, the warming of climate or the slightest move away from artificial fibres could threaten the long-term survival of thermolactyl. If the Damart brand had been left to become synonymous with thermolactyl, it would have been bound to decline, hence the strategic importance of diversifying the brand, making it more independent and giving it a greater meaning, so that it could become a force in, for example, the senior ready-to-wear market.

This finding testifies to the limitations of product brands, long regarded as the ideal model of brand management. A product brand more than any other brand must ensure its survival and not get caught in the product life-cycle. This leads, for example, to the complete modification or transformation of the product: for instance there was Dash 1, 2 and 3. The Ariel of 1996 has little resemblance physically and chemically to the Ariel of 1969. And during the launch campaign of the latest Golf it was announced: 'Everything has changed except its name!' This shows the peculiar relationship between the brand and the product. This relationship makes the classic conception of the product brand obsolete, and a major hindrance to modern brand management.

THE LIMITS OF THE CLASSIC CONCEPTION OF BRANDING

The classic conception of branding rests on the following equation:

(1 brand = 1 product = 1 promise)

For instance, in the Procter & Gamble tradition, every new product receives a specific name which is totally independent from the other brands. Ariel corresponds to a certain promise, Dash to another, Vizir to a third. Mr Proper is a household detergent, and nothing else. Let us compare this policy with that of Colgate-Palmolive: Palmolive is a toothpaste, a soap, a shaving cream and a dishwashing liquid. Ajax is a scrubbing powder, a household detergent and a window cleaning liquid.

The classic conception of branding leads to an increasing number of brands. If a brand corresponds to a single physical product, to a single promise, it cannot be used for other products. Under this conception it is a rigid designator, the name of a product, a proper noun, just as Aristotle is the name of the famous Greek philosopher (Cabat, 1989). It names a specific reality, as a commercial name is linked to a specific company.

Under this conception of the brand, few extensions are possible. The brand is in fact the name of a recipe. All that can be done is range extension, that is a variation around the central recipe either by:

- ameliorating the quality of its performances. The brand then gets a series number: for example Dash 1, then Dash 2 and Dash 3;
- increasing the number of sizes in order to adapt to the changing practices of the consumer (packet, tub, mini-tub);
- increasing the number of varieties (Woolite for wool and Woolite for synthetics).

The classic conception of branding is actually limiting. It does not differentiate the history of the brand from the reality of the brand. Of course, a brand originally begins with a new single product which is better than the competition, thanks to the know-how of a firm.

With time, and through communication, packaging, advertising, etc the brand becomes rich with features, images and representations which give it its style. The brand thus has personality along with know-how. After designating an origin (the manufacturer's brand), or a place of sale (the commercial name), the brand conveys after some time the signs of non-material elements, which take root in physical production (the products) and iconic production (advertising images, logos, symbols of visual identity). The relationship between the brand and the product is therefore reversed: the brand is no longer the name of a product, but the product itself carries the brand in a sense that it reveals the exterior signs of an interior imprint. The brand has transformed the product, endowing it with both objective and subjective features.

In this reversed perspective, there is no other limit to brand extension than that of the ability of the brand to leave its mark on a new category of product, ie to segment it according to its own attributes. Bic, ignoring the dissimilarity of products, left its mark by creating sub-segments of simple, cheap and efficient goods wherever these attributes are valued. Bic failed where these were not valued – in the perfume segment.

The classic conception of branding is nominal: the brand is the name of an object. If one looks beyond this object, and wonders what project it conveys and what vocation it embodies, one can grasp the full meaning of the brand, its etymological meaning (the brandon), the exterior sign of an internal transformation.

Nothing stops the luxury butter brand Président from extending to Swiss cheese or to Saint-Paulin. By giving them its name, it would signal their taste and psychological qualities. Président can go wherever it wants to. The brand is autonomous. It fixes its own ambitions. Because it is subject to profitability constraints, it must reflect on its actual ability to modify the products that it wants to extend to, and also on the attractiveness of this transformation to the consumer of that product category. What would be the taste, the texture, the colour and the personality of a Roquefort cheese once it was marked by the Président brand? Is this new offer capable of attracting enough consumers to justify this new extension of the brand?

The history of brand extension follows and yet has contributed to the awareness of what a brand really is. The brand has evolved from a rigid denominator of an object to a sign, an image, demonstrating an internal and external transformation. The first extensions were timid, using similar recipes to those which founded the original product. Président ceased to be a top-of-range butter only and put its name to a camembert. Another level of extension shatters the traditional method of distinction according to different know-how: bringing together very different products is achieved through common values. What is the link between McCain Pizzas, McCain French Fries and McCain Iced Tea? Simply the image of McCain American food.

What do the Palmolive shaving cream, soap and dish-washing liquid have in common? A common cult of softness. Following this logic, the brand extends along an axis, a value, wherever this value can be materialised in a strong and pertinent way. Bic is not simply a brand name for pens: it is to be seen as simplifying utilitarian objects, as expressed by the 'disposable' characteristic. It therefore went from the ball-point pen to the lighter and the razor (its experiment in wind-surfing and perfumes will be analysed later). As for Gillette, it does not define its territory as a product – the razor – or an attribute but as all that concerns the modern man in the bathroom. As a specialist on razors, it can extend to more feminine products such as eau-de-toilette, skin-care products, etc. The last and broadest stage of brand extension is when the brand signifies a common spirit, an ambition, an allegiance to shared values. What else is the relationship between Nina Ricci haute couture and the men's ties of Monsieur Ricci? Or between all the products sold under the St Michael brand?

Thus, the classic conception of the brand takes the history of the brand for its long-term reality. But, although the brand originates from a product, it is not the product. The brand is the meaning of the product.

Products cannot speak for themselves. The consumer is perplexed in front of a tin of brandless frozen lasagna. How can he or she foresee the satisfaction that will be derived from this tin? The brand reveals the intention of the maker:

what values did he try to into this tin? What did he want to introduce in this product: the love of tradition, an example of work well done, a respect for modern tastes, the will to find a compromise between fat and light food?

Extensions cannot be made in all directions. The direction is defined by the brand itself. A brand works as a genetic programme. It carries the code of the future products which will bear its name.

What does this new conception of branding change for brand extension? According to the classic conception, brand extension barely goes beyond technological know-how. The key concept is that of know-how. The only question asked of the entrepreneur is: is it or is it not within your industrial know-how? This does not explain how perfumes by jewellers – Van Cleef, Bulgari, Boucheron, etc – are successes. It reduces brand identity to one single facet, the physical. This logic would exclude the idea of a Swatch car.

The larger conception of branding leads to extensions out of the initial field of know-how. The brand is different from the technological know-how. It is a way of dealing with products, of transforming them, of giving them a common set of added values, both tangible and intangible: this way, a Swatch car is possible. An alliance with a company which has the technical know-how (Mercedes for example) will suffice. This alliance, eventually made explicit through co-branding, will give reassurance as to the car's quality and free consumers' desires.

The case of Lacoste helps to compare the operational consequences of each of these conceptions of branding. Lacoste gained its reputation in sports shirts made out of knitwear (called the 12 × 12), so a logical extension of Lacoste could be made not only toward other knitwear products, but also to polo-shirts, T-shirts, sportswear and textiles in general. Under this conception, shoes and leather items are excluded (apart from tennis shoes), since they do not use the same know-how as textiles and knitwear. Under Lacoste's broader brand conception, the crocodile signals a typical attitude: with Lacoste, one is casual when smartly dressed, and smart even when dressed casually. Lacoste is beyond fashion: it is a classic. From this perspective, Lacoste can brand shoes or leather goods as long as they preserve the brand's originality: it must not brand products that have already been seen. The other condition is to brand only products which embody the values of the brand: flexibility, casualness, extreme finish, durability, distance from fashion, unisex use, etc. What enables Lacoste to brand a product is not the physical know-how – which can always be delegated under licence – but whether the product belongs to the Lacoste culture.

Most of the decision grids of the strategy consulting firms are based on the know-how approach, as viewed from the supply side: they have not yet taken on board the fact that brand logic is different. Far from remaining within its original product, brand reasoning leads to new questions and decisions. For example, the question 'what product should the brand cover in order to regenerate itself?' led Marlboro to create a ready-to-wear line: 'Marlboro's Classics'.

Trying to manage, maintain and fuel the capital of the brand, its status and its imaginary dimension leads to extension decisions that are beyond the original 'job' of the brand. Retroactively, by covering all these far-fetched products, the brand gains significance, evolves and remains up to date. Indeed, brand logic is additive. The brand is the sum of its attributes: it is revealed by the products that it covers. The case of McCain is typical. The brand generally penetrates new countries through its frozen fries (it is actually the main supplier to McDonald's). They later introduce a frozen pizza ('deep pan', typical of the American way of life and of eating). They then launch buns to aim at the snack market. McCain also launched an iced tea to penetrate this high growth market. Brand identity is actually uncovered by the sum of all these products. McCain's identity in Europe is that of 'American fun and generous food'. Generosity is both a relationship trait and a physical trait: all portions should be bigger when signed by McCain. Hence the surname 'deep pan pizza' or the higher cap of its iced-tea (surnamed Colorado to refer to a mythical view of America). Future products may come from anywhere as long as they embody this enlarged identity of the brand, and fall within the territory of legitimacy the brand has created step by step, through each of its product launches.

History should not determine the future. In order to remain up to date, the brand must also be able to evolve: this is achieved through extension towards products which lead it in new directions and modify its meaning. Nestlé, known for dry foods (its prototypical products are instant milk and chocolate), did not enter the ultra-fresh market of yoghurts by killing the Chambourcy brand just to increase its turnover. The move was also intended to develop its image thanks to this more modern segment, capable of updating its traditional and classic image traits.

ECONOMIC CONSEQUENCES OF BRAND EXTENSION

By capitalising on the brand awareness, the esteem and the qualities attached to an existing brand, the practice of brand extension can help to increase the chances of success of a new product and lower its launch costs. These two alleged consequences have been verified. In 1990, the OC&C consulting firm compared the rates of survival of new mass consumption products depending on whether they had been launched under a new brand name or under an existing one.

As shown in Figure 8.1, only 30 per cent of new brands survive longer than four years, whereas the rate is over 50 per cent for brand extensions.

How does extension increase chances of survival? First, distributors themselves will allocate more space to an already well-known brand than to a newcomer. But brand extension also has an impact on the consumer (see Figure 8.2):

- in the trial rate, inducing a higher rate (123 vs 100);
- in the conversion rate (17 per cent vs 13 per cent);
- in the loyalty rate (index of 161 vs 100 for new brands).

Thus, for an equal facing and an equal unweighted distribution/weighted distribution ratio, consumers have a higher probability of trial, conversion and loyalty when the product bears an existing brand name, as this second OC&C analysis shows.

As far back as 1969, Claycamp and Liddy had measured the impact of a 'family name' (extension) on the trial rate of the new product. Their forecasting model, known as Ayer's model, rested on a database of 60 launches in 32 categories, half of these being in the food sector. The basic structure of the model is presented in Figure 8.3.

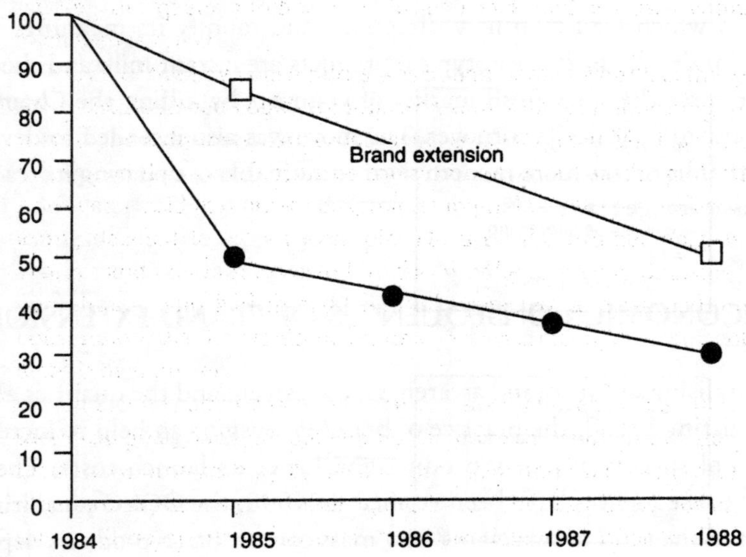

Figure 8.1 Rate of success of new brands *vs* brand extensions

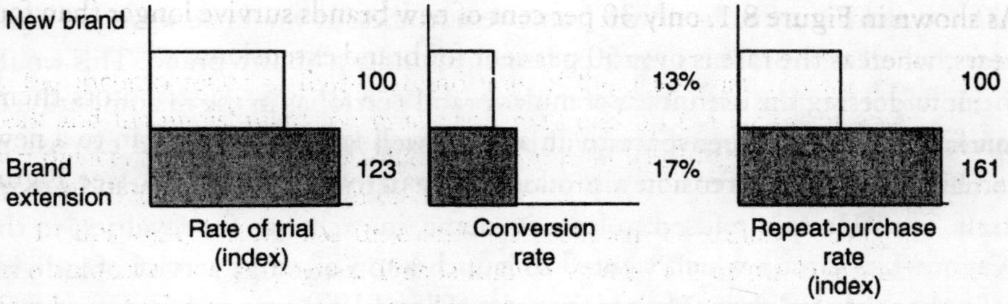

Figure 8.2 The impact of brand extension on the consumer adoption process

The estimate of the parameters of the model (through double regression) resulted in a very positive weight for the 'brand extension' variable. A previously known name directly and strongly induces the consumer to try the product. Moreover, Liddy and Claycamp noted that this variable was not correlated to advertising recall or even to weighted distribution. This last point is surprising: perhaps American distributors do not act as barriers to entry as much as their European colleagues.

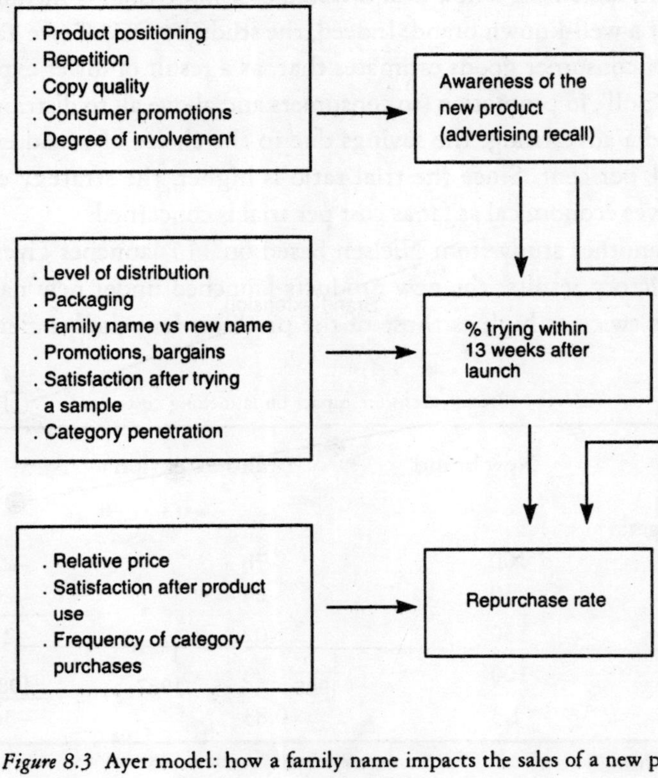

Figure 8.3 Ayer model: how a family name impacts the sales of a new product

What conclusions can be drawn from these studies? It would be wrong to think now that all new products must be launched under a known brand. This would mean forgetting the usefulness of multi-brand portfolios in the maximisation of market coverage. Moreover, as will be discussed later, some brand extensions can hinder the success of a new product, or be detrimental to the brand capital itself. Thus Hermès refused to lease its name, in exchange for royalties, to the Wagons-Lits Group which wanted to launch a top-of-range service of individual or package holidays. The service risks of hotels in exotic and far away countries were too high for Hermès to be willing to associate its name with that venture.

These figures also reveal that the consumer's view of the product is generally far less conservative than that of management itself. Quite often the latter is too blinkered by the origin of the brand and considers the manufacturing history of the brand as its definition. For management, Mars could not mean anything else but the chocolate bar. And yet the Mars ice-cream bar is a success. This proves that the consumer distinguishes rather well the brand from the product, or at least that he does not associate them irreversibly.

The second economic argument put forward to justify brand extension has to do with cost: launching a new brand would cost more than launching a new product under a well-known brand. Indeed, the study by OC&C (see Table 8.1) on the basis of consumer goods estimates that, as a result of lower expenses in 'push' and in 'pull', in promotion (to consumers and above all to distributors) as well as in media advertising, the savings due to the choice of brand extension amount to 21 per cent. Since the trial ratio is higher, the strategy of brand extension proves economical as far as cost per trial is concerned.

However, another study from Nielsen based on 115 launches gives apparently contradictory results: the new products launched under new names get market shares twice as high as those of the products launched under known

Table 8.1 Brand extension impact on launching costs

	New brand	**Brand extension**	**%**
Launching budget:			
— pull	100	78	–22
— push	30	24	–20
Total	130	102	–21
Trial rate	100	123	+23
Cost/trial	1.3	0.83	–36

Source: OC&C (Paris).

brands (except for health and beauty products, for which the results are identical: 2.7 per cent vs 2.6 per cent) (see Figure 8.4). The reason for this difference can be seen in the second column. The extension strategy would not in fact be less efficient: the lower market shares are due to the fact that management uses smaller communication budgets in cases of brand extension, which lowers the share of advertising presence.

For an equal percentage of advertising presence, brand extension results in equivalent or even greater market shares in the field of health and beauty where, the risk perceived by the consumers being higher, there is a preference for known brands.

What can be deduced from these two studies? Are they contradictory? OC&C concludes that extension is more efficient even with a lower budget. The contradiction could be solved by considering the fact that many managers, confident in the productivity of brand extension, under-assess the media advertising budget (thus the results of the first column of Figure 8.4). For equal budgets, the extension strategy has a slight advantage which is not significant in the cleaning products and food sectors but significant in the health and beauty sector (0.46 vs 0.39). In addition, the fact that OC&C analyses efficiency in terms of trial rate (very tightly linked to the familiarity of the brand name) whereas Nielsen's is based on market share over 24 months, which reflects the marketing mix and product quality as a whole, may have some bearing. Finally, this under-assessment of the launch budget of the extension may be linked to a desire to keep the bulk of advertising on the core product of the brand to preserve its sales.

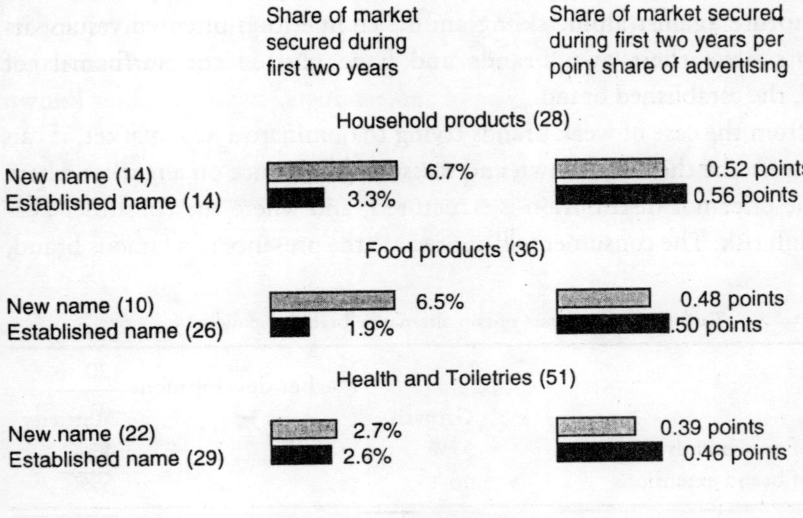

Figure 8.4 Comparative sales performance during first two years

A hidden factor in each of these two studies is the moment of entry on the market. A risky, new market cannot be approached in the same way as the same market at a more mature stage. Sullivan's (1991) analysis of 96 launches in eleven categories of products gives interesting descriptive results (see Table 8.2).

First, this analysis noted that companies preferred to penetrate new markets with new brands. Of the 48 launches studied which had taken place on emerging markets, only 13 were brand extensions. However, in mature markets, 40 out of the 48 launches analysed were brand extensions. Sullivan also noted that the brands which used their own names in order to penetrate a young market were rather weak brands. For example, in the United States, Royal Crown Cola was the first brand to penetrate the diet cola segment under its own name. It was followed by Pepsi-Cola with Diet Pepsi. Coca-Cola had preferred to launch Tab and not to put its brand capital at risk. It introduced Diet Coke last. The survey shows that the brands which have become leaders in these markets were almost always new brands (Diet Coke is an exception).

Why do strong brands hesitate to penetrate young markets? Of course, they would benefit from the fact that there is no competition yet. But creating a market entails more risks for the creator (Schnaars, 1995) and a negative effect on the brand and its capital. In a young, badly defined market, a brand must be flexible in order to find the best positioning. Brand extension does not permit such flexibility. The attributes of the brand must be respected. Furthermore, launching a brand which is specific to a new market enables the brand to become the reference on that market, by benefiting from what is called the pioneer advantage (Carpenter and Nakamoto, 1991). Finally, many new markets are created in reaction to old ones. For example, the snow surfing market is a counter-culture against alpine skiing and its competition-oriented values; its proponents have their own brands and have refused the surfboards of Rossignol, the established brand.

Apart from the case of weak brands trying to dominate a new market, it can be attractive to be the only known and reassuring reference on a market where neither the offer nor distribution is structured, and where the consumer perceives a high risk. The consumer will appreciate the presence of a famous brand,

Table 8.2 Success rate of two alternative branding policies

	Market development	
	Growth	Maturity
Launches of new brands	57%	43%
Launches of brand extensions	46%	68%

Source: Sullivan (1991).

even if it is far from its original market. Only its fame and serious reputation count. That is why Tefal penetrated the fledgling market of domestic appliances under its own name.

Finally, the analysis of success rates of the two launch strategies, depending on the degree of maturity of the markets, reveals a slight advantage for the new brand strategy in the market creation phase. But with time, the brand extension strategy seems more successful (see Table 8.2).

EXPERIMENTAL STUDIES ON BRAND EXTENSION

After having looked at the factors which explain brand extension decisions, we will now examine the main results of research on that subject. The problems arising during the implementation of this strategy for a given brand will be examined further in this chapter.

Research on brand extension is new (Aaker and Keller, 1990), since academic researchers have only recently made the distinction between brand and product. Most research on brand image is in fact research on product image. Therefore, the notion of brand extension did not fit in with this way of thinking: research used to be cut off from real practice which has indeed been dealing with extension for a long time. The trend has changed since then and research on brand extension is now being carried out everywhere. We will present the most significant findings published to date in so far as they reveal a consistent pattern. This research examined is both descriptive and explanatory.

The first study was presented in 1987 during a symposium on brand extension at the University of Minnesota. The attitude towards a fictitious brand of calculators (Tarco) was manipulated through the presentation of the results of tests evaluating six Tarco calculators. These tests concluded, according to the cases, that none of the six calculators was of poor quality, or one out of six, two out of six ... up to six out of six. Naturally, the general attitude towards Tarco was much influenced by this manipulation. Then a list of new products to be launched by Tarco was presented: these ranged from a new calculator and 'close' extensions (microcomputers, digital watches, cash registers, etc) to 'further' extensions (bicycles, pens, office chairs). The interviewees in each group were asked to state their feelings about each of these new Tarco products before having even seen them. The correlation between the attitude towards Tarco and the attitude towards these extension products of Tarco was measured. As shown in Table 8.3, the correlation is stronger when the extension is close. In short, the transfer of attitude increases with the perceived similarity between the category of brand origin and the category of the product extension.

Table 8.3 Is reputation transferable? Correlations between the attitude towards a brand and the attitude towards each of its extensions, ranked in order of increasing dissimilarity

Extension		Correlation
Close	Another calculator	0.85
	PC computer	0.76
	Cash register	0.75
	Digital watch	0.63
	Video recorder	0.62
	Radio	0.58
	Colour TV	0.51
	Office chair	–0.11
	Bike	–0.11
Remote	Ball pen	–0.17

Source: Consumer Behaviour Seminar (1987).

Naturally, the bases of 'perceived similarity' vary with the individuals. As another study has shown, experts and non-experts use different indexes to evaluate the degree of similarity between two products. For example, the two following types of extension were shown to two groups of individuals, non-experts and experts:

- one was a superficial extension, using superficial similarity and relatedness (from tennis shoes to tennis rackets);
- the other was a 'deeper' extension, using the same know-how (that of carbon fibre, enabling a brand of golf clubs to introduce tennis rackets).

When asked about their perception of similarity between the starting category and the final category (tennis rackets), non-experts found the superficial extension very similar, but the experts not as much. On the other hand, an explanation of the process and material used convinced the experts more easily of the fact that tennis rackets and golf clubs are close products, while for non-experts they remain quite dissimilar. Thus, identical composition is not a factor of perceived similarity for non-experts: they base their opinions on more superficial signs. They are sensitive to extensions based on relationships of complementarity or substitutability between products:

- Uncle Ben's sauce is complementary to Uncle Ben's rice;
- Nesquik cereals are substitutes for Nesquik milk chocolate.

Experts are not satisfied with these peripheral cues. They need a stronger rationale, such as that of Look's extension. This brand, famous for its ski bindings, was extended to the upper-range mountain-bike market, for it could apply here its mastery of the automatic grip pedals and of new composite materials.

In the first study, the fact that Tarco was a fictitious brand was intentional. This way, the brand had no capital – no particular quality and image was associated to the brand. This explains the importance of the criterion of similarity of products to facilitate the transfer of attitudes. In a normal situation, if the brand is a strong one, the relevance of its differentiating attributes in the product class it wishes to enter is what determines the attractiveness of the extension even if the categories of products are very different (Broniarczyk and Alba, 1994). The success of Bic in pens, razors and lighters illustrates this fact. In a pioneer study, Aaker and Keller (1990) presented a series of possible extensions for well-known brands (for example Heineken pop-corn or McDonald's films). Each consumer had to indicate his attitude and interest towards these extensions, and at the same time explain why. The independent variables were:

- the perceived quality of the brand;
- the impression of transferability of know-how from the category of the original product to that of the extension;
- the degree of perceived complementarity between the two products;
- the degree of perceived substitutability;
- the perceived difficulty to manufacture the extension product.

In all, each interviewee answered on several extensions and the study was based on 2100 observations. In order to isolate the variables explaining the attitude/interest for the extension, the authors used the regression method. The results are listed in Table 8.4. The conclusions to be drawn were as follows.

- The degree of perceived quality of the brand does not directly influence the opinions on the extension. This can be explained – as shown previously by the Tarco study – by the fact that the transfer of attitude from the brand to the product of extension depends on the perceived similarity between the category of origin and the final category.
- The feeling of transferability of know-how does influence the attitude towards the extension.
- Complementarity does not guarantee the extensibility of the product. For example, the success of a pasta brand extending to tomato sauce is not assured.

Table 8.4 Explaining consumer attitudes towards specific brand extensions

	Regression importance weights	Statistical significance	
Perceived quality	–0.01	NS	
Know-how perceived transferability	–0.15	$p<0.05$	facets of perceived similarity
Product complementarity	–0.02	NS	
Product substitutability	–0.08	NS	
Quality × transferability	0.12	NS	
Quality × complementarity	0.25	$p<0.05$	
Quality × substitutability	0.18	$p<0.05$	
Perceived difficulty	0.56	$p<0.05$	
(Perceived difficulty)^2	–0.47	$p<0.05$	
R^2	26%		

Source: Aaker and Keller (1989).

- The same goes for substitutability (for example skis and ice-skating shoes): it does not guarantee positive attitudes *vis-à-vis* this extension.
- As indicated by the two positive interactions, only brands with a high perceived quality can hope to see this perception transferred, provided that the extension seems either complementary or substitutable.
- Finally, the perceived difficulty of the extension is linked in a non-linear way to the attitude towards this extension. It is negative for extensions which are either too easy to manufacture (the Chanel T-shirt) or too difficult (the Bic perfume). Intermediate levels of difficulty, however, lead to a favourable attitude.

However, one must be aware of the fact that this research gives only limited explanations, as the R^2 shows: over 75 per cent of the variance remains unexplained. This is a lot, even for an analysis made at an individual level.

In this type of study, the authors still do not differentiate a brand from a product. They give no autonomy to the meaning of the brand. The entire analysis rests on the intrinsic perceived similarity between product categories. This denies the brand its unification, transformation and identification powers.

The first sign of awareness of a mechanism independent from the product and stemming from the brand itself appeared in 1991, among Park and his colleagues. Two lists of products were given to the persons interviewed: functional products and expressive products:

TV	perfume
compact disc	shoe
cassette-player	wallet
radio	shirt
video tape	bag
VCR	pen
walkman	ring
car-radio	watch
video camera	belt
record-player	crystal
headphones	tie

Two questions were asked:

1. the traditional question about the degree of similarity between the products of each column;
2. a question about whether the products of each column 'fit' together.

The researchers asked these two questions in two ways:

- blindly, as above;
- using a brand, here Sony for the first list and Gucci for the second.

What were the results?

- For the symbolic products, the fact that the brand was mentioned or not did not modify the judgements of low perceived similarity between the products. However, the presence of the Gucci brand name created a considerable link between products which did not seem to fit much without the brand (3.68), but suddenly fitted together (4.74) under the brand.
- For functional products, the presence or not of the brand did not modify the judgements of perceived similarity and of 'fit'.

In short, the authors hinted at two processes by which consumers build an opinion on an extension:

- If the brand is mainly functional, the extension is evaluated according to inherent links between the category of the original product and that of the extended product. The consumer's evaluations rest on the degree of perceived similarity between product categories.
- If the brand is symbolic, the concept of brand creates a link between products which otherwise would not have one. In this case, the judgements on extension are independent of the intrinsic characteristics of the product categories. The extension is evaluated according to its belonging to the brand and to its coherence with the value system of this brand.

Some extensions bear the risk of dilution of the brand. Like an elastic band which has been pulled too much, the brand can become weak. Many factors explain the weakening of a brand by excessive extension. Evaluating this risk is no mean task: what would be the impact on Tuborg if a sparkling mineral water were introduced under this brand (such an extension does exist in Greece)?

A recent study demonstrated the existence of this risk. It focused on a well-known health and beauty brand, Neutrogena. Two extensions were presented to the consumers, one very unusual for Neutrogena, the other very typical of Neutrogena. The experiment consisted of informing the consumers that both extensions did very poorly in the two dimensions which make Neutrogena famous, softness and quality. What would be the impact of such a statement on the image of Neutrogena itself (Roedder, 1993)? Would the image of softness and quality of typical Neutrogena products be affected, too? The study considered product A1, the brand prototype associated with Neutrogena by 83 per cent of consumers; product A2, associated by 61 per cent; product A3, by 55 per cent; product A4, by 39 per cent; and product A5, by 5 per cent of consumers. Here are the conclusions:

- Although of poor quality, the unusual extension did not stain the image of the brand, nor the image of its other products. This phenomenon is well-known to researchers on stereotypes: the exception does not harm the rule. The extension is atypical, therefore without influence on the heart of the brand.
- The situation is different for the more typical extension of Neutrogena. Its poor quality had a negative influence on both the image of the brand in its key attributes, and that of products typically and spontaneously associated to the brand. (A1, A2 and A3 had a statistically significant poorer softness image after exposure to the extension.) There has, indeed, been a negative impact on the brand and on its most significant products, but only in the case where the extension is typical of the brand. An obvious danger therefore underlies extensions which do not fulfil the implicit contract implied by the brand.

TYPICALITY AND EVALUATION OF EXTENSIONS

Above we have spoken of typical and unusual extensions. This raises the question of how to judge whether the product resulting from an extension is at the heart, at the limit or outside the territory of a brand. This question is one more application of a more general question at the heart of research on cognitive psychology: according to what criteria is an object considered part of a category?

Indeed, the psychological study of classification by categories aims at identifying the processes by which we form categories, and assigns certain objects to one category rather than to another. The brand is, in that sense, a category.

For decades, the dominating, or 'classical', theory answered this question in the following way: a product or an object belongs to a category if it has the necessary and sufficient features of this category. This leads one to question 'the' definition of the concept (or the category), ie about the nature of these features determining the belonging or non-belonging. This model works well for certain categories (for example the category of 'even numbers'), but it seems less reliable for others. Specialist or niche car makers such as BMW or Saab have definite image and physical traits which can qualify a new car as belonging or not to the brand. This is not the case for the generalist brands such as Ford, Opel, Vauxhall, Renault etc. The same holds true for Braun vs Philips.

Indeed, in this classic model, all examples of the category are equivalent since they all have these necessary and sufficient traits: two is an even number as much as 18 or 40! All BMWs are BMW.

Experience proves that the situation is different for many categories: for example, some birds are more 'birdlike' than others, and even a butterfly is more 'birdlike' than an ostrich. Belonging to a category does not seem to be a clear-cut binary function (yes/no) but a probabilistic one. The frontier between the 'bird' and 'insect' categories is unclear. This does not nullify these two categories: indeed, we all have in mind the prototype of a bird and that of an insect, and these two prototypes cannot be mistaken one for the other! However, the frontiers of each category are not that separate.

Thus the new tendency of research on categorisation, led by Rosch (1978) and Lakoff (1987), admits that categories can also be groups with unclear boundaries which are not defined by a series of necessary and sufficient features: what common features would link bridge, hopscotch, a doll and Monopoly? All are prototypes of games, but games in a different way for each one of them. This is important as these objects are more linked by a 'family resemblance' than by the possession of specific features common to all. Family resemblance means that if A resembles B, B resembles C in a different way, and C resembles A in an even more different way. The same goes for mega-brands such as

Danone, Whirlpool or Philips, which are characterised by typical products more than by typical image traits (see Table 8.5).

Although the theory of categorisation has evolved and its authors have reintroduced the possibility of features that define the meaning of natural categories – called 'most typical' features – various consequences can be drawn from this new approach.

Basically, an extension is considered acceptable if it 'fits' the idea that consumers have of the mother-brand. This feeling is based either on a high perceived similarity to the most typical product – or products – of the brand (also called pivot products), or on the coherence between the extension and the brand contract (also called its concept or identity). Figure 8.5 sums up this evaluation process.

Table 8.5 Typicality of the products

	Philips	**Whirlpool**
Television	9.10	5.06
Magnetoscope	8.65	4.97
Hi-fi	8.45	4.61
Electric razor	7.82	4.01
Walkman	7.73	3.44
Video-disc	7.68	3.34
Compact disc	7.64	3.49
Vacuum cleaner	7.57	5.85
Video cassette	7.45	3.65
Refrigerator	7.40	8.69(1)
Hair-remover (woman)	7.21	4.19
Coffee machine	6.97	5.06
Food-processor	6.94	6.05
Freezer	6.86	8.57(3)
Washing machine	6.83	8.69(1)
Dish washer	6.81	6.37(4)
Microwave oven	6.81	5.87
Iron	6.73	4.77
Hair dryer	6.67	7.83(7)
Cooker	6.60	8.12(6)
Tumble dryer	6.47	7.83
Electric oven	6.38	8.16(5)

Base: How typical of each brand is each product?
(Answers range from 0 to 10)

Source: Kapferer and Laurent (1996).

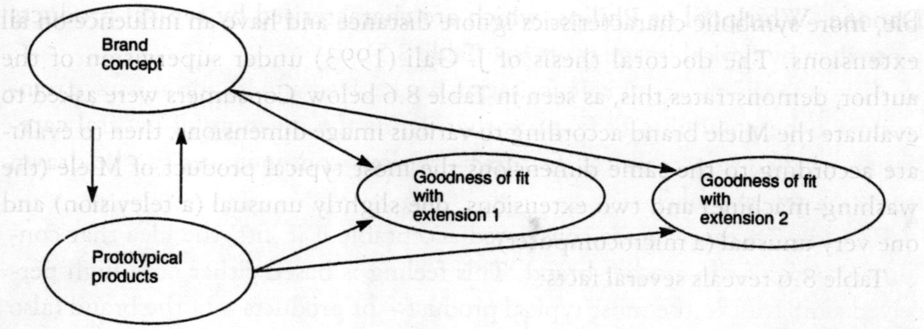

Figure 8.5 Typicality and brand extension evaluations

Indeed, the analysis of possible extensions for Danone shows that the less typical of Danone they are considered, the less attractive they are to the consumers (see Figure 8.6).

When the extension is distant from the mother-brand, which attributes of the latter are transferred to the extension product, and which are not? As the notion of distance is linked to a comparison with the pivot product – or products – of the brand, the objective characteristics of the brand are the ones which will be transferred the least to remote extensions. On the contrary, the intangi-

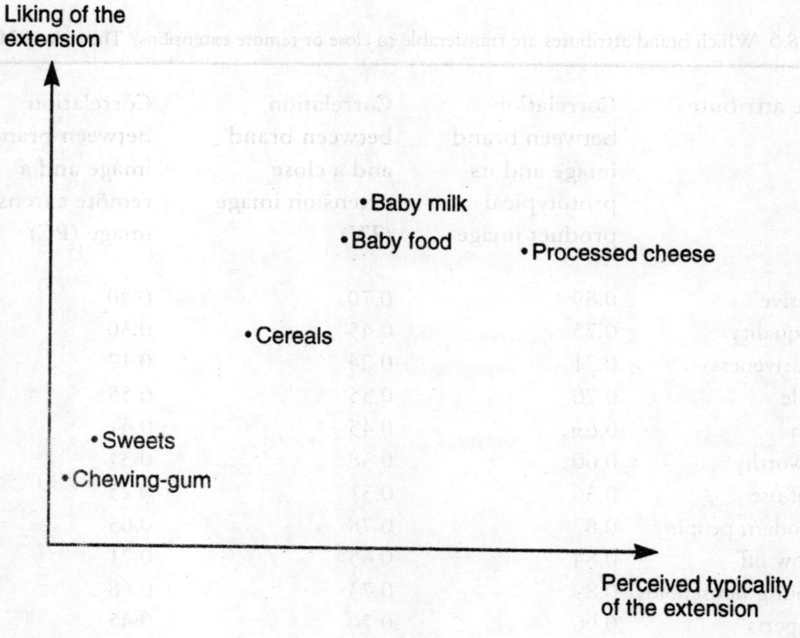

Figure 8.6 The Danone case: how typicality impacts attitudes towards brand extensions

ble, more symbolic characteristics ignore distance and have an influence on all extensions. The doctoral thesis of J. Gali (1993) under supervision of the author, demonstrates this, as seen in Table 8.6 below. Consumers were asked to evaluate the Miele brand according to various image dimensions, then to evaluate according to the same dimensions the most typical product of Miele (the washing-machine) and two extensions, one slightly unusual (a television) and one very unusual (a microcomputer).

Table 8.6 reveals several facts:

- First, the very unusual extension receives very little of the Miele values, as shown by the comparison of correlations in columns 2 and 3. Its role could be the opposite: to introduce into Miele values which the brand lacks. The more typical extension (column 2) receives more values from the brand.
- Generally speaking, objective qualities are not transferred as well as symbolic qualities. Thus, typical physical features of Miele – quality, innovation, reliability – are weakly correlated to the image of the two extensions on the same features. On the contrary, the extensions receive the following features: for the young, to show off, for innovators. For that reason, in a different context, luxury brands have little difficulty in practising extension even into dissimilar categories. Their primarily symbolic qualities ignore the distance between concrete objects.

Table 8.6 Which brand attributes are transferable to close or remote extensions? The case of Miele

Image attributes	Correlation between brand image and its prototypical product image	Correlation between brand and a close extension image (TV)	Correlation between brand image and a remote extension image (PC)
Expensive	0.89	0.70	0.40
High quality	0.75	0.45	0.30
Innovativeness	0.71	0.24	0.17
Reliable	0.70	0.55	0.55
Design	0.61	0.45	0.41
Trustworthy	0.60	0.38	0.31
Ease of use	0.36	0.31	0.25
For modern people	0.87	0.78	0.63
To show off	0.84	0.65	0.71
For young households	0.89	0.73	0.68
For experts	0.90	0.70	0.45

Source: Gali / Kapferer (1993).

This selection of the major studies on the process of evaluation of extensions by consumers is summarised in Figure 8.7. Starting from the right of the diagram, the attitude of the public towards an extension depends on the added value of the latter as compared to other offers on the market. This added value rests primarily on the intrinsic quality of the product itself. The fact that the extension of Oasis, a former orange crush, into new markets should come along with an innovation in packaging is significant. In all the extensions of the Andrex brand in the UK outside its original market – toilet paper – where it is the leader, the new product was perceived as superior to competition in blind tests. The Look extension did bring a significant improvement in the pedals of mountain-bikes. The success of Yamaha in guitars or classical pianos rested on the superiority of the products themselves. The brand then brings its own added value: awareness, esteem and spontaneous attribution of certain intangible attributes (solidity for Siemens, precision for Salomon, romanticism for Cacharel). These attributes only produce added value if their presence on the market for the extension is relevant.

The ability of the brand to transfer its objective attributes depends on whether the public feels the extension fits the brand. This feeling is determined by:

- the perceived distance to the pivot product (or products), the family resemblance between the extension and this (or these) products;
- the feeling that the product stays within the boundaries of the know-how of the company as it is imagined. For an unusual extension, the reputation of the company and its history of undisputed quality for a very large number of

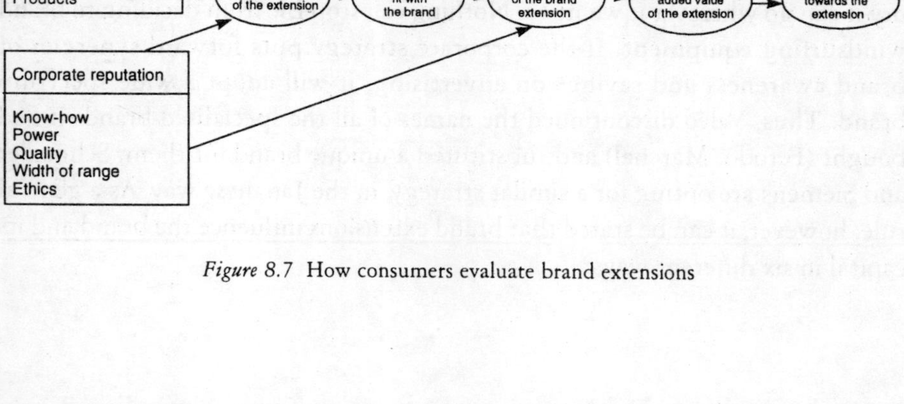

Figure 8.7 How consumers evaluate brand extensions

very different products are sources of credibility. This is the base of the Japanese approach which, for purposes of economies of scale, puts all the activities of the company under the same name (Mitsubishi for example). This is also the case for distributors such as Carrefour and Marks & Spencer;
- the belonging of the extension to the same concept as the brand.

Finally, one must acknowledge that different countries weigh certain elements of the model differently. German consumers give preference to notions of closeness between products and know-how. The idea of a Swatch automobile seems to them incongruous. The French, more used to abstraction, to concepts, put forward the notion of adequacy to non-tangible values, to the extent that they sometimes forget about very concrete constraints of brand extension.

TYPOLOGY OF BRAND EXTENSIONS

Brand extension is a leap out of the category of origin. Here again it is necessary to see the difference between close extensions, also called continuous extensions, and discontinuous extensions. A brand of spark plugs for automobiles can undertake a close extension into other automobile accessories (batteries, windscreen wipers, etc), as is the case for Bosch and Valéo. A brand which masters optics can extend into photocopying: this is the case for Canon, Minolta, Ricoh, Kodak and Agfa. A sports brand can cover other sports goods (Adidas, Salomon). Discontinuous extensions eliminate technological synergies and physical links between products: they are real diversifications, for example Yamaha has brands for motorbikes and classical pianos. The Carrefour distributor's brand covers the entire field of mass consumption goods and even quality goods.

Thus, there are extensions which are far from the original territory of the brand, and extensions which are close. This leads to brands with a narrow spectrum of products – specialised brands – and brands with a wide spectrum (such as Philips or General Electric). Is it better to be a specialist or a generalist? This question cannot be answered, generally speaking. A brand is arbitrary, in theory it can go wherever it wants to. Nothing can stop Bic from deciding to brand windsurfing equipment. If the corporate strategy puts forward synergies of brand awareness and savings on advertising, it will adopt a wide spectrum brand. Thus, Valéo discontinued the names of all the specialised brands it had bought (Ferodo, Marchal) and substituted a unique brand for them. Schneider and Siemens are opting for a similar strategy, in the Japanese way. As a general rule, however, it can be stated that brand extensions influence the brand and its capital in six different ways:

1 Some extensions take advantage of the brand capital: the product sells thanks to what it receives from the brand. This is what happens when the product receiving the brand is no different from the existing competitors on the market: the brand has not entirely played its transformation role, but it enables the product to benefit from its image. By using this practice too frequently – through a loose licensing policy for example – the brand capital wears out as the brand becomes associated with these now commonplace products, and with their unjustified price premium. Industrial brands often fill up the gaps in their lines by buying the missing items from their competitors. This is typical of the copiers' market.

2 Other extensions destroy the brand capital, for instance when the extension is downwards. Flaminaire wanted to cover three markets: the upscale market (to compete with Du Pont and Dunhill), the middle-range market, and the market of disposable lighters (against Bic). The brand has now disappeared. The low-range extension destroyed the legitimacy of the top-of-range products, which were profit generators. Porsche has cancelled its 924 range, cars which only justified their considerable price difference against their competitors (the Gti) by the prestigious name. None of the objective or subjective values of Porsche could be found in the 924 model: neither masculinity, nor technology. This model seemed to announce the end of the Porsche myth. Since at that time the brand no longer took part in Formula 1 racing and was losing in the Le Man 24-hour endurance race, the only communication element of the brand was advertising, of which a large part was dedicated to the 924. To return to its source, the brand ceased to manufacture the 924 and even the basic 944.

3 Some extensions have a neutral effect on the brand capital. The product is not out of place but is in tune with what is expected from the brand. Significantly, in the field of home appliances, some brands are thought to offer many more types of products than are actually produced, but if they decided to actually penetrate these markets, their image would not suffer. This shows that consumers have a perception of the brand which is different from that of those who manufacture it. They attribute to the brand areas of competence which are larger than and not limited to just the existing products.

4 Some extensions influence the meaning of the brand: when Rossignol added branded tennis rackets, the status of the brand changed. It is now less specialised and is characterised by a wider range of interests. Yet the two sports covered by Rossignol were not chosen randomly: the brand is still offering the equipment which extends the individual's body to help gain access to pleasure and performance. When Tefal, the home appliance brand, endorsed

telephones and entered domotics, it modernised itself through these extensions and acquired a new meaning: that of a brand whose purpose is to bring together technology and aesthetics in the service of the home. Nestlé increased its modernity by competing upfront under its own name with Danone on the ultra-fresh market (ie yoghurt).

5 Some extensions are regenerating. They revive the brand and its core, and re-express its base values in a new, stronger manner. Thus, the classic green blazer is a regenerating product for Lacoste. It represents a rare symbiosis between the features building the Lacoste brand: conformity, discretion, sociability but also a certain distance on fashion. As for the green colour, it is more casual than the blue blazer (too uniform for Lacoste) and refers to the green grass of the original tennis courts at Wimbledon. The green blazer brings Lacoste up to date and at the same time expresses its roots. The 'Marlboro Classics' line allows the brand to recommunicate its history, its roots and founding values.

6 Finally, some extensions, although not desired by the brand, are necessary to defend the brand capital: their purpose is, above all, to prevent the use of the brand name by another company in another category of products. Thus, Cartier may not want to develop along those lines, but they have to in order to prevent another company from registering the brand name Cartier on an international scale in the textiles category.

STRESS ON THE BRAND THROUGH EXTENSION

Not all brands lend themselves to extension. Some brands are defined only through their precise know-how – they are positioned in market segments where consumers expect very high performance and specific benefits. The brand reduces the consumer's perceived risk. This is the case with cosmetic brands such as Clarins, Roc and Vichy. Their field of extension has to be limited within appropriate boundaries which combine both science and beauty. Other brands, on the other hand, are symbolic of certain things – for example, Dim is the mark of the French woman, the young and casual Parisian. Its extension into the male world is possible provided that the male client targeted is the man suited to this kind of woman, the ideal man that this woman would create: not a dandy or effeminate man, but rather her very symbol of masculinity.

Other brands are almost like sects and have quasi-religious principles: St Michael, the brand owned by Marks & Spencer, covers everything from food to clothes, from toys to para-pharmaceutical products and furnishing. Through its signature it imparts legitimacy to all that is in conformity with the Marks &

Spencer ideology. Like a patron saint (etymologically, patron means pattern, ie model to be followed), the brand transforms and elevates all the products that it sanctifies.

The manufacturer could deliberately give a brand a very precise function, that of a specialist with very specific benefits. This is what the group L'Oréal does with its multiple cosmetic brands. Each one aims at a specific target market and its level of use. On the other hand, if it decided to follow a strategy of remote extensions, it would have to take account of factors that are necessary conditions for their success. In fact, such extensions exert a very real pressure on the brand and many are unable to stand up to it. Consumers may not believe that such extensions involve the same brand, but are rather from a company with the same name. Is the Bosch of household appliances the same as the Bosch of car accessories? It is rather incredible that the same principles should lie behind both detergents and cigarettes as is seen in the case of Ariel.

If the brand is to remain intact in the eyes of the consumer and not be split into disconnected units, the prerequisites of a large extension must be taken into consideration. For the extension of one brand into various remote categories to look coherent, one has to draw upon the deep meaning of the brand. This supposes that the brand either has such meaning or has the potential to acquire it. If this was not the case, the brand would be economically meaningless after extension. The Swiss brand, Caran d'Ache, built its reputation through up-market pencils and writing tools. Its extension into scarves, wallets and leather items failed. The brand was missing the necessary deep meaning.

Figure 8.8 demonstrates the demands arising out of brand extension. Every degree of product dissimilarity changes the meaning and the status of the brand. Close extensions (B) are compatible with formula brands: Heinz can market not only ketchup, but also mustard sauce. Extension one degree further (C) corresponds to brand know-how: Palmolive softens all that it embraces and Bic simplifies everything from pens to razors to lighters, making them disposable and cheap. A further extension (D), in order to be coherent with the initial product (A), assumes a brand defined by its focus and its interest centres. Tefal is interested in the entire house, not only the kitchen. In the beginning, Sony was a brand exclusively for hi-fi systems. But in a few years it has acquired fame in the field of television sets and videos and has therefore modified its image and its significance, but its core values still remain technology, precision and innovation. The last extension (E) assumes a brand that is defined by deep values. General Electric sells nuclear reactors as well as toasters. Certain brands encompass clothes and porcelain, all very naturally. They transform everything. This comes so naturally that few people know that the famous Lanvin chocolates are not made by the brand Lanvin. For the consumer they are one and the same brand.

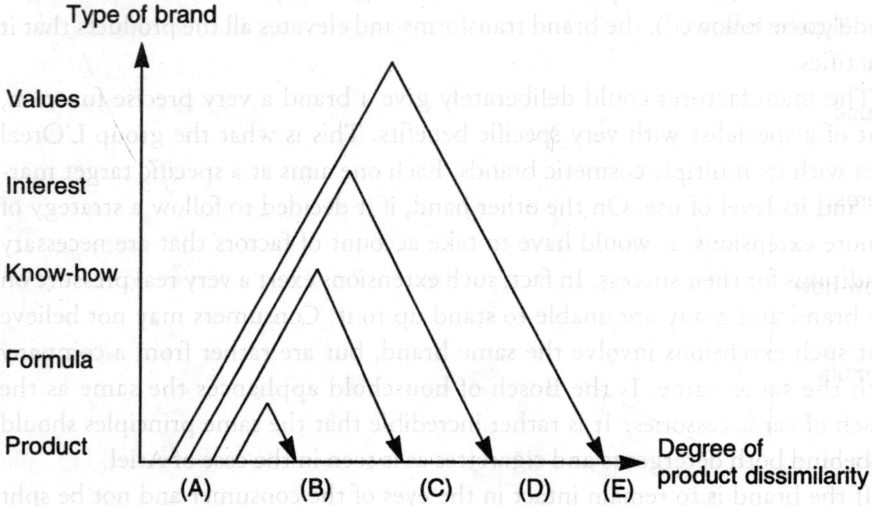

Figure 8.8 Type of brand and ability to extend

Thus, the only way for a brand to give a single meaning to a collection of extensions is to regard them from a higher viewpoint. To make distant extensions more meaningful, the brand has to distance itself physically and serve more as a source of inspiration and a value system that can embed itself in different functions. This is the case with Nestlé, a brand with a very large spectrum of offers. The distance helps to maintain the angle between the brand and its capacity to lend itself to different products. The steeper the angle, the greater force it exerts on the products (from A to E). The flatter this angle, the less is the force available to the brand to unify the products. Like an over-stretched rubber band, the brand becomes weak, loses its grip and finally breaks.

More concretely, brands having only a physical facet (a product, a recipe) and no profound identity do not lend themselves to large extensions. If extended, they decline and regress to the level of a proto-brand: that of a factory brand with only a guarantee of origin. They become diluted and are no more than numbers (see X in Figure 8.9). This is the case with Mitsubishi. It no longer operates as a unifying brand but is only a corporate name and a factory trademark. It carries no signification other than the generic characteristics of Japanese technology and the image of industrial power that is associated with the group. Mitsubishi cars do not seem to embody any particular ideal and neither do Mitsubishi televisions or tools. This is also the case with Philips to a certain extent.

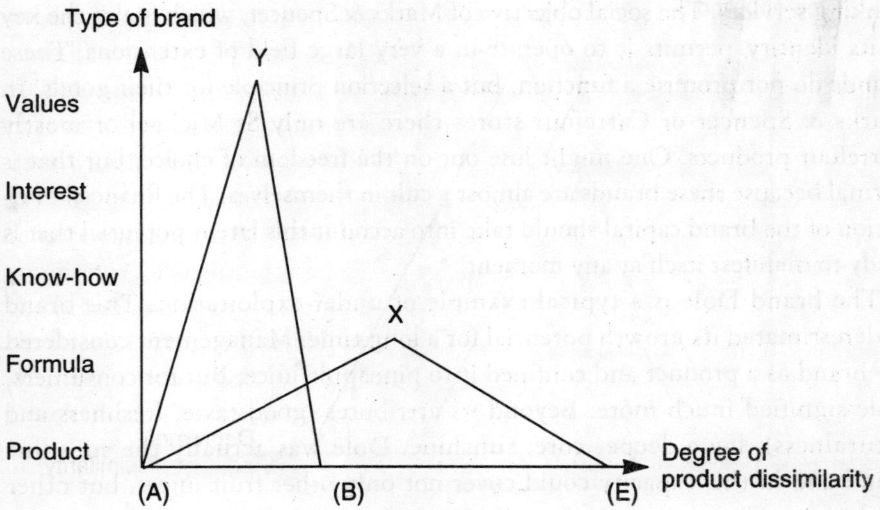

Figure 8.9 Under- and over-exploitation of a brand capital

Originally Philips signified a certain know-how associated with products such as televisions, videos and hi-fi systems. But the brand did not carry with it any other meaning. Therefore, its extension into small household appliances and white goods was too far-fetched given the elasticity of the brand capital. Consumer surveys are proof of this fact: 80 per cent of people interviewed stated that Philips was a specialist of brown products, that these products belonged to its domain and that it was competent in this area. Only 60 per cent of the respondents thought the same for the household appliances and 40 per cent for white goods. Thus, Philips lost half its credibility as far as washing-machines and refrigerators were concerned. On these products the name was scarcely more than a simple guarantee, like that of a retailer or a quality seal. The need to economise having led to the policy of a single brand, its limitations were seen in the fact that different signatures were used for different products. But the brand signature should not exist in different forms. The brand is, after all, unique. The multiplication of slogans reflected the tensions imposed on the brand which was looking in vain for a unifying factor. The subsequent (and foreseen) phase was a concentration on only the core business of the brand and the sale of the white goods unit to Whirlpool in 1989.

At the other end of the spectrum are the underexploited brands. These (see Y in Figure 8.9) cover a very narrow product field but have an inner meaning which makes them legitimate over a large range of products. The initial objectives of the multiple retailer, Carrefour, were limited to the food sector, but soon found larger and larger areas in which to express themselves: textiles, bags, banking services. The social objective of Marks & Spencer, which is also the key to its identity, permits it to operate in a very large field of extensions. These brands do not promise a function, but a selection principle for their goods. In Marks & Spencer or Carrefour stores there are only St Michael or mostly Carrefour products. One might lose out on the freedom of choice, but that is normal because these brands are almost a cult in themselves. The financial evaluation of the brand capital should take into account this latent potential that is ready to manifest itself at any moment.

The brand Dole is a typical example of under-exploitation. This brand underestimated its growth potential for a long time. Management considered the brand as a product and confined it to pineapple juice. But for consumers, Dole signified much more. Beyond its attributes (good taste, freshness and naturalness), lay a deeper core: sunshine. Dole was actually the sunshine brand and in this capacity could cover not only other fruit juices, but other products, eg ice-creams. Very well known for a long time as a shoe brand, Salvatore Ferragamo has now successfully diversified into ladies' handbags, cardigans and ties.

INCREASING THE BRAND SCOPE THROUGH GRADUAL EXTENSION

As shown in Figure 8.8 (see page 256), the further a brand wants to move from its origins, the more it needs to have acquired a relevant surplus meaning. The senior citizens' brand, Damart, did not progress in one step from being an anti-cold mono-product (thermolactyl underclothes) to light ready-to-wear clothing for the summer and even swimming costumes. After 20 years of intensive television communication focused exclusively on thermolactyl, to the point that it was practically considered to be a product brand, the offer of ready-to-wear clothing was totally unacceptable under this brand. Furthermore, leaving aside all considerations about the brand, even in product terms the Damart ready-to-wear line did not offer anything more than the catalogues of the large direct-mail companies. The extension procedure consisted of two parallel actions which reinforced each other:

- The evolution of the brand concept and its disconnection from the strict physical, material plane was achieved by giving it more scope so as to allow it to legitimise and nourish, equally, the ready-to-wear line offer and the traditional offer of winter underwear. As a result the brand changed its signature also: moving from the product slogan 'Cold? Me? Never!' to the brand slogan 'Living Fully'. This corresponded perfectly to the lifestyle needs of senior citizens. The latter slogan is based on the need for warmth in winter and the accent on active lifestyle in summer.

- Gradual extensions were made, starting from underclothes. Damart was a manufacturer's brand and had to propose a product that offered more. They first extended the thermolactyl to corsets, sports undergarments, panty-hose and socks. Then they developed a line of snug-fitting products that were both well adapted and comfortable. Finally, even in the ready-to-wear line they sought to develop clothes where a special product could be introduced.

This same gradual and methodical procedure was followed by Tefal. Going from pans to Teflon covering, Tefal first diversified into small kitchen appliances (grills, barbecues etc) and then to electronic weighing scales. The next step was the offering of wall telephones under the Tefal name in large multiple retail stores, the objective not being to sell them, but rather to prepare for their entry into the world of domotic appliances. This entire process took five years.

Being well aware of the gradual nature of the process, Salomon did not want to repeat the failure of Rossignol in the field of snowboards and snow-surfing. This culture, which arose in opposition to the traditional skiing environment, refuses to support existing well-known brands. It looks for and worships its own cult brands. So, before entering the snowboard market with an innovation, the company decided to spend some time getting accepted by the youth, penetrating their world through another of their sports where a real value-added product could be offered: roller skates and inline skates.

Research does, indeed, demonstrate that the order in which intermediate extensions are made affects consumer reaction to the final extension. Thus, in an experiment, consumers were presented with a sequence of five extensions for a number of brands. These extensions were chosen to represent five degrees of perceived distance or fit with the brand. In one case, consumers viewed an ordered sequence of extensions (from the closest to the farthest); in the second case they saw an unordered sequence of extensions (Dawar and Anderson, 1992). Two results emerged from this laboratory experiment.

As expected, there is a decrease in perceived coherence due to the distance between the extension and the brand's present product. However, the decrease in perceived coherence due to the distance is less steep when consumers saw the remote extension after a series presented in order of increasing distance. Each one may have acted as a stepping stone and prompted a category (brand) extension mechanism known as 'chaining' (Lakoff, 1987). The same result held true for the purchase likelihood for extensions.

Interestingly, it took less time to evaluate the farthest extension's coherence with the brand when that extension was seen at the end of the ordered sequence (4 seconds vs 4.34). Actually, the ordered sequence had itself modified the meaning of the brand, making it clear that it was not a product brand but a larger brand with a wider territory.

Again, a real-world illustration of this process is that of McCain. This brand entered the market with its frozen fries. After two years, it moved to large American pizzas, then to buns and recently to the fast-growing iced tea market. The meaning of McCain is now clear: American food, simple products, generous portions, fun to eat and innovative in their category. This brand territory will determine McCain's future extensions.

A second experiment demonstrated another basic rule of brand extension: only the coherence between extensions can create a brand territory. Two extensions may be equally remote from the core of the brand but not in the same direction. When a remote extension is presented to consumers after an intermediate extension in the same direction, this sequence increases the perceived coherence of that remote extension and its purchase likelihood (compared to the case where the intermediate extension is not in the same direction) (Dawar and Anderson, 1992).

CHOOSING THE RIGHT BRAND EXTENSION

It goes without saying that before making any brand extension it is imperative to know the brand well. What are its attributes? What is its personality? What identity does it convey to its buyers and users? What are its latent associations or traits? The answers to these questions are based on both quantitative polls (to discover the popularity and the image of the brand) and qualitative interviews of the target public. A simple listing of the image characteristics does not give a full picture of the brand or its sources. Access to the prism of identity and its motivating force requires qualitative investigation.

Armed with this information, the second step of the investigation procedure involves the extrapolation of the brand's distinctive features in order to assess their consequences. If Dove is personified by gentleness, then what other products need to be gentle? If Christofle is a brand for knives, forks and spoons, could it, by metonymy, be extended to glasses, plates or other tableware in general? Since Rossignol is active in one area of sport (skiing), could it not also extend into tennis rackets and golf clubs?

Luxury product brands often find the reason and the inspiration for their extensions from within their own history. Thus René Lalique, founder of

Lalique, made jewels, scarves and shawls. The extension of Baccarat into small items of furniture, jewellery, perfumes and lamps is also symbolic of the reconquest of unexploited areas.

Whatever the source, a long list emerges from this process of introspection and investigation into brand identity and extrapolations based on it. It is then subject to internal feasibility filters. Brand extension is a strategic choice that is also accompanied by other changes: in production, know-how, distribution channels, communication, corporate culture. These have to be financed either internally or by forming alliances. Thus, Boucheron sold 22 per cent of its shares, not those of its core business (high-fashion jewellery), but those of the company that managed the so-called 'first circle' extensions (jewellery, watches, spectacle frames, pens and perfumes).

This shortlist is then tested with the target public. Opinion polls are often used to achieve this. For every extension proposition consumers evaluate the product on a scale of interest to them such as 'very much, so-so, not much'. This leads to a popularity rating of the possible extensions.

This method is advantageous in that it is simple and that the grading is done by numbers. Its one drawback is that it is conservative. When a series of questions about a multitude of products are thrown at them, interviewees tend to comment only on the salient and most striking features of the brand. Therefore, this technique is biased towards only those features. Thus, when Bic was only making ball-point pens, this strategy would have ended up by exhausting all the possibilities in stationery and completely rejecting the idea that Bic should sell razors.

Davidson (1987) distinguishes a number of concentric zones around an inner core: the outer core, the extension zones and finally the no-go areas (see Figure 8.10). Close-ended questions in surveys provide information on the immediate vicinity of the brand (the outer core). In-depth qualitative phrases explore the remote extension zones.

Once again, it is necessary to proceed with a qualitative investigation to bring out the latent potential of a brand and to see how it can or cannot adopt each of these extensions. Through this same investigation we can also tell whether the resulting refusals were due to a conservative attitude linked to the actual situation, a lack of imagination on the part of the interviewee, or due to incompatibility with the brand.

The qualitative phase is a constructive one. Bearing in mind that a brand has to bring some added-value to the product category, one would also like to know under what conditions the envisaged product would be legitimate for the brand. What attributes – objective and subjective – would be necessary for it to be able to bear the brand name? How is the product superior to the present market offer?

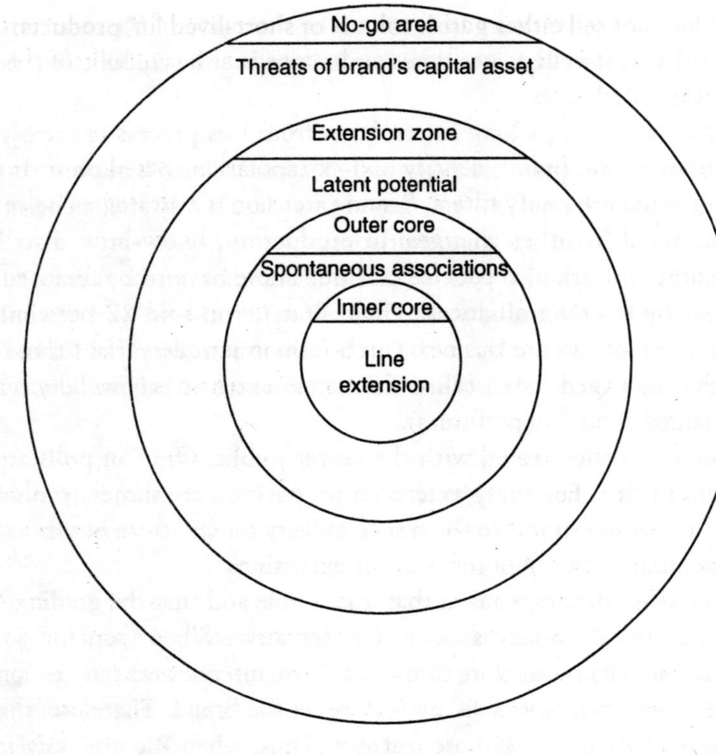

Figure 8.10 Perimeters of brand extension

Thus, it is not enough to say that Lacoste could make jackets. One also has to describe what the characteristics of a Lacoste jacket would be and those of a 'non-Lacoste' jacket. The Lacoste identity prism encompasses the following characteristics: knit, finish, durability, discretion, harmony, social aptness, conformity and adaptability. The reputation of the original Lacoste product is that of a second skin: it induces a distancing effect which constitutes the central value of the brand. It nurtures an image of supple transition between the personal and social – personal ease and social ease. The aerated knit is analogous to the skin and its pores. This identity prism defines the territories which are not Lacoste and which should be avoided for fear of losing the very meaning of the brand:

- since it conforms to a sporting ideal, Lacoste is transversal and cuts across all barriers of age and sex, thus it should not put its name to products which are exclusively feminine (in fact, the Lacoste aerobic line was a big failure), or hyper-masculine (eg hunting);

- Lacoste does not sell either garish colours or short-lived 'in' products;
- being a 'second-skin', Lacoste does not make either heavy knitwear or shiny leather clothes.

One understands why there are no Lacoste leather jackets. They are very masculine, virile and fashionable, and they do not last. Only the suede jacket is capable of possessing Lacoste characteristics.

The qualitative stage also permits an understanding of the functions of the brand for its users. Is the brand a sign for itself or for others? Where would consumers like to see the brand signed? This information is essential for branding. On the pocket of a Lacoste blazer should the signature be Lacoste, the crocodile or Lacoste Club?

Fundamentally, the testing phase should not only find out whether the brand extension is coherent with the brand, but also whether the product is superior to its competitors when deprived of its brand. In spite of the many explications about image failure, many extensions fail simply because they are inferior to existing products and are more expensive. Above all an extension is an innovation and its added-value should be considered. Finally, these projection techniques allow the tricky question of the boomerang effects on the brand capital to be dealt with. Reliability also needs to be mentioned here. Group simulations of natural processes that take time reveal the need for a methodology and extreme prudence in interpretation. The experimental simulation of 'before and after' differences in image are also hardly reliable, because of research bias.

A FEW CLASSIC ERRORS

Brand extension is a strategic procedure which deals with both the future and the capital of the brand. It is a delicate act which explains the need for a safe methodology and studies of potential. There are certain pitfalls along the road of extension and we will study them presently.

A restricted vision of the brand

Many companies have a very restricted vision of their brands. They take them to be nothing more than descriptive names. Thus, the brand extension programme is limited to a few variations of the main product. It is this conception of their brand that prevented Lesieur (the culinary oil) from benefiting from the rising popularity of sunflower oil at the outset. Clinging to a notion of groundnut oil = Lesieur and therefore Lesieur = groundnut oil, the brand shut itself off from thinking in terms of the grain and therefore could not enhance its capital with all the image characteristics of sunflower. Palmolive does not contain any extracts of olive either in its soaps, shaving foam or dishwashing liquid. As for Petrol Hahn, a Procter and Gamble hair lotion, there is hardly any petrol in the lotion, shampoo or the conditioner. Yet these brands would have had much more reason to limit themselves to such a physical vision of their identity because it was part of their name: olive, petrol. To have done so would have been an error. In fact the brand obliterates the semantic associations of the words that support it: when one thinks of Palmolive, one never thinks of olives.

Does this mean that the presence of the word 'olive' has been completely neutralised? The reality is that the meaning of the word has been suppressed but it still remains deep within the brand as latent potential. Palmolive carries in its name a vision linked to the olive which entrenches itself in the objective and subjective qualities of the products that are signed with the name. There is no need for these products to have olive extracts; it is the signification of the olive and not its physical presence which forms the extension programme for the brand.

Keeping the brand locked up

Having concluded that the Maggi image was rather old, the directors of new product launches at Sopad-Nestlé were quickly convinced that it was better to launch their new instant purée with as little connection to Maggi as was possible. The same thing happened for Bolino, ready-to-eat meals.

They had fallen into the trap of the self-fulfilling prophecy. Having said that the brand Maggi was old, they concluded that it could not cover new and modern products. Thus they closed the brand in a ghetto by disassociating it from these products. This only reinforced its old and outdated character and made it even less apt for extension.

Many believe that the only way to save the brand is by advertising and the adoption of the latest trends. But a brand proves its modernity through the products that it creates and brings to the market. The Maggi syndrome results from the failure to remember that the firm builds its brands through a long gradual process. Product launches have to achieve sales targets, but the longevity of a company depends on its few brands which themselves cover a large range of products. Had they paid greater attention to the brand equity perspective, they would have associated the Maggi name with the new line and increased its value. This is what was done by Knorr when it launched Knorr purée.

When the past determines the future

Another reason for the excessive limitations put on brands is the preoccupation with past decisions. But one cannot manage a brand by staying in the past. Admittedly, the brand is a memory as far as products are concerned, but over time it acquires and emanates its own meaning. It has its own identity. This does not imply that the future should be an extrapolation of the past. The brand drives itself through its own energy and inertia, but in the long run it is strategic decision-making which determines its direction.

It sometimes happens that the extension or non-extension of the brand can be defined as a function of the products that have already been signed by it. Before having been acquired by Danone, the management of the biscuit brand Lu stated clearly in all its documents that being the 'mother' of all French biscuits and deeply embedded in the roots of history, Lu could not be extended to cover any foreign brands: neither Pim's nor Prince because they were English, nor Sirtaki because of the Greek connotations associated with it. But we know how easily the brand today not only embraces all these biscuits, but also enriches itself through them. The brand is one of the strongest in the market and a strong candidate for European globalisation. One could have limited Lu to a brand that was an upholder of tradition but it was a strategic decision to do otherwise. It was decided to make it the brand for biscuits in France and in Europe. Its latent potential allowed this, even though this was not evident at the time. The nationality of a biscuit is nothing but a surface characteristic. Lu, on the other hand, is different: the brand changes and creates, updates recipes and innovates indefinitely in an infinite range of sense and taste. Lu is an artist and not an artisan.

Strong brands can overcome wide extensions. That is why Chanel for Men did not harm the image of Chanel. One can imagine how passionate were the debates on the extensibility of the brand into the world of men's fashion. Very often, brand extension is hindered by the excessive attention that is accorded to the overt attributes and the physical characteristics of the brand which leads to a conservative attitude which sticks too much to the present.

The first three attitudes that we have examined so far all serve to restrict the brand. The following five have the opposite effect: the brand is not only over-stretched, it is in a risky position. These decisions often result from a desire to profit from commercial opportunity: faced with a profitable market, an opportunity to exploit the brand or to enter into a licensing agreement, the company becomes preoccupied with short-term gains and underestimates the long-term risks to the brand capital.

Harmful extensions

Aware of the boom in the sector of 'light' foods, many companies jumped at the opportunity to profit from it. But, it was a wrong move for quite a few, which is why there is no 'Heineken Light'. By launching Bridel light, Bridel, a camembert brand, perhaps committed a mistake because by making it light they probably destroyed some of the most important characteristics of Bridel: excellent taste, authenticity and respect for nature. It was therefore a big risk for the entire brand because 'light' products do not usually taste as good as the original product. On the other hand, Président foresaw this risk and decided to put much more distance between its name and its range of light products by calling them Présilège and by treating them differently from Président for advertising purposes. Conversely, Lipton's extension from tea to soups led to a weakening of the brand.

In general, extension into lower quality segments is destructive. That is why Lycra would never have a quality sub-brand. It might imply that there are different levels of quality associated with Lycra.

Opportunism and identity incoherence

Extension is rife in the luxury goods market where opportunities for licensing abound. One can thus find china and cutlery in a Nina Ricci boutique. It is not the right brand for such extensions. What is right for Hermès isn't necessarily so for Nina Ricci because Nina Ricci's identity is based on the image of the woman whose virginal symbol is the hymen, and china belongs to the social universe of the lady of the house, the lady with status. It is compatible with brands such as Hermès or Dior which are based on a social status, or a brand such as Yves Saint Laurent which is based on seduction. It is not coherent with the identity and the universe of Nina Ricci.

Prototypical brands

In some markets one brand may represent the entire product category. It is the prototype of the category. Coca-Cola is therefore the symbol of all colas and Levi's that of jeans. Having established such a brand which is universally recognised and has an incontestable reputation, the company is naturally tempted to use this precious capital for the new products that it creates. But it runs the risk of losing the legitimacy and the power of the brand in its original market.

A prototype brand should also not try to venture into categories where other prototypes exist. In having to recognise the authority of the other brand it itself declines a little. Lacoste, the well-known symbol of sportswear, therefore lost out when it tried to venture into the jeans market, dominated by the creations of Levi's. It could not impose its brand, that is, change the product category and establish its own references. One can always stick a crocodile on a pair of jeans, but it is a superficial act and it weakens the brand because it serves as proof of its lack of meaning.

The trap of mundane products

Choosing a category of very simple and mundane products prevents a brand from segmenting the category and leaving its own traces. The brand can only add its name as an imaginary halo but cannot change the product category in any distinctive manner. In the short term this can lead to an additional flurry of sales due to consumers attracted by a well-known brand name and its promise of excellent quality. In the medium term this can weaken the brand. Attaching the brand to a product whose added-value as a result of the inclusion of the brand name is not immediately obvious renders the brand artificial and only an act of communication. A true brand is one whose image is embedded in the product's characteristics.

A category of mundane products does not permit the establishment of qualitative differences so a big brand cannot exploit all its potential and knowledge and therefore fails. For example, Thomson did not benefit from the image of Thomson Industry (radars, weapons and electronics) when it tried to sell household appliances.

The case of luxury goods: Licenses and accessories

Are Chanel T-shirts and Cardin cigarettes examples of this syndrome too? Big signatures expand into mundane categories such as handkerchiefs, socks, cigarettes, etc through licensing agreements. The only difference between a handkerchief and a Cardin handkerchief is the brand name. There is, however, a structural difference between a Thomson television and a Chanel T-shirt. The television is the brand's own product and a concrete manifestation of some of its characteristics. The T-shirt merely supports the brand through the motif and the consumer wears it as a sign of his allegiance just as people wear religious symbols or their candidate's logos during elections. That is why the watch is adopted by any and every brand. In showing the time, it serves as a medium to display the brand also.

The brand, as we have said, is additive – it is the sum total of its own attributes. The long-term danger for Chanel is that their T-shirts might come to be considered as an attribute of Chanel. And one has to accept that the T-shirt is an uninspired garment which is worn by people who do not exactly have the Chanel look. A very wide distribution of the garment can be detrimental to the guarantee of refinement which is one of the pivotal features of the brand's identity.

When a brand proliferates, not in all directions but into uninspiring products such as cigarettes, handkerchiefs, ties and various other accessories, the brand's capital asset is drained. Cardin is the prototype of this phenomenon. When the name is splashed on all kinds of products, it becomes insignificant just like the word 'de luxe' which is today used for everything from cars to cheap beers. Or was it perhaps part of Cardin's plans to exhaust the brand by spreading out in all 'cardinal' directions?

Finally, there is a last group of difficulties associated with brand extension which is related to a disregard for the customer's point of view and a preoccupation with the technological conception of the brand.

Complementarity is not guarantee

The graveyard of brand extension is littered with extensions which were considered risk-free. Panzani pasta failed in their efforts to sell Panzani tomato sauce. Yet one can understand the temptation to market the sauce, an indispensable accompaniment to a good pasta dish. Campbell, the soup brand, considered it quite natural to launch a spaghetti sauce. This seemed obvious for a brand whose leading products included tomato sauce. But, it was a failure and was relaunched under the name Prego. Similarly, Astra margarine was never able to launch Astra oil.

Therefore, it is not the products themselves which determine the possibilities of extension, rather an adherence to the brand's core identity. Barilla succeeded where Panzani could not, and it was not because Panzani's management was incompetent. The pure Italianness of Barilla legitimised its extension. Such a consideration also explains the reticence on the part of Lacoste to enter the jeans market. Market studies show that the garment worn most often with the famous Lacoste knit shirt, are blue jeans. It would be tempting for any trader to try to capture the market for its complementary product. But it would have been an error even when considered without the existence of a prototype on the market. When worn with jeans, a Lacoste makes its wearer stand out. If it were to sign the jeans also, Lacoste would create a kind of uniform and renounce its brand identity. Similarly, Lacoste signs tennis rackets but not the strings. These always wear out very quickly and disappoint the player. No brand proclaiming durability would want to attach their name to such a product.

THE MARKETING MIX OF BRAND EXTENSIONS

Once the brand extension has been decided upon what kind of precautions are necessary, and what principles of direction should be followed to make the most of the extension?

Foreseeing the risks for the brand

Certain extensions include some risks which cannot be excluded. This is the reason why, in spite of all temptations, Fisher-Price did not enter into the child-care products market. This would have been consistent with the brand, but accidents are very common with these products and the resultant publicity could have had unwanted repercussions on the other activities of the brand.

In 1989, the group Wagons-Lits decided to enter the market for luxury travel that was targeted towards the elite. Approached for the use of their name, Hermès eventually refused. The unforeseen risks of the service sector – especially the travel world – would have exposed the brand to risks that it did not want to undertake. They are well able to control events in their shops in the Faubourg St-Honoré, but would be helpless when it comes to problems with hotels in Tibet.

Anticipating the risks for the extension

On a psychological level, brand extension assumes three hypotheses: first, that the positive associations linked with the brand will be transferred to the new product; secondly, that negative associations will not be transferred; third, that a positive trait of the brand will not become negative when associated with the new product. The purpose of market research is to verify these hypotheses. The role of communication is to ensure that the second and the third hypotheses continue to hold true.

Thus, the notion of Colgate or Signal chewing gum will spontaneously evoke the sensation of a pharmaceutical taste. This attribute may be positive when associated with toothpastes, but becomes negative when linked with chewing gums. Moreover, it would be a mistake to focus communications around dental hygiene as that would only serve to reinforce the negative associations stemming from the imagined taste. Communications should, on the contrary, stress the pleasure of the taste of chewing gum and the taste of mint. Communication therefore helps to block the risks of the transfer of the negative aspects of the brand.

What names for brand extensions?

Proper branding also helped the sun-tan products line of Lacoste. The brand lacked credibility in this segment and lacked all dermatological know-how. This could have seriously handicapped the line and made the products less attractive to the buyers. Also, they did not want to call it the Lacoste Sun Range. The line needed its own more meaningful name to compensate for the deficits of the Lacoste name and to endow it with all the technical credibility necessary for its success. The name chosen was Sun Technics from Lacoste.

Generally speaking, the more a brand expands its field, the greater is the need to add sub-brands to help these extensions. This leads to a multi-level brand structure: the mother-brand level and another level made up of the names of the products. The problems of different brand structures were dealt with in Chapter 7.

As a rule, when the extension is close to the core, it should not receive a specific brand name. When it is remote, it should be helped by a specific surname or a sub-brand. For instance, Danone's core values are health and nature. The new products close to the core must reinforce this identity and avoid fragmenting it. Hence, one finds highly generic extension names such as Bio, Danone with fruits, or Danone Velours. The further the extension, the less it can capitalise on a process of affect transfer: it should express its own personality to take off and eventually bring its genuine personality to the mother brand. Thus, when it entered into iced-tea, McCain did not call the extension McCain's iced-tea but Colorado by McCain. Figure 8.11 presents Nivea's branding system.

Co-branding to enter new territories

In the summer of 1995, M&M's chocolate launched a line of cookies with Kraft's toffee, Sunkist's lemon or Hershey's chocolate. Compaq and Mattel work together on a new line of Fisher-Price products. Kellogg's launched an extension with the help of Pop Tart, a well-known brand of biscuits. Beyond classic competitive enhancement due to alliances of corporate know-how, co-branding adds a communication dimension by means of the visibility of the alliance. Each brand brings part of its equity to the other and makes its extension more credible. Yoplait's upmarket extensions were helped by the reputation of Côte d'Or chocolates, a brand of Kraft. Compaq will bring its industrial know-how to Mattel, but also derive from it a closer brand relationship with millions of households, a step towards further Compaq market entry.

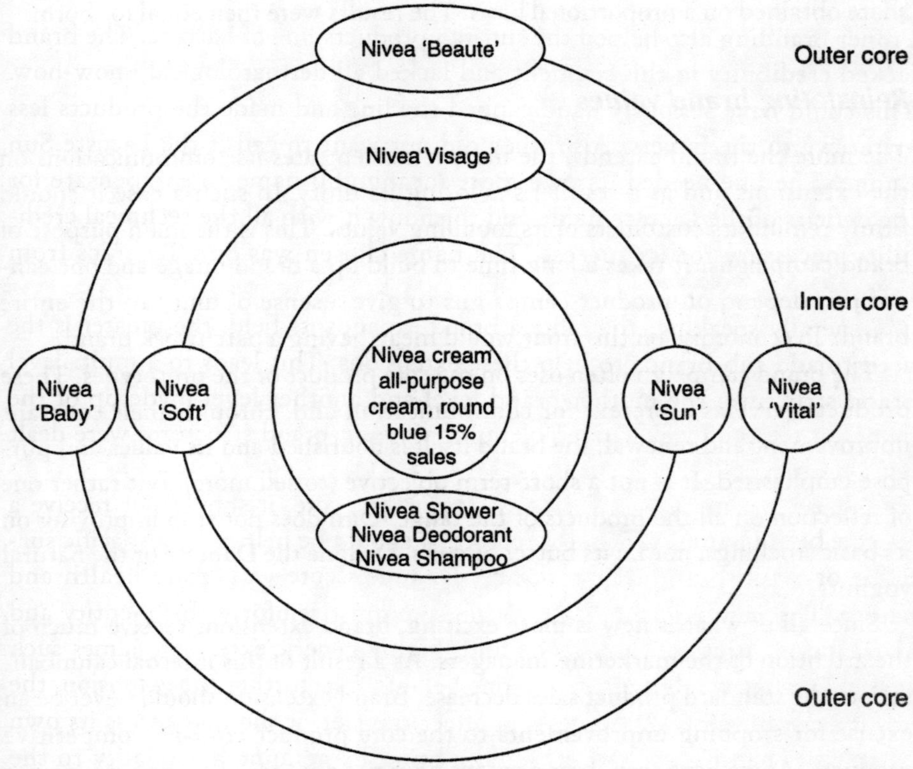

Figure 8.11 Nivea's branding system

The temptation to under-invest

Many extensions are brought about for economic reasons. But advertising costs cannot be supported for too many brands and so the brand portfolio has to be trimmed. Furthermore, since the brand is already known, its seems normal to under-invest on communication for an extension as compared to the launch costs for a new brand. An analysis was carried out by Nielsen under the supervision of Peckham (1981) illustrating the dangers of such an attitude in the consumer goods market (see page 239).

Nielsen studied 115 new product launches in three segments: body-care, food and hygiene. Results showed that within two years new products launched under their own name achieved twice the market share of products launched under an already existing name (6.7 per cent versus 3.3 per cent for body care, 6.5 per cent versus 1.9 per cent for food). Is brand extension a mistake?

Deeper analysis revealed the true reason for this difference in performance. Products launched under their own name had launch budgets twice as big as those for brand extensions. To eliminate this bias they recalculated market share obtained on a proportional basis. The results were then equal for both.

Reinstating brand values

The more the brand extends, the more it concentrates its communications on the extensions and as a result risks losing its unity. In such a case it should firmly remind its customers of its founding values. This is the main purpose of brand campaigns. It takes a long time to build up a brand image and one cannot just depend on product campaigns to give a sense of unity to the entire brand. To economise on this front would mean having a patchwork brand.

The brand campaign often uses on the core product or the prototypes. These products serve as a pretext for communication and, through their constant improvement and renewal, the brand itself is nourished and its values and purpose emphasised. It is not a short-term objective (to sell more), but rather one of reflection on all the products of the range. Dim does not stop improving on its basic stockings, nor Lu its butter biscuits, Danone the Danette or the natural yoghurt.

Since all of what is new is more exciting, brand extensions receive much of the attention of the marketing managers. As a result of this internal cannibalisation, the standard product sales decrease. Brand extension should never be an excuse for stopping improvements to the core product *vis-à-vis* competitive products. As we have seen, brand extension is not a source of economy. One not only has to provide support to the extension, but also reinforce the brand core products which still bear most of the brand sales and image.

Management of luxury brands also necessitates double communication: offensive – working towards territory expansion – and defensive – safeguarding its actual legitimate territory. The defensive form of communication highlights product origins and sources of value at the core of the brand. Even while expanding into new areas (golf), Lacoste takes great care to reinforce its roots by sponsoring the Davis Cup and the Roland Garros tournament. Advertising is concentrated on their symbol, the crocodile, and on the famous shirt, but also covers other diversifications within the same brand code.

Coherence of the marketing mix

Brand extension is not limited to applying the brand name to new products beyond the original areas covered by the brand. It is often accompanied by development of a marketing mix different from that of previous products.

Thus, Armani decided to target a younger and different clientele with outfits that were 50 per cent less expensive. These bore the name Emporio Armani and were sold internationally in boutiques different from the original Armani stores.

When Vuitton launched its watches, they only sold them in the already established Vuitton showrooms. Would it not have been better to take advantage of this extension to establish a position as a true watchmaker by placing them in the specialised watchmaker jeweller boutiques of New York, Tokyo or Paris? On the other hand, Cartier launched the 'Must de Cartier' collection to benefit from brand recognition and fame in order to leave the hallowed world of jewellery and its limited clientele. Extension on a price parameter had to be accompanied by a change in the distribution network.

The failure to master the marketing mix of the extension is the true reason behind the failure of many. For example, Pernod decided to launch Pernuts, a range of peanuts and grilled almonds packed in nitrogen and distributed in coffee shops, hotels and restaurants. This simple idea appeared promising on paper. The problem was logistics and stock management. Considering the long life of a bottle of Pernod, stocks were managed on a LIFO basis (last in, first out). Thus, whether a case of Pernod stayed in the warehouse for months or not was of little consequence. But it was completely different for peanuts. It was essential that the first stock in should also be the first to go out. Failure of this system led to clients often receiving stale peanuts that were unfit for consumption.

Signal, the toothpaste brand's, extension into chewing gums was also a failure, attributed partly to the fact that the chewing gums were displayed on the toothpaste shelves in stores and not along with other sweets. But the key question here is: 'Is a chewing gum marketed by Signal enough of a chewing gum to be able to fight market leaders such as Freedent, X-Tra and also Wrigley's, who communicate on the pleasure of taste, and hold strong positions in the sugar-free and healthy chewing gums segment?'

When the brand hides the new product

Well-known brands should treat with extreme prudence the forecast sales figures emerging from market studies and test market simulations (like Bases or Assessor). In these studies consumers are well aware that they are dealing with new products, but in national launches of extensions many of the target clientele might not even know that it is a new product. The advertisement is well seen, but not the product. This risk is augmented when the brand uses a symbol or a person who has become so familiar that the public no longer awaits (and therefore, does not hear) any informative message. They believe that every appearance of the brand is a friendly reinforcement and not an announcement for a new product. In fact, people often attribute to well-known brands products that are not actually made by them. This is exactly what happened to Andrex when they decided to challenge Kleenex in the paper handkerchief market in the UK. The attack tactic was the development of a family-size format in combination with the inherited values of the Andrex name (Yentis and Bond, 1995). Based on test market simulations, sales were predicted at 11.6 million units. In reality, they were only 10 million units in the first year. The reason for this was that even before the launch, Andrex handkerchiefs had 6% spontaneous awareness and 60% assisted awareness. These users were therefore not even conscious of a new launch (unlike the consumers used for the simulation and the test marketing). Thus, the commercial had to be reshot a second time to highlight the real novelty of the product both for Andrex and for the market. This problem is aggravated when one can only use the press as the medium of communication for a launch.

THE LIMITS OF BRAND EXTENSION

A chapter on brand extension cannot conclude without a word about the present dangers resulting from extension practices. Sometimes an extension is chosen through simple laziness or for the sake of conformity. In reality, it would be better to launch a new brand. This is certainly more risky, costly and needs more effort, work and energy, but the future of the company rests on its portfolio of strong brands. There is an unmeasured opportunity cost for brand extension that is not quantifiable: it is the strong new brand that was not created. This new brand could have allowed a better coverage of the present market, or a deeper penetration of new, young and emergent markets which could bring much growth to the company.

9

Multi-brand portfolios

The question of how many brands should be kept in each market has become a primary concern of all senior marketing managers. The fact is that, due to historical reasons, most firms have to manage a large portfolio of brands. The natural tendency during the growth of firms has been to add new brands each time they wanted to penetrate new market segments or new distribution channels. This was done so as not to create conflicts with former segments and channels which could have endangered their old brands. The vogue of company mergers and acquisitions brought additional brands that managers were reluctant to dispose of or merge with other brands. The size of brand portfolios, therefore, just grew and grew.

Times have changed though, and now the trend is to reduce the size of portfolios as quickly as possible. There are several reasons for this reverse in trends.

- Although it is easy to maintain several brands simultaneously in industrial markets where different brands are sometimes used for the same product to ease relations with distributors, in the retail market it is nearly impossible. Given the cost of advertising and promotion, any attempt to finance too many brands would only result in making the creation of a strong brand impossible. A brand is more than a mere name on a product, a brand must have public significance, which can only be achieved through communication. But since the volume of mass communication in every sector is soaring, it is becoming more and more expensive to successfully get one particular message across. The direct consequence is that only a few brands in a portfolio will be promoted, to gain a significant market share.
- The concentration of the distribution trade has reduced the number of retailers and has even almost suppressed certain retail channels and small businesses. Brands which were previously uniquely handled by specific distribution channels and sold only in certain stores may now be found in a

single wholesaler or purchasing group. This tends to lead to the reduction in their numbers. This concentration has enabled the distribution trade to invest proportionately far greater sums in advertising their own trade names than those spent by individual manufacturers' brands. While the Thomson Multimedia Group spent 45 million francs advertising its best brand of television sets, Darty, a French subsidiary of Kingfisher, spent 200 million francs on its own advertisement. The distribution trade has also pursued a policy of creating distributors' own brands. This, coupled with the fact that supermarket shelf space is limited, leads to the reduction of space allocated to the other brands, another factor causing a reduction in the number of references or brands themselves.

- Industrial production has also become concentrated. International competition has put the emphasis on high productivity and low costs and has led to the regrouping of production units and research and development activities. There is less justification for large brand portfolios when the products, however varied, come from the same factories.
- Consumers, however, still have the last say and despite the fact that the objective of a brand is to clarify the market, their most frequent complaint is that they are confused by the growing number of brands. Too many brands were created in the 1960s and 1970s selling the same product under different guises: this approach was a classic in the white goods markets. Justifiably, consumer groups fought to have the number of me-too brands reduced. A company is fooling the consumer if it sells two identical products under two different brand names. Manufacturers responded by rationalising their brands. In this respect it seems paradoxical that just when manufacturers started cutting out their own me-too brands, hence clarifying the market, retailer brands took their place. All retailers developed their own brands which often originated from the same supplier. What is more, distributors, for their private label, ask the suppliers for similar products to their own brands. The result of this pressure from distribution is that, again, the same products are sold under two different brands, the manufacturer's and the distributor's, for two different prices.
- The last point, but not the least, concerns brand internationalisation. In many areas today, national barriers no longer make sense. In Europe, for example, class, lifestyle and consumer needs are no longer exclusive to a single country. The luxury goods industry has long been targeting the world market, as indeed have most industrial companies. Not all brands are suited to the international arena, however. The investment required to establish a significant global presence means that firms can only maintain a small number of brands to enable a multibrand approach, or indeed just a single one for

a mono-brand strategy such as that of Philips, Siemens, Alcatel, Mitsubishi or ABB.

How many brands, therefore, should be retained in a portfolio? It is obvious at this stage that there does not exist any magic formula or number. The question of the number of brands to retain is closely linked to the strategic role and status of the brands. In keeping only a single brand, we are assuming that an umbrella brand policy is possible and indeed pertinent in the market being considered. For decades, the Philips brand included both brown and white products, yet they parted with the latter in 1989, selling them to the American company Whirlpool. The decision regarding the number of brands to be retained should therefore be closely linked to an analysis of the brand's function in its respective market. Every market can be segmented, by product, customer expectation or type of clientele. This does not mean, though, that a market divided into six segments, for example, should necessarily call for six brands. This depends on their function (do we need endorsing, umbrella, range or product brands?). It also depends upon the long-term corporate objectives, the degree of competition and the resources of the company. The appropriate number of brands results from a multi-stage, multi-criteria decision process whereby various scenarios are presented and evaluated. A good example of this approach is that of the hotel division of the Wagons-Lits International Company.

BRAND PORTFOLIOS AND MARKET SEGMENTATION

In 1986, the Wagons-Lits International Company carried out an audit of its portfolio of international hotel brands (Frantel, PLM, Etap) in the three- and four-star hotel market. They drew the following conclusions:

- Since this portfolio was formed by a process of external growth, through successive acquisitions, there was a big overlap between all three names. Far from defining separate products and services, the brands overlapped.
- There was too much variance within the same individual brand. PLM, for example, ranged from bush stopover camps in Kenya to the smart St Jacques hotel in Paris.
- Frantel was considered similar to Novotel, and therefore represented a too standardised product. Little known outside France, the name had a French

resonance which was good from the point of view of gastronomy, but not so good where hotel service was concerned.

- Etap had made its mark in Turkey and was well-known in Holland. In France, they were looked on as two-star hotels or motels.

The company decided to rationalise its brand portfolio and to start a chain of prestigious international hotels to be found in capital cities, with four-star status just below that of the Hilton or Sheraton. This created a dual problem: (a) They had to determine the number of brands required to cover the three- or four-star hotel market on an international level; (b) they had to find appropriate names for their brands which could come from the original portfolio.

In the hotel trade, in order to gain brand awareness, particularly at an international level, one must have a large number of hotels. This reduces the number of brands as do high commercial and advertising costs. Considering the presence of Arcade in the two-star market and the plans for the one-star market, Wagons-Lits International concentrated on the three- and four-star market. This market was also of interest because it covered both the business and leisure travelling categories.

At least eight possible brand scenarios could have been adopted (see Figure 9.1): a single brand (1), four brands (2), two-brand scenarios (3 and 5), two scenarios with line extensions (4 and 6) and two three-brand scenarios (7 and 8).

The primary concern when creating a new luxury chain is to avoid all risks and any false steps which might hinder the slow progress towards a successful

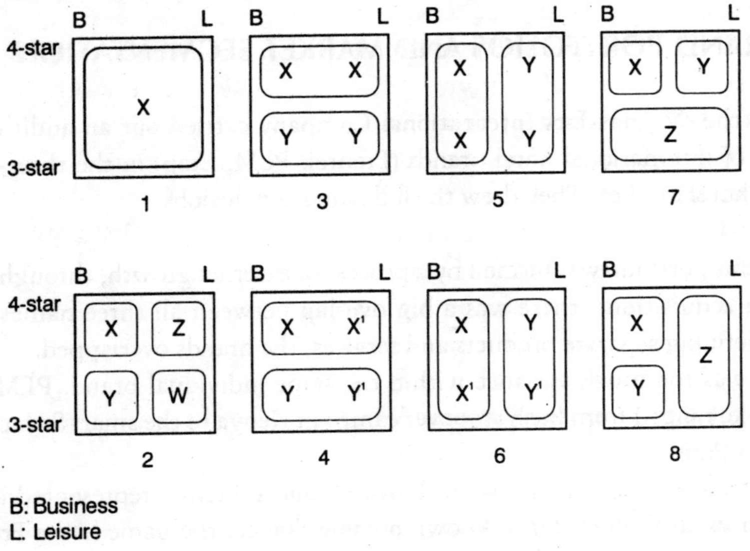

Figure 9.1 Options for a brand portfolio in the hotel industry

reputation and image. While Hilton, whose reputation is now well established, can leverage its name on both business and leisure hotels, Wagons-Lits International had to avoid this during the early years of the new luxury chain's existence. In order to avoid getting unfavourable reports they had to begin with a level of service which they could tightly control. A certain standard can be reached in Vienna, London or Prague, but not so easily in Nouakchott, Dakar or Lagos.

Could the prestige chain remain credible if its name was also used for three-star hotels, albeit with a special qualification (X Confort, for example, as with the Holiday Inn Garden Court Hotels). Any risk of association with the lowest level rating had to be excluded and the X name should only apply to the few hotels offering the high standard of service expected by senior managers on business trips.

In targeting this specific clientele, the brand must designate a no-compromise offer: it is a product brand and is associated with a specific level of service. On a two-day trip to Ankara or Munich, a business manager wants to reduce the risks of not finding all he expects and requires (24-hour service, air conditioning, information desk, etc). All these features are identified with the brand, which is the customer's only source of reference. There shouldn't be, therefore, any variation in service from one hotel to another. On the other hand, in order to avoid a monotonous repetition of identical hotel layouts in every city, there can and should be personal touches to the surroundings. Hence, the X names being defined by a different suffix in each city.

The holiday guest is another kettle of fish. His first contact with the hotel is through detailed brochures. The role of the brand name here is less significant. The guest wants to get away from it all. The hotel needs an evocative name in tune with the guest's holiday dream and which adds to the appeal of its photographs (eg the Malibu, the Saint-Tropez Beach). Is there a need for a common brand name, or even several, for the holiday segment? Here the brand's only function is that of a guarantee of quality and efficiency. It simply indicates that the hotel is under *controlled* management. The brand has only an endorsing function and as such could support a wide range of hotels. These differences no longer pose a problem, since they are clearly shown in the brochures and as such no longer constitute a surprise but rather a goal.

With these considerations in mind Wagons-Lits International chose scenario 8 from Figure 9.1:

- Brand X constitutes the new top-of-the-market chain, limited to business hotels. A few exceptions are acceptable if a leisure hotel already has a luxury reputation (eg X-Cataract in Assouan). The nominal identity takes the form

X-p, where the suffix p is a minor addition which personalises the hotel (eg X-Astoria in Brussels). X is the leading name, the one which does the talking and the selling.

- Brand Z guarantees a vast range of hotels in the Caribbean, Morocco and North Africa. Z is only the endorsing brand which follows the hotel's name: the Carrayou-Z in Martinique or the Marissol-Bas-du-Fort-Z in Guadeloupe.
- Brand Y indicates three-star business hotels in a regional metropolis (the Y Lindau in Germany or the Y Clermont-Ferrand in France).

Once the architecture of the brands is defined, the choice of the three names X, Y, Z supposes that there exist precise concepts of the identity each brand is to have. Would it be a good idea to give the prestigious chain a French connotation or should all French links be hidden? With its objectives in mind and after considering all legal and financial constraints Wagons-Lits International chose the following names: Pullman for X, Altea for Y and retaining PLM for Z. All the brand names were changed on the same day, 25 March 1987. In order to preserve the reputation of the Etap brand in Turkey, a transitional programme was devised, which initially incorporated Etap in the new name (eg the Pullman Etap Izmir or the Pullman Etap Marmara) with the long-term goal of its removal.

Another good example of brand portfolio management is the defensive strategy adopted by Hollywood, the chewing gum brand of Kraft General Foods, faced with the competition of the American giant Wrigley's. This world leader, irritated by the fact that it was excluded from the French market, introduced the brand Freedent in 1987 in order to try to remedy the situation. Freedent, a sugar-free chewing gum, targeted the mouth hygiene market and contributed to the expansion of the sugar-free chewing gum market, which in 1994 represented 41 per cent of all chewing gum consumption. It also toppled Hollywood Light, a former line extension which was positioned on weight-control, as the best seller.

The temptation would have been strong to extend yet again the Hollywood brand and launch a new chewing gum to counter the Freedent invasion. But a straightforward combat in the dental hygiene market was not coherent with the Hollywood brand identity in March 1992. The group chose to launch a new brand, Tonigum, with calcium, a complete innovation which strengthens teeth enamel. At the same time Hollywood Light's market positioning was changed through a new packaging and advertising campaign. The new promise was that of a longer lasting fresh taste. With this strategy, Kraft thought it had cornered Freedent but, in April 1993, Wrigley's launched a second brand, Extra, on the

French market. Its positioning was identical to that held by Hollywood Light and it succeeded in showing the fragility of its competitor. The fact was that whether or not one liked it, and despite the advertising campaigns to the contrary, the term 'light' carries a negative aspect, that of lack of taste (this is why Pepsi light was named Pepsi Max). In 1995, Kraft General Foods launched a new product (which exploited an innovation giving a strong sensation in the mouth) with a promise of intense taste. They named it Cristal, but this time with the Hollywood guarantee. Customers in the sugar-free market are not faithful to one brand but change regularly, so Cristal provides a new alternative. Besides, both Extra and Cristal refrain from advertising the fact that they are sugar-free in order to increase their attraction.

This example illustrates the need for a global vision when defending one's market share, either using new product brands or extending existing brands to new market segments. It illustrates certain parameters that should be taken into account when deciding the ideal number of brands to have. The first concerns market segmentation. It demonstrates that there are no strict parallels between product policy and brand policy: the brand portfolio can easily cover every market segment without needing a separate brand for each one. A brand name is an indicator, a cue. The analysis of consumer behaviour and of the information need in the decision process enables one to be more precise: What should it indicate? What exactly is the brand role?

A multiple brand policy corresponds to a segmented market, where the various expectations in each segment are not only different but are also seen as incompatible by consumers and industrial buyers. For instance Alezo-Nobel coating division considers that the paint market should be divided along three criteria, each of them commanding separate brands: is it for professionals or for the do-it-yourself market? Is it a specialised paint or a generalist one? Is it an upmarket, a mainstream or a low-price offer?

MULTI-BRAND STRATEGIES

At the beginning of this chapter, we looked at the practical reasons why the number of brands had to be reduced, sometimes even to a single brand. They all correspond to a strategy of domination and competitive advantage via low cost. While recognising the market segmentation, it has been decided not to take it into account at brand level, but only in terms of products.

The multi-brand approach, on the contrary, is the logical consequence of a differentiation strategy and as such cannot coexist with a low cost policy, in view of reduced economies of scale, technical specialisation, specific sales networks and necessary advertising investments. Nevertheless, with the exception of exclusive luxury brands, pressure remains. In order to take advantage of productivity gains, there is a tendency to fragment the production chain in the cause of differentiation at the last possible moment, thus exploiting the benefits of the learning curve. This is the case in the domestic appliances industry, making industrial regrouping a necessity, as well as in the food processing or automobile industries. The policy of having general car brands makes the most of all possible production and corporate communication synergism, and breeds the loyalty of the customer who progresses from one model to another within the same make.

With all the advantages of a mono-brand policy, what makes it necessary to have several brands on the market at the same time?

To start with, market growth. No single brand can develop a market on its own. Even if it forms the sole presence at the outset, once the brand has created the market, its development requires a multiplication of players, each investing to promote their respective differences. The collective presence of a number of contributors helps to promote a market. Beyond their differences, their combined advertising accentuates the common advantages of the product category. A multiple presence is necessary to support the market as a whole. It would not be in Philips' interest to see its competitors in the electric razor market disappear. This would only decrease the number of messages praising the merits of electric razors, which could only benefit Gillette and Wilkinson Sword. Philips should acquire a brand and maintain it as an active brand in the market. In the pharmaceutical industry, a laboratory discovering a new formula could certainly profit from 'co-marketing' it with other laboratories in order to accelerate its impact. An example of this is found in the case of aspartame.

Multiple brands allow for best market coverage. No single brand can cover a market on its own. As a market matures there is a need for differentiation and it becomes necessary to offer a wider range; the market is becoming segmented. A brand cannot be targeted at several different qualities at the same time without running the risk of losing its identity. In any case, consumers and retailers themselves will object to further brand ascendancy. This dual process is illustrated by the case of Rossignol. The company Rossignol follows a dual brand policy:

- a mono-brand multi-product policy: the hallmark Rossignol covers its skis, ski suits and ski boots (those coming from its acquisition of the Le Trappeur Brand, since then debaptised);
- a multi-brand mono-product policy, with the Dynastar brand on skis, Kerma brand on sticks and Lange brand on boots.

With 20 per cent of the world ski market, Rossignol is the leading manufacturer. Their share in the upmarket ski sector is thought to be even greater, of the order of 40 per cent or more. This is an area where they should not offend people's susceptibilities by expecting them to dress from head to toe in Rossignol products. If the world leader wants to grow even bigger, it should be the one increasing the choice, rather than its competitors. In this market, the distribution is still handled by a large number of small independent retailers, who fear the control of a single supplier. This is why each company brand has its own sales force. In the United States the Rossignol company presence is assured by two separate companies, Dynastar Inc. and Rossignol Inc. In the industrial sector, Facom and Legrand, two dominant leaders, successfully increased their hold on their market by creating apparently separate and autonomous brands. This enabled them to find new distributors, who were only too happy to have at their disposal a near exclusive brand, different from those of other retailers in that zone.

Multiple brands offer a tactical flexibility which also enables one to limit a competitor's field of extension. In this way Delsey, the leading European luggage manufacturer, cornered Samsonite. They created a new brand, Visa, positioned to undercut Samsonite prices, while at the same time Delsey restrained them from moving into the top-of-the-range market.

A multi-brand policy can stop any new competitors entering a market. A strong entry barrier to a market can be created by offering a complete range to retailers, with a brand name for each sector of the market. This is why in the European market, Pepsi-Cola and Orangina have distribution agreements, Coca-Cola itself having in its brand portfolio the world leader in the carbonated orange sector, Fanta.

A multi-brand policy is necessary to protect the main brand image. This partly explains why the Disney Corporation uses a number of brands in film production, for example Buena Vista and Touchstone. This enables them to produce films of every type without endangering the revered Disney name. Similarly, when the success of an innovation is not certain, it would be foolish to risk associating it with a successful brand. This is why Procter & Gamble launched their first liquid detergent under the brand name Vizir and not under the name of the leading market brand, Ariel. The inverse policy was adopted by the Cadbury Schweppes group when it decided to launch its new fizzy drinks not under the brand Wipps but as Dry de Schweppes. This was not only because Schweppes' name helped the sales but because it was thought that the new brand Wipps would reinforce the slightly old and stuck-up image of Schweppes, and would have, in the long term, threatened the value of the brand. In order to avoid having to lower the prices of its leading products, 3M created the sub-brand Tartan which only covers the products where 3M is the dominant leader. This minimises the risk of unwanted cannibalisation. Where 3M is not dominant but a challenger, retailers might be tempted to move directly to the lowest priced alternative from 3M.

The distributive trades also play a part in the brand multiplicity in a market. Each type of retailer has a specific function and is aimed at the clientele which shops there precisely because they do not want to go elsewhere. Loyal perfumery customers are looking for the atmosphere which is to be found there, far removed from the perfumery corner in a supermarket. The identity of these distribution channels is partly created by the selection of products which are unique to each one. This is why L'Oréal elaborated several brands targeted at different channels. For example, Plénitude is aimed at super- and hypermarkets while Vichy can be found in pharmacies.

In industry, different brand names are used in order to minimise the risks of price competition between retailers selling the same product.

The increasing number of brands finally comes from the segmentation of the market and the limits of brand extension. When a market is sophisticated, one brand cannot meet all the demands of the customers without leading to confusion. This is why Lego, in order to cover the children's market, multiplied its brands. Duplo is aimed at the very young of both sexes. Then, at about the age of three, the child moves on to Lego. The problem then arises with age – girls lose interest in the toy: 90 per cent of six-year-olds who play with the building blocks are boys. This is why the company launched Belville, a game targeted at girls, involving less building and more figures and varied settings.

So as to avoid diluting the strength of its brand, Reebok created the brand Box aimed at the casual streetwear market, keeping its original brand uniquely for the sports market. The Thomson Multimedia group targeted each of its four brands of television set according to the segmentation of the consumers. Typologies have shown that consumers have very varied attitudes towards television. Four separate attitudes can be identified, each associated with specific brand attributes and names:

- the Thomson name is reserved for the innovative brand, aimed at the *involved consumer* who values technological progress and wants to be up to date;
- Saba is an economical brand aimed at a modern consumer who is looking for a product which looks good but which is above all user-friendly;
- Telefunken is also an innovative brand, but suited to a consumer who is looking for reliability and well established value;
- finally Brandt is cheap but reliable. It is rarely found at specialised retailers but it is a popular bottom of the range brand for mass retailers.

This segmentation also defines the order, from Thomson to Brandt, for the introduction of innovations. When the group asked the designer Philippe Starck to revamp the style of its entire range, he worked according to each brand's image. The Thomson design could not be the same as that of Saba or Telefunken. The identity of each brand is reflected by its exterior casing. Each of the brands has it own well defined segment competitors. Brandt is targeted against Schneider and Radiola, Saba against the Japanese and Korean brands, Telefunken against Grundig, and Thomson against Philips and Sony.

Finally, very few brands have successfully managed to cover sectors representing substantially different price ranges. It is true that large car manufacturers like Renault build a wide range of cars, from the Twingo to the Safrane. But they cannot really enter the top of the range saloon market, even when they add a flattering extension to their brand name such as Baccarat. This was also one of the aims of their association with Volvo, a brand more easily associated with top of the range cars. Toyota took the approach of creating a separate brand, Lexus. A brand portfolio makes it possible to cover the different price sectors without affecting the reputation of each brand. The Gillette group, having taken over Parker, Waterman and Paper Mate, can specialise its brands in terms of price and style. By reputation, Parker represents the top of the range in each product segment, from the ball point pen to the ink pen. Waterman represents the middle of the range. The Whirlpool group allocates to each of its brands a price bracket. The average price of the Whirlpool brand itself must be that of the middle of the market. The average price of the Laden brand corresponds to the lower quartile of the market price range and that of Bauknecht the higher quartile (see figure 9.2).

A multi-brand portfolio only makes sense if, in the long term, each brand has its own territory. This is not always the case – companies hang on to brands whose images are not different enough to justify the economies of the multi-brand policy.

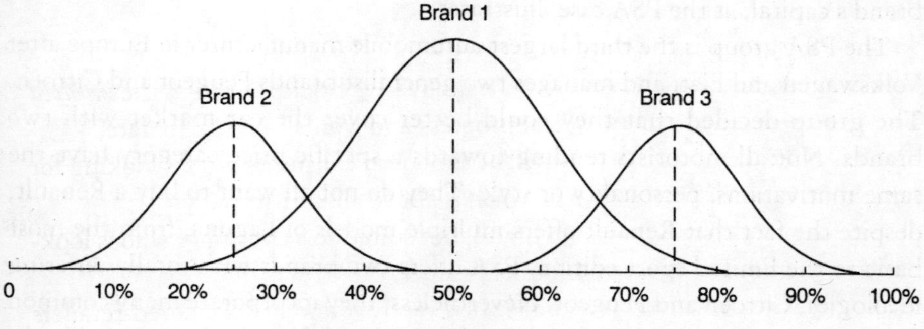

Figure 9.2 Segmenting the brand portfolio by price spectrum

Each brand must have its own clear meaning. This calls for a disciplined approach in handing out innovations among the brands of a portfolio. Gone are the days of a slow trickling down of innovations from the most expensive brand to the most popular. But we should not move to the other extreme. In order not to offend the sales teams, innovations are often distributed to all brands in the portfolio at the same time, and one waits to see which performs best. This policy is commercial and opportunistic in the short term but inevitably drains the image capital of each brand in the long run. A brand policy has to be properly managed. If brands are to make sense, they must guide the structure of the range and the management of innovations. Distributing an innovation to all brands minimises the ability to justify a premium price for the top innovative brand. In any case it is foolish to believe that all innovations can be attached to any brand. Certain innovations clearly go with certain brands. In the case of the Thomson group there is absolutely no need to update its Saba brand with the latest gadgets. Besides, the Saba public (looking for simplicity of usage) do not immediately demand them. A further point is that retailers do not stock full ranges, but only select parts. The manufacturer cannot just wait and see which brand was selected by the retailer to represent the innovation. To a manufacturer, conducting a brand policy means making this selection himself by awarding the innovation voluntarily on the merits of individual brand meaning.

The second constraint is linked with cost management. Even though the multibrand logic is not part of a competitive price strategy, but aims at a better adaptation to specific market needs, the price factor cannot be ignored. Productivity gains are a constant necessity. To achieve the maximum overall saving, in spite of brand differences, manufacturers incorporate identical features in their brands as far as is 'desirable'. 'Desirable' is preferable to 'possible' in this respect. Indeed, there have been too many dummy brands which have differed only in their packaging, destroying the belief in brand differences. Similarity between products should not reach the point where it endangers the brand's capital, as the PSA case illustrates.

The PSA group is the third largest automobile manufacturer in Europe after Volkswagen and Fiat, and manages two generalist brands Peugeot and Citroën. The group decided that they could better cover the car market with two brands. Not all motorists tending towards a specific price category have the same motivations, personality or style. They do not all want to buy a Renault, despite the fact that Renault offers multiple models of Laguna, from the most basic to the limited sport edition. PSA offers two brands with totally differing ideologies, Citroën and Peugeot. Nevertheless, they incorporate many common parts so as to avoid diseconomies of scale and the higher prices that would otherwise result from excessive brand specialisation. This enables them to remain competitive with the prices of Ford or Honda.

It is notable that while PSA chose to manage two full-range brands, VAG handle three specialist ones Seat, Volkswagen and Audi, each targeted at different and complementary segments of the market. PSA's reasoning was that you can better cover the whole market with two brands. To encompass every segment from the bottom of the range to the top necessitates cars which have variations from one segment to another. This limits the inclusion of common parts and also economies of scale. They therefore needed a larger number of cars in each segment, which could be more easily achieved with at least two brands. In fact, PSA started with three brands, Citroën, Peugeot and Talbot, the last of which was later abandoned when the demand for cars dropped during the first oil crisis.

The advantage of a generalist approach like PSA's can be found in the marketing process. A generalist brand benefits from customer loyalty, maximises advertising synergy and allows for the existence of two separate dealers. A brand logic is only complete when it structures the whole business from the initial products to its distribution, advertisement and after-sale service. Having two parallel and distinct networks, PSA had to have a generalist brand policy.

One particular danger threatens all companies which opt for a multi-brand strategy, that of over-exposing the commonalities between brands. This was the case with monospace cars. For economic reasons Ford, Volkswagen and Seat joined forces to produce such a car, imitating the joint venture of Peugeot, Citroën, Fiat and Lancia. These agreements, when systematically repeated, end up generating a common product but with several different brand names. This only succeeds in making the brand a mere superficial gimmick, devoid of real differentiation.

Unlike manufacturers, major retailers do not suffer from communication budget constraints, for they do not need to pay a listing allowance since they are in their own stores. The distributors' own-brands benefit from the corporate endorsement, either explicitly on the packaging or implicitly. Each individual product benefits from the distributors' communication budget focused on the trade name. Finally, since these are often tactical copycat brands, the problems of defining a territory do not exist. The packaging and content of each copycat brand has already been defined by the manufacturer's brand. All that is left to do is copy as closely as possible a known brand, place the cloned version on the shelves and confuse the customers. It is an effective ploy – detailed studies reveal a high level of confusion. For instance, when presented with the trade brand Clair (a copycat brand of Cif, or Jif in English), 42 per cent those questioned declared that they had seen the brand Cif (Kapferer, 1995).

THE CASE OF INDUSTRIAL BRANDS

In the industrial world, multi-brand strategies either have very few constraints, or there is a multitude which is very often underestimated.

The first case is illustrated by the chemical industry in the agricultural market. As each herbicide brand is associated with one unique active principle, a single company often stocks 500 trademarks or even more!

When a brand is strategic and the portfolio corresponds to the segmentation of the final market, the brand must mean more than a mere difference in name or logo on the product. In this way BASF sells paint to coach builders worldwide under two brands, Glasurit and RM. They are, in fact, the same product. In the car world there is a difficulty with the idea of two different qualities – no one would buy the inferior one. The two brands are thus supplementary and not complementary.

Glasurit is aimed at the technically minded coach builder. As its international slogan points out, Glasurit is the 'Preferred Technology Partner'. As its slogan indicates, RM is the thoughtful coach builder partner, 'The key to your success'. It is aimed at the other segment of coach builder who expect service to increase their activity. They see themselves rather as company directors than as painters.

To maximise their chances of success, BASF gave each brand the necessary means to defend itself. Dictating who did what would only weaken both brands and give the advantage to their competitor Akzo. Instead BASF decided to:

- create two separate management teams (as opposed to a common marketing department which was for a long time the case), based in two different countries;
- have two separate sales forces in charge of the distribution, so as to minimise cannibalisation from the inside;
- avoid all references to the parent company BASF, in order to increase the perceived difference between the two brands;
- develop services in line with the positioning of each brand;
- have different advertising campaigns on a worldwide scale.

This is how BASF maximised its cover of the market. It adapted itself to the two distinct segments of the car re-finish market and to the psychology of the constructors. Mercedes, for instance, would not like the idea that its paint supplier also supplied Lada!

The constraints associated with multi-brands are often underestimated in the industrial world, where a brand is considered just a name or a reference in a catalogue. When a brand corresponds to a strategic segmentation this underestimation can undermine or even break the strategy. In the industrial electrical equipment market, the manufacturers have to decide whom to favour, the installing company, the wholesaler/distributor or the end user. It is impossible to favour all three at the same time. Merlin-Gerin, who concentrated on the distributors were losing touch with the fitters. For the latter, the Sarel company was created. This increased the proportion of the market that could be reached, provided that all links with Merlin-Gerin were hidden. In practice, in the various countries they operated in, because of the different turnovers of Merlin-Gerin and Sarel the constraints of their multi-brand strategy were soon forgotten:

- Sarel could sometimes be found in the same office block as Merlin-Gerin's local headquarters.
- The published organisation charts did nothing to hide the Sarel–Merlin-Gerin link. Sound management on the organisational front should instead dictate that, despite its small size, Sarel be directly linked with Schneider's, their common parent company, and not Merlin-Gerin's local manager.
- On occasions, in order to save money, both Sarel and Merlin-Gerin shared the same trade exhibition stands.

GLOBAL PORTFOLIO LOGIC

For the last few years big groups have been carrying out a policy of stuffing their portfolios with additional brands, either through acquisition or partnerships, at the same time as extending the product range of some of their brands. Nestlé has become the world's number one food processing company thanks to its acquisition of Carnation and Stouffer in the US, Rowntree in the UK, Buitoni-Perugina in Italy and Perrier in France. Philip Morris is another busy company; its foodstuffs division is made up from Kraft (cheeses), General Foods (coffee, corn-flakes, confectionery, chocolate) and Jacobs-Suchard (coffee, chocolate).

In the mineral water market, outside Evian and Badoit, the Danone group, which already owns Volvic, has bought La Salvetat, a sparkling mineral water spring. Kraft General Foods owns three strategically important chocolate brands: Milka, Suchard and Côte d'Or.

This trend towards company size growth is partly motivated by the gains that can result from joining forces in research and development, logistics, manufacturing, distribution and sales. Another reason is due to the levels of financial and human resources that are now necessary to compete on the world market. A third reason is the desire to buy a dominant position and be able to restrict the market to a duopoly or an oligopoly. A final reason is to be able to resist the pressure exerted by the concentration of distributors.

It is worth remembering that besides this quantitative aspect, the idea of a portfolio implies a global vision of the competition in a market or category. A portfolio also forces the relationships between one brand and the others in the portfolio to be considered, the idea being that a brand's value can be enhanced by belonging to a larger portfolio. There are several decision grids, the most famous being the Boston Consulting Group's. Hence at Pernod-Ricard one speaks of growth products (Clan Campbell, for example), contributors (Ricard, Pastis 51, Orangina) and the famous cash cows. To these can be added the concept of a 'strategic brand': Pacific, a non-alcoholic aniseed drink, may not be financially interesting but is vital for the long-term prospects as it accustoms future customers to the aniseed taste. Unisabi (Mars) control half the cat food market thanks to a portfolio which is made up from the following brands: Ronron, Kit-e-Kat, Whiskas and Sheba. These can be classified into strategic, value and tactical brands. Whiskas is strategically aimed at being the invincible brand in the market, with the biggest range, large profits, central consumer benefit (best nutrition) and the most expensive advertising campaign. Sheba is a value brand: its market share in money is three times as much as its market share in volume. Sheba, a high quality product, is targeted at the most dedicated owners. Ronron is a buffer brand, low in price and hardly given any advertising support; it is there to counter-attack the distributor own brands. Strategic, niche and tactical brands can also be distinguished in the Heineken Breweries.

DISTRIBUTORS' OWN-BRAND PORTFOLIOS

Distributors' brand portfolios have specific characteristics which are worth looking at separately. The question for distributors today is no longer whether or not they should have a DOB but what importance it should be given. This leads to the necessity of addressing the following questions:

- What spread should be given to a DOB (number of products, categories and segments concerned)?
- What types of brands should a distributor retain: store name brands, an endorsing brand or product brands?
- What positioning should be adopted in terms of targeted customers, quality and price? What type of products should be offered: standardised, sophisticated or highly specialised?

For a retailer a brand is a means and not a necessity. This is why the different configurations of DOBs observed in stores cannot be analysed without first understanding the function of DOBs. Is it a means of pressurising manufacturers or of creating a differentiated image, or is it a source of profit? From retailer to retailer the function varies, with the consequence that the approach to the DOB phenomenon within each sector is very different.

In the hypermarket business the aim is to differentiate the stores. The DOB is often purely tactical. Faithful to their strategy, discount stores use private labels so as to be in a better position to negotiate with their suppliers. On the other hand, certain stores have added an image objective. This is the case of Marks & Spencer and Sainsbury. Their aim is to differentiate themselves in the long run by offering high quality goods, in the main under their store named.

DOBs will necessarily progress in the future. Their first factor of growth is the size of their distribution. New sectors are taking the same route: computing (Vobis), television/hi-fi/video (Firstline), and industrial, mechanical and electrical equipment. Pharmacies have merged under one name and created their own brands, as has Boots in the UK. The new problem that is going to have to be addressed is how to determine the optimal balance between DOBs and national brands, and between premium price products and DOBs. Concerning the convenience goods market, hypermarkets as a whole no longer have any new customers to gain and the classic alternative of increasing the quantities bought by each customer cannot be called upon. No one in the coming years is going to eat or drink more – the reverse is more likely. So the priority must be to maximise profit margins and to do all that is humanly possible to reinforce store loyalty. In France, according to IRI, the average family visits 3.3 super- and hypermarkets a month. The presence of national brands tends to make customers unfaithful because it enables them to compare prices between stores. In order to avoid such comparisons stores are replacing known brands by DOBs. These products are exclusive and can to an extent create loyalty among the clientele. The problem is that the absence or under-representation of a brand can also have the opposite effect. A shelf without the favourite market brands is unattractive in the eyes of the customers. It is more a sign of the store's impoverishment, unless it is a deliberate choice, like those of a hard discount store where only the price rules. The paradoxical situation can occur where a retailer has to solicit a manufacturer to retake shelf space which had been formerly set aside for DOBs. This was the case with Intersport, who preferred to reintroduce the Lafuma brand of mountain bags and reduce the place previously allocated to its own brand MacKinley. However, Lafuma was only able to return on the terms and conditions set out by Intersport which included a strict positioning of its sale prices.

10

Handling name changes and brand transfers

One of the most spectacular aspects of brand management, but also one of the most risky, is the changing of brand names. Some cases immediately spring to mind: Philips–Whirlpool, Raider–Twix, Treets–M&M's, Pal–Pedigree, Datsun–Nissan, CGE–Alcatel-Alsthom, Pullman–Sofitel. The industrial world is now used to external growth by company acquisitions and to the creation of large groups such as Novartis, Zeneca, Alcatel and Schneider by the fusion of identities which were previously separate and independent. In the United States in 1991, 154 brands changed names. In 1993, the figure was 197, a 29 per cent increase (Schechter, 1993).

This growth is normal: it is the consequence of capitalisation, the key to modern brand management. The reorganisation of multi-brand portfolios and the reduction in the number of brands has meant that the products under brands due to disappear will have to be transferred to one of the remaining brands. The same applies for companies themselves. This approach is risky: the abandonment of a brand means that the market is going to lose one of its benchmarks, one of its choices or even one of the loyal customers' favourite choices. The risk of losing part of your market share is high. This is why the transfer of a brand is a strategic decision that is not to be taken lightly. To this day, empirical studies on the question are either scarce (Riezeboos and Sneller, 1993), or private and confidential (Greig and Poynter, 1994). It is possible though, thanks to the accumulated experience of ten or so cases, to define the conditions for successful name changes on a local level or multinational plane.

TYPES OF BRAND TRANSFERS

Brand transfers are too often thought of simply as name changes, though admittedly this is the most risky facet of the change. In the customers' minds a well known name is linked with mental associations, empathy and personal preferences. However, a brand is made up of many components which cannot be reduced to just one, the name. In fact, when you examine the numerous examples that have occured both in Europe and the United States, the situation is far from simple, so much so that they cannot be described as simple trade mark transfers or name changes. Many of them involve other changes in the marketing mix. To forget this would be dangerous, especially when analysing sales results for example. The cases that will be looked at will show changes in one, a few or all aspects of the brand (see Table 10.1).

Some brand changes are also product changes. What disturbed Treets fans, apart from the loss of a product they loved, was that M&Ms included two different products: peanuts covered in chocolate and a sweet similar to Smarties. It was therefore a transition from a simple and familiar situation to a totally confusing one where all references had changed, as, indeed, had the product itself. When Shell changed the name of its oil from Puissance to Helix it also modified the characteristics of the product. However, the fact that these characteristics

Table 10.1 The different types of brand transfers

What brand attribute was changed?	Typical brand transfers Treets M&Ms	Raider Twix	Shell Puissance/ Helix	Philips Whirlpool	Chambourcy Nestlé
Name:					
Umbrella name				X	X
Product name			X		
Product-brand	X	X			
Visual Identity:					
Colour	X		X		
Packaging					
Logotype	X			X	X
Visual symbol	X		X	X	
Audio identity		X		X	
Brand Character					
Physical product	X		(X)		
Consumer benefit or brand positioning	X			X	(X)

are 'hidden', hardly perceptible by the customers, meant that this was not a risky move for Shell. The change of the oil formula could be used as an alibi for the introduction of the new name.

As regards name changes, the risks associated vary immensely depending on whether we are dealing with product brands, umbrella brands, endorsing brands or source brands. Examples of the first two cases are Raider/Twix and Philips/Whirlpool respectively. The change only affects the one and only nominal indicator of the product or products. Conversely, Puissance has become Helix but still remains under the mother brand Shell. Changing a name when the product is defined by a hierarchy of brand names is far less problematic.

With self-service, visual identity has become crucial as an aid to customers to quickly pick out their brand. Distributors' own-brands capitalise on this: their imitations, which aim at confusing the customer, rely less and less on similar names (for example Sablito against Pépito) and more and more on near identical copies of colour codes of the national brands that are targeted on the shelves (Kapferer and Thoenig, 1992; Kapferer, 1994). In this way, in the UK, a fierce conflict arose between Coca-Cola and the retailer Sainsbury, whose colas totally imitated the Coca-Cola colours: red for classic cola, white for sugar-free cola and gold for sugar- and caffeine-free cola. Conversely, some brand changes are accompanied by profound modifications of the colour codes. Thus, the brown Shell Puissance 5 oil can became the yellow Shell Helix Standard oil can. The long and gradual change from Pal to Pedigree was accompanied by the adoption worldwide of a new colour, bright yellow, striking and eye catching, to reinforce the impact on the shelves. Since colour is the first thing that consumers notice in a self-service situation, how risky such modifications can be is all the more evident.

The shape of packaging is the second most important visual recognition factor. This is why, despite the savings that could have been achieved by adopting a unique European oil can, Shell France refused to abandon its easily recognisable and very practical 'spout' can. Part of Shell oil's added value comes from this can. Finally, brand transitions can be accompanied by changes to the logo or trade mark as well as to visual symbols. As regards this last point, the impact of the disappearance of visual brand symbols shouldn't be underestimated. Replacing Nesquik's gentle giant Groquick by a rabbit in some countries for reasons of international coordination is playing with the relationship children have with Nesquik. The same applies to people associated with a brand: one day Lancôme had to replace Isabella Rossellini, just as Chanel No. 5 will have to replace Carole Bouquet. The disappearance of emblematic figures can have drastic consequences for a brand.

Finally, with written and musical slogans now under copyright, it has to be realised how important they are, as they are what people will remember. When Raider was changed to Twix, Mars hesitated but decided not to keep the same brand music. Music is one of the vehicles of a brand's personality. A slogan is also, in the long run, an integral part of a brand and can now be put under copyright. The famous slogan 'Melts in your mouth not in your hand' was lost when Treets became M&Ms.

REASONS FOR BRAND TRANSFERS

What are the aims behind the numerous brand changes that we are witnessing? The reasons are numerous.

- Many brands are bought with the intention of transferring their activities to the buyer's own brand. In this way, as there is only room on the market for two national brands, the third brand sometimes decides to buy the second one. British Airways bought the French regional airline company TAT with the perspective of creating BA France.
- Firms decide to transfer brands when they decide to stop some of their activities. So when General Electric wanted to withdraw from the small domestic appliances market, Black & Decker took over with the agreement that they could only use the GE name for a limited period. No brand would want part of its image to be controlled by another company. It was the same for Philips and Whirlpool: the takeover of the former's 'white goods' activities by the latter included the agreement that the Philips name could only be used for a limited period. Looking to concentrate only on its 'brown' products and small domestic appliances, Philips only conceded temporarily its name to Whirlpool. Whirlpool bought the white activities for the European market share it immediately gave them, as well as the chance to be the world's number one domestic appliances manufacturer.
- The search for the ideal size also provides an explanation for brand transfers. The Mars group abandoned its European brands Treets and Bonitos to merge them into the global brand M&Ms. To compete against McDonald's, the European Quick bought Free Time and changed its trade name. The Accor group wanted to buy the Méridien chain in order to merge Sofitel into it. Sofitel had itself previously absorbed the Pullman chain of hotels belonging to Wagons-Lits International. If this had come off, the Accor group would have been in control of a truly global hotel chain enabling them to respond to the demands of the world market and of global buyers. They

would have been able, for example, to compete for the international senior executive travel market of large multinational companies.

- The creation of worldwide companies leads to the same results. Ciba-Geigy and Sandoz merged under the new name Novartis. Alcatel was born out of the joint venture between CGE and ITT. In a few years all the company brands of both companies and even a few product brands (such as their telephones) were given the Alcatel brand. This is how Telic became Telic-Alcatel, then Alcatel Business Systems. In order to preserve Telic's contacts with small businesses, the sales network kept the Telic name, but was not the sole distributor of Alcatel Business Systems. The emergence of the Schneider Group as a force able to compete against the likes of ABB and Siemens was brought about by replacing the Merlin-Gerin and Télémécanique companies by Schneider throughout the world. These two companies disappeared in 1994 but they both became brands to preserve the market share associated with their names.
- Brand transition is a common tactic used when trying to access a foreign market. It is basically the same ploy as the 'Trojan Horse'. The local industries in a country are often highly protected using all kinds of domestic regulations to prevent foreign product invasions. The electrical equipment market is a typical example. Desperate to grow internationally, Merlin-Gerin bought the famous Yorkshire Switchgear company as a way to penetrate the British market. The transfer was carried out progressively. Yorkshire Switchgear received the endorsement of Merlin-Gerin, then the names were switched round before finally being replaced uniquely with Merlin-Gerin UK, now Schneider. To get a foothold in the German market, the L'Oréal Group bought the Dralle company which sold the shampoo Beauty in supermarkets. L'Oréal is now going to launch Ultra Beauty from Dralle, with, as an endorsing brand, the signature of Laboratoires Garnier. The third step will be to split this new product into Ultra Doux and Ultra Rich, Garnier's leading European shampoos. In time Dralle will give way to Laboratoires Garnier. This is how L'Oréal will slowly implant Laboratoires Garnier and its products in Germany, as in Europe as a whole.
- The fact that international markets are now more homogeneous than ever before is also an explication for the number of brand transfers. Companies that favour global brands are replacing all their local brands with global ones. This is why Raider in continental Europe became Twix, Pal changed to Pedigree, and why the paint brand Valentine will be transferred to Dulux, the worldwide brand of ICI. In order to make sure European motorists can spot their products in all European countries, Shell gave their lubricant a unique name, Helix, and where possible used the same colour codes. This

sometimes meant having to go to court when the local competitors already used the chosen European colour.

- In order to capitalise on a restricted number of strong brands and stop investing in a string of small brands, companies tend to eliminate the latter in favour of the former. In 1992, the former BSN decided to capitalise uniquely on Danone in the 'ultra fresh' market, turning Gervais into a line brand in the Danone range.
- The retreat of hypersegmentation, handicapped by the absence of economies of scale, leads necessarily to brands vanishing and hence to a transfer. This is why the Accor group eliminated Urbis, its chain of two-star hotels situated in urban areas, in favour of Ibis. In the 1970s there had been a clear segmentation between towns and the countryside, to which Urbis and Ibis corresponded. But with urban spread came the problem of where the boundary actually was. Should new sites be called Urbis or Ibis? For this reason, plus the desire to reach a critical size, everything was called Ibis.
- Along the same lines, the defence or consolidation of a strategic brand can lead to it entering markets where it had not been before and in which specialised brands had been developed. Confronted with the rise of supermarkets, pharmacies and their customers expect more from the brands exclusively distributed in the latter. The generalist brand Vichy, owned by L'Oréal, felt the need to give itself a more professional and expert image in the dermo-cosmetic market. This led it to take on problems like juvenile acne, dandruff treatment or skin problems related to the menopause. These three activities constituted up to then the territory of the brand Laboratoires d'Anglas, also owned by L'Oréal. Vichy was further strengthened by the transfer of the d'Anglas products to it.
- With time, the name attached to a brand can become a burden to the brand's development, for example when wanting to access new activities, international markets or simply when wanting to rejuvenate a brand. The Chargeurs group looked at the possibility of changing its name on several occasions. Chargeurs as a name was deemed not to be compatible with quality textile activities. BSN became Danone in order to instantly gain international recognition, which would have been lengthy if not impossible with an acronym. Leaving aside the legal problems in the US due to the similarity of the CGE acronym to that of General Electric, GE, it was in order to quickly gain awareness and stature that CGE decided to adopt, on 1 February 1991, the name of its two strongest brands: Alcatel-Alsthom. To aid Eurodisney's relaunch and repositioning it was renamed Disneyland Paris in 1994.
- Brand transfers can also be the result of lost court cases. For example, Yves Saint Laurent had to abandon the name of its brand of perfume Champagne

in several countries, turning it into Yvresse. The sportswear brand Best Montana lost its case against the luxury brand Montana and had to become Best Mountain.

Finally, distributors are themselves responsible for brand changes. In convenience goods, retailers with European establishments demand strong brands with justifiable European appeal. This is why, despite the fact that the Valentine company was taken over by the British group ICI in 1985, it was not until 1992 that the hesitation over what the brand should be called was put to one side. It had become essential for ICI to have one European brand. So in France its internal brand Dulux, used in 41 other countries, was introduced. This was done using the mixed name ICI Dulux Valentine as a first step. The date when the local reference Valentine will be abandoned has yet to be fixed, the equity of that brand being still too important to take undue risks.

Before recommending how to maximise the chance of success of brand transfers, it would be helpful to study in depth several significant cases. Each of them illustrates a particular situation or category of products.

FROM RAIDER TO TWIX

In the autumn of 1991, continental Europeans were informed by a massive advertising campaign that the chocolate bar Raider was to be henceforth called Twix, Twix being the name used everywhere else in the world from New York to Tokyo and London. The difference from the Mars group's previous brand transfer (from Treets to M&Ms) where everything had changed, including the product, was that this time, great care was taken not to disturb the customers. Nothing was changed apart from the name. It was a success.

Why was the brand change necessary? Philippe Villemus, the marketing director of Mars, explained (for more details see Villemus, 1996) that Mars was a worldwide group with six brands each worth more than a billion (US) dollars, and that it wanted only to have mega-brands which satisfy the five following conditions:

- is able to meet an important, durable and global need;
- represents the highest level of quality;
- is omnipresent all over the world, and within every one's reach both physically and financially;
- creates a high level of public confidence; and

- is the leader in their segment (when this is not the case the brand is simply removed, like Treets and Bonitos).

For legal reasons it can happen that a trade mark cannot be registered in a particular country or region. This was the case with the Twix name in continental Europe. As soon as the legal aspect had been dealt with by the acquisition of legal rights in certain countries, the group did not hesitate to rename Raider and to give Europe the global name.

What were the objectives behind this change of brand? In the first instance, it was to gain more market share and increase sales, otherwise, according to Villemus, there would have been no point to the operation. It is important to remember that a brand transition is not an exercise in style, but a unique opportunity to increase the share of the market. It is a competitive move. A second objective was to have a global brand. A third objective was to reduce production, packaging and advertising costs. A fourth objective was to make its management easier. Finally, it was desirable to have one brand name so as to make the preparations easier for the intended brand extensions towards new sectors such as ice creams.

Raider had a strong brand equity in Europe so the transition was no small matter. It was the second most popular chocolate bar after Mars and it had an annual volume growth rate of 12 per cent. This was thanks to its specific concept and its slogan, which included a physical description of the product as well as its benefits for the customer. In France, for example, spontaneous recognition was 43 per cent, assisted recognition was 96 per cent and that of the slogan was 88 per cent. Eighty-five per cent of all adolescents had tried Raider and 44 per cent bought it on a regular basis. Knowing this, Twix was marketed as the ideal snack for adolescents and young people between the ages of 15 and 25.

Even though the customers thought that the transition was rapid, in truth it took over a year. From October 1990 to October 1991, the Raider's wrapping carried the words 'known globally as Twix' and for six months after the transition 'Raider's new name'.

The communication objectives given to the campaign by the marketing director were:

- to communicate clearly and simply that only the name was changing;
- to transfer all Raider's values to Twix;
- to quickly obtain a high brand awareness within the target group of young people (30 per cent unaided, 80 per cent assisted);
- to make the change popular using the alibi that the new name was in tune with the rest of the world, and that Twix was a global brand for young people all over the world.

The key elements of the success of the operation were due to the flawless implementation of the strategy:

- it was very rapid: 15 days to change everything in one country (the whole transfer in Europe took three months);
- Mars made a big event of it which maximised its visibility and the awareness created;
- promotional activities at sales outlets contributed to the impact and trial of Twix;
- finally, great care was taken to ensure good co-ordination with field activities. It was decided that, even if it meant buying back stock, on the day of the transfer no stocks of Raider should be left in any shops.

Looking more closely at the different means of communication that were used, we see that the packaging was the first medium used. It was used for one year before the transfer to warn the customer of, and to familiarise him with, the new name. It was used for six months after that to explain the transfer. In order to meet the communication objectives the advertising campaign was characterised by:

- a strong emphasis on the pack-shot to maximise the recognition;
- the interruption of all communication of the Raider brand six months before transfer day to hasten the drop in its awareness;
- a high impact European commercial starring David Bowie;
- a strong concentration of means: in three weeks as much as the total advertisement budget for two years was spent on television advertisements alone (it is now easy to understand why it was absolutely vital that all Raider packets were removed from all sales outlets).

In shops Twix was given prominence and was put on visible display. Twix was the focal point of all the sales force, and all other brands were sidelined in terms of priority. Supermarkets had of course been informed well in advance. The bar code was kept the same so that supermarkets did not take Twix to be listed as a new brand and hence claim a listing fee.

Six months after the operation, Twix's market share was the same as Raider's had been. But from then on there was only one brand name, one factory and far less complexity. Due to its young and international status, Twix's image was more modern than Raider's.

Looking back, all the decisions taken seem logical. All successful operations give the impression of being easy. But the decisions were not taken without debate. For example, some people recommended improving the recipe and announcing 'even better'. In the end it was decided, after reflection on the opposite approach of Treets/M&Ms, to change the product as little as possible. It might also have been a good idea not to change the Raider music in the change-over film to Twix. Was the modification necessary? It is said to have disturbed some customers, which goes to show just how much the brand's music is an integral part of its identity and personality.

FROM PHILIPS TO WHIRLPOOL

On 1 January 1989, Philips and Whirlpool joined together to create the world's biggest household appliances group, Whirlpool International, owned 53 per cent by Whirlpool and 47 per cent by Philips. This partnership was formed with the intention of attaining a significant global size which would enable and ensure the development of a long lasting manufacturing firm. Besides, Philips wanted to concentrate on its core activity. Finally, both companies were highly complementary, in their plant layout and industrial capacity, in innovation and in their geographic market coverage. Philips was the most important domestic appliances brand in Europe. Whirlpool, for its part, was the number one in the United States, Mexico and Brazil. With 11.1 per cent of all the goods manufactured, Philips Whirlpool overtook Electrolux (9.6 per cent) to become the world leader in the household appliances market. In 1990 the Philips Whirlpool brand was launched in Europe by a spectacular advertising campaign (50 million US dollars). In 1991, Whirlpool bought the remaining 47 per cent held by Philips. In January 1993, the Philips Whirlpool brand became Whirlpool in all communications, but the dual brand was kept on its products. In the last countries to make the switch, Philips was removed from all products in 1996. Via this brand transfer Whirlpool became the world number one domestic appliance brand. The importance of what was at stake and the risks involved during the brand transition become evident when one looks at the significance customers put on a brand when buying durable goods which are perceived as high-risk investments. According to a study carried out by Landor, in Europe Philips was the second most powerful brand over all sectors. In France, another study showed that when customers were asked to mention names of brands from any sector off the top of their head, Philips was placed fifth after Renault, Peugeot, Adidas and Citroën (Kapferer, 1996). Nevertheless, it is worth noting that Philips' market share and its public brand recognition differed from country to country. This is why it was quickly apparent that it would be impossible to carry out the change in different European countries simultaneously. In the same way, the guarantee role of brands in the domestic appliances market rules out a sudden, quick transfer as was the case with Raider/Twix.

In January 1990, the assisted brand awareness of Whirlpool in Europe was non-existent. This was why a stage-by-stage progressive approach was decided upon. This included a Philips Whirlpool stage before Philips was abandoned. The case is different, therefore, from that of Black & Decker's takeover of General Electric's domestic appliances activities in the US where both names already had a good reputation.

Another reason favoured the stage-by-stage approach. In order to ensure global coherence, Philips' products left in stores would have had to have been bought back, as Twix had been for the transfer to Raider. But this of course would have been impossible for both practical and financial reasons.

So what was Whirlpool's transfer strategy and why did they choose it? In the first instance early research had shown that customers perceived favourably the Philips Whirlpool partnership. Both companies had very different images. Whirlpool had potential, it evoked change, fluidity, movement and dynamism. It had the ideal qualities required to give the brand transfer a positive image. The fusion of both companies gave the Philips Whirlpool brand an ideal image, the dynamism of one was tempered by the solidarity of the other. Research showed that the Philips Whirlpool couple was perceived as 'sure and dynamic, solid and robust, classic and stylish, reliable and innovating'. In Europe, the arrival of Whirlpool was seen by consumers as bringing new impetus to Philips, a touch of high-tech to a reliable classic brand, imagination to a brand characterised by experience.

The first thing that needed to be done was to decide upon the nature of the dual brand and its visual form. To start with, should it be called Whirlpool Philips or Philips Whirlpool? Tests revealed that the first option did not inspire confidence and that it evoked a confused perception. People associated it with jacuzzis and all 'water equipment'. On the other hand, Philips Whirlpool evoked a healthy equitable partnership or even a slight predominance of Philips. Only a minority thought that it referred to a Philips product range like that of the Philips Tracer razors. The second question regarded the graphic trade mark. Should both names be written on the same line or one on top of the other? The first choice was adopted because it inspired an image of partnership and looked better. Figure 10.1 shows the synergy brought by Philip's association with Whirlpool. It represents brand images, in terms of innovation, in France before the launching of the transfer campaign.

With regard to the communication, what target should it be aimed at? Obviously the priority was the distributors. Only 20 per cent of domestic appli-

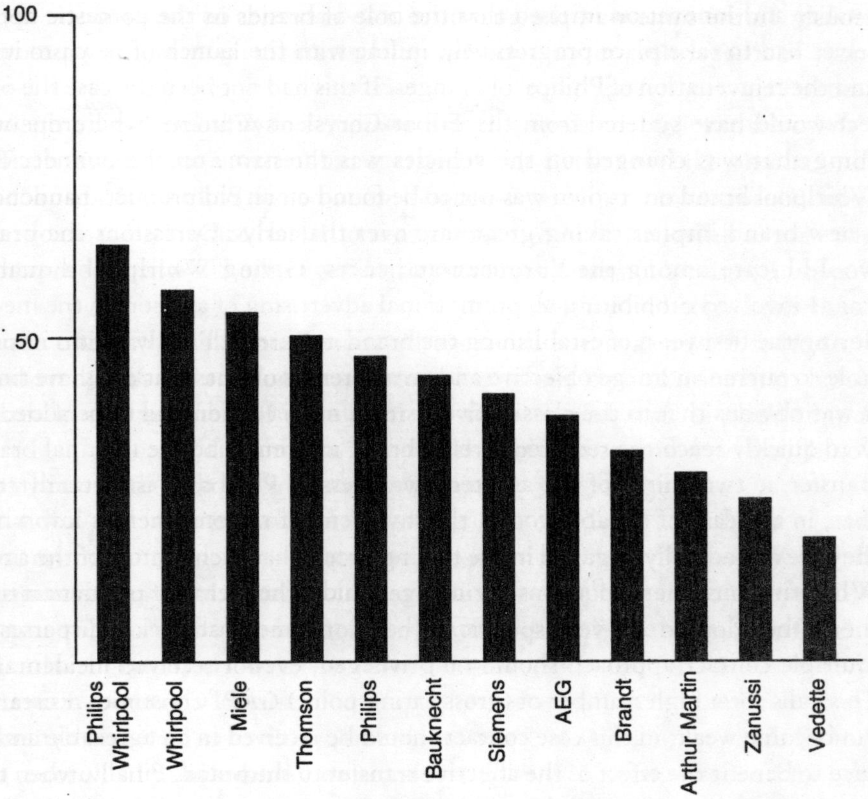

Figure 10.1 Perceived innovation of Whirlpool before its introduction in Europe (1990)

ance customers visit a shop with a specific brand in mind, and only 10 per cent ie half of them, actually buy that brand. This shows the importance of sales outlet staff in the sale of these products. Whirlpool started in 1990 a considerable communication effort aimed at retailers – this is a little known facet of brand transfers. This of course was addressed to the big European or national retail bosses, but it was also used by Whirlpool's sales force with customers, shop owners and sales staff whose opinions were so influential on consumers. Moreover, Whirlpool's image was that of an innovating leader, so merely confining oneself to innovations in products and services would have been limited. Whirlpool brought about a revolution in producer–distributor relations, a new approach which distributors weren't accustomed to, which not only touched on services but market information and more besides. As regards the consumers, the plan was to reassure them as quickly as possible by the rapid acquisition of brand awareness and a strong image of quality and innovation.

These communication objectives had several important operational consequences. On the one hand, wanting to associate with Whirlpool an image of quality and innovation implied that the brand transfer on the products themselves had to take place progressively, in line with the launch of new products and the rejuvenation of Philips' old ranges. If this had not been the case the project would have suffered from the Talbot-Chrysler syndrome, where the only thing that was changed on the vehicles was the name on the bonnet. The Whirlpool brand on its own was not to be found on an old product. Launching a new brand implies taking great care over the early impressions the brand would create among the European audiences. Giving Whirlpool a quality image involved prohibiting all promotional advertising of any sort in the media during the first years of establishing the brand in Europe. Finally, as it is impossible to pursue an image objective and an awareness objective at the same time, it was obvious that to the classic advertising a media action had to be added so as to quickly reach the required level of brand awareness before the final brand transfer, ie two-thirds of the assisted awareness of Philips. It is certainly true that, in the case of durable goods, the involvement of consumers is low when they are not actually engaged in the buying process – which is most of the time. When the consumer is not considering a purchase, the means of persuasion that should be adopted are very specific. When consumers' attention disperses, a multiple contact approach should be privileged, even if received incidentally. This calls for a high number of (gross rating point) *GRP*. Consumer resistance can become weak; in this case contact should be received in an agreeable ambience to benefit the effect of the affective transfer to the brand. Finally, when the consumer is not ready to make a cognitive effort one must repeat the consumer benefits of the brand rather than point out the difference between specific products.

This is why, in some countries, Whirlpool invested large amounts of money sponsoring prime-time TV programmes. This choice was no coincidence; they represent viewers' favourite moments on the most popular channels, and are often associated with a relaxed family atmosphere. Thanks to this strategy, the brand awareness made considerable progress, as shown in Figure 10.2. In all the countries where only traditional commercials were used, the awareness reached was less significant.

Figure 10.2 also points out the structural relationship between assisted and spontaneous awareness, as described earlier (see page 139). On first analysis, it might be thought that for durable goods only assisted brand awareness counts (recognition being reassuring) but this cannot be the case for a brand aiming to be seen as the quality reference and the leader of the sector. Yet, it is known that a high level of assisted brand awareness must be reached before there is any hope of increasing spontaneous awareness. This is even more the case when the market is 'closed', ie when there are already three brands with high levels of

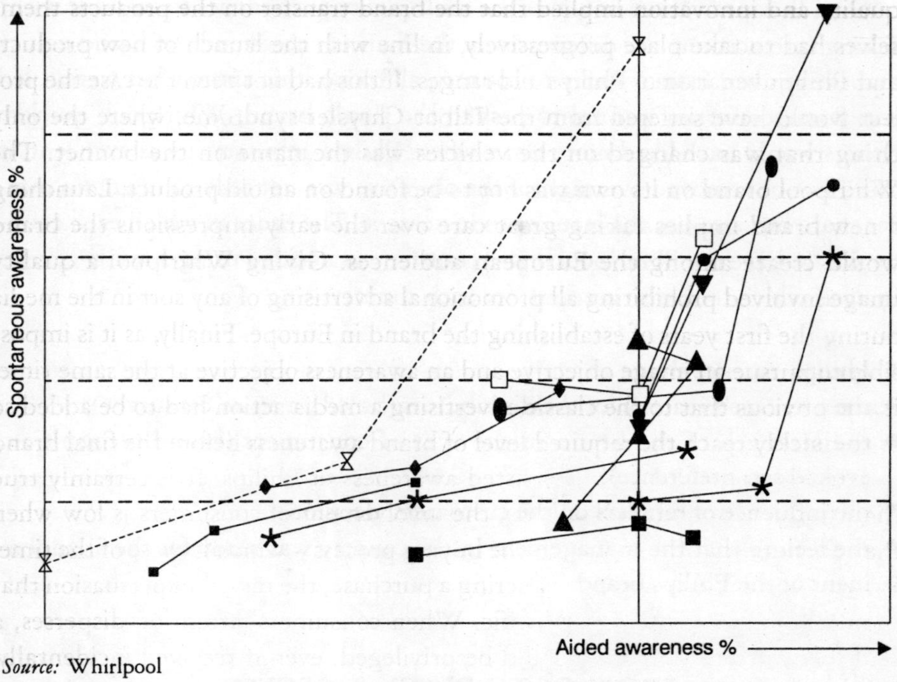

Source: Whirlpool

Figure 10.2 Growth of Whirlpool brand awareness in eleven European countries

spontaneous awareness. This is why Whirlpool wanted to reach the critical zone of 70 per cent assisted awareness as quickly as possible. Thus it would be possible to gain the status of market leader associated with spontaneous awareness. Then it would also be possible to safely remove the Philips brand from the products in the shops.

It was indeed important to separate the treatment of the Philips brand in the media and in sales outlets. In the media, it was necessary to stop mentioning the brand as quickly as possible, otherwise the brand would only have been reinforced when the objective was to see a decline in its spontaneous awareness. This is why, during the short period when the dual brand existed, Philips Whirlpool adverts finished with the dual brand but the signature tune only mentioned Whirlpool. This was to ensure that only this brand was associated with the innovations.

As early as January 1993, it was decided to remove Philips from all TV adverts. This put an end to any reinforcement of Philips' awareness. What is more, it sent the message to retailers that Whirlpool, the market leader, no longer needed the Philips guarantee and that the transfer programme was ahead of schedule.

On a European level, how was the multiplicity of countries to be dealt with? Taking into account the differences in the market shares and the brand equity that Philips had from country to country, all monolithic approaches were ruled out. Some countries wanted to pass to the single brand, Whirlpool, quickly. Others would have liked more time: where Philips' reputation was excellent, it could not be removed overnight if the objective was not only to maintain market share but also use the transfer to increase it. The order in which each country was to have the Whirlpool brand transfer was decided using a multi-criteria analysis which took into account, for each country:

- Philips' market share;
- the presumed reaction of the distributors (based on an *ad hoc* survey);
- the strength of the brand in the eyes of consumers (brand recognition, evoked set, preference);
- the influence of retailers on the customers' decisions;
- the feeling that the management in the country was ready for the abandonment of the Philips brand.

FROM GE TO BLACK & DECKER

It is interesting to compare the Philips Whirlpool case with a similar example, that of the transfer in the United States of all of General Electric's domestic appliances to the Black & Decker brand, which up till then had only been known for its drills and other DIY tools.

In April 1984, the Black & Decker Manufacturing Company bought the entire small domestic appliance division of General Electric for $300 million. At the time, General Electric was not only the market leader, but was a well-known brand with a long history, almost an American cultural institution. In buying GE's electrical appliance division, Black & Decker realised the dream of every market competitor, the elimination of the market leader.

General Electric sold the division because it no longer held a strategic interest and did little for their corporate image. From Black & Decker's point of view, having seen its cordless vacuum cleaner take off, this presented a good opportunity to branch out beyond electrical tools to cover all equipment in general, including small electrical appliances.

Black & Decker found itself owner of a range of 150 products with the General Electric brand. The countdown had already begun: the company could only use the GE name until 1 April 1987. The brand merger had to be completed within three years. In this short time, it had to:

- establish a new positioning and identity for Black & Decker;
- keep all of General Electric's former loyal clientele;
- try to retain the brand's capital in the crucial sector of electrical tools.

This posed several fundamental questions from an operational point of view: What name would be used to replace GE? Should the Black & Decker brand, which up till then had been very specialised, be extended, or, on the contrary, should it be protected by launching a new brand, X? What should be done with the inherited General Electric image and reputation during the three-year transitional period? Should it be referred to or should it be pushed into the background? What timetable should be followed? How should the transition be managed within the appointed period? Should they make an immediate clean break, or proceed in gradual stages? Finally, with 150 products on their hands, should the brand be changed for the whole lot simultaneously, one category at a time, or product by product?

To avoid losing the equity associated with the GE name and to eliminate any confusion in customers' minds, Black & Decker decided to hasten the process by finalising the entire transition in less than three years. The Black & Decker brand was retained for electrical domestic appliances. It was felt that the name already enjoyed a wide reputation and that its image was as strong as that of GE on two counts, quality and reliability. On the other hand, Black & Decker was not perceived as innovative as General Electric. A $1 million advertising-communication strategy was immediately put into action in order to establish the brand's awareness in this new segment and thus to transfer its positioning. The Black & Decker Manufacturing Company became the Black & Decker Corporation. The brand slogan became 'Ideas at work' in order to enhance its image as an innovative force both outside and inside the home.

As regards the products, each underwent the transition. The whole programme comprised 140 steps. The first wave of brand transfers affected:

- GE products which had a real edge over the competition, and all new products;
- products for which consumers' choices did not rely too heavily on the brand, ie those where a brand name did not make that much difference. In the same string of TV commercials, for example, there would be almost identical adverts for literally the same product, but one under the GE name, the other under Black & Decker;
- products which already had their own name, thus their own identity, under the endorsement of GE. Thus, the new advertisement for the Spacemaker range ended with the words 'Spacemaker, now by Black & Decker'.

The second wave of brand transfers dealt with those products where the brand was of real significance. For example, the name of General Electric irons had been passed down from mother to daughter. The strength of their inherited reputation could not simply be ignored, and there was no way that the Black & Decker brand could be slipped in on the sly. This is why their commercials only covered their new products and always ended with the qualifying words: 'Its predecessors bore the General Electric name. My mother told me not to buy anything unless it was General Electric, this is why I bought Black & Decker.'

So as to give credibility to the brand change, the company relied largely on an offensive approach of new products and services. Black & Decker relaunched practically all the 150 products as if they were completely new, introducing changes varying from simple differences in colour or reshaped handles to major innovations. Furthermore, the company extended the General Electric one-year guarantee to two years.

Black & Decker's approach with the distributors was no less vigorous. General Electric had always been treated favourably by retailers and had enjoyed regular shelf prominence. Black & Decker though, in their eyes, did not have a good company image as a result of their inflexible approach and poor service record. With the competition taking the opportunity to bombard retailers with promotions and special offers, it was vital for Black & Decker to protect their profit-generating products. They introduced promotional offers on their most threatened lines without, as such, having to concede on price. In addition, the company launched a 'service plus' programme whereby retailers who participated in promotional events would have their names appear in Black & Decker commercials.

FROM CHAMBOURCY TO NESTLÉ

In 1985, Nestlé bought out Unilever's European activities in the chilled foods sector. Nestlé had been synonymous with milk worldwide, but knew little about refrigerated dairy products. The buy-out presented a particular problem in France, that of the coexistence of two brands, Chambourcy (Nestlé) and La Roche-aux-Fées (formerly of Unilever). They both enjoyed an equal share of the market (11 per cent). Like Chambourcy, La Roche-aux-Fées was a range brand with the exception of the Créola, Yoco and Félicie product names. The two brands both covered numerous market segments thanks to a complete range of 99 items in the case of La Roche-aux-Fées and 74 for Chambourcy. The Chambourcy–La Roche-aux-Fées case illustrates the problems that arise when two complete ranges are merged.

Having considered the capital and potential of these two brands, together with that of Nestlé itself as a likely candidate, they decided to retain Chambourcy as the sole brand for the European market. Having done this, a single product that would limit any serious loss of sales quantity had to be chosen for each market segment to replace the previous two. This implied detailed questions on name, taste, container format, packaging and price structure. The difficulty lay in the contrasting regional popularity associated with these two brands. If the 5000 tonnes which were sold of La Roche-aux-Fées' 'Bulgarian yoghurt' were stopped in favour of Chambourcy's 12,000 tonnes of its equivalent, 'Kremly', there would be a risk of losing the 5000 tonnes of the former in the regions where Kremly was hardly known. In fact, despite extensive advertising, this amount was absorbed by the competitors' brands. Retailers allocate shelf space on a brand-for-brand basis, and in a sector where market share is strongly correlated to shelf prominence, some loss could not be prevented if one brand was to disappear.

Whenever products had two names, a product name as well as the brand name, the transfer was carried out using a fade-in fade-out process. A brand transfer is easier when a product has its own identity. In this way, in the derived milk products market, where Créola from La Roche-aux-Fées and Chamby from Chambourcy had the same output of 6000 tonnes, it was decided to allow the two ranges to run parallel for a while. This allowed a gradual merger which would not alienate consumers who favoured one or other of the two brands. The process is illustrated in Figure 10.3.

Children's preference for either Créola or Chamby was very much based on each product's visual identity, Créola carrying the picture of a parrot and Chamby the faces of two children. The removal of Chamby could only be successfully carried out in a gradual process. The first step was to amalgamate its visual identity with that of Créola, the two children being replaced by a parrot. As for Créola, it immediately lost the La Roche-aux-Fées logotype and visual identity symbol, taking on that of Chambourcy, with a transitional reminder of the La Roche-aux-Fées name. The final product had the original Créola container format, the best recipes (Chambourcy's vanilla and La Roche-aux-Fées' chocolate and caramel), the more popular brand according to the latest tests (Créola), the Créola design and, of course, the Chambourcy brand. No tonnage was lost in this segment and the operation was a success overall. Despite losing one-third of the items during the merger (from a total of 173 items for the two brands combined, to 111 items after the transition), the company only lost 13 per cent of its volume in 1986, which it regained the following year.

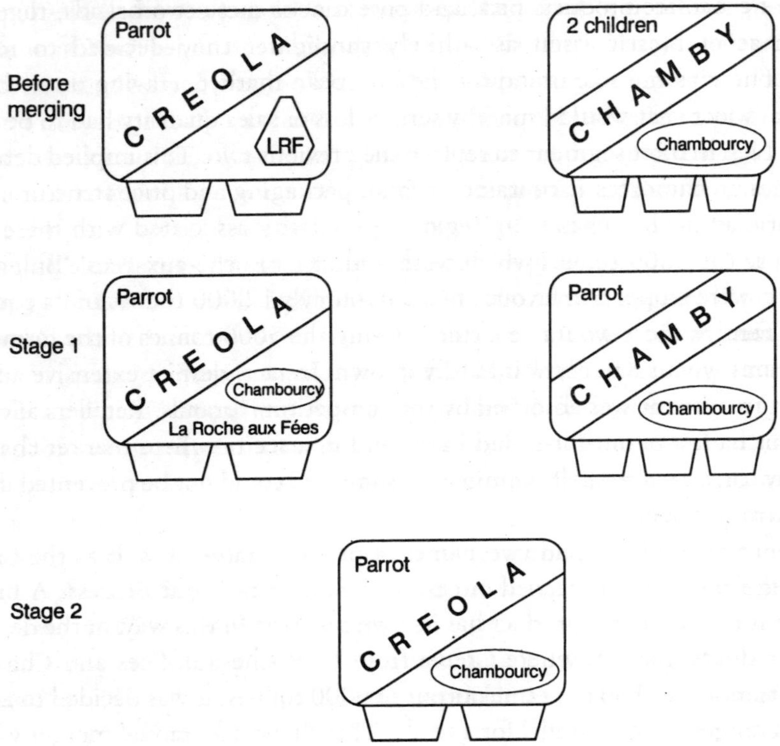

Figure 10.3 Merging of brands and product concepts

Ten years after, in 1995, it was decided to transfer all of Chambourcy's products to the Nestlé brand. It was true that Chambourcy seemed to be threatened in several segments in the 'ultra fresh' dairy market and there was no way that on its own it was going to reduce the market share margin that separated it from Danone (17.6 per cent vs 33.6 per cent). As for the segments of products where the brand was either leader or in second place, it was the daughter brands of the products that carried the image and the preferences of the customers: La Laitière, Viennois, Yoco, Kremly, Sveltesse, Marronsuiss. The consumers of these products did not take any notice of the mother brand, Chambourcy. The advertising war was very uneven: in France, for instance, Chambourcy spent around 70 million francs in 1994 compared with Yoplait's 100 million and Danone's 260 million. Danone's strength enabled it to invest heavily in its strategic products: 23 million francs on Danette, 25 million on Velouté and 30 million on Bio. The conquest of market share had therefore to be accompanied by an increase in the advertising budget, something which was difficult to justify for the Chambourcy brand. The fact was that all adverts on

Nestlé's chocolate products had a positive knock-on effect on all Nestlé products in general, apart from the 'ultra fresh' segment under the Chambourcy label. The effects of brand awareness synergy could not be counted upon. Besides, without having to spend as much as Danone on advertising, a transfer to the Nestlé brand name would instantly benefit all the 'ultra fresh' range. Nestlé, according to a Landor study, is the most powerful foodstuffs brand in the world after Coca-Cola.

In any case, it also seemed necessary that a brand as valuable as Nestlé should finally put its name to 'ultra fresh' products. There is, in fact, an evolution of food products over time, starting with dry products, then dry groceries, then frozen goods and then finally fresh products. It is the case that the future of the agricultural processing industry lies with fresh goods, that is goods that have not had to endure the physical shock of being transformed into powder, put into cans or frozen. It would not be prudent for the Nestlé brand to be absent from this evolution. Not doing so would have branded Nestlé a manufacturer of dry foodstuff, products for the cupboard, therefore 'not fresh' and far removed from modern healthy produce. Quantitative research carried out on clients and non-clients to test the acceptability of the Chambourcy–Nestlé transfer in several market segments (fitness and health, desserts, children's products and traditional specialities) revealed that the Nestlé brand was already starting to suffer from such an image.

Indeed, it was desirable to know what the public would think of the brand change. Wasn't there a risk in updating the 'powerful multinational' facet with the removal of Chambourcy in favour of Nestlé? The credibility and legitimacy of Nestlé's penetration into each of the 'ultra fresh' segments, either as a signature on daughter brands or as a direct product brand, also had to be evaluated. In fact, some of the Chambourcy products were likely to be ill at ease under the Nestlé umbrella, others would benefit from it, while others would inject it with new life.

As regards the operational strategy, a decision had to be taken as to whether or not the same logic should be followed as with the Chambourcy–La Roche-aux-Fées transfer. The 1996 brand transfer posed several strategic questions:

- How to convince the customers that the arrival of Nestlé, normally associated with dry produce and far removed from Chambourcy territory (natural, gourmet), in the 'ultra fresh' market was legitimate?
- Should the change be given a high profile with extensive communication at the time of the transfer, or, on the contrary, should the consumers and the distributors be disturbed as little as possible?

- Should a global 'ultra fresh' brand communication be adopted or should it concentrate on individual products according to each item's market segment?
- What should be retained of Chambourcy: the signature tune associated with desire and pleasure? The joyful 'Oh Yes!' slogan? Should Chambourcy become a daughter brand like Danone had done with Ch. Gervais?
- Should there be a transitional period where both brands exist side by side on the products or should there be a quick break changing from Chambourcy to Nestlé in one go, as in the Raider–Twix case?

The answers that were adopted resulted from the key parameters of the image of Nestlé, of Chambourcy and the different products involved, and the possibly exploitable negative facets of the image of Danone. Finally, the attitude of the distributors had a strong influence on the decisions. Knowing that, in the short term at least, the products would not evolve, one could not make an event of a simple name change. Similarly the desire not to disrupt the consumers demanded that some of Chambourcy's communication codes should be maintained even after the removal of the brand. Finally, to preserve as much as possible the core of Chambourcy's loyal customers, Chambourcy became a product name on three prototypical products.

WHICH BRAND TO RETAIN AFTER A MERGER

Reductions in brand portfolio sizes are often a source of brand transfers. As soon as a brand has been diagnosed as weak it naturally follows that its flagship products will be transferred over to strong brands in the portfolio. When a company gives up part of its activities to another company, it is the brand of the latter which inherits the products of the former. This we have seen in the Black & Decker–General Electric and Philips–Whirlpool cases. But it can happen that the decision of which brand to keep after a merger is not as simple. For example, which of the following names currently used in different countries will Johnson keep as its European brand name: Pledge, Pliz or Pronto?

These decisions are not necessarily rational. More Pal was sold in continental Europe than Pedigree in the UK, yet the decision was taken to use the British brand name hitherto unknown on the continent.

One can also assume that Pedigree has an international feel understood by all dog owners, and that this name is closely tied to the creative concept which presents the product as the one preferred by pedigree dog owners. The Merloni group was wise, too, when it chose its European portfolio brand, opting for

Indesit rather than Ariston. Indesit had an image of lowest price products but was well known in Europe. Ariston was the group's historical brand and had a good image but was hardly known in Europe.

A good illustration of a methodological approach worth following in such situations is that of the Accor group's takeover of Pullman International Hotels. Looking to reach a critical size, the group found itself with two international prestige hotel chains, Sofitel and Pullman. Capitalisation meant that one of the two trade names had to go, but which one? In order to make that choice both names were compared using 12 criteria judged to be important for the decision. They were:

- The degree of spontaneous awareness of each brand among top executives.
- Clients' preference for one or the other brand. Clients from each chain were asked if they preferred that the new chain be called Sofitel or Pullman.
- The level of customer satisfaction with the service of each chain. This was calculated using the following style of question, 'overall Pullman (Sofitel) is a hotel chain that meets my needs'.
- Customer tolerance of the other name in case of a change. When questioned about their hotel preferences in the case of the disappearance of their usual chain, the Pullman clientele preferred the Hilton first and Sofitel second, and the Sofitel clientele preferred Novotel.
- Customer preference based on the level of service associated with each chain. This was tested with the following question, 'would you like the new chain amalgamated from the previous two to have the Pullman or the Sofitel level of service?'
- The difference between the name and the reality of the product.
- The perceived positioning of each chain compared with a luxury chain.
- The perceived clientele satisfaction and pleasure.
- Staff attachment to their chain.
- The financial consequences of choosing one or the other name and the necessity of constructing a homogeneous network at the level required by the positioning.
- Contractual constraints resulting from the trade names, where renegotiating difficulties are foreseeable.
- The risks that the change would inflict on the hotels which were particularly sensitive to a change in their name.

The analysis led to the abandonment of the Pullman name. Its hotels were, depending on their location and level of service, transferred either to Sofitel or to Mercure or sold off.

MANAGING RESISTANCE TO CHANGE

It is a fact that brand changes arouse hostility which can be a real danger in terms of the effect on market share. The source of the opposition can be found with consumers, with distributors and also internally. From the clients' point of view a brand change is not a superficial act, but it affects the very identity of the product. There is therefore a perceived risk of altering the implied contract. This is especially the case in the service industry. When there is a lack of any tangible element the brand becomes the heart of all contractual relations. Besides, we have already seen that a brand can only be successfully extended to cover a new category of products if it is seen to be legitimate (Chapter 8). This was Black & Decker's principal challenge when it took over General Electric's domestic electrical appliance activities. A successful brand transfer also has to deal with distributors. In the industrial world with long distribution channels, retailers tend to choose a few complementary brands which they stick with. Having promoted these brands, they have inevitably linked their reputation with them and their customer loyalty derives from them. To change a brand is therefore like questioning ten or 15 years of good and loyal service. A retailer loyal to a brand expects something in return from the company. A simple presentation of the strategic reasons why a company should replace brand X by brand Y is not enough, even if the products are identical. There must be some compensation. The situation is completely different when dealing with supermarkets who care far less about brands apart from their own. Here their analysis is much more down-to-earth: is this an opportunity to receive a listing allowance for the new brand or a contribution to the temporary hassle incurred by the transfer? Also, distributors will not hesitate to criticise any operations aimed at placing a weak brand under the umbrella of a strong one in order to improve its shelf prominence.

Finally, one must not forget the internal and human elements of resistance. Generally speaking, all brand changes have to pass through managers who will inevitably be attached to their own brand. When L'Oréal decided to give Ambre Solaire a modern technological dimension by placing it under the umbrella brand Laboratoires Garnier, the division came up against numerous pockets of resistance in Europe. In the UK, where Ambre Solaire had a good name and Laboratoires Garnier was unknown, the partisans against the change pushed forward the fact that the future signature brand Laboratoires Garnier had little recognition. The opposite was true in France: the Garnier management argued on the basis that Ambre Solaire suffered from a bad reputation, and that the change might devalue their brand. In the end the operation did take place and Ambre Solaire sales increased from 25 to 130 million francs.

The precautions taken by the British group ICI when it made an apparently insignificant brand change, transferring the leading paint brand in the French market Valentine to 'ICI Dulux Valentine', illustrate the need to take into account these three stumbling blocks. The precautions aimed solely at the personnel showed just how much they were involved. The personnel at Valentine were attached to their brand so much that they saw themselves as its trustees and looked after it as if it were their own. This is why they took any brand modification to heart, and the dividing line between evolution and dispossession was very fine. The importance of internal communication during this brand change was therefore absolutely crucial if feelings of loss of identity were to be avoided and all thoughts of disappearance kept at bay.

As a result, one of the first things to be done was the setting up of a selective information policy. Only the people who worked closely on the project were informed of progress. The project itself was given a code name rather than a title which would have given the game away. Afterwards, when the deadline date was imminent, the personnel were told. The operation was presented as a step forward and not as the end of the Valentine company once bought by the ICI giant.

The sales force was gathered for a big presentation on the evolution of the European market, on ICI and on its Dulux brand. Particular attention was given to the worldwide importance of Dulux, to its long history (founded in 1930), to its sympathetic and relaxed communication strategy (projection of advertisements), to its content and to its corporate values. The change was presented not as a big event but rather a natural evolution which would bring real and important benefits to the customer.

This gathering was held six months before the brand change. A notable consequence of this date was that all internal rumours were avoided, at least on a large scale.

Some of the distributors were informed very early on of the name change. It is worth remembering that they were part of the cause of the decision to change, because they also favoured a European extension and therefore wanted a European brand. They could not therefore oppose the principle of a brand change. All that was needed was to show them that everything would be done to assure a smooth transition.

Some retailers were informed a whole year before the name change directly by Valentine managers, when internally only the people responsible for the project knew about it. On the other hand, shopkeepers were forewarned by Valentine sales representatives only three months beforehand. Finally, department or shelf managers were informed by mail, just before the change, that on 23 March 1992, ICI Valentine was to become ICI Dulux Valentine. The letter was accompanied by a free luxurious badge of the Valentine mascot, a panther. And when the Valentine sales force next came by they distributed an ICI Dulux Valentine watch (blue background, 12 yellow stars for the 12 hours of the clock and a black panther in the middle) which was such a great success that some people still wear it.

In fact, if this brand transfer was carried out without any hitches, it is because it was presented as an adaptation to meet the constraints of the retailers, and therefore more for their benefit than a revolutionary brand change. What is more the new packaging was intended to make the distributors' life easier and the product clearer and more comprehensible for the consumer, and it permitted a more homogeneous organisation of the shelves.

It had already been established that it was more practical, from the clients' point of view, to organise shelves according to purpose (paint for floors, for ceilings, for wood, for steel, etc), rather than according to brands. Thanks to the new packaging, customers could easily find all the information they needed, paint for the kitchen, for the bedroom, etc.

What is more, Valentine made sure that the brand change would not upset the shelf layouts and that no extra work was needed by the distributors. They also decided that at no point should there be the two different brand names on the same shelf. This is why 180 people carried out the necessary relabelling when the transfer took place in each of the 620 shops concerned. What is more, a freephone number was made available to the retailers should any kind of problem occur.

Tests to measure consumer reactions were also carried out before the brand change. Tachytoscope tests (successive presentations of the old and new packaging) revealed that both versions of the packaging were equally well associated to the brand.

Another benefit for the customer was the opportunity to quickly reorganise the whole range of paint products into sectors according to the main kinds of uses. In normal circumstances this would have taken three years. This makes the customers' choice much easier when they do not know what kind of paint to use in the room or on the surface that they are repainting.

KEY FACTORS FOR A SUCCESSFUL BRAND TRANSFER

Although the cases looked at and their particular situations vary a lot, it is still possible to draw an overall lesson from the principal experiences in this domain. A good summary is by Philippe Villemus, former marketing director of Mars, who remarks:

Above all, this kind of operation requires a combined effort from all the company departments: production, logistics, sales force, marketing and general management. All will be concerned and any false note will be a source of problems.

Secondly, it is vital that this event be considered an opportunity and not a constraint. The transfer must be an occasion for reappraisal, when the strengths and weakness of the brand can be rethought, and an occasion to gain new market shares by profiting from the extra attention that the new brand will have for a while. In this respect the transfer has to be seen positively by the personnel, the distributors and the consumers, so the benefits that the new brand will bring for each of them must be specified.

A brand transfer cannot be improvised, it must be well prepared. The retailers, prescribers, opinion leaders and the personnel must all be warned well in advance.

The time factor is crucial: one must wait until all the customers are aware of the change, and if the operation has to be carried out quickly, one must have, at one's disposal, the communications means necessary to be able to let them know.

You cannot force a brand change on retailers. Not only should they be informed but everything possible should be done to facilitate their work. That means no double stock. The same product codes should be maintained. This approach not only reduces demands for listing allowances, it makes the rotation of the new brand easier. In the case where a new code is introduced, the chances are that the optical check-outs will not be able to read them because the new reference has not been registered at a central level nor in the shop's computer system.

Even when the transfer is to take place in transitional phases, like a double brand phase before the actual inversion, one should still opt for the quickest time frame. It is true that the average purchase frequency should be taken into account; the frequency of paint purchases compared to that of ultra-fresh produce leads to very different minimal transitional periods. To linger too long only results in being bogged down and losing one's way. This was the case of the Pal to Pedigree transition which took several years. Retrospectively, the process would have benefited if it had been shorter, or even, as in the Raider/Twix case, instantaneous and accompanied by a strong advertising campaign.

Nothing is more shocking to the customer than the strategy of 'fait accompli', imposed without warning, information or explanations. The loyalty to the brand is dented by this sudden disaffection and lack of consideration. Lessons have been drawn from the Treets/M&Ms mishap.

(Villemus, 1996)

It is worth noting that the sudden change from Coke to New Coke on 8 May 1985 nearly brought about a revolution in the United States which forced the return of classic Coca-Cola to the sales outlets and the disappearance of New Coke. The Night and Day case illustrates the preventive and transparent approach.

Launched in 1976, Nuit et Jour coffee became the second brand behind Sanka in the decaffeinated segment. This it achieved thanks to an original positioning (The pleasure that lasts all day long), much sharper than Sanka's health approach, which was backed up with a far superior advertising campaign. The brand went from strength to strength. In 1985 Nuit et Jour had a market share of 42 per cent. Encouraged by this success, the majority share holder, Mr Jacobs, launched the product in several countries with a brand name adapted to the local market; Nacht und Tag in Germany, Austria and Switzerland, and Night and Day in the United States and Canada. Each country adapted the original concept to its local market.

In 1987, Mr Jacobs decided to create an international top-of-the-range coffee brand signed with the Jacobs name. This brand was to rely on the existing leading products under the old brands. In France, for example, the products looked at were Nuit et Jour and Carte Noire, both leaders but also weakly associated with their respective mother brands (Jacques Vabre and Grand-Mère). Mr Jacobs decided to retain the name 'Night and Day' as the world brand and chose an advertising agency which had offices in 40 countries. The new brand would be introduced using the opportunity provided by a change in the decaffeinating process. The transition took place in June 1988. There were two communication phases:

- Before June all the packages had highly visible labels forewarning the name change ('Nuit et Jour will soon be called Night and Day').
- Starting from June an intermediary package explaining the transition was brought out. On the back of the packet there was the following notice: 'From now on your decaffeinated Nuit et Jour coffee will be called Night and Day. It has changed its name so that it can be set free from our borders and seduce European decaffeinated coffee consumers. They will now be able, like you, to savour the dense and generous taste of our coffee. Night and Day is decaffeinated using a natural element, clear water, and has the aroma and richness of a luxury coffee.' At the same time, in July 1988, a wave of radio advertisements sold the name change: it made the operation totally transparent and gave value to the international aspect in the eyes of the consumers.

Last, but not least, to achieve successful brand transfers it is important to know what the customer identifies with the brand. The Shell Helix case is revealing in this respect. Having decided to replace all its local lubricant brands with one European brand, Shell left the coordination of the transition to its subsidiaries. France was a particular problem in view of the share of the automobile oils market enjoyed by the self-service supermarkets (more than 40 per cent). The strategy which was adopted consisted of the launch in September 1992 of a top-of-the-range oil called Shell Helix Ultra. It was added to the local Puissance range of products, keeping the characteristic can with a practical spout, but in a different colour, grey. Shell Helix Ultra was launched in the automobile press and sold only in Shell service stations. The print advertising campaign slogan, aimed at making Helix the market reference, was: 'One day all oils will be like Helix'. In the meantime the name Helix Plus was added in small letters to Puissance 7 and Helix Standard to Puissance 5. In October 1993, in order to follow the European transition, all the 'Puissance' brands were replaced by Helix. All the same a small mention of Puissance under Helix survived for a few months. The Puissance 7 blue can became the Shell Helix Plus blue can, but the Puissance 5 brown can became the Shell Helix Standard yellow can. The advertisement campaign put the old Puissance 7 can and the new Helix Plus can side by side under the slogan: 'It may have changed its name but the spout remains'. The problem was that the advertisement agency focused on the name change while the clientele paid more attention to the colour of the can. Yet nowhere in the advertising campaign did the yellow can appear. The customers looking for their brown can could not find it, instead they could only find a yellow can the name of which they had never heard of. In reality, despite the brand awareness scores of the name Puissance, the strength of the brand was in fact associated with its colour! The customers should have been informed of a transition from brown to yellow rather than soley a name change from Puissance to Helix.

MERGING CORPORATE BRANDS

On 1 January 1991, CGE became Alcatel-Alsthom 'to have a brand with a higher profile'. It had up till then been handicapped by the confusion that was occurring due to its similarity with General Electric. In September 1989 CGEE-Alsthom became Cegelec but this name, unpronounceable in the Anglo-Saxon world, hindered international expansion and the effectiveness of all communication. To the precautions to take when changing a brand name a few more can be added when dealing with company names. These are based on the fact that there is always a strong internal public and a multitude of external micro-publics.

The first problem that should be avoided is that of rumours, which will always portray a different picture of the change than the reality. The internal public is quick to interpret any change in terms of a crisis, serious problems or shareholder pressure, especially when new majority shareholders have arrived.

A big effort is therefore needed to explain the situation. As regards the external public, they generally under-evaluate internal problems. The name change does not bring them any specific advantages so there is no reason for them to pay too much attention. But if they did understand they might go along with the decision, so the name change must be made relevant to them. Finally, each micro-public demands a specific action. In this way, with regard to the transfer from GCE to Alcatel-Alsthom, the first problem that had to be resolved was that of the stock market traders. The company was quoted in about ten markets around the world, so they had to be certain that right from day one all financiers would be looking for the letter A and not C in the finance sections of their newspapers.

11

Decline, ageing and revitalisation

Following the analysis of the factors of a brand's longevity in Chapter 5, one could simply say, *a contrario*, that brands decline when they are not respected. In fact, their decline always comes from mismanagement. When a manufacturer ceases to be interested in his brands (due to lack of innovation, advertising or productivity), he can expect the consumer also to lose interest. And if the brand loses dynamism, energy and shows fewer and fewer signs of vitality, how can one possibly hope that it will arouse passion and proselytism? Apart from these rules, which are so basic that it is astonishing that they can be forgotten, there are some factors which accelerate the decline and which will now be studied.

THE FACTORS OF DECLINE

The first and surest road to decline is through the degradation of the quality of the products. The brand ceases to be a sign of quality. Economic factors oblige companies to cut corners with regard to quality, albeit in minor steps, and unfortunately, far too frequently. For instance, when L'Oréal bought out Lanvin, its leading perfume Arpège was a mere shadow of its former self. The fragrance had originally been made up of natural oils but by then included a fair amount of artificial ingredients. The bottle had even lost its round shape. Consumers around the world were conscious that they were no longer respected since Arpège had been so badly mistreated. L'Oréal's first step was to give back to this perfume the case, the bottle and the ingredients of the quality that it deserved. This task, which was not spectacular but was expensive, was absolutely necessary. It enabled contact to be reestablished with the consumers who had been forsaken, and the rebuilding of acceptable foundations for the brand.

The change in the level of quality of a product is rarely abrupt, but results from the insidious logic of statistical tests. Each change is tested against the product's previous version: if consumers have a lower opinion of the changed product but statistical analysis reveals that the difference is not significant, the company will not hesitate to carry out the change to provide a source of financial savings. The problem entirely rests with the expression 'significant difference'. All the decisions are based on the so-called 'alpha risk threshold' (generally 5 per cent). As long as the difference observed in the sample, just due to chance, affects less than 5 per cent of the cases, it is declared non-significant. In sciences, the aim of this high-risk threshold is to avoid taking for real a phenomenon which would not exist in reality. The problem is that in marketing, it is the beta risk which should be taken into account, the aim of which is to avoid considering as false a hypothesis which is in reality true. For, through modifying a product even by the smallest amount which each time has been declared 'non-significant', a considerable risk is taken. Consumers are not fooled. They avoid the product, then abandon it, even sometimes spreading by word of mouth a very negative opinion. From then on, any modification of the product must be approached with caution if it is rated below the standard product, even if the difference is said to be non-significant.

The second factor of decline is the refusal to follow immediately a durable change. Thus Taylor Made, for a long time the world reference for golf clubs, did not believe the gigantic head launched by the Callaway brand under the suggestive name of 'Big Bertha' would catch on. By clinging to a different conception which was more demanding for the average player, ie for the majority of the market, Taylor Made suddenly lost its leadership. In the same way, Banga orange juice continued to believe in glass bottles when the market, following the market leader Oasis, turned towards plastic.

Still at the level of the product policy, the brands associated with a single product are more vulnerable. They risk being carried away by the decline of the product, particularly if nothing has been done to help its evolution. Damart thermalwear barely escaped that risk. Having focused their advertising exclusively on a single product – thermolactyl underwear – the brand quickly inherited an ageing image. At a time when winters seem to be getting warmer, who could still want to buy a product created in 1950 which had not evolved and favoured practicality at the expense of style? The brand's image then acted as a foil, evoking a person very sensitive to cold, someone joyless, colourless, a caricature of old age. In order to receive a new burst of vitality, the brand had to be freed from its obsession with the cold and engaged in an extension towards ready-to-wear clothes. In the meantime a rejuvenation of the entire line of thermolactyl underwear was required, including other fibres (silk, cotton, wool) and a concern for aesthetics. This type of syndrome could also affect other single-product brands, like Seven Up, Sprite, Gini, Cinzano and Pernod. Acknowledging the difference between the brand and the product, the latter needs to be adapted to consumers' new expectations. Such is the function of line extensions: to bring the product into line with current taste by multiplying its versions, while retaining its identity.

This example is a reminder that certain brands hesitate to produce extensions while the market they depend on is in decline. Resting on their laurels and high margins, they discover that the market has collapsed when it is too late: at a time of microcomputers, who will still buy Letraset transfer letters or Caran d'Ache colour pencils? There are fewer smokers of heavy tobacco, which is why Gauloises had to produce light cigarettes in order to stay alive.

Pricing policy can also accelerate the decline of a brand by displacing it from the centre of the market, and by inviting the premature arrival of distributors' brands. The example of Carlton is revealing. Truly innovative, this sparkling peach wine, presented as a champagne, had a very successful beginning due to a remarkable strategy based on word of mouth, presence in selected fashionable places on the Riviera and later in Paris, and a good brand name. But when the manufacturing cost of the product became known, the mark-up or profit margin could not but excite imitators' desires. And as the product could be copied, imitations took off in supermarkets under names which were conceptually close (eg Claridge) and at a much more attractive price. In a way, the excessive price premium attracted the competitors who proposed cheaper me-toos. Carlton, a new and hence weak brand, could not resist the attack. In addition, having refused to change the alcohol content to benefit from lighter taxation, they made it even easier for the newcomers. In a similar way, distributor brands, which had taken on a policy of positioning themselves 20 per cent below the price of national brands, followed them in their rise. And by so doing, they made it easy for hard discounters and budget products to enter. They gave birth to their own competitors.

The relationship with the distribution channel can be a factor of decline if the brand does not live up to the new expectations of it. What is obvious in the sectors requiring mass distribution also applies to the channels for pharmaceuticals for instance. Because companies such as L'Oréal developed particular brands for supermarket distribution, such as Plénitude for cosmetics, Vichy's status in the field of pharmaceuticals is under threat. Consumers who go to a chemist shop to buy such products expect from them a higher level of quality as befits the laboratory guarantee. But over time, Vichy had become a generalist brand more focused on lifestyle than scientific quality. Moreover, since L'Oréal's division, Cosmétique Active, had assigned its curative products (Normaderm, Dercos, Quintessence) to the young pharmaceutical brand Laboratoires d'Anglas, Vichy found itself, in 1995, surrounded by products which no longer corresponded with the products which consumers wanted to buy in a chemist shop. Vichy's survival was contingent upon a qualitative upgrade of all its products and its repositioning by absorption of the best performing products of Laboratoires d'Anglas.

Other brands have collapsed because they have allowed themselves to become trapped in a declining distribution network. Before being bought up by the Rolot corporation, the Murat jewellery brand was only to be found in the less dynamic jewellery shops. Before its purchase by Procter & Gamble, makers of the brand of shampoo Petrol Hahn refused to allow it to be sold in supermarkets, though this was where consumers of this type of product wanted to find it. In the UK the Smith brand, which was for a long time the leader in the crisps market, declined to the benefit of a newcomer from General Mills, Golden Wonder. Smith's success was due to advertisement and consumption by adults outside the homes. Golden Wonder developed family consumption at home by proposing a wide line to supermarkets, a growing form of distribution.

Finally, communication can accelerate the decline of brands. Beyond the obvious fact that ceasing to advertise means ceasing to exist in the market and ceasing to be a key actor, the sensible management of communication consists of modernising the signs, but keeping the essence. After having abandoned its connection with the concept of vitality, Vittel could not halt its decline whereas Contrex never gave up its connection with slimming. What had dated in Vittel's case were the codes and expressions which were very much in the 'Club Med' spirit at a time when 'Club Med' itself was ageing and seemed old-fashioned to a large sector of its main clientele.

If the daughter brands are too much in the spotlight, the mother brand can be adversely affected and give the impression that it is in decline. This happened with Dim between 1991 and 1994. Although the brand was by far the main advertiser in its hosiery market, and even in the textile market in general, it seemed to be lacking, remaining in the background. Such an imbalance between the actual share of voice and the feeling of loss of energy felt by the market worried the management of the Sara Lee group. In fact, the diagnosis was clear: the promotional tactics of the daughter brands had been carried so far that they had fragmented Dim's image. Indeed, it was appropriate – as we have seen in Chapter 7 – to clarify Dim's wide range by attributing first names to different product segments which did not propose the same customer benefits, hence the appearance of Sublim, Diam's and other lines. On the other hand, this measure produced a dispersion of the Dim image, even the disappearance of Dim to the benefit of the daughter brands. The first symptom of this condition was the packaging. There was no longer any homogeneity between the different packagings, and the mother brand appeared in a minor role in variable places. Moreover, in the context of the organizational change, further divisions had been introduced (tights, lingerie, men's items). Unfortunately, there was no longer anybody in charge of coherence between the divisions and of the defence of the Dim mother brand's capital. Finally, since the Dim hallmark only appeared clearly on bottom-end products and was concealed on advanced products, this increased the perception that its quality had declined. At the same time, the market was moving towards opaque tights, a more durable and more top-end product, which could easily make Dim the symbol, not of today's woman, but rather of a poor quality.

In order to correct these dangerous impressions, Dim undertook to increase the added value of all its products, including the basic product, to upgrade all its packagings, to return the status of source-brand by replacing the first-name brands under its umbrella, and to clearly advertise 'Dim presents the new Diam's' instead of 'This is the new Diam's by Dim'. (This example illustrates, in passing, a tendency which is fatal for a brand: its systematic absence from the best new products, thereby confining it to an offer which is static, obsolete or old-fashioned.) To complete the story, it should also be mentioned that, in parallel with the excessive exposure of the daughter brands, the Dim brand had been extended to leisure and indoor clothing. This created an added danger for the brand, that of dilution. On leaving its field of competence (everything which is worn close to the body) to enter the sector of regular clothes, its added value belonged only to the intangible realm of lifestyle. The existence of clothes with a Dim label without any tangible added value could only raise doubts about the brand's actual contribution, not only in this new market, but also in its basic markets: tights and lingerie. So, in the context of Dim's renewal plan, an end was put to this extension which was causing the dilution of the brand's capital. The priority was to return Dim to the field in which it was recognised to have expertise. The history of ready-to-wear clothes contains too many examples of brands which have abandoned their initial concept to experiment with new extensions and so lose their identity. This has been the case with Newman, which can no longer be associated with a typical product, of Daniel Hechter which has moved away from its founding style, of Ted Lapidus, and so on.

WHEN THE BRAND BECOMES GENERIC

The highest degree of dilution of the brand's added value occurs when the brand becomes generic. The brand is considered a descriptive word, part of everyday vocabulary with no distinctive properties. The classic examples are well-known: Scotch, Kleenex, Xerox, Nylon. What causes a brand to be reduced to the point of becoming generic? Market domination along with the abandonment of any communication on the brand's specific nature and purpose can cause its decline. Thus, any dominant brand of a new product risks becoming a generic name. This can be prevented by taking certain precautions, for example:

- create a word to designate the product of the brand;
- never mention the brand's name alone, but together with the product's generic designation;
- never use the brand's name as a verb (in the United States, for instance, to xerox means to make a photocopy);
- systematically protest whenever the brand's name is used as a common noun by third parties and the media; for instance, request that an erratum be published. Through not having reacted strongly enough, Du Pont de Nemours lost the ownership of Nylon and Teflon, which have since become generic terms;
- nurture the perceived difference between the brand and competitive products, either with tangible attributes or with intangible values.

THE AGEING OF BRANDS

It is frequently said that a brand is ageing, shows signs of ageing or seems aged. This impression may be felt by customers, non-customers, suppliers, distributors or employees themselves, who acknowledge a difference between them and their competitors. Ballantines, Martini, Black & White, Club Med, Yves Saint Laurent and Guy Laroche have all been described as ageing.

The concept of ageing has in fact two different meanings:

- The general meaning suggests a slow but systematic decline over a long period of time. The brand is not destined to end rapidly but seems likely to be inevitably phased out with time. Yesterday strong and active, it appears today much more mundane, as if it no longer had anything to say or to propose to the market and lived exclusively on its loyal clients. One symptom of this is the widening gap between the spontaneous awareness and the assisted awareness. The brand still rings a bell, but it is not one of the brands which has an impact on the market. This is the case with Johnny Walker, Ferguson, and so on.

- The second meaning refers to the reflected image of the customer. Everything points to the typical customer being older. And even in the case of a company whose marketing is deliberately targeted at older customers, it is never advisable for the image of a brand to be too closely associated with an older clientele. Although it is aiming at the flourishing older customer market (that is, customers over 50), Damart must make sure not to be associated with the clientele who are 60 or 70. Without going to that extreme, the Yves Saint Laurent label appears to young people to represent a clientele older than that of Dior's and Chanel.

What is that produces these impressions of ageing? Most of the time these impressions are well founded: the brand no longer seems to belong to its time and has lost its inner energy.

Many brands allow themselves to be associated with the products of another age. With the acceleration of time, the notion of another era now refers to a close past. In all markets dominated by technology, obsolescence can occur very rapidly. Little can be done for brands linked to a dated technology, or those which seem not to have kept up to date with progress.

A brand can be eighteen years old and threatened with ageing. The challenge for the eau de toilette Eau Jeune (ie Young Water), launched in 1977 by L'Oréal for supermarket distribution, is to be still considered Eau Jeune by the next generation of 18 to 25-year-olds, but who are so different. If this brand had remained a single product, it would have disappeared. What symbolised youth in 1977 no longer symbolises it in 1997.

The point of view expressed by the brand on its market can also sometimes seem to be suddenly behind the new dominant values. As long as decisions regarding Playtex in Europe were taken in the United States, the brand never seemed to take into consideration the role of femininity in women's choices. Even though the products were of high quality, they were purely functional, that is based on the tangible problem of breast support. What was relevant in the United States was totally opposite to the way European women related to their bodies. In its tone and inflexibility, Playtex seemed to be addressing the mothers, not the daughters.

Although it is still the world's leading brand for shoes and ski bindings, Salomon has recently realised that it was in great danger of ageing within a few years. In fact, Salomon, in the same way as Rossignol does, has represented the values of alpine skiing for half a century: effort, order, competition, gaining one hundredth of a second, beating all others by a microsecond. The new generations no longer subscribe to these values: a counter-culture, originating in the surf, is now growing on the slopes, bringing with it new sports and new values.

What has been called the 'glide generation' has not learned alpine skiing and probably never will. They instinctively practise snowboarding on the slopes in winter and roller-skating or roller-blading in the streets. They put as paramount values friendship and emotion: they eschew competition and the brands associated with yesteryear. They have elected their own gods: Burton, Airwalk, Quicksilver, Oxbow. All these brands are new and symbolise another vision of sport.

The lack of evolution in a brand's outward signs indicates its present lack of interest in attracting the customer. The brand seems to have come to a standstill. Relying on its unexpected success with its fabulous 205 car, Peugeot decided to extend variations on the 205 look to its entire line of upcoming cars, up to the 605. The problem is that, in the meantime, the 205 had begun to decline, a symbol of the 1980s which had passed. Lacking a new model, Peugeot's dynamism seemed to have come to a dead stop. While Renault was multiplying its innovations in terms of design and concept (the Twingo, the Safrane, the Laguna), Peugeot's monotonous repetition of the same design seemed to signify a return to the brand's past image.

Certain brands also come to a standstill because they remain associated with the same images. The fact that Yves Saint Laurent seems more dated than Dior or Chanel is connected with the omnipresence of the ageing creator himself and association with Catherine Deneuve. Lancôme was sensible enough to bring in Juliette Binoche, and turn its back on Isabella Rossellini even though she was only 40 years old! A more serious problem, since it is more structural, is that certain brand names are a sign of their time. Just as Christian names go in and out of fashion, brand names can also suffer from obsolescence.

As for the clientele, the loss of direct contact with young people is the surest symptom of ageing. This is what differentiates Johnny Walker from Jack Daniel's or Citroën from Renault. In the alcohols sector, the link between generations is broken. Gone is the time when the father initiated his sons to alcohol and its brands. It is now the responsibility of the brands themselves to make sure that this connection is made. Since tradition has become of doubtful value, the brands have to be accepted by each new generation. This continuing need to conquer tomorrow's consumers is difficult, for it goes way beyond the simple updating of advertising. It must be adapted to the new habits of the younger generation, to their modes of consumption, to the places they go. Whereas Cognac is confined to the status of an after-dinner drink, Ricard has developed its relevance from 10 o'clock in the morning to 10 o'clock in the evening, from the coffee-shop to the night-club. It has to adapt itself to young people's tastes and so has created an extension of its line, an alcoholic soft drink. After all, Smirnoff too has recently launched Moscow Mule for the new generation.

Finally, it is important to develop close contact with the young, to be part of their world and share their expectations. This is the motivation behind Paul Ricard's Formula 1 car racing circuit, and behind the very impressive series of free concerts entitled 'Ricard Live Music', which take place from June to September and have become a sign of quality. This drink also invests heavily in order to participate in the organisation of parties in universities and business schools. In a totally different sector, Chanel was able to recapture a younger audience by launching Coco with the help of the rock starlet Vanessa Paradis and by publicising a new and spectacular creation under the direction of Karl Lagerfeld on the body of the top model Claudia Schiffer. For all that, however, the brand did not betray its roots and its older clientele: hence the presence of Carole Bouquet behind the classic No. 5 perfume and the relatively conservative ready-to-wear line of clothes for the well-to-do which ensures that the boutiques remain in business. If this were the only clientele, the label would only appeal to buyers in their forties. This would be fatal: it is the balance between today's and tomorrow's clientele which constitutes the success of the brand.

Without necessarily having to appeal to young people between the ages of 20 and 25, the brand should always be attractive to tomorrow's consumers. The buyers who are today in their forties will modify their functional expectations when they reach their fifties. But they will also like to show that they have not changed by staying with their usual brands. They will refuse to support the ghetto brands which signal their entry into old age. This is why Damart's future depends on its image among 45-year-old men and women even if its marketing is rather targeted at the 55-year-old consumer. Damart has to work on the evolution of its image, not of its target clientele. To do so, they must improve their image so as not to appear a last-frontier brand. This is why, besides the modernisation of their main product, underwear, they have left behind their old methods of distribution: some department stores now have a Damart lingerie department next to Playtex, Rosy or Warner. Damart also advertises products which cross the generation barrier, allowing them to dissociate their image from one based merely on age: thick and coloured tights are just as appropriate for a young girl in a short skirt riding a motorbike as they are for skiers and autumn hikers. Through these significant actions, they address their future customers and put an end to the stagnation of their clientele, for in 1990 Damart was attracting hardly any new buyers, but was selling more and more to loyal customers.

As has been noted, keeping in touch with young people implies a cultural revolution among management. The efforts to be made may seem huge to an older internal team who often do not appreciate the danger they are facing as their own reference points always seem secure. Finally, with consumers living longer, the effects of the clientele's ageing may pass unnoticed. The decline is slow and never spectacular. But unfortunately, as with a cancer, without an obvious sign of decline to react rapidly to, it may sometimes be too late.

To make the radical internal changes required to energise an organisation which has aged with its own reference points, there should be no hesitation in rejuvenating the entire management with young people. This is what Paul Ricard did by appointing a young 35-year-old president to head the Ricard brand, the main asset of the Pernod-Ricard organisation. The revitalisation of brands always starts with a major work of internal rejuvenation.

REJUVENATING A BRAND

The awareness of the value of brand capital has led companies to re-examine their portfolio of weak brands, not with the intention of phasing them out, but to give them a second life. The costs of launching a new brand are such that they justify the savings to be made by resurrecting an old and weak brand which may even have disappeared, but is still remembered and above all is legally registered. This is why brands which had disappeared from the market such as Talbot, Bugatti, Sunsilk and Argus were reborn. The concept of revitalisation, however, is more than just tactical opportunism by which, for managerial reasons, names already owned by the company are chosen to launch a new activity or a new brand.

The notion of renewal covers a wide range of cases, including the following:

- To halt the abrupt fall of sales of a leading brand to enable the recovery of a company on the verge of bankruptcy. A typical example of this is the action led by Robert-Louis Dreyfus and his associates after they bought Adidas from Bernard Tapie in February 1993. Adidas' sales had gone down from 11.5 billion francs in 1991 to nine billion in 1992, a year when the net loss neared 500 million francs. Two years later, it was positive again (with 515 million francs profit), the sales almost reaching 11 billion francs.
- To halt the slow but systematic fall of sales of a leading brand in its market. This is what the Bel cheese dairies succeeded in doing for La Vache-Qui-Rit whose sales had imperceptibly dropped from 30,000 tons in 1980 to 20,000 tons in 1987. Refusing to accept the brand had come to the end of its life-cycle, a new marketing team reorganised the entire marketing mix of La Vache-Qui-Rit from factory to shelf, including packaging and advertising. This drastic programme covered all aspects of the marketing mix, even those which were supposedly sacrosanct, and enabled the management to bring the company round.

- To halt the fall of sales of an ageing brand which has almost lost contact with the opinion-leaders and the younger generation. This is the task of Ballantine's marketing team. Another example is Citroën's revitalisation. This prestigious brand was first taken over by Michelin and later by Peugeot. The AX's failure against the 205 and the Renault 5 gradually separated the brand's image from young people and women, even if in the meantime they received awards for their spectacular advertising.
- To revive brands which have become marginal in terms of market share but still have goodwill among the public. The doubling of the market share of Henkel's Le Chat washing powder after its ecological repositioning, and Omo's recovery after it adopted the detergent micro formula and invested in new advertising, are examples of this. The expected revitalisation of prestigious but forgotten labels such as Balmain and Lanvin fits into the same category.
- To revive marginal brands which still have a certain fame but whose goodwill has disappeared or has been replaced by ill-will among distributors, opinion leaders and the media. This is the task of the new holders of the Ted Lapidus label and was the case when Atari decided to turn from video games to microcomputers.
- An extreme situation is the resurrection of brands of another era which have already disappeared from the market. Examples are Bugatti, Talbot and Sunsilk.

To these cases, must be added the possibility for the holders of brands which have disappeared to transfer them under licence: if they wanted to, Nestlé could transfer the brand La Roche-aux-Fées, a former yoghurt brand, to a franchise of children's clothes. The images spontaneously evoked by this name would fit.

Is it possible to formulate rules based on such a variety of situations that are not too general to be of real operational interest? However, the prospects for revival are not the same in the presence or absence of the following parameters:

- Does the brand still have goodwill among distributors or the public? The rescuers of the Ted Lapidus label which had been neglected for years know that, in Europe at least, the name has lost its celebrity status and that most fashionable multi-brand boutiques have crossed it off their lists. The label, however, still has a residual international fame and may arouse interest in licences in the emerging market of Asian and Eastern Europe.

- Is it the brand itself or the company which is responsible for the decline? In the case of Adidas, the decline was clearly due to the company's mismanagement. Robert-Louis Dreyfus diagnosed a lack of innovation, the products being good technically but not very interesting in terms of design or creativity for the bulk of the consumers, that is young people under 18. The advertising and marketing budget was multiplied by five while many sponsoring activities were cut down. Finally, the designs were changed, and the development and even the marketing were reorganised according to sectors where a sport prevails: basketball in the United States, football and running in Europe. In the same way, in the United States where the brand was marginalised, Adidas remained faithful to its origins in popular sports, and adopted a grassroots strategy targeted at the black youth from the ghettos rather than the yuppies from Yale. It excited interest by sponsoring youth and rap group competitions. They got rid of all products unworthy of the brand, eg. shoes under $50, and offered the distribution channels an opportunity to regain strength from Nike and Reebok. Adidas' market share in the United States went up from 1.9 per cent to 3.8 per cent in 1994 with the expectation of reaching 15 per cent in 1998.

  In the automobile industry, when Ford took over Jaguar, they understood that they had to invest a sum equivalent to or even greater than the purchase price in order to place the factories, the production methods and the mentalities, at the quality level which was required by a prestigious car manufacturer.
- Does the brand's product correspond to the market's expectations? This is the problem of Suze, a bitter gentian alcohol. While sweetness is spontaneously liked, the taste for something bitter needs to be cultivated. And Suze is very much an acquired taste: young people coming across it for the first time generally do not find it very attractive. Indeed, this is the case with any taste one is not accustomed to – one could argue that whisky does not taste particularly good either but everybody drinks it. The main difference is the effect of fashion: the American cinema and the GI's have widely contributed to making this drink popular. Suze may be dominant in its segment but it has to do all the work itself – unfortunately, it cannot make the fashion on its own.
- Is there anything in the company itself blocking the change? In the hygiene and beauty sector, does the Elida-Gibbs salesforce still believe in Sunsilk, a brand which disappeared at the end of the 1970s and has been revived twice since with mixed success, the last being its association with the hairdresser J.F. Lazartigue?

- Is there still a group of loyal buyers who offer potential for growth tomorrow? According to the morally correct principle that a brand must always respect its faithful customers, one should not touch the root product, but rather develop more modern extensions adapted to new targets.
- Does the firm have long-term plans or does it expect quick results? Time and a lot of perseverance are required to revive labels such as Lanvin or Balmain or the Caron perfumes. The unrewarding nature of the initial work is that it does not produce any visible result. But, like the foundations of a building, it forms the basis on which the rejuvenated brand can prosper. All products have to regain the level of quality expected by the market, but which for years had been cut back for economic reasons. A relationship of confidence must be restored with the agents, importers, wholesalers and distributors who may have been turned off by years of bad commercial service and disappointing products. It will be necessary to invest in a new team of creators who are able to bring modernity to the brand while not betraying its roots.

THE FACTORS OF SUCCESS

In spite of the wide range of situations and parameters, several leading principles in successful revivals may be discerned, which we will study in turn.

The term 'revival' of a brand is not quite accurate since it always implies a change in the product. In other words, a new product needs to be launched which meets the expectations of the new clientele and brings a true plus in comparison with the competitors. The brand must on the one hand become a model of quality (which often is a real challenge in sectors like the automobile industry, luxury products and domestic appliances), but also represent a concrete and significant change for today's customers who are already widely solicited by an over-abundance of brands they are happy with. Campari's decline was turned around by the launch of the pre-mix Campari Soda, sales of the latter now representing 20 million litres as against 10 million for Campari. This was also the case for Martini and Martini Bianco.

In fact old brands need to be innovative. Smirnoff is a perfect example. Challenged as the best vodka by Absolut, it launched Smirnoff Black, revitalising the authentic imperial Russian roots of this famous brand of vodka: Smirnoff Black is the authentic Russian super-premium vodka. In the meantime, to keep in touch with the youngest opinion leaders and consumption trends, it extended its red version by means of modern pre-mixes sold in small individual bottles: Moscow Mule and Smirnoff Singles Beach, neither needing a glass to be drunk. Revitalising a brand is first of all a task of creating innovative products in line with the tastes of today's new consumers, not those of yesterday's.

Even when it is very old, the brand leaves in the memory some traces that should not be abandoned when it is revived. These traces define the maximum territory of legitimacy and evolution that will be acceptable. Therefore, while the brand is still alive, any necessary changes must respect the brand's identity. The study of any latent potential, hitherto unexploited, is a necessary preliminary stage for any attempt at revival (see page 119). In Ted Lapidus's revival, the point was not to put back in boutique windows the famous safari jackets which first made the brand famous, but to make the consumer wonder what the former designer Ted Lapidus would do today. For that, it is essential to understand the brand's roots, that is, what inspired Ted Lapidus' products during the 1960s.

The revival of a brand sometimes requires a change of market. Rather than persevere with the impossible, it may be advisable to use the brand in markets which are related and rapidly growing. This has been the approach of Oasis, a brand of orange juice before it was bought out by Schweppes. Abandoning its historical mundane market, it now encompasses pure fruit juices, fruit nectars and iced tea drinks.

There is a big difference between respecting one's roots and cultivating the past. Revivals are based on an update of the overall offer of the brand while staying true to its identity. From this point of view, the original approach linking the designer Claude Montana to Lanvin's revival was perhaps more appropriate than the brand's big return to a classic style of men's ready-to-wear clothes. Luxury stands half-way between pleasure and modernity. Looking to the past sometimes indicates an actual lack of inspiration.

Co-branding is an efficient tool for brand rejuvenation. Considered in its home country as a soft drink for children, Orangina had to show to modern adolescents (the heavy buyers of soft drinks) that it was now in tune with their values. In addition to a high-impact new advertising campaign, the brand developed specific cans designed around typical brands beloved by teenagers – Lee Cooper, Swatch, Reebok, and so on. By so doing it could send out new signs of modernity.

Rejuvenation may also entail a name change: thus Motobecane was transformed into a technical acronym MBK when the brand was bought by the Japanese Yamaha, who later totally modernised the product line. Dim was first called Dimanche (Sunday in English) until its name was changed into the brisk and more modern Dim.

The issue of price is a very sensitive one when rejuvenating or trying to bring back old brands. If during the decline the price had been slashed, a come-back will be almost impossible. Not only will consumers resist, but so will distributors who used that brand as a promotional bait.

Finally in this chapter, a new opportunity to revive brands which have disappeared, but which are still known and appreciated should be pointed out: an exclusive transfer to a multiple-retailer for a determined period of time. This particular method of trade marketing has been used by the Heineken breweries: they transferred the Mützig beer brand to the Cora chain of hypermarkets for a three-year exclusive period. This brand had practically disappeared from the market, its distribution was scarce and its sales had reached rock bottom. In 1993, they were only selling 600,000 litres as against 80,000,000 in 1985. The agreement with Cora multiplied Mützig's sales volume by eight in 1994. Both producer and distributor profited. The former sells the brand to the latter at a better price than a simple distributor's brand. And the distributor has exclusive control of a truly well-known brand. This contributes to differentiation from competitors and avoids the price war on national brands. In the sport sector, Spalding is now exclusively sold by the Intersport network. It seems likely that this method will expand. Once again, and at no cost, manufacturers will be able to profit from the numerous brands in their portfolio which were very well known yesterday but which are today more or less absent from the market.

12

Making brands go global

Geographic extension is built in to the brand concept. On it, depend the brand's growth, and its ability to explore fresh avenues and to sustain its competitive edge in terms of economies of scale and productivity. As such, marketing directors are no longer questioning the principle of international expansion, but are preoccupied with the means by which this can be accomplished. They ask themselves: Where should we go? Do we traverse the Single European market and enter the world arena? What balance do we maintain between a global brand which shuns linguistic and national frontiers, and one which makes provision for local requirements and context? Which brands are destined to have global significance and which should remain on a national footing? Finally, how do we condense the present multitude of national brands into a small number of global brands? Reappraisal of the brand portfolio in this context will cause the necessary demise of a large number of national brands which have their identical counterparts in other countries. Any such transition must be carefully administered, as we have seen in Chapter 10.

The debate between advocates of brand globalisation and those of a sound adaptation to local markets was set in an academic fashion in the 1980s through the articles of Levitt (1983), Quelch and Hoff (1986), Kotler (1986) and Wind (1986). One had to choose sides almost ideologically. Ten years later, we are able to learn from past experience which was more or less successful. If on a global scale we cannot deny the existence of certain factors which bring together countries and cultures, we must not forget that the speed of this coming together is sometimes slower than reckoned. Moreover, if at a certain level of generality or social and cultural trends consumers in many countries declare the same motivations and expectations, a closer look reveals slight differences that must be taken into account. This chapter urges us to a pragmatic approach. The empires built by Marlboro or Coca-Cola will never be replicated, as they benefited from particular historical and time factors. The international expansion of Coca-Cola was fostered in great part by the wars and the presence of GIs in Europe and Asia. It took Marlboro 35 years to conquer the world and McDonald's 22 years! A contemplation of these models, however agreeable it may be, is quite useless for Danone, for example, whose brand image varies from one country to the next because the products through which it penetrated these countries are simply not the same: creamy desserts in Germany, plain yoghurts in France, fruit yoghurts in Great Britain. How do you then create a uniform image around the concept of health if in concrete terms the brand does not have the same products in each market or country? This is the reality for European brands today. The ways leading to a certain type of globalisation have to be drawn up from scratch by these multi-product mega-brands. The approach will have to be pragmatic and modular.

GEOGRAPHICAL EXTENSION: A NECESSITY

A sound understanding of a brand's functioning leads to a permanent search for new openings. A brand can only survive if the product is kept permanently on its toes. Far from representing a source of guaranteed income, the brand is an obligation for perpetual endeavour. Customers quickly grow accustomed to the latest in technique and performance to the extent of considering them normal. In order to survive, competing brands must strive constantly to match this level of performance and if possible go beyond it. This explains the virtuous spiral of the brand: in order to survive, it must always strive to better the products it puts its name to if it wants to keep the promise, that implicit contract binding it to the customer. If Ariel wishes to hold its positioning as a state-of-the-art washing powder, it must adapt itself to new washing processes and incorporate every latest chemical innovation into the modern day household. Apple – the brand which changed the human–computer relationship – cannot rest on its laurels. Having established new standards, it has led IBM, Atari and Amstrad to achieve new heights. It is now endangered by even higher standards set by competitors such as Microsoft.

Research and development are therefore the mainstays of brand achievement. Behind all great manufacturing brands, however vain they may appear, there are whole departments of R&D. L'Oréal is supported by over 1000 researchers, 3M by more than 3000, while Unilever's R&D division tops 4000. When an innovation seems promising, considerable financial investment is required before it can reach the production stage. Today, it is no longer possible to delay the full effect of an innovation by initially offering it to a minority at a high price and then gradually extending its market. If the brand is to remain competitive, the innovation must be offered immediately to all at the lowest possible price. The marginal cost of each progressive feature rises day by day. Hundreds of researchers are needed to even hope to innovate. Industrial investments and research costs must now be set against low unit margins. Using the awareness and public confidence which it has acquired, the brand provides the firm with access to outlets on an ever-widening scale. Without these, such investments could not be economically justified. The manufacturer's brand opens the way to progress and, at the same time, makes it available for all.

In the competitive race, economies of scale provide a strategic lever in that they contribute to competitive pricing. A company designing a car with worldwide market potential in mind has a competitive advantage over the manufacturer who only sets his sights locally. Even though the latter may produce a car which better reflects the tastes of his own country, the difference in price from that of a Japanese or a Korean car designed from the start with a worldwide market in mind will naturally make even the most patriotic motorist hesitate. This is why Renault's Twingo, whose low price is a key element of positioning for the easy-to-live-with car, was designed from the start for a European level: the same product everywhere.

The local company – even if it is positioned in a niche – has no other way of overcoming the price handicap than to extend its outlets while innovating. Geographical extension is an essential condition in the race for survival.

To summarise thus far, globalisation particularly affects products by allowing overall savings and leaps in the experience curve. The same product can, however, be marketed under different brand names in different countries – Ariel in Europe is Tide in the USA and Cheer in Japan. Omo Power in Holland is Skip Power in France. Ricoh photocopiers were called Savin in the USA and Nashua in Europe. Each of these brands has acquired a national reputation which in itself commands sustained cost-effective investment in R&D and production through the outlets which it accesses. But a global product does not necessarily signify a global brand, in other words moving from a single product to a single brand needs further discussion on the subject of economy of signs and symbols.

THE GLOBAL BRAND: A SOURCE OF OPPORTUNITIES

In certain market areas, the global brand is a necessity, whereas in many other cases it is a means of exploiting and taking advantage of new opportunities in communication.

The single brand is a necessity whenever the clients themselves are already operating worldwide. Firms using IBM or Compaq in London would see no sense in having the same equipment in their Bogota or Kuala Lumpur offices under a different brand name. The same applies to most technological industries. Caterpillar, Sumitomo, Schlumberger, Technip and Alcatel are of necessity world brands – quite apart from the fact that they are global enterprises. After it bought Square D in the US, the Schneider group undertook a brand globalisation programme to make its brands acceptable for a buyer who wants all his subsidiaries to be equipped with the same brands and who is negotiating a worldwide contract.

It is also necessary to retain a single brand when the brand itself corresponds to the signature or *griffe* of its individual creator. Take the luxury trade – Pierre Cardin is Pierre Cardin wherever his products are found, just as Yves Saint Laurent is Yves Saint Laurent. Their creations are bought around the world because their signature bears witness to the values of their creator. Whether or not the creator lives on in body or in spirit does not change the rule: from a single source comes a single name.

These cases apart, the single brand permits a product to adapt to new international opportunities:

- As tourism develops, for instance, it is a disadvantage that certain products have different names in different countries. If this were not the case, tourists could find their brands. Seeing the queues of comforted tourists from all countries in front of McDonald's instead of Quick is enough to convince anyone. This argument applies, however, more to some sectors than to others: to food more than lingerie and to car oil more than cooking oil. But the main advantage is linked to the synergy: the exposure of an American executive to Nashua in Europe will in no way benefit the renown and the reputation of Savin in the USA (who market the same products). A young person from continental Europe visiting the UK to perfect their English might see Pledge, a dust remover, advertised on television without realising that it is the same as Pliz in Europe. If Johnson had adopted a single brand name, its international significance would have been understood. Brands acquire additional credibility when they prove to have international appeal. This is why in 1989 Ariel brought out the first advertising commercial featuring testimony from housewives from different European countries.
- The more international media develop, the greater the opportunities they provide for the single brand. This has long been the case with traditional media; it now concerns the Internet. For instance, the French speaking population of Belgium, Switzerland and North Africa watch French television

channels and therefore see French television commercials. This has obliged brands with different marketing mixes in these countries to avoid making use of TV advertising, so as not to contaminate one area with the commercials made for another. Global television channels such as Sky, aimed directly at an international audience, are also on the increase. However, the language factor – particularly where English is concerned – has resulted in hitherto moderate audience ratings for such channels. The Lintas agency tried, in this regard, an interesting experiment. A representative sample of adults from six different countries was asked to translate this English sentence: 'I think that films and series should be viewed in their original language rather than with a translation.' The percentage of adults who were able to translate the sentence correctly is as follows: 46 per cent of Dutch, 46 per cent of Flemish, 31 per cent of Germans, 7 per cent of Spaniards, 6 per cent of French-speaking Belgians, 4 per cent of French and 3 per cent of Italians! The real opportunities for worldwide coverage are provided by such events as Grand Slam tennis tournaments, the Tour de France, the World Soccer Cup, the Olympic Games, Formula 1 motor racing, etc. Through its sponsorship of the Roland Garros tournament, the BNP is known as far afield as California where they speak of the tournament as the 'BNP Tournament', just as there is a 'Volvo Grand Prix'. These programmes reach an international audience and therefore in practical terms exclude on-the-spot local brands, since the costs involved in appealing to only part of the audience would be prohibitive. Only global brands can be present in worldwide events such as the Olympic games or Formula 1 motor racing. Compared with the share paid by Mars France to finance the sponsoring of the Olympic Games by Mars, the local repercussions are considerable. Mars, Coca-Cola, Sony, Canon, Bacardi, Campari, Martini, etc draw a super-brand status from it that none of the brands in the Danone group can reach. Only the global brand can justify the cost of sponsoring such worldwide stars as Steffi Graf, Tiger Woods, Michael Jackson, etc. In a similar way the Internet favours international brands.

- When a brand goes international, it can further benefit from the internationalisation services of certain retailers, brought about by the international extension of their outlets or by agreements made by them with foreign retailers. The concentration of European retailers and the creation of global purchasing centres are working towards the same goal. The brand escapes the stranglehold of local distribution through its globalisation, which is a source of power. What can happen in this or that country is therefore seen with much more ease of mind and strength to resist.
- Finally, the single international brand is easing the process of brand extension. The worldwide single brand allows the firm to capitalise on its own

name sooner than normal, since the brand acquires a wider international presence and awareness, and – if the products and services make an impact – a corresponding reputation. The goodwill thus achieved by the single name on a worldwide scale provides a priceless lever for entering other markets and other areas. This conforms with the typical Japanese approach. They invest in awareness and reputation over the long term and on a global scale, without regard to the short-term effects or for immediate returns on investments in communication. Using one particular sector as a launch pad, they allow this reputation to permeate a public who are not interested in that sector alone. It thus becomes a key to entry into other sectors whose companies are caught off guard. The example of spectacle lenses is significant. The top worldwide manufacturer of lenses for spectacles is Essilor. We owe to this company all the significant progress in the field of eye-sight correction, eg the famous Varilux – the brand of variable focus lenses for the long-sighted. Essilor built its worldwide market share on R&D and assistance to opticians. In this market, up until now, the brand of the lens did not matter: the consumer trusted the optician and his advice for the choice of lens. This is why Essilor did not develop a communication policy for the greater public around its own name, either as a brand or as a company.

However, structural factors are changing the logic of this market in depth: the 'advice-giving optician' is becoming a salesperson more than an advice-giver and therefore expects pre-sold brands. More importantly, Nikon and Seiko have entered the market, strengthened by the reputation they have acquired elsewhere, the former in optics (which is not far from eye-sight), the latter in clock- and watch-making (which yields an image of meticulousness, precision and exactness). From now on, some opticians may ask consumers a new question: do you want a Nikon, Seiko or Essilor lens? All of a sudden, Nikon and Seiko have made brand awareness a key decision factor in this market, which was not the case until recently. Unknown to the greater public, Essilor is a strong company but a weak brand, handicapped on this ground compared to the new entrants that have capitalised for more than 20 years on a single international name, and are ready to reap the fruits of this thanks to brand extension.

FROM SINGLE NAME TO GLOBAL BRAND

How far do we push the global idea? To what extent do we continue to make marketing decisions on a national level? Should we globalise positioning, creative concepts and even the products themselves? The fact is that, though no one denies that a single name is often an advantage, there is some dispute over the brand strategy to be adopted, together with the form it should take. For some, the essence of marketing policy is to stick close to the markets, while for others, the advantages offered by homogeneous marketing on a global scale offer no alternative.

Before dealing with the respective arguments, it is important to be precise about the terms used. Global marketing implies the wish to extend a single marketing mix to a particular region (eg Europe or Asia), or even to the world. It also denotes a situation in which a firm's competitive position in one country can be significantly affected by its position in other countries. The global approach sees the role of individual countries as only part of a wider competitive action.

The global approach considers countries and their roles in a widened competitive field. The aims of marketing in each country are no longer determined by the local subsidiary, but are decided upon according to the global competitive system. Thus, whereas traditionally each subsidiary planned their activities based on their own resources and the domestic market, within a global strategy the following is the case:

- Certain countries have the task of developing a marketing mix for a new product, testing its capabilities in their home markets before its extension to other countries. This therefore constitutes a test, not of the best marketing mix on single national lines but of a global marketing mix prior to extension. As a consequence, nowadays it is insufficient to keep an eye on the competition in one country alone – every country should be included.
- Certain countries are assigned to develop know-how on a particular brand or a type of product brand so that they can act as a precursor and coordinator for others.

In contrast to the global approach, many multinational firms follow a 'multi-local' philosophy, preferring to follow specific trends in each country's market. Not only will the same brand differ from one market to the next both in positioning and in price level, but it is also supported by its own specific advertising campaign. Coca-Cola follows a global marketing policy, while Nestlé prefers multi-local marketing. Thus Maggi ready-snacks were launched:

- in Germany under the name 'Maggi, 5 Minuten Terrine' and positioned as a practical nutritious food for men and women and between 30 and 40;

- in France under its own name 'Bolino' (with Maggi in small print) and positioned as an instant snack for the young single person;
- in Switzerland under another name, 'Quick Lunch', and positioned as a quick meal approved by mothers.

In these three countries, the product achieved its sales objectives. Manichean comparisons should, therefore, not be made between global and multi-local policies in terms of either customer appreciation or sales. However, a company's ultimate aim is not simply to achieve maximum sales – marketing globalisation leads to profitability.

- In the first place, it cuts out duplicated tasks. For example, instead of bringing out different TV advertising for each country, the firm can use a single ad for the region in mind. Bearing in mind the high cost of producing these ads (up to US $1 million), the potential for savings is considerable. The McCann-Erickson agency are proud of the fact that they have saved Coca-Cola $90 million in production costs over the past 20 years, thanks to producing ads with world appeal. Even if production costs are, from now on, low compared to the investment in the media themselves, rendering the economy argument less forceful, it is still worthwhile for middle brands used to developing one campaign per country!
- By launching a product in several countries simultaneously, it eliminates the problems which arise when a new product appears at staggered intervals from one country to the next, depending on the local situation. This has the drawback of allowing competitors time to pre-empt certain ideas in one country which they have seen in another.
- Globalisation allows a firm to exploit good ideas wherever they come from. Since good ideas are rare, they must be made maximum use of. By getting representatives in several countries to put their minds to a particular question, there is a better chance of coming up with a strong idea that can be used on a global plane. This is how the global idea 'Put a tiger in your tank' came to be used around the world. The Timotei shampoo was developed in Finland and spread to other European countries to benefit from the emergence of a trend towards natural goods. The worldwide drink Malibu was created in South Africa.
- A global policy allows a firm to slip the stranglehold of the major retailer, whose commercial demands are closer to a systematic toll than to a payment for real services to the producer. A national brand may have few means of extricating itself; such is the intensity of distribution concentration that it is forced to use a small number of major retailers in order to reach the consumer. The global brand is fortunately less susceptible to local pressures.

Arguments against globalisation point to the specific nature of each market and the differences in product lifecycle depending on the product. In fact, there are plenty of examples of failure resulting from undue haste in adopting a global marketing policy without certain precautions.

The overall culture which has made Procter & Gamble a general success is that of calculated risk and the principle of caution: it employs everywhere what has already worked elsewhere. Thus, in January 1984 Procter & Gamble launched in France the anti-dandruff shampoo Head and Shoulders relying on exactly the same marketing mix and positioning which had led to its success in the UK and the Netherlands. At the end of 1989, Head and Shoulders still had only 1 per cent of the French market. The problem was that they had not taken sufficient account of a feature particular to the French market and present nowhere else. Consumers either buy anti-dandruff shampoos in pharmacies, the pharmacy being a guarantee for efficiency and treatment, or they pick up the variant of their usual brand in their hypermarket (Palmolive dandruff shampoo etc) for everyday use. In between these two brand groups, there is scarcely room for a brand positioned on efficiency, sold in hypermarkets and much more expensive than usual brands, unlike other countries where these cheap brand variants do not exist. The adopted communication mix in no way bettered the situation of this shampoo:

- Procter & Gamble had decided not to translate the name, relying on the evidence that it had been well accepted in Holland as it stood. However, outside the UK, Holland is the EU country which speaks the best English, so there is a considerable inherent risk in extending a policy tested in Holland to a country such as France.
- For its launch, Procter & Gamble used their British film showing a face divided in two so that the results could be seen. The punchline was 'Dandruff talks behind your back'. In France, however, dandruff is seen as a social problem – one should not point the finger in blame, but should sympathise with the problem. The tone adopted in the British approach was perhaps in keeping with Dutch levels of sensitivity, but scarcely applicable to the French.

Head and Shoulders illustrates the harsh realities of different levels of sensitivity and competitive forces in the market place, both of which make a monolithic global policy a perilous strategy. Difference in lifecycle can also bring about failures in over-hasty global policies. Polaroid, for instance, decided to enter the French market by using the popular Swinger – the first Polaroid camera to be sold in the US for under $20 – introduced in France at less than 100F as a call-in product. With a global policy in mind, they used the same advertisements for the Polaroid Swinger as they had adopted in the US. 'The Polaroid system now at only 99F!' It was a commercial failure. Though the Polaroid system was already well known in the UK and in the US, it wasn't in France. The Polaroid company should therefore have first set out to educate the public in the finer points of the instant Polaroid system before concentrating on the Swinger's price.

Such reverses do not, as such, amount to a rebuttal of global policy, since we have such universal successes as Marlboro, Coca-Cola and Mars. The idea of global marketing has an inescapable draw, even though its implementation has been seen to vary considerably in speed according to the markets, the public and the companies themselves, and in spite of the fact that certain idiosyncratic brands are destined to remain on a local footing. If we look at consumer habits, we can see the reasons for this drawing power and identify the conditions which favour the global brand, together with those which impose limits.

CONSUMERS AND GLOBALISATION

The global brand results from a deliberate will to rationalise its management and less from a demand from the market. The consumer does not buy a global brand *per se*, but on the contrary, individualistic brands that correspond exactly to his/her specific needs. Even when it is global, the brand is bought in an individualistic fashion. The buyer of Mr Propre in France compares it to Ajax and to other local competing brands: she has no notion of the existence of Mr Propre in another country, with the same positioning and the same promise of shine. She is sensitive to the latter and to the personality of the brand, just like the buyers of Mr Propre in these other countries. Thus, when in several countries, groups of buyers appear sensitive to the same advantages and expect the same features, there is an opportunity for a global brand. People have rightly spoken of 'coincidence of globalism', referring to the fact that globalism expresses a corporate view, whereas at the consumer's level in each country, in spite of so-called similar needs, their choice remains individualistic and egocentric (Buzzell and Quelch, 1988). The brand must therefore often be a chameleon and seem 'just like back home'. This does not apply to international high-tech, service, luxury or alcoholic beverage brands. But Kodak and Philips are considered French by a third of the French population, as Bic is thought to be an American brand in the USA.

European studies all point to new examples of coincidences of globalism. Whether we are discussing European studies on lifestyles from the CCA or social and cultural trends from the Cofremca or the Risc system, all underscore the convergence of lifestyles. There are less differences between top executives in Italy and in Germany than between executives and employees within Germany. Increasing awareness of this feature is apparent in all countries, though to differing extents. We are not yet at the stage of the Euroconsumer, though there is a representative number in each country. It would therefore be preferable to speak of Eurosegments or Eurotypes. We could also extend the analysis beyond this continent to North America. However, this does not replace a certain local adapting. The trend for 'well-being and harmony with one's body' is indeed European but these words do not have exactly the same meaning in Sweden and in Italy. One must take this into account when devising the advertising strategy.

The existence of Eurosegments is not sufficient justification for a global brand policy promoted in each country using the same name, positioning and advertising material. The competition must be studied at a national level – as we saw, and Procter & Gamble underestimated the market structure in France, so Head and Shoulders was squeezed out. Apart from this factor, psycholinguistic and cultural differences have a real bearing. From one country to the next, any given symbol does not necessarily have the same meaning and vice versa.

That the same word has different meanings according to the country is a known fact. It is one of the major obstacles to the globalisation of names, even to their Europeanisation. Thus, in 1991, the Glaxo laboratories launched a revolutionary medicine, with the ambition of making it the first worldwide pharmaceutical product. Glaxo had in fact just finished the developmental phase of a new formula called Sumatriptan, which alleviated migraine attacks hitherto unresponsive to medicine. The brand name, which was withheld on an international level, was 'Imigran', and had to be adapted in France after an outcry from doctors and general practitioners in a climate where immigration was a sensitive topic. It therefore became 'Imigrane'.

Descriptive names are a handicap on the international scene, since they lose their meaning and impact in other countries as they cannot be pronounced and sound 'imported'. Hence the preference for non-semantic names with no implications. It still has to be verified that they have not been previously registered in any country, and the necessary formalities have to be complied with. Even in Europe, this involved a long and costly process. As long as there was no single procedure, it took many months to complete the necessary searches, checks and registration procedures required to establish a European brand. At the end of this, there was a fair chance that the brand had been registered in some country. Thus, Eurostar, the name of the bullet train between London and Paris had indeed already been registered!

According to the country, the same idea must be expressed through different symbols. This established fact has the paradoxical consequence that it is not by using the same brand name from one country to another that one stays closest to the initial brand concept. The concept behind Jif is better expressed by Viss in Germany and Cif in France. One can change a local name to a global name when the former has little intrinsic meaning and the name precisely encompasses the concept of the product. Otherwise, a fundamental element of the identity is shattered. The diversity of names draws the product closer to its consumers in each market. This is why Playtex applies a modular policy: the Playtex name is worldwide. On the other hand, the company adapts the names of individual products to the markets. Indeed, Playtex only launches new product concepts if they are international. The marketing strategy is homogeneous within large geographic areas (Europe for example): thus the 'Cross Your Heart' range has the same positioning, the same consumer benefit, the same advertising theme and the same execution in all countries. Cross Your Heart adapts to local markets in terms of fabric (cotton in Italy for instance) or of packaging (to take into account differences in distribution circuits). As for the name, it is 'Coeur Croisé' in France (a direct translation), but 'Crusado Magico' in Spain (a slight shift to a 'magic cross'). To stick to the common concept and convey it as best it can, Playtex does not hesitate to change the name of the products if necessary, to provide a more appropriate translation.

- Thus the line of bras without underwires is called 'WOW!' in the US ('WithOut a Wire'), but 'Armagiques' in France.
- The line of girdles that feature long-lasting comfort is called '18 hours', which can be translated in each country.
- A line of bras is called 'SuperLook', a name which in this case needs no translation. Wonderbra itself was launched untranslated.

Despite the legitimate willingness to globalise, we must not overlook real cultural differences and differences in perception. This is why Procter & Gamble has created different versions according to the country for the Mr Clean brand, while nevertheless remaining within the limits of a common strategy (shine). Indeed, the symbols of 'shine' change with the culture. In France, it is expressed by the idea of the mirror ('You can see yourself in it'), while in the US, the emphasis is on reflection off water ('Is it water? No it's the shine!'). Throughout the world, Camay is the soap which implies 'seduction'. This is the line which Procter & Gamble have always taken. However, though customer habits and expectations are the same the world over where soap is concerned, cultural blocks call for different approaches when speaking to a woman about intimate moments.

- In France, the seductive power was portrayed from 1965 to 1985 by a woman beautifying herself in her bath for her husband. The success of this commercial tempted the Japanese to introduce it in their market where it caused fury when the advertisement was screened. In Japan it is considered an insult for a man to enter the bathroom while his wife is performing her ablutions.
- In Italy, they preferred to show a fawning wife and her macho man.
- The Austrians just use Paris as a backdrop to signify seduction.
- In Greece, they added a more sensual note, bringing in the proverbial vamp.

Flexibility at the creative stage not only satisfies local cultural requirements, but also allows Camay to establish its own status in different countries. In France, Camay heads its market segment, with 10 per cent of the whole market. The nucleus of its faithful clientele is made up of 50 to 60-year-olds who have been using the soap since their younger days in 1958. The aim is to regain a younger clientele without losing the loyal core. In Greece, the brand is recent. It does not carry the weight of identity and of a traditional clientele built throughout the years.

Ethnocentrism being what it is, consumers cannot imagine that Camay's advertising could possibly be different elsewhere. They expect global communication to be a straightforward extension of seduction as depicted in the commercial they see. This imagined global process constitutes an elevation of their own national system of values. The same would be true for consumers in other countries. From an operational point of view, although a commercial may be made for a global audience, it should not give the impression of having been 'exported', but must seem coined specifically for the local consumer in front of his/her TV screen that evening in Munich, London or Barcelona. Thus it is difficult to detect the global character of Coca-Cola commercials, whereas the advertising for some brands seems directly imported. Created to address everyone, such ads do not succeed in giving rise to personal involvement.

CONDITIONS FAVOURING GLOBAL BRANDS

Certain situations make global communication and brand policy easier. They are linked to the product, to the markets, to the force of brand identity and also to the organisation of companies.

Social and cultural changes provide a favourable platform for global brands. Under these circumstances, part of the market no longer identifies with long-established local values and seeks new models on which to build its identity.

Turning its back on prevailing national values, it is open to outside influence from abroad. In drinking Coca-Cola, we are drinking the American myth – in other words the fresh, open, bubbling, young and dynamic all-American images. Youngsters form a target in search of identity and in need of their own reference points. In an effort to stand out from the rest, they draw their sources of identity from media-personified cultural models. Levi's are linked with a mythical image of breaking away down the long, lonely road – an image part Dean, part Kerouac, tinted with a glimpse of the North American Eldorado. Nike encourages them to strive to surpass themselves, turning its back on the national confines of race and culture. Women also constitute a clientele looking for new models: Dim could portray the free, independent and seductive woman, and use this image for its own globalisation. Brands corresponding to new eating habits also have to impose forcefully their view of the world in order to rally consumers in search of change. In this way, the brand is seen as a new flag-waver.

New, unexplored sectors have not, by definition, inherited a system of values. Everything is there for the making, and it's up to the brand to do it. This is why there is nothing to prevent the global marketing of high-tech, computer, photographic, electronic and telecommunications or service brands. Apple can, and must, spread its apple everywhere, because brands themselves are the only point of reference in these markets. Only the themes of the campaigns will change to take into account the country's level of economic development, hence its preoccupation. Globalisation also applies to new services: Hertz, Avis and Europcar globalised their campaigns by portraying the stereotype of the hurried businessman – and in any event an Italian businessman wants to identify more with being a businessman than with being an Italian. The argument of novelty works also for McDonald's, Malibu or Corona!

The world has been standardised by the increasing and levelling power of technology – this is Levitt's point (1983). Its products no longer stem from local culture but belong to our times. They are the fruit of science and time. They therefore escape the local cultural contingencies that hinder global communication.

In general terms, globalisation is possible – and indeed desirable – in markets which revolve around mobility. This applies to multi-media, the hotel industry, car rental, airlines, and also the transfer of pictures and sounds. When the brand is perceived as being international, its authority and expertise are automatically accepted. Again, brands have a clear opportunity to organise and structure those market sectors which symbolise the disappearance of time and space constraints. It is their role to deploy their system of values, which can only be unique faced with mobile clients.

Products recently reported can virtually become standards. The globalisation of coffee brands is linked to the particular space left for it amid all the food products in Europe. We know that food consumption habits are closely bound to culture. But this is less true for the coffee market, since coffee is a product with no specific national legitimacy in any country in Europe because it is perceived everywhere as an imported product. Its collective image reflects the traditional representations of South America and Africa that are the same throughout Europe.

Globalisation is therefore possible when the brand is totally built into a cultural stereotype. AEG, Bosch, Siemens, Mercedes and BMW rest secure in the 'Made in Germany' model, which opens up the global market, since the stereotype invoked is a collective symbol breaking national bounds. It conjures up a meaning of robust performance in any country. The Barilla name is another stereotype built on the classic Italian image of tomato sauce, pasta, a carefree way of life, songs and sun. Volvo, Ericson, ABB and Saab epitomise Sweden.

Finally, certain brands represent archetypes. Snuggles fabric softener not only arouses the same notion in every country – that of gentleness (which is not in itself original) – but also the image of reliance, love and security as in one's childhood, as symbolised by the teddy bear. This is why, in order to express the notion of 'snuggling, caressing, cajoling', the brand name is translated as Cajoline in France, Kuchelweib in Germany, Yumos in Turkey, Mimosin in Spain and Cocolino in Italy. La Vache-Qui-Rit, which corresponds to the archetype of the providing mother, is likewise translated (Die Lächende Kuhe or The Laughing Cow). Marlboro embodies the archetype of the Rousseauist man – alone and untouched, authentic, yet modernised and popularised throughout the world in Western sagas of the conquest of America. Drakkar Noir is machismo wherever you see it. Lancôme expresses the French woman.

Several of the above factors explain why luxury brands and *griffes* have gained a worldwide appeal. In the first place, they bear a message – each creator is expressing his own personal values. They were not conceived as a result of any market study or consumer analysis from one country to the next. It is the creator's identity and his desire to express his own values which form the automatic basis of the brand's identity, in no matter what part of the world. Secondly, behind every luxury brand there is a guiding standard – sometimes even an archetype. Cacharel and Nina Ricci represent the dawning of femininity, a dawn tinted with shyness and modesty. Yves Saint Laurent stands for female independence, even rebellion. Finally, the 'Made in France' label and the myth of Paris imbue these brands with definitive cultural undertones. All these are reasons why such brands are able to impose their own vision of the world on national outlooks. Like any religion, brands which set out to convert must believe in their message and spread it unerringly among the multitudes.

On the whole, brands whose identity focuses on the product and its roots can more easily go global. Jack Daniel's whisky builds the pivot of its brand identity from its distillery and its tradition, which leads to advertising which has been remarkably stable throughout time and similar in all countries. Even though it is working with different agencies, the articles and conditions are such that each one produces commercials or announcements that are typically Jack Daniel's. In the same way, with the good fortune to inherit the Clan Campbell name, that of a real and vigorous Scottish clan, the cement of globalisation is evident: a country would be crazy not to try and exploit this unique edge and the images it brings to mind. In fact, all the advertising executions of Clan Campbell in Europe portray the notion of participation in the noble values of this real clan. It is not the same for Ballantines or Johnny Walker, for example, for which the pivot of the identity is no longer clear. In fact, these brands give rise to different advertising creations and positioning in each country.

A strong identity often rests on what gives the product its edge, an advantage which structures the whole marketing mix whatever the country. It is striking to see how alike the clients of the warm underwear of Damart are, whether in the UK, the USA, France, Belgium, Switzerland, Australia or Japan. The exclusive consumer benefit naturally attracts the same customers in all countries: the seniors. There may well be local differences in the the various percentages of sales made in shops compared to catalogue orders or to the share of ready-to-wear in the offer of the brand. But these differences do not alter the profoundly global character of the product offer and the advertising themes which it leads to. As for the execution, it is decentralised, which allows for local optimisation, as in Japan where since the Emperor once declared he wore Damart, the product is almost a luxury good.

Certain organisational factors also ease the shift to a global brand. One-man companies and brands which bear the name of their creator who is still alive are from the start more global. Countries have less ability to modulate locally the identity of Ralph Lauren since the head of the company is precisely Ralph Lauren. It is also true for Bic or Paloma Picasso.

American companies are more ready to globalise because marketing on the domestic market is in essence global, considering the social and cultural diversity of the American melting-pot. Organisational factors also point in the same direction. When expanding towards Europe, these companies created European headquarters from the beginning, based most often in Brussels or London. Individual countries therefore had to account for their results to these European centres. As seen from the US, there was very early on the need for a centre for 'European operations', for considering Europe as a single and homogeneous area.

Finally, a single centre for production in Europe is also a strong factor for globalisation, at least for products. The fact that a factory in Amiens centralises the production of detergents for Procter and Gamble in the whole of Europe leads to a standard product offer throughout and to the spread of technical innovations to all countries at the same time. In markets where the product advantage is key in the positioning of the brand, this centralisation of production and of R&D leaves little room for differentiation on a local basis. Common progress impacts on the brand.

DISRUPTION *VS* OPTIMISATION MARKETING

Apart from factors linked to the market or to the organisations themselves, the same company may have to follow two different policies according to the status of its products. One analysis that explains the differences in observed behaviour is linked to the type of marketing. Certain products are the optimisation of an existing offer. Others are complete breaks from what is on offer, innovations even to the extent of creating a new segment which did not exist before. Taking Renault as an example, the Clio is an optimisation of the R5 and the Safrane an optimisation of the R25. On the other hand, the R5 in 1961, the Espace in 1984 and the Twingo in 1993 were completely new in the automobile market. These cars did not respond to the specific and explicit expectations of consumers but to a latent demand which was not declared. This distinction has an impact on the chosen international policy. Optimisation marketing leads to more flexibility when there is a need to adapt to local conditions. Strong innovation, however, that which conveys new vision, tends to impose itself on all countries and hardly needs any adapting. This is how the Safrane gave birth at once to a specific version for the German market. Two German chassis-builders received the unchanged Safrane and improved it, making it compatible with the upscale demands of the German market by giving it a technological and a luxury start (Safrane Baccara Bi-Turbo). The R25 did not have a strong image in Germany; it was up to the Safrane to prove Renault's technological mastery. The launching was intended to be as homogeneous as possible throughout Europe, because each product is built in a deliberate effort to establish a common image for the manufacturer. But, even by the second year of production, adaptations and local refinements were coming into play. The launching of the Laguna in Germany required from the start a specific approach. Indeed, in that country, the segment which this car belongs to (the so-called 'upper medium') is that of frustrated consumers who cannot buy a Mercedes. Their choice therefore had to be prompted by adding a technological start to the Laguna, a slant all the more necessary since the technological image of cars 'made in France', and even more so that of those made by Renault, does not stand out despite Renault's five years' continuous success in Formula 1 motor racing.

The Twingo shows the opposite approach. From the start it was devised for a specific target, defined socially and culturally as little involved in cars, even to the point of rejecting the automobile and its constraints, costs, etc. The existence of the target was quantified: although strongly present in France and West Germany, it is, however, less developed in countries where a car is still a symbol of status and personal worth (eg Italy, Spain). The chosen European concept – 'the car which you thought was impossible' – signified the break brought about by this car. The advertising campaign was Europe-wide with some minor exceptions and only one product was distributed.

Generally speaking, a strong new concept is capable of breaking the rules and borders. For example, alcoholic beverages are generally promoted using local strategies. What is more cultural than alcohol? Moreover, it is drunk by adults and as we get older our tastes and preferences solidify (unlike with soft-drinks for teenagers). However, very new concepts in this field are able to have a worldwide impact: Corona, Absolut, Bailey's, Malibu. It is the same for cheese: La Vache-Qui-rit is a global concept. Indeed, countries in the Middle East have a local strategy but it is much more to bring the brand closer to the public than to offer a very different promise. The price of the coffee brand Carte Noire is the same in France, Germany and in Japan! Indeed, this coffee was intended to build a new segment, the over-the-top coffee capitalising on aroma. The new concept was based on 'quality and luxury' (as its name evokes), on the pure arabica and the innovation of a soft packaging that locked in aroma. Breaking away from the usual advertising themes of tradition, know-how and quality of the raw materials or of the congeniality evoked by drinking the product, the creative concept put forth emotion and sensuality. Carte Noire took 10 per cent of the market between 1985 and 1991.

It was decided that the concept could become global because it fits with the representation of France abroad: that of upmarket foods. The positioning as *nec plus ultra* was thus extended to all countries ('Gives you the ultimate coffee experience'), and the strategy subjected to as little local adaptation as possible. The brand is Carte Noire everywhere, without translation or local umbrellas, the packaging is the same, the coffee is a blend like that used in France if this is acceptable to local tastes and if it is on par in blind taste-tests with the qualitative reference on the market. The commercial is the same as that which launched the new brand/product in France, though sometimes slightly adapted to reinforce the product benefit (aroma) and the French image which benefits any exported product. Thus in Japan a sequence was added to signify that the coffee is not instant and the word 'Paris' was mentioned.

Many conclusions can be drawn from this example. First, good product concepts, good ideas and advertising transcend borders. Thus it is for all Ferrero products in Europe: Kinder, Nutella, Tic Tac, Mon Chéri, Roche d'Or. An innovation such as Toilet Duck with its revolutionary format becomes without difficulty Canard WC or Pato WC. Examples are just as numerous in the luxury, food, clothing, computer and car industries. Secondly, even with global brands, local adaptations are either necessary or desirable. For example, certain brands are at very different stages in their lifecycles in different countries. Where the brand is new, its commercials must include many sequences featuring the product. The important point is to include everything in the construction of the global commercial from the start. Different versions at the appropriate level can then be used without having to reshoot the whole production. If a testimony-type advertising format is chosen, the casting will obviously have to be adapted to each country to help the identification between audience and person endorsing the product. On the physical side, that of the content of the product itself, what counts is the concept, the benefit for the consumer. In this, local factors will always lead to slight modifications. The example of Orangina is revealing.

In Asia, and in the Third World in general, soft drinks are one means by which consumers achieve a daily intake of sugar (in Asia, for example, there are no desserts served at meals). The Orangina product must therefore be sweeter in these countries. Moreover, in these hot and poor countries there are no refrigerators at home or in the large number of mobile selling points. Orangina is therefore drunk with ice which dilutes the taste, a second reason for the sweeter version of the drink, the unique taste of which is the key weapon in the current globalisation. The natural aspect of the orange pulp in the drink provides the secondary promise. However, this natural aspect is not a strong motivation for buying in the Third World: this is why in South East Asia the advertising signature positions Orangina rather as a bubbly orange drink from France, to exploit the local lever of attractiveness linked to the international character of the beverage. On the other hand, the emphasis on the orange pulp remains a point from which there is no local exception. However, in Asia it is not considered a positive attribute, but an odd deposit at the bottom of the bottle. Further communications in Asia will therefore need to educate the consumer.

BARRIERS TO GLOBALISATION

The debate on globalisation vs localisation was launched ideologically by Theodore Levitt, with a clear preference by him for a globalisation of brands and their marketing mix. The arguments are well-known: the homogenising character of technology, the convergence of lifestyles, the global village created by the transnationality of the media, economies of production, mobility of buyers because of tourism, etc (Levitt, 1983). If there are any lessons to be learned from the simple alternatives, it is that the reality is often a shade of grey and brand management must be pragmatic. Even if the trend is towards standardisation, there are market factors which may render it impossible, even undesirable.

The example of yoghurt is relevant. At first glance it would seem possible to sell plain Danone yoghurt to everyone in Europe in the same way, whether it be flavoured Danone Kid or Danone Bio. However, despite appearances, yoghurt is a typical case of non-transversality because of the different circumstances in each of the markets when yoghurt was first introduced. In France, the market is still influenced by the fact that yoghurt was first introduced as a health product and therefore was sold exclusively in pharmacies (in much the same way as mineral water). Though this is no longer the case and most younger consumers would not be aware of it, this has a deep and unconscious impact on attitudes in the market. Thus in France the product reference is a plain yoghurt, a symbol of good health, while fruit and flavourings were only added a long time afterwards. In Anglo-Saxon countries, on the other hand, where there weren't any pharmacies in the French sense, yoghurt was first introduced as a low-fat product containing fruit for enjoyment, and in this sense it was a product for adults. The motivation to purchase in the yoghurt market therefore comes from very different impulses in different countries because of the way the market was first created in those countries. Moreover, as a result of these differing motivations, the same product will be regarded in a different light in the various countries involved.

For example, in the UK, the origins of the yoghurt market mean that the product is regarded as being one for pleasure, for the enjoyable experience of eating. Flavoured yoghurt, ie yoghurt without the fruit, is therefore a lesser product, and also means it cannot be positioned in the market for children. Moreover, plain yoghurt without either flavouring or fruit – and therefore without pleasure in the eating – is thus a boring product only for those on a diet. In Spain and Portugal, on the other hand, where fruit is abundant, the fruit yoghurt does not have the position of product reference in the market. Indeed, there, where the standard of living is lower than in other European countries, flavoured yoghurt constitutes the main segment, and is eaten as much by children as it by adults: it is a family product and does not need a first name (such as Kid). Again, in Italy, the reference is blended yoghurt with a different texture, and flavoured yoghurt is positioned for very young children. Yet again, in France, flavoured yoghurt is regarded simply as a plain yoghurt with added flavouring, so the logic of the health benefit prevails, as testified by the slogan 'Petit à petit on devient moins petit' (literally 'Little by little we become less little'). To emphasise this promise and to differentiate it from competitors, Danone chose to give the first name 'Kid' to this type of yoghurt, thus identifying it with a child reaching a later stage of development.

In a similar way the reaction to Bio is different depending on the country. In France Bio is perceived as the rebirth of plain yoghurt, conveying health and pleasure. In the UK Bio was the first to introduce the health aspect of the product to the market. In Italy, on the other hand, cultural morality frowns upon the taking of pleasure in the taste of food and it is not considered possible to taste good and and be healthy at the same time. This is reflected in the related commercials – the internal body clock of the UK commercial instead of the nude woman chosen in France.

Thus by considering one of the few food markets which does not have a long history but is actually an industrial product, we can clearly see that the conditions under which the market was created in each country have determined the long-term perception of that product in each specific market. Only Yop crosses these borders. Positioned for teenagers like a soft drink around the concept of freedom, Yop has a European commercial which works well in all countries, provided of course the market understands the concept of a drinkable yoghurt.

Other examples of this kind are abundant. In the car industry, the small car segment represents 38 per cent of cars on average in Europe, with extremes reaching 59 per cent in Portugal and 18 per cent in Austria or Germany. In Italy, the small household car is nevertheless the main car, in which the whole family fits. This determines a stream of structural expectations (five doors for example) very different from France where the segment corresponds to the second or even the third car. Another problem arises when Germany is considered: in this country the segment simply does not exist. Here it is the Golf that is considered the small car, when it is in the middle range segment everywhere else in Europe. It is, therefore, difficult to speak of the Peugeot 106, for instance, in the same way in all countries. In France, in order to compete with the Renault Clio and not to poach sales from the Peugeot 205, the amount of interior space was emphasised, despite the small size of the car (hence the slogan 'la surprise de taille' – 'the size surprise'). In Germany, the 106 was positioned like the Austin Mini, as a second car, small, feminine and urban, and after that as the most environmentally friendly because it was the smallest. In the countries of Southern Europe the interior space was again emphasised to make it a good first family car. In the UK the 106 was positioned as a feminine car which was small but which allowed escape through its comfortable and dynamic aspects – two qualities that make Peugeot a valued brand in this country.

The conditions of consumption of a product often prevent any possibility of applying a transnational approach, even sometimes of exporting a brand. Ricard, an aniseed drink, is the third most popular spirit worldwide after Bacardi and Smirnoff. However, 95 per cent of its sales are domestic, despite relentless efforts to export it. For instance, even after 15 years of heavy investment, the penetration of Ricard into Spain remains very little, since the brand is only drunk by Algerian-born French who emigrated to Spain. Indeed in Spain cocktail type drinks are not all that common. This is a structural problem for this alcoholic beverage: when do you drink it? Moreover, water does not have a good image in Spain: you do not put any in alcohol in case it alters the flavour. Ricard, however, is drunk with five times the quantity of water. Finally, in France the brand is strongly associated with Provence and holidays: it embodies optimism, it is the sun in a bottle. This attracts people in the North, but has little effect in countries situated south of Provence (Italy, Spain). Finally, the brand image is not valued in Spain: it is associated with French tourists spending their summer holidays in that country. The same structural difficulty forbids any hope of penetration into the US: Americans do not mix water with alcohol. They drink their whisky or bourbon on the rocks, a mode of consumption which is hardly favourable to Ricard.

As soon as one touches on products with cultural foundations, the difficulties of a global approach are enormous and they command adaptation. Cheese is typical: there is a wide range of very different traditions, cultures and competitors. There are considered to be 52 food regions in Europe. This is why Bongrain follows a strategy of adaptation: one must utter the right words, address the consumer within his/her own culture. The technological research which is at the basis of cheeses at the Bongrain group does indeed create single products for the European market, but the company adapts its communication to the country and is flexible on the brand name. Tartare is called thus everywhere except in the Netherlands, where it is Paturain. In France, a waterfall evokes the fresh positioning of Tartare. In Germany, it's a peasant who speaks of French freshness. As for the Paturain commercial, it is set in a camping ground. Saint-Moret has the same name everywhere in Europe except in Spain, where it is called Saint Millan. The promotion of cheese from Holland in Europe is also tailor-made, country by country. Indeed the status of cheese in the country, the conditions of its use and the competitive situation define the problems to be solved, which are totally different from one country to the next. There is indeed no proper brand in the strict sense but the country of origin, the 'Made in Holland' label being a collective brand which makes its own promotion.

In the Netherlands, national cheeses control in an almost monopolistic fashion this little market, which is nevertheless a heavy cheese consumer (13.6

kg/year/inhabitant). The product is most often eaten at breakfast or at lunch. The penetration of cheese is very high: 98 per cent of Dutch eat cheese. The role of marketing is to induce new modes of consumption. In France on the contrary, cheese is served on a platter after a meal and in prepared meals. One French person out of two eats cheese. But cheese from Holland is still considered more as a cheese for children than as a cheese for gourmet adults. Hence the chosen communication: 'La Hollande, l'autre pays du fromage' ('Holland, the other cheese country'). And in the UK cheese is consumed at lunch, at dinner, in sandwiches, in salads and as a snack. Dutch cheese only has a 5 per cent market share which overall remains small, all things considered (7.5 kg/year/inhabitant vs 11.5 in France). It was decided that communication here would focus on Edam because of its reduced fat content, and show different ways of eating it, the advert stating 'Dutch Edam, ready for anything'.

MANAGERIAL BLOCKAGES

Barriers to globalisation come from two sources: external and internal. We have already examined the difficulties arising from structural market differences and from behaviour patterns in different countries. It must also be acknowledged that the positioning of exported goods in terms of price is rarely the same as in their country of origin. This leads to differentiated communication positioning, as illustrated by the approach of Perrier in Europe and in the United States. The high price per bottle in America – a country scarcely used to paying for water – completely changes the status of Perrier compared with that in France. Moreover, the 'Made in France' connotation accentuates the fact that it is an import. The same situation arises with Evian. Barilla is a popular but medium range brand in Italy. Outside Italy, it is becoming the symbol of the best Italian food. In the US, Levi's is not an upmarket brand of jeans. Everywhere else, it represents the American myth, the rebel, the sign of youth and seeks to be the most expensive brand of jeans. The same holds true for McDonald's.

Many obstacles to global branding do, however, arise within the company itself. Globalisation is a voluntary step. It was Theodore Levitt who said, 'I know that the world is round, but from a practical point of view, I prefer to think of it as flat' (1983). The global approach tends to concentrate more on similarities of behaviour among countries, rather than to exploit their pertinent differences. It is therefore understandable why certain companies either favour or reject the global attitude, depending on their backgrounds and internal organisation.

One-man firms, as we have seen, are more easily suited to global marketing. Such is the case for luxury goods and for designers from Cardin to Benetton:

whatever the country, the physical and spiritual message of the brand's founding figure is always the same. It is not by chance that Mars is a global brand: the company is dominated by the Mars family. Decisions are centralised. They personify Mars. The uniqueness of the brand – based on universal themes of energy and sports – translates the strong-willed single decision-maker. It was conspicuous in Europe when the Treets brand was cancelled and replaced by M&M's. The Mars brothers had in mind to make M&M's the premier chocolate brand in the world. They disregarded all the arguments concerning Treets' past success, awareness and value at national market level, in favour of their own resolute intentions. In the same way, it took all the authority of Mr Jacobs to overcome the German idea of translating the successful decaffeinated coffee 'Nuit et Jour' into 'Nacht und Tag' in Germany. The fact that the main shareholding boss was at the head of the operation eased the extension of the 'Nuit et Jour' marketing mix to Germany – an operation which, incidentally was a success (later Jacobs decided to name these brands 'Night and Day').

At another end of the scale, decentralised firms whose power lies within their subsidiaries are less capable of brand globalisation. The difficulty is that the ideal career pursued by an executive in a subsidiary is to become the local CEO, and to achieve this he must concentrate on the specific requirements of a particular market territory covered by a wide range of products. The global ideal is the opposite, based on expertise in one product and one brand at a transnational level. Decentralised organisations rely on their specific, ethnocentric attitude backed by the well-known byword 'not invented here'.

Such an attitude is above all an automatic means of defence on the part of organisations and does not always reflect the reality where individual countries are concerned. In 1987, the Toshiba corporation asked its French subsidiaries to include the world brand slogan 'In touch with tomorrow' in all their communication. The answer came back that, since France was a specific case, such a slogan may not readily apply, especially since Philips already signed all its advertising on brown products (hi-fis, TVs, etc) with the slogan 'It's already tomorrow'. With their expert knowledge of brands, the local advertising agency was asked by Toshiba to come up with other possible brand slogans. In accordance with brand identity logic which states that the truth of a brand lies within itself, all the products, speeches and presentations from Japanese presidents were scrutinised to draw the contours of Toshiba's identity prism. The study revealed five communication axes: each one of them was expressed with several slogans. In all, around 40 slogans were tested. The one which received unanimous acclaim among French dealers, company personnel and consumers alike was the slogan 'Toshiba, l'empreinte de demain'. This was in fact almost the exact translation of 'In touch with tomorrow'. The above ethnocentric attitude had therefore revealed the relevance of the worldwide slogan when applied at a national level!

Many companies prefer an approach adapted to each market due to their corporate culture. Pernod-Ricard was built worldwide around local businesses in each country, with a strong practical culture and a lot of autonomy. It is also the case for Nestlé, which is very attached to the democratic respect due to local specificity and which conducts taste adaptation policies. Hence, there are across the world close to a hundred different varieties of Nescafé. There is no global or even European communication. It would be more appropriate to speak of a global concept rather than a global brand, even if Nescafé is present throughout the world. In another area, being close to the people, being within reach and understanding them well is one of Apple's major strengths: it would be impossible to enforce a rigid world-wide communication policy. There is nevertheless a common platform for new product launchings because of the technology and identity, but it allows for adaptation to keep a local flavour each time. Pepsi-Cola develops a pioneer spirit which is very challenging, and gives a great deal of local autonomy to very motivated teams. This also leads the important countries to develop their own communications. These serve common values, tracing the contours of the identity of Pepsi. With its humanist culture Renault accepts more easily than other manufacturers some exceptions to launchings which are more and more transnational, in Europe at least. As for Japanese manufacturers, because of the need and desire to avoid the criticism of seeming like an invading force, they try to blend into the background of each country by giving a great deal of autonomy to local teams. Beyond the brand signature, advertising for Mitsubishi, Honda and Toyota in Europe is far from homogeneous.

Another factor largely explains whether or not brands are managed on a global basis: the relationship between the mother company and the various countries. When a country represents an important part of world sales, its desire to make independent decisions comes up against little resistance. This was the case for Apple France, the third biggest worldwide subsidiary of Apple. While being in the same advertising network as the other subsidiaries (BBDO), the French subsidiary has long applied its own communication policy, albeit taking account of Apple's brand basis and its identity. On the other hand Austin Nichols leaves much room to individual countries to define the strategy of the Wild Turkey brand of bourbon, because for now the share of exported Wild Turkey is very low. Since the majority of sales are in the domestic American market, Austin Nichols lets countries locally optimise their strategy.

Finally, the price factor will be a key component of the homogenisation of brand strategies in the future. Indeed everything points to reducing the price span within which the same brand can evolve from one country to another, from one area to another.

- The existence of a concentration of distributors on a European level creates a major destabilising threat to brands that optimise locally their price policy. There is nothing to prevent the distributors from demanding the lowest price to be seen in Europe, which may be in Portugal for instance, or in a country which has lowered its prices as a means of competition.
- The emergence of parallel markets needs to be avoided as these would destabilise the normal distribution channels of a country and therefore the relationship between a brand and its distributors.

There is indeed a close relationship between price positioning and market positioning. A brand cannot be the most expensive on the market in one place and in the mainstream in another. The price level situates the brand in terms of perceived quality, performance and prestige. In the market for special vintages of champagne, for example, to be the most expensive, on a par with or cheaper than Dom Perignon, does not position its challenger Veuve Clicquot in the same way. Reducing the international price variance of a brand is a factor which encourages uniform positioning and, by extension, affects the whole brand policy. Unless a policy is explicitly chosen that allows optimum prices locally and strong price differences from one country to another, identical products need to be sold under different brand names in each country. This is the strategy followed by Benckiser which buys strong local brands. R&D are indeed by necessity European, using the principle of a 'lead country' for the development of new products and the definition of the marketing mix. On the other hand, however, brands stay local and keep their autonomy of expression. Large groups with local brands are less subject to the inconveniences of competitive devaluation of some countries such as England, Italy and Portugal.

THE IMPACT OF THE SINGLE EUROPEAN MARKET

Even if the ultimate goal of every company is to conquer the world, Europe is the primary natural market for brands originating within its borders. So how far have we got in the standardisation of European brands? Does it vary according to the product category or the country of origin? Does the media profile of the brand (whether it invests in television or not) impact on the globalisation of the brand at a European level?

A study conducted by the author and by the Eurocom network with 210 European brand managers gives us the answers to these questions. In words at least, the great majority of brand managers interviewed declared they were working towards increased homogenisation and standardisation of their marketing mix in Europe. Only 12.9 per cent openly preferred a marketing policy adapted to each country. As Table 12.1 shows, there is a strong relationship between the type of European strategy followed and the country of origin of the brand under consideration. Analysis of the results suggests a strong difference in attitude between Latin and Anglo-Saxon countries. Certainly the trend towards globalisation is massive everywhere, but brands born in Italy or in France are more likely to have local adaptation policies. Can this be interpreted as culturally-based management styles, certain countries having less qualms about establishing a deliberate policy to accelerate the standardisation of brands in Europe? Another explanation is possible: some product categories are overrepresented in certain countries. For example, food brands are a significant part of French brands, and we know how sensitive food is to local culture, unlike high-tech products for example. In fact Table 12.2 shows how great the difference is between product categories when a single marketing mix is to be adopted in Europe.

On the whole, 40 per cent of European brands interviewed declare having a common marketing mix in Europe, 34 per cent vary the marketing mix according to different regions in Europe and 26 per cent prefer to adapt to each country. Food brands are the most reluctant to go totally global: they would rather segment according to 'culinary regions'. At the other end of the scale, luxury and cosmetic brands are the most likely to globalise. Indeed, they are aimed at the same clientele who are mobile and international in their taste for luxury. On the other hand, cosmetics respond to totally universal motivations (anti-ageing, sunscreen, acne treatment) with heavy investments in R&D, therefore their innovations have a scientific basis.

The impact of technology is a recognised factor in standardisation: the investments demand widespread diffusion of innovation. The technological argument implies heavy globalisation percentages as observed for hi-fis, videos,

Table 12.1 How country of origin impacts globalisation tendencies

	Subsidiary free to decide (%)	Push towards standardisation (%)	No response (%)
Germany	4.5	95.5	—
Great Britain	5.3	94.7	—
Japan	0.0	85.7	14.3
Switzerland	20.0	80.0	—
USA	5.7	77.2	17.1
France	24.0	69.0	7.0
Italy	30.0	60.0	10.0
Mean	12.9	81.0	6.1

Table 12.2 Which products lead to marketing standardisation?

	Same marketing mix in Europe (%)	Same marketing mix within regions (%)	Marketing mix adapted per country (%)
Luxury goods	64	28	8
Cosmetics	61	30.3	8.7
Hi-fi/TV/video	54.2	20.8	25
White goods	54.2	37.5	12.5
Detergents	53.8	30.8	15.4
Beverages	40	30	30
Textiles	39.1	39.1	21.8
Cars	35	35	30
Services	28.6	21.4	50
Business to business	25	16.7	58.3
Food	23.5	50	26.5
Mean	40	34	26

household appliances and detergents (accruing from advanced chemical research). On the other hand, sectors where a direct relationship with the client is the basis of the marketing mix are by their nature more inclined to adapt a lot more to local requirement. Unlike the single product that can be manufactured in Amiens and sold across the whole of Europe, service provision involves a transaction in which the consumer participates actively. In 'business to business', the relationships with the technical team and sales force are largely responsible for loyalty to corporate brands.

Lastly, analysis of brands according to their profile in the media shows that the use of television advertising favours the trend toward standardisation (85 per cent of brands advertised on TV declare themselves to be partisans of the latter). The reasons (for economies or the desire to seize opportunities) were stated earlier on. On the other hand, even those which do not advertise on television prefer for the most part (70 per cent) to globalise as much as possible.

What are the strongest barriers to globalisation? What are the parameters that, according to Euro-managers themselves, make difficult, even impossible, brand globalisation? Table 12.3 is particularly revealing in this regard.

The first and only factor which justifies for most people interviewed (55.2 per cent) the non-application of a global strategy is legal differences. It is true, for example, that laws which deal with the authorisation and manner of advertising of alcohol and the use of children in advertising vary considerably. However,

Table 12.3 What differences between countries would compel you to adapt the marketing mix of the brand?

Type of difference	Necessary adaptation (%)
Legal differences	55
Competition	47
Consumption habits	41
Distribution structure	39
Brand awareness	38
Brand distribution level	37
Media audience	37
Marketing programme success	34
Consumers' needs	33
Media availability	32
Brand images	30.5
Norms for products manufacturing	27.5
Brand history	25.2
Lifestyle differences	25
Cultural differences	25
Subsidiary sales	23
Consumers' buying power	22
Consumers' age differences	12

Source: Kapferer/Eurocom pan-European survey

because of the Single European Act, these differences in legislation will have to be evened out, thus suppressing the major obstacle to globalisation. The second factor is linked to the local competitive situation (number and strength of competitors, levels of brand awareness, type and level of distribution, stage in the product lifecycle). Taking the example of Orangina once more, it is not possible to approach the French market where Orangina is a close second to Coca-Cola in the same way as the English market, where it occupies a niche in the premium segment of carbonated orange soft drinks and competes with Fanta, Sunkist and Tango, the local dominant brand. This has a deep impact on market strategy, but the Orangina brand is nevertheless the same, as much in its distinctive signs as in its differentiating attributes and its brand kernel. Moreover, since they are known in advance, these very different market situations can be integrated when filming European commercials. Some commercials destined for countries where Orangina is not known will need longer sequences on the product and on shaking the pulp. At the other end of the scale these sequences can be reduced in France or in Belgium. The significance of this factor concerning the local competitive situation explains in some measure global success of brands such as

Mars, Gillette, McDonald's, Coke, Malibu, Bailey's, Damart, etc. They didn't really have any competitors in the market, and they were new products, creating new segments or revealing the start of a latent transnational demand. They were driven by the feeling that they had an excellent product and extended their programme to all countries. The third factor hindering globalisation is the differences in consumer habits: these are, as we have seen, fatal for products such as Ricard which are deeply rooted in a particular culture. Moreover, to become truly global, a brand must play down its ethnic component. As long as Bailey's was an 'Irish Cream' its potential was limited. An 'exotic' beverage coming from afar, its 'strangeness' relegated it to small sales volumes, to fans of Ireland who would sip it in the evening by the fireplace. But how many people know Ireland throughout the world? Who will still drink alcohol as a liqueur? The globalisation of Bailey's consisted of breaking away from the association with the liqueur set ('The Bailey's moment is whenever') and the promotion of Ireland as a tourist destination.

The discussion above on the impact of the competitive situation on the opportunity to lead a global approach underscores the need to state precisely which of the brand facets can or cannot be globalised. In the case of Orangina, the fundamental attributes of the brand and its identity signs remain intangible. The execution can indeed vary: the product adapts to local tastes and legislation and the global advertising shown in Europe is adapted in Asia because humour is difficult to export. Table 12.4 presents the facets that are most easily globalised for pan-European brands.

Table 12.4 Which facets of the brand mix are most often globalised?

	%
Logotype, trademark	93
Brand name	81
Product features	67
Packaging	53
After-sales service	48
Distribution channels	46
Sponsoring (arts)	32
Sponsoring (sports)	29
Advertising positioning	29
Advertising execution	25
Relative pricing	24
Direct marketing	18
Sales promotion	10

As we can see, the percentage varies from 10 per cent to 93 per cent. Such a variance is linked to the fact that the word brand refers to identity and to action (the marketing mix). It is the fixed image of the brand (its fixed logo) which is the most globalised, a sign that image precedes sound. What counts is that the exclusive typography and the red colour of Coca-Cola can be found throughout the world, even if it isn't written 'Coca-Cola'. Unilever does not use its Motta brand everywhere in Europe, but its local equivalents use the same colour and signal codes. The brand name comes in second. It is true that most companies have inherited some odd situations where what is called Dash in Italy is called Ariel in France, and so on. When brands are local strengths it is not a good idea to risk standardising too fast. The operational facets of the marketing mix are naturally adapted to local markets, all the more so as we approach below-the-line activities or local financial optimisation regarding the price. In the era of television and multi-media, image wins over word. All the more so in Third World countries where illiteracy is common. Colour codes and graphics must be global: Coke is red, Orangina is blue. However, even the strongest brands hesitate when the question arises of what to call them in the enormous Chinese market.

The dilemma is as follows: should one respect the sound of the name even if it has no local meaning and is therefore difficult to pronounce or to memorise, or should one respect the concept, the consumer benefit even if it means parting with the international sonority of the brand? By chance, Coca-Cola benefits from a Chinese equivalent which sounds close and is endowed with positive signification: Keu Ko Keu Leu means 'good to drink and make happy'. In the same way the premier worldwide brand of insecticide Decis from Agrevo is pronounced Di-Cha-Seu in Chinese which luckily means 'at them until death'. Pepsi-Cola chose ideograms pronounced Bai Seu Keu Leu, a little farther from the international pronunciation but signifying 'lucky and happy'. The question is of some importance when the size of the Chinese market is taken into account. A strict adherence to the phonetics of the brand name often leads to a series of ideograms which have little local meaning and therefore are a handicap against appropriation by the consumer. It must be remembered that we are not selling a name but a consumer benefit. It is the latter which must be conveyed. In the case of soft drinks, the question then becomes what is the consumer benefit? Is it the taste, the subjective effect, or the cosmopolitan and prestigious aspects that accrue from them? This lever would lead to a preference for an international name even if it has little meaning for the Chinese consumer and would be pronounced or memorised with difficulty. The example of Bisquit Cognac is in this regard symptomatic of the dangers of a policy seeking meaning. This Cognac was brought into China – where one drinks Cognac as wine – with a Chinese-like name Ba-Ksi-Kat, which means 'a hundred good things'.

On this label the Chinese name was just above the Bisquit brand. This was a success, but more than ten years later, it appears that Bisquit is sometimes mistaken for a cognac made in China, a local product trying to look French, which makes it inferior to similar brand names such as Remy Martin or Martell whose international image is intact. Meanwhile, Remy Martin had capitalised on its visual symbol and was the 'Cognac of the man with a horse'.

Indicative as they may be, statistics from the pan-European study are only averages and conceal the diversity of European brand types. On the basis of a study of the 210 Euro-brand responses a typological analysis revealed four brand profiles, each one characterised by a tendency to globalise either all the facets of the brand and its marketing, or only some of them.

The first type of profile revealed is flexible. Such brands do not hesitate to adapt their advertising, promotion, direct marketing, media and sponsoring to conquer local market share. Although the advertising strategy is one and the same all over, there is no hesitation over adapting the creative idea and the advertising execution to local requirements and demands. One finds in this category brands such as Apple, Ray Ban and Evian. The car industry is over-represented in this field (12 out of 20 brands are of the flexible kind), applying 'global' marketing techniques: Renault is a typical example, as shown in Table 12.5.

The second type is the beginners. They are at the first stage of Europeanisation. This type covers many brands that have inherited a European patchwork, and are seeking to create the basis of a long-term convergence. We

Table 12.5 Renault's branding policy in Europe

	Global	Local
Corporate brand and logo	Yes	—
Corporate slogan	Yes	UK
Product names	Yes	—
– Limited series	—	Yes
Product features	Yes	—
– Options	—	Yes
Product price	—	Yes
Distribution	—	Yes
Communication		
– Product positioning	If possible	Yes
– Advertising execution	If possible	Yes
– Media	—	Yes

therefore find a hodgepodge of brands whose logos are not only different from one country to another, but whose names, packaging, product characteristics and even advertising promise are also different. The third type is the tactician. It standardises the heart of the brand, its products, its advertising strategies and its execution (to a certain extent). On the other hand, it adapts its channels of distribution and the price level to those of its competitors. We find in this type Club Med, Polaroid, Kodak, Vizir, Rank Xerox and Levi's. Finally, the fourth type corresponds to the image that one has of a truly global brand: almost everything is standardised, except perhaps the sales tactic (direct marketing, promotion and the advertising sales ratio). Luxury brands are over-represented in this category. But we also find brands such as Playtex, successfully using the same product concepts and marketing mix in Europe under the umbrella of a brand well-positioned on support and seduction, since it managed to gain its autonomy from Playtex USA, which has retained a purely functional image due to the nature of the American market.

The preceding typology is descriptive. Is there a winning strategy? To answer this question we have examined the behaviour of the market leaders in all 18 European countries: they are over-represented in the first category (that of flexible brands), as are the brands which are either leaders or not but are present in these 18 countries. These two cases alone represent 51 per cent of so-called flexible Eurobrands, 36 per cent of so-called globalising Eurobrands, 26 per cent of so-called tactician Eurobrands and 20 per cent of so-called beginner Eurobrands. Correlation does not at all mean causality but these results tend to prove at least that leaders know how to adapt. It would be wrong to believe that big leader brands apply standardised marketing: on the contrary, it is the mixture of consistency and flexibility that makes their competitive strength.

WHICH ORGANISATION FOR A GLOBAL BRAND?

Since it marks a profound cultural revolution, globalisation necessarily entails a change in decision-making procedures and in the general underlying structure. Although it is not necessary to go so far as Mars, which has completely eliminated the position of local marketing manager, globalisation does mean transferring the marketing function, which used to be a very decentralised operation (unlike the R&D, planning and finance functions), up to headquarters, or at least to regional headquarters. The subsidiaries focus on sales, distribution, the promotion of products and adaptations in brand communication. To counterbalance the highly negative underlying effects of this structure on the involvement, motivation and loyalty of marketing executives, companies with global brands are developing multinational career options for their executives. It is a question of 'de-ethnocentralising' local management. This leads to international staff recruitment and transfers from one country to another. This structure also favours the entry of people with no marketing training into marketing departments. Indeed, the natural leaning of marketing is more towards responding to specific expectations rather than common and converging transnational factors. Where budgets are concerned, a major proportion should remain under local control in order to preserve the existence of decision-making challenges, and thus the very challenge of the job.

As for advertising, globalisation implies adopting a single network. This favours creative standardisation, the easy exchange of information and people, and the creation of a circulating *savoir-faire*. From a procedural point of view, certain differences in emphasis may be observed according to the company:

- Some companies ask a number of agencies to propose a campaign on the basis of the same brief. The best campaigns are then tested in each country in order to determine which global campaign should be selected. This campaign is either 'imposed' or suggested, bearing in mind that any subsidiary always has the right to refuse. The execution of the global campaign is either centralised, which maximises economies of scale (this is the case for Coca-Cola), or it is decentralised. Thus, brands either choose international stars (Tina Turner and Michael Jackson for Pepsi, Borg for JVC), or national celebrities (local actresses for Woolite), which in this case leads to the decentralisation of each commercial.
- Some companies appoint an agency in the network as head of production and initiator of advertising campaigns due to the significance of the market where it is located.
- In any case, even when under highly centralised management, globalisation requires structures and procedures for information, persuasion, coordination and approval. European companies are all developing multinational teams which unite European managers for the same brand under the direction of one head manager. Let us not forget that brand globalisation is not limited to economic concerns, but also seeks the best ideas whatever their source, in order to use them in other countries. Thus, the idea of comparing a creamy dessert for children, *Le Petit Gervais aux Fruits*, to the protein contained in a piece of steak was coined in Brazil and thereafter spread to Europe. Brand globalisation need not imply the need to water down versions of advertising copy – on the contrary. The opinion of European brand managers on the impact of the Single Market on communication attests to this fear: in a European survey 46 per cent of interviewed managers felt that 'if campaigns

are unified throughout Europe, good creative ideas risk being lost'. The objective of sound globalisation is precisely the opposite: it is to provoke good ideas in order to spread them.

The survey which was carried out by the author and the Eurocom network makes it possible to join types of organisations to types of brands (see Table 12.6).

Nowadays the dominant forms of organisation in Europe are those allowing subsidiaries autonomy with some central coordination (46 per cent of the cases), the constitution of transnational teams to establish a strategy (31 per cent), or else complete centralisation as is the case with many European advertisers (13 per cent). This last figure should grow significantly in the years to come despite the risk of decreasing involvement that this type of organisation provokes among local managers.

Comparison of these forms with the types of European brands is revealing. It comes as no surprise that Euro-beginner brands are the quickest to let each subsidiary decide their own strategy and produce the advertising. So-called flexible brands navigate between many types of organisation. Tacticians prefer central coordination, which in their case leaves little room for local adaptation where the core of the brand and its advertising are concerned. The purists of globalisation, however, represent the majority of brands adopting the 'lead country'

Table 12.6 What organisation for Euro-brand management?

Organisation / Euro-brand type	Beginner	Flexible	Tactician	Global
Decentralisation: full autonomy of subsidiaries (4%)	150	92	85	99
Autonomy with central coordination (46%)	116	96	129	100
European team (31%)	96	112	96	95
Lead country (6%)	–	117	90	191
Full centralisation (13%)	117	55	35	193

Base 100: mean of each line

approach or total centralisation. Even though trends are appearing, it is nevertheless quite amazing that there is such a wide variety of organisational modes according to the type of brand: this is the sign of an activity which is in the course of structuring itself.

Obviously companies experiment in the search for the solution which suits them best, independent of fashion and trends. Nevertheless, it is suggested that with time they will go through the following phases: starting from a very (perhaps too) decentralised position, they will move to the creation of collective structures and more or less strong centralisation, but as rigidities appear as well as a loss in the quality of the relationship with the market itself, they will evolve once more towards decentralised structures, though under strong coordination (see Figure 12.1).

It is these intermediate policies which are the most successful. The opposite leads to significant energy losses to impose obvious local decisions to a management which is far away and rigid. For example, for a local subsidiary of Procter & Gamble, it took close to eight months of fighting and the production of three commercials to prove that the testimony-type advertising format imposed in Europe for the launching of Always, the new product for female sanitary protection, was less efficient than a whisper-type format, which was used in Japan with success. The testimony-type of commercial received bad scores among all age segments. The whisper style had the best scores among the target audience

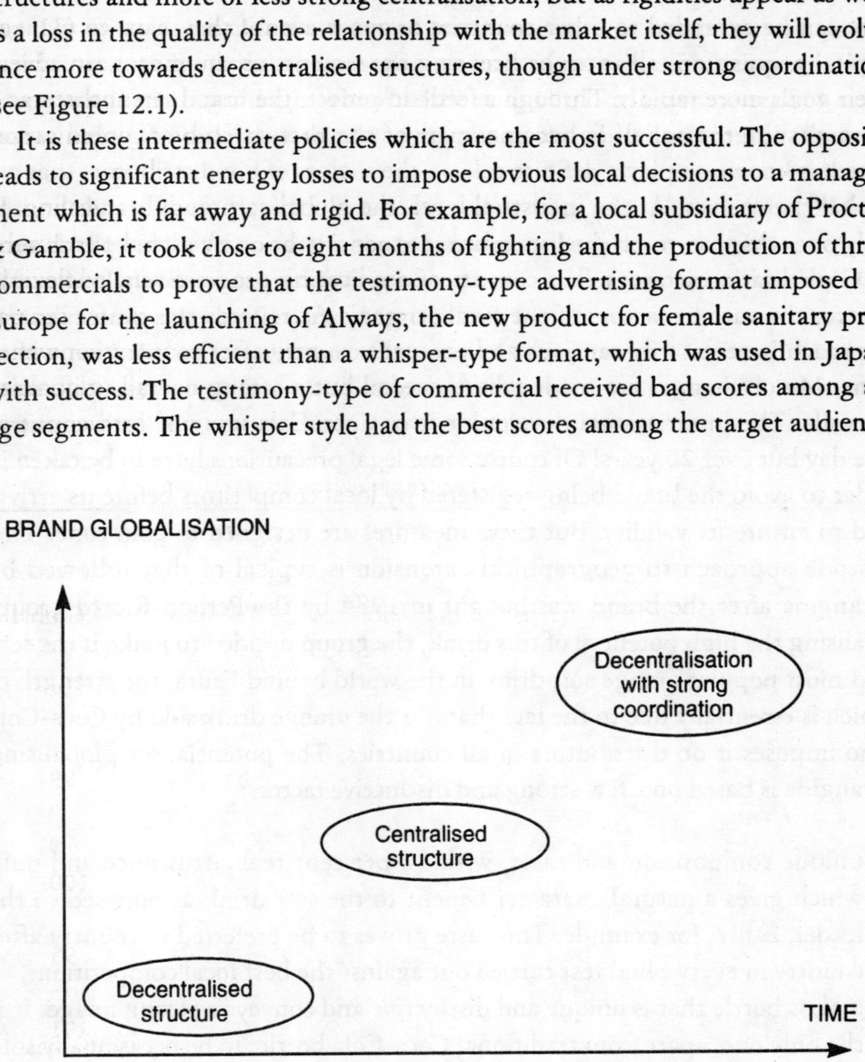

Figure 12.1 How Eurobrands move from one type of organisation to another

of women over thirty. Because of rigidity and centralisation, Procter was taking unnecessary risks.

THE PATHWAYS TO GLOBALISATION

What are the main strategies for brand globalisation? Corporations now understand that some of their brands have the potential to seduce consumers or industrial clients beyond their national borders and that their local success factors can be extended to other countries or zones even if they have to manage capital acquisition, alliances or licensing agreements as the means to achieve their goals more rapidly. Through a feedback effect, the brand strengthens as it becomes international. It becomes part of the private club of global actors which is known to play a definite role on the shelves of big distributors that are global themselves. At the industrial level, the global corporate brands are the only ones that can reach the lists taken into consideration by global purchasers.

Globalisation strategy first consists of duplicating progressively, but everywhere, the success factors of the local strategy. As regards the timescale, the approach is necessarily cautious and proceeds country after country, zone after zone. Minor changes are made where needed but a strong overall uniformity prevails. The international development of Coca-Cola was not carried out in one day but over 20 years! Of course some legal precautions have to be taken in order to avoid the brand being registered by local competitors before its arrival and to ensure its validity. But these measures are designed to gain time. This cascade approach to geographical extension is typical of that followed by Orangina after the brand was bought in 1984 by the Pernod-Ricard group. Realising the high potential of this drink, the group decided to make it the second most popular orange soft drink in the world behind Fanta, the strength of which is essentially due to the fact that it is the orange drink sold by Coca-Cola who imposes it on distributors in all countries. The potential for globalising Orangina is based on a few strong and distinctive factors:

- unique composition and taste, with 12 per cent real citrus juice and pulp which gives a natural character benefit to the soft drink as opposed to the leader, Fanta, for example. This taste proves to be preferred in country after country in every blind test carried out against the best local competition;
- a glass bottle that is unique and distinctive and conveys a strong image. It is the only one, apart from traditional Coca-Cola bottle, to be occasionally sold without a label, the brand name being engraved on the bottle itself;

- a name that is easy to pronounce and means the same thing in most countries;
- a colour code that is specific and arbitrary (blue) which protects it from various imitations produced by distributors. The visual symbol of orange pulp is also strong, exclusive and international.

The conclusion of the strategic analysis carried out by the Pernod-Ricard group was that the orange soft drink segment was not dominated by a brand, unlike that of colas, and that there was a big opportunity for a worldwide soft drink which could bring a real added value to the table. The selected strategy consisted of consolidating the growth of Orangina in its source country and its status of second most popular domestic soft drink after Coca-Cola, France also being tested for line extensions (Orangina light, Orangina Plus, Orangina Red). This market is still under-developed in terms of soft drink consumption per capita and offers strong growth potential. On an international level, the group now opens new markets for Orangina on the basis of one key country per year. The selection criteria are based on the potential for market growth, the absence of entry barriers, a prior brand awareness for Orangina (because of trips and vacations) and the market price level. Finally, of course, excellent bottlers must be available and ready to associate with the Orangina venture. In every country, the same strategy proves to be a winner. It consists of imposing the distinctive attributes of the brand – the unique product made out of 12 per cent citrus, the pulp, the round glass bottle (even in markets where glass bottles are no longer sold), the blue code, the orange pulp logo and now the musical jingle. As stated previously, the sugar content can indeed vary to take into account the specific requirements of Third World or Arab countries, but the physical identity of the brand is intangible. The launching process systematically begins with an education phase and the creation of a strong 'premium' soft drink image, the emphasis being put on its consumption in cafes, hotels and restaurants, product-tasting and the priority distribution of the little round bottle. The next step in the strategy consists of achieving sales volumes via mass distribution, PET formats (two litre bottles), cans and advertising campaigns.

In terms of advertising, the type of advertising hitherto developed using themes such as the South and emphasising Spanish or South American values had to be abandoned in order to fit with the global strategy of Orangina. Indeed, for an Australian or even an Italian consumer, the very concept of 'South' has little meaning. The brand had to start all over again on a sound footing with a proposition to suit the whole world and the priority target of the soft drink market: teenagers. A proposition consisting of several commercials was selected in 1994 whose function was to put forward the advantages and the unique personality of Orangina. Indeed, in all markets, and even in its domestic one, today, teenagers from 13 to 18 must discover what Orangina is.

The second global strategy consists of launching the brand from scratch simultaneously in several countries. This is a typical approach used by the large multinationals in creating new brands from scratch for an international market incorporating the occasional local adaptation of the product or the advertising execution as soon as the product is conceived. This is how the Gillette G2 and the Sensor, the Ariel micro formula and the Skip Power, the Ford Mondeo, etc were launched. It is typically the approach used for luxury brands, for example for the worldwide launch of a prestigious perfume such as that produced by L'Oréal. Details of the launch of the Renault Twingo have already been presented.

The third strategy for globalisation is the most common in Europe. It consists of unifying the local brands inherited during the growth of the groups. Big groups have, historically speaking, often chosen a strategy of external growth through the buying up of strong local brands. The industrial sector typically uses this strategy: Merlin-Gerin has never stopped purchasing local leading brands of electronics for instance, Yorkshire Switchgear. In buying these well-established reputations, these companies were able to smooth their way through local markets. This approach also involves fast-moving consumer goods. The former BSN took over the famous Belgian biscuit brand, Beukelaer, the local equivalent of Lu. The Swedish group Molnycke bought Nana in France, which then joined the Scandinavian brand of sanitary protection, Libresse.

Given this patchwork type of situation where there is not much standardisation in the brand portfolio, companies proceed to regroup brands around the same positioning.

Two scenarios are then possible:

- The company changes the names of the local brands by substituting the name of its own brand. Thus, ICI bought the French company, Valentine, and gradually substituted its own international brand's name, Dulux (for more details see page 315). Merlin-Gerin first placed its logo on the British company, Yorkshire Switchgear, then signed as an endorsing brand before appearing as the only brand name, Merlin-Gerin UK (before finally becoming Schneider). The entire process took two years. To launch Laboratoires Garnier in Germany, L'Oréal bought out the well known local brand, Dralle, which already owned a local product, Beauty. In 1995, this range was relaunched as Ultra-Beauty of Dralle, with the signature of Garnier Laboratories in fine print. It was easy then to introduce Ultra-Doux or Ultra-Rich, other famous Garnier products, into this market, and then the whole range of Ultra products. Eventually, Dralle disappeared completely.

- In the second scenario, the company decides to keep the local brand equities connected to the brand names. General Motor's branch in Europe is called Opel while in the UK it is known as Vauxhall.

The harmonising process of a European brand portfolio is quite tricky and should always be conducted on a voluntary basis, since the initial situations of each separate brand name are never the same. A systematic programme of unification according to the style, but above all according to the product basis, must be implemented. The example of Mölnycke is interesting from this point of view. In the female hygiene market, the intimate relationship which has slowly been built up with the client is a key factor in the capital of the brand: of course, there is the product benefit, but there is also the climate of a relationship within the brand identity. This relationship must be maintained. Having judged it necessary to preserve the brand capital attached to Nana in Southern Europe and to Libresse in Northern Europe, at the same time as Procter and Gamble was entering the market with Always, the Mölnycke group progressed in three steps.

The first step consisted of determining together what the unique positioning of these two brands could be. The positioning revolved around the concept of what is 'natural'. Deeper examination revealed that this concept gave rise to different readings, according to the country under examination. In Scandinavian countries, the home territory for Libresse, nature in its strictest sense was evoked, whereas in the home countries of Nana nature connoted spontaneity. The whole example emphasises once again the importance of looking beyond the superficial impressions created by the similar expectations expressed by Euroconsumers. The second step consisted of bringing the brand image of Libresse and Nana closer together as they were quite different to start with. Libresse had to develop a more feminine image and more humour, going so far as to include a man in the advertisement for the first time. As for the Nana woman, she had to evolvé in her commercials, become more natural with less frivolity, more pared down to the essential, more thoughtful, as can be seen in Figure 12.2.

This second step was brought about by specific communications, but then having achieved a single concept for the brand, the third step consisted of launching new products shared by both brands with the same commercial.

In conclusion, analysis of this third strategy for internationalisation enables the definition of the typical pathway to follow in all countries with similar constraints. The process is made up of five basic steps (see Table 12.7). A consensus of opinion about the kernel of the brand, the deep identity to which all subsidiaries must adhere, is the essential starting point of these five steps. This

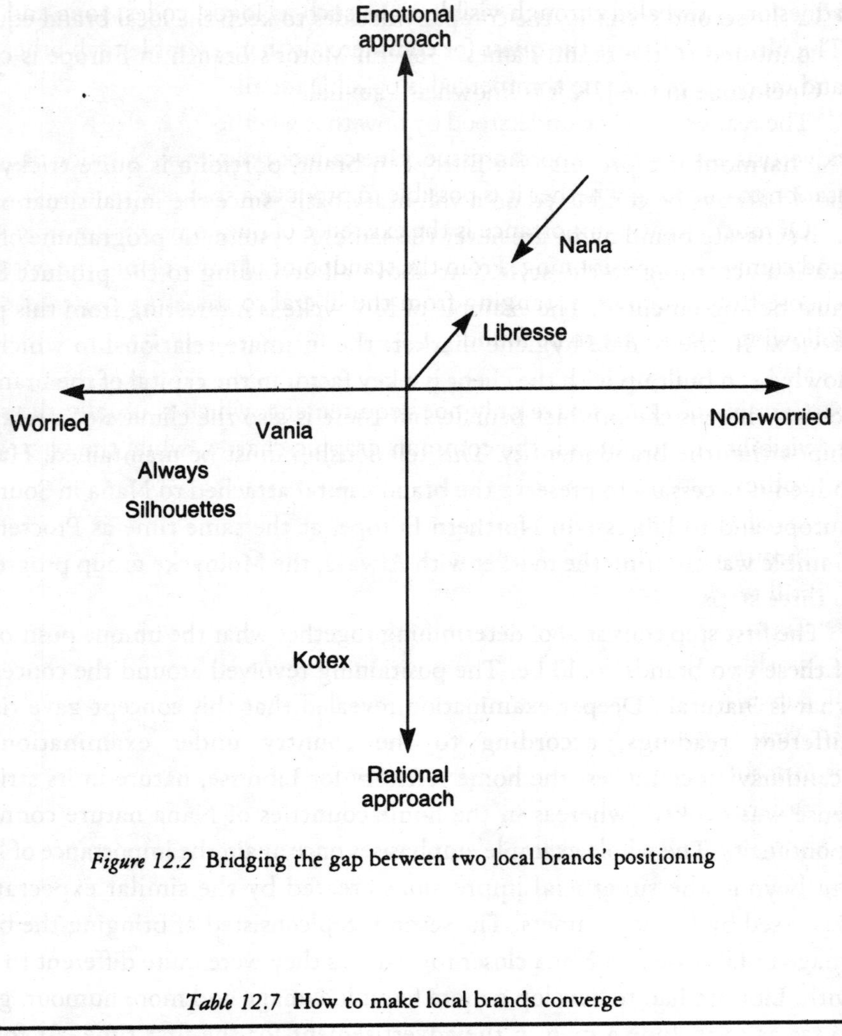

Figure 12.2 Bridging the gap between two local brands' positioning

Table 12.7 How to make local brands converge

Step 1	Is internationalisation necessary?
	Pertinence of globalisation for the brand or brands?
Step 2	Which brand facets should be internationalised?
	Which ones should not?
Step 3	Agreed-upon description for the network of the common kernel, brand platform, prism of identity and concept
Step 4	Definition of the common visible facets, of the graphic charters, packaging charters, charters of advertising expression
Step 5	Definition of the common copy strategy
	Definition of the common advertising execution
	Global launching of common products

Source: Adapted from F. Bonnal/DDB

adhesion is revealed through visible signs such as logos, codes, tone and style. The ultimate phase is the quest for commercials that resemble each other more and more, until a single commercial is possible for all.

The reader will have understood by now that whether or not to have common advertising is not the important issue. One cannot reduce the question of globalisation to knowing whether it is possible to produce a standard commercial.

Of much greater importance is the existence of one common invisible kernel and competitive positioning. From the standpoint of advertising, the options to choose from are diverse, ranging from the liberal to the most centralised. The following policies are to be found:

- Certain companies have only one requirement, which is usually the strong visibility of the brand, the common graphic charter, while the strategy for and execution of the advertising remains free but centralised around the invisible but precise brand kernel. Volkswagen adheres to this approach throughout the world. Although very different, the commercials for the Golf still reveal a strong common trait.
- Certain companies go even further by producing advertising campaigns worldwide (brand or company), leaving, however, the possibility for local subsidiaries to produce their own. Such is the approach of Mars, British Airways and McDonald's.
- Another solution is found in the creation of a pool of advertising which subsidiaries may make use of: such is the approach used by Coca-Cola, AT&T and Jack Daniel's.

Part Three

BRAND VALUATION

Part Three

Financial evaluation and accounting for brands

13

Financial evaluation and accounting for brands

Financial evaluation and accounting procedures for brands have become subjects of considerable debate, as can be seen by the numerous articles which have been published on the subject, particularly in France and England, and also by the number of *ad hoc* committees which have been set up nearly everywhere by national accounting institutions. This intense interest in the subject has several technical, economic and fiscal aspects but especially reflects the discovery of the importance of intangible investments in modern companies and of the growth that a brand can generate in certain cases. The debates are becoming international as they concern the financial information of large multinational corporations holding brands which are strong or presumed to be. However, from one country to another differences exist between accounting procedures for brands and their place on the balance sheet. This could greatly affect the interpretation of the health of these companies. On top of this within the same country, the accounting text and regulations may be contradictory, thus creating certain possibilities which may be seized by certain innovating companies. In this instance the practice was ahead of the rules and indeed shaped the accounting regulations.

The reason for the sudden interest in this subject – it was hardly mentioned before 1985 – is the large increase in the number of takeover bids for companies with brands, in view of the single European market beginning in 1993. The financial and tax implications of the new problems posed by goodwill were considerable.

THE DISCOVERY OF THE FINANCIAL VALUE OF BRANDS

The first people to reveal the monetary value of brands were financial analysts. These were not any old analysts, they were those of hostile companies who were trying to take over companies with brands or of companies fighting to buy firms that were found to have, after careful examination, either modest net assets or negative net assets when accumulated debts are taken into account. Since 1985 there has been a huge increase in the number of mergers and acquisitions with totally new norms. Until then, acquisition prices were determined by the financial results of the target company. The norm was to pay eight to 10 times its profits. If this firm possessed brands, it was believed that their effects were already incorporated in the profits. Brand value was considered to be included in the earnings, and it was thought that if a company made a loss, its brands were worth very little. This explains why companies that were in financial difficulty were bought for virtually nothing; for example, in July 1983 Bernard Tapie took control of 66 per cent of the equity of Look (a company famous for its ski bindings but which made a loss of 53 million francs from sales of 133 million) for one franc. Six years later Bernard Tapie Finance resold Look for 250 million francs to Ebel-Jellinek, an American Swiss duo, even though the company made a loss of more than 41 million francs and was 250 million francs in debt. Its turnover had increased from 133 to 350 million francs thanks to a successful diversification into automatic pedals and composite bike frames which are sold internationally. In order to justify this high price considering the poor financial results, John Jellinek declared: 'The brand has kept all of its potential; we are counting on a boom in the American bike market.' This key sentence reveals a new conception of the brand: it is no longer included in the actual earnings but guarantees future earnings. It is the future that justifies its price.

This is not the only example of this. In 1985, the Italian financier Carlo de Benedetti bought Buitoni for a few hundred million francs. BSN was after Buitoni for a number of years but believed that it was too expensive. The company's financial performances were poor, its guaranteed loans were uncertain and the quality of its products was seen as mediocre. Three years later, de Benedetti resold Buitoni for eight billion francs (35 times its profits) to Nestlé. In the meantime, this financier had transformed Buitoni into a truly European brand, becoming the leader in pre-cooked food and diversifying well beyond its original activities. From this moment onwards products as diversified as tinned and frozen couscous, paella and the truly French gratin Dauphinois would be produced under Buitoni, an umbrella brand. Throughout the world there were more than 100 products all having one thing in common: the same Buitoni logo which was drawn in an identical manner and imposed on all the subsidiaries by de Benedetti after he bought the company.

The skill of this financier is to have bought Buitoni in the traditional way – focusing on the book value of the company – even though he had clearly seen that the real value of Buitoni was not written anywhere but was nevertheless a certainty for anyone who would be able to exploit the potential linked to the brand name, Buitoni, which was already present in all the principal European countries. This is exactly what he did when he extended the brand and globalised it throughout Europe. Within three years, Buitoni, from very little, had become a brand leader, enjoying the benefits of well established European brands. These benefits (and immediate entry as market leader) were estimated to be worth eight billion francs by Nestlé considering the shortage of such brands on the market. In 1985, even though the other bidders had calculated their propositions as if they were only buying a manufacturer of tinned food and Italian pasta, de Benedetti knew that he was buying more: a fantastic brand equity which was ready to be exploited in order to deliver profits.

There are many more cases like these two. On the other hand, since 1986 we have seen a frenzy of mergers and acquisitions, with many brands at stake. This explains the overbidding and the multiples which occurred during these takeover bids and raids. It became normal to see multiples of more than 25 times the company's earnings or two or three times the company's share price. In April 1988, Nestlé bought the UK company Rowntree (with the famous brands KitKat, Polo, Quality Street, After Eight) for £2.4 billion, even though its market capitalisation was only £1 billion. These amounts were reached because Nestlé was reacting to the first offer made by Jacobs Suchard on 13 April 1988 offering to buy the shares which were then worth 450 pence for 630 pence. On 26 April, Nestlé offered 890 pence. On 26 May Suchard bid 950 pence, leading Nestlé to offer 1075 pence.

This high bidding can be explained by the prospect of a European single market and the need to take over these dominant positions. To be able to compete against Mars in the confectionery and chocolate markets, it is no longer possible to create new brands. The market is not growing, and established brands (Mars, Nuts, Treets, KitKat) are sources of loyalty. To recreate a brand from scratch would cost a fortune, take years and would probably fail! Suchard and Nestlé had thus no choice other than external growth. However, there are very few potential candidates in the world: Cadbury and Rowntree in the UK, Hershey in the United States or the Swiss competition. It was normal for the two Swiss companies to increase their bids because their strategic interests were at stake. Even when bought for a high price, the global brands of Rowntree amount to less than the cost would be of the unlikely success of new own brands. On top of this, besides the immediate access to this existing market share, there would be considerable synergistic benefits between the activities. These benefits are attached to the goodwill of the merger: having only one top management rather than two, one sales force, further discounts from suppliers, a stronger position with distributors.

The size of these transactions gives us an indication of the financial value of brands, at least in the eyes of the buyer. This value is, at most, equal to the difference between the price paid and the value of the net assets, the book value of the company. In fact, the value of the brand is not necessarily all of this 'overvalue'. There is part of it which can be attributed to overbidding. In June 1989, Hermès made a proposition to buy Cristalleries de Saint-Louis for 27 million francs. As the book value was negative, we could think that this price was equivalent to the estimated value of the Cristal Saint-Louis brand. However, faced with a competing offer from American Brown Forman (Jack Daniel's whisky and Lenox china), Hermès bid 250 francs per share or 68 million francs. This overbidding effect can be estimated to be the 150 franc difference between the two bids. The price paid also includes the cost of removing a competitor. Commenting on the price paid by BSN for Nabisco Europe ($2.5 billion and a multiple of 27) *The Financial Times* wrote (7 June 1989): 'Just like Nestlé, BSN pays twice: once for the brands and once so that these brands are not found in a competitor's brand portfolio.'

The specific value of these purchased brands is announced during the presentation of the company's consolidated accounts. In France, accounting rules (Agefi, 1990) stipulate that goodwill has to be included in the balance sheet as an intangible asset and amortised over a period of five years. However, companies may attribute part of this goodwill to specific items (just like patents). Brands can be depreciated over an even longer period, or maybe not depreciated at all (as BSN decided to do). In the UK the custom is to eliminate all of the goodwill by deducting it from owner's equity, thus avoiding having to include the depreciation in the income statement (which would lead to a reduction in profits). This custom was broken by Reckitt & Colman. After having bought Airwick (and its brands) from Ciba-Geigy in March 1985 for £165 million (which was equivalent to a record multiple of 41 times profits), Reckitt & Colman decided to post £55.8 million on the asset side of the balance sheet as the value of the brands bought. The difference between the price paid, £165 million, and this amount corresponds to the tangible assets (plant, machinery, inventory) and to the unassumed overvalue also known as goodwill. This non-attributable goodwill was deducted as before from the reserves. Through this technical measure, Reckitt & Colman were anxious to expose their increase in assets to everyone, in this particular case through the buying of intangible assets: well-known brands.

In 1988 in the UK another obstacle was overcome when Rank Hovis McDougall took the decision to include in the asset side of its balance sheet an estimated value of brands which it had created and developed. Although this was not strictly forbidden, this decision was the first of its kind and started a debate which is currently still unresolved on the capitalisation of home-grown brands on the balance sheet. The debate which started in the UK (due to its specific treatment of goodwill which consisted of getting rid of it) spread to Australia and Europe because of the necessary harmonisation of accounting practices. Rank Hovis McDougall's decision, which was followed by many other companies in the UK, is in contrast to European and American practices which forbid any re-evaluation of intangible assets which are bought (and thus forbid the inclusion in the balance sheet of any intangible assets which are created by the company).

Apart from the debate on the accounting principles, this decision resulted in a really fundamental problem: why are companies who buy brands allowed to include them on their balance sheet thus resulting in an increase in all of their assets, whereas companies that prefer to grow internally by developing their own brands are not allowed to do this, thus giving the impression that their assets are undervalued? The consequences of not including internal brands on the balance sheet may be weakening for the company, thus making it a prey for raiders. In fact if the market undervalues the company, the value of the share will make a low priced takeover bid with the hope of a certain profitability possible. This argument was started by the Rowntree incident: in March 1988 the market capitalisation of Rowntree was only £1 billion. Nestlé bought all of Rowntree for £2.4 billion in July. Were the brands and their future potential not undervalued by the market? Threatened by a takeover bid, Rank Hovis McDougall preferred to take the initiative and highlight openly not only the presence of brands (everybody already knew this) but their estimated value. The company's assets increased in value in the eyes of the investors and shareholders after this announcement.

The debate on the inclusion of all of the brands, whether they be purchased or created, raises basic questions about the very essence of accounting. Why do balance sheets and company accounts exist? Is it to give an estimation of the true financial value of the company (which of course is very subjective) or, following the accounting prudence principle, to include only objective data and to assess only past and recorded transactions? Until now the second idea has been chosen in all countries: therefore only transactions involving external brands are recorded. If the internal brands were to be noted, the principle of reality would be respected at the expense of reliability and of the consistency of accounting. In fact, what would we think of a balance sheet which was based on non-uniform and sometimes subjective methods of evaluation? The inclusion of an acquired brand does not violate the principle of book-keeping at historical costs which is a fundamental accounting principle. How then can internal brands be valued? As we will see later on, the valuation methods which are based on historical costs or replacement costs are not good enough. The best methods are those based on projections of future income which are highly subjective. A certain amount of uncertainty and heterogeneity, which are against the rules of caution, would be created if these were included in the balance sheet.

But one may contend that the function of accounting is to present a framework to identify and deal with a company's commercial expenses which are accumulated in the form of intangible assets which are developed internally. For the moment, these outlays are treated as expenses and are deducted from the company's income for the year in question; this in turn reduces the amount of tax that the company has to pay. However, the French tax authorities are beginning to clamp down on the payment of back taxes. For example they now consider that the money spent to produce advertising commercials can no longer be classified as expenses but are rather investments and thus are no longer exempt from tax.

Accountancy, just like taxation, is interested in the recording of costs (as expenses or as investments). Financial analysis estimates the discounted value of certain assets as a function of the probability of the future income that they are supposed to generate. Thus, there will not be only one value of the brand because valuation methods depend on the goals of the valuation. The accounting principles already exist and can integrate with some reservations the costs accrued during the creation of a brand. It is for the finance people to estimate the market value of these assets according to their own methods. This reasoning already exists for buildings and thus can also be applied to brands.

Here, a first conclusion is taking shape concerning the monetary value of brands: ideally for a valuation method to be acceptable it should be possible to apply it equally well to brands which are to be bought and to brands which already exist within the company, with a financial aim as well as an accounting aim. However, this is not possible.

The notion of value is highly dependent on your position. Rowntree was worth £1 billion for its shareholders and £2.4 billion for Nestlé! For Midland Bank, Lanvin was worth £400 million; for Henri Racamier and L'Oréal it was worth £500 million. On top of this, accountancy is controlled by a principle of prudence, objectivity and coherence through time. By definition, in its own evaluation, a raider thinks and acts differently. He does not want to be prudent and is rather subjective. The valuation of brands in the context of mergers and acquisitions is a one-off operation: it aims to fix a price at the start given the intentions and synergies which can be expected by the potential buyer. Accounting for brands should obey different norms since their value derives from a different point of view. When there is no transaction involved, the internal brand is valued either as a function of accrued costs or as a function of its everyday usage (and not what another party could do with it). Therefore, there will definitely be a gap between the value of the brand which is bought and of the brand which is created. Moreover the need to constantly revalue brand values either up or down, in a subjective manner, if they are legitimately noted in the balance sheet introduces fluctuations which undermine the reliability of company accounts. We can reply that the value of the inventory which, in France, is indicated annually in the notes to the accounts does not have this effect. It is understandable why the accounting experts at the London Business School who were studying the case for the inclusion of all brands on the balance sheet gave an unfavourable opinion (Barwise, 1989) concerning home-grown brands.

It is a paradox that those who support the most the argument of posting brand values are the marketing people. Perhaps they are hoping to find a method accepted by accountants and financiers of valuing the long-term effects of marketing decisions. However, even though everybody agrees orally that, for example, advertising has both short- and long-term effects, controllers analyse brand performance within a short span of time. Product or brand managers have to produce positive annual operating accounts, positive profit and loss accounts. Thus evaluation and control are done on an annual basis. This type of behaviour encourages all decisions which are profitable in the short-term. Marketing people would like to have a way to counterbalance this short-term bias which has the effect of ballooning annual earnings but of eventually undermining brand equity through rapid promotions and brand extensions which are too far from the core activity. On the other hand, looking for gains in awareness at any price may not always add to the marginal increase in brand equity and thus should be halted with the money put to better use.

More generally, the value of a brand can be measured if the sources of this value can be located, in other words to measure is to understand. Therefore the resulting figure does not interest marketing as much as the process by which it is acquired, that is, the understanding of how a brand works, of its growth, of its increase or loss in value. This understanding is a learning experience and introduces logical and analytical elements to areas where magical beliefs dominated. It also supplies the means for a real communication between people working in marketing, accounting, finance, tax and law. Finally, even if, for reasons linked to tax or respect for the principle of objectivity and accounting coherence, the inclusion of internal brands on the balance sheet is still not recommended and should not be practised by the company, brand valuation remains a worthy exercise to be carried out internally, for all the above mentioned reasons. Mergers and acquisitions are in the end exceptional events even though they do catch the media's attention. The coming of 1993 resulted in companies taking up strategic positions but this trend soon slowed down. The valuation of brands should not be restricted simply to these occasions, it is also needed for the benefits that can be obtained from the point of view of management: for help in the decision-making process, for management control, for information systems, for marketing training and for education of product and brand managers. At this time when much is being said about the decline of brands, it is healthy to wonder what the real value of their awareness, image and public esteem is. Brand equity is based on psychological indicators which are measured from the consumers' point of view and is only worth something if it results in extra profits. The demands which arise from the presentation of company accounts and from shareholder and investor information are one thing, those arising from a management control system are another. The two should not be mixed up because they do not have the same objectives nor are they faced with the same constraints.

The notion of value is ambiguous and a source of several misunderstandings. It is important to understand that there is no single value for a brand; in fact there are several because the valuation will be different depending on its aims:

- the value of liquidity in the case of a forced sale;
- the book value for company accounts;
- the value needed in order to encourage banks to lend the company money;
- the value of losses or damage to the worth of the brand;
- the value in order to estimate the price of licenses;
- the value for management control which depends on the behaviour encouraged in managers;
- the value for the partial sale of assets;
- the value in case of a takeover or of a merger and acquisition.

For the last case the buyer only asks one question: by how much will actual income rise due to the acquisition of a company with a strong brand? In order to reply to this question the company will evaluate any possible synergies that may exist between the two companies, any resulting cost savings (due to production, logistics, distribution, marketing), any extra capacity to impose one's decisions on distributors or the possibility of brand extensions or internationalisation. The proposed price for buying the company will be shaped by these questions. However, none of these questions will have any influence on the book value of the company's brands.

What conclusions should be drawn at this stage? Financial valuation of brands allows for the multi-disciplinary meeting of all the company's departments: marketing, audit, finance, production, tax, etc. A capitalistic perspective is introduced in the long run, counterbalancing the logic of annual valuation perspectives. It acts as a reminder of the fact that a company's wealth no longer comes solely from the land, plant and equipment but also from its intangible assets (know-how, patents, brands, etc).

The debate on the value of brands and the way to account for them as assets is essentially an accounting one. This is not the essential benefit, but rather the integration of brand value in evaluating marketing and advertising decisions, which have been up to now subject to one single criterion: the preservation of the annual operating statement of the brand. Before we start to talk about the different valuation techniques, it is important to remember that the real objective of a valuation (for an acquisition or for the presentation of company accounts or for management) modifies the criteria of valuation for these methods. Depending on this objective we will have to choose between these demands which are, unfortunately, not very compatible: more validity or more reliability? more subjectivity or more objectivity? more present value or more historical costs?

WHY INCLUDE BRANDS ON THE BALANCE SHEET?

Marketing and advertising people are well disposed to the idea of including brands on the balance sheet because they see this as proof of all their good work. It marks the passage from the status of commercial expenses to one of investment in assets that bear future financial results which are virtually certain.

Curiously, the question is of little interest to those who use company accounts, those who use financial information. Otherwise the problem would have come up a long time ago. When bankers value a company, they are very wary of intangible assets. They are right to be so because the amount written in the consolidated accounts and/or the company's accounts reflects more the reasoning that led the company to write one particular amount rather than another. More precisely, in France companies would be less interested in this subject if the value of brands included on the balance sheet had to be depreciated. Paradoxically you could say that it was accountants who created brands and made them visible. By refusing to follow the American method which allows for the depreciation of goodwill, or the English approach as outlined in SSAP 22 which includes goodwill in the company's reserves thus leading to a deterioration of the net income of British companies and making them very attractive to raiders, the French National Accounting Committee (the CNC) encouraged companies to include a large part of the goodwill under the heading 'brand' which is not depreciated over time. In a cynical way some companies include the difference between the price paid for the firm and the amount of net assets, without any justification and just like any valuation method. In order to avoid this, the CNC asks companies to base their estimates on a method which can be used as an annual estimation of the evolution of the value of the assets and thus of the posted brands.

The decision of the CNC resolves the difficulty of posting a large amount of goodwill to the consolidated accounts by offering the possibility of not depreciating the largest part. In France consolidated accounts are not subject to tax. On the other hand company accounts are. This explains why companies are reluctant to include on the balance sheet the brands that they have created themselves because the incurred costs would no longer be considered as expenses and thus no longer tax deductible. What is more, if the Commission des Investissements Immatériels recommended that these created assets could be depreciated, just as the tax authorities do not recognise the principle of deduction of brand depreciation, the tax burden on the individual accounts of the company would be more important.

This is why the only companies who wish to include their created brands on their balance sheet are those that have nothing to lose. During recessionary times the equity of a lot of companies does not do well. Brands may be a means of improving fictitiously the net accounting assets. Companies that are losing money, an accounting loss, will not be liable to pay taxes but by including brands on their balance sheet they will be able to boost the company's outlook, or more precisely its balance sheet. As we have seen, the accounting principles governing intangible assets are a long way from being neutral and sometimes show a manipulative tendency among companies; analysts realise this.

Is it necessary to include brands on the balance sheet? This question is already out of date. Acquired brands must be included, whether it be in consolidated accounts or company accounts. Created brands may be included. The accounting framework which allowed for the capitalisation of a part of R&D expenses also gives an adequate answer to those who ask about the capitalisation of commercial expenses. Nevertheless, for the moment, those in favour of including created brands on the balance sheet have been kept quiet by the tax issue. This said the tax authorities will probably quicken up the process. It is tempting for the tax authorities to point out that a sudden emergence of large amounts of goodwill in the consolidated accounts means that there was none in the accounts of the individual companies. Logically it would perhaps be better to include goodwill in the accounts of the latter because it would disappear when these companies merge. The tax authorities are correct when they point out that companies cannot both treat brands as assets in the consolidated statements and yet make sure that they are not treated as such in the subsidiary company's accounts. It is because of this that more and more companies are paying back taxes as a result of the Fiscal Administration questioning the tax deduction for certain communication costs. As we have seen, if brands appeared in consolidated accounts because of accountants, it will perhaps be the tax authorities who will hasten the inclusion of created brands in company accounts. To prevent handicapping French companies against their competitors in other countries it is important that the depreciation of brands is tax deductible. For the moment the administration does not allow this because it is believed that the brand *a priori* has an infinite life (it is legally renewed every ten years). However, it is not clear why brands are not treated in the same way as buildings which can also last for one or two hundred years. Generally speaking people are still very wary of intangible assets, as can be seen by the number of conditions that they, and not buildings and machinery, must satisfy before they can be included on the balance sheet.

Therefore when does the question arise about the development of brands and what are the rules and regulations governing each case?

For consolidated accounts the problem arises when a subsidiary enters the field of consolidation. The goodwill which emerges must be allocated. Three situations can lead to inclusion an individual accounts: a once-off acquisition of a brand, the creation of a brand, and finally a merger or a partial exchange of assets. As we will see below, in each one of these situations it is best to distinguish the accounting problem for brands (Is it necessary to include them on the balance sheet? Is it necessary to depreciate them, and if yes over what period? Can they be revalued?) and the problems of the proper valuation methods used, for example in order to attribute to brands a part of the goodwill or in order to determine the stock value each year of brands included on the balance sheet.

The following accounting rules already exist for the first problem (see Viale 1994, 1991; Viale and Lafay, 1990):

- For consolidated accounts the CNC issued a guideline on 15 January 1990 which made obligatory the allocation of goodwill to identifiable items and notably intangible assets which are not included on the individual accounts of consolidated entities. By identifiable, the CNC means that the item has to have a defined valuation method which has sufficient precision that allows it to monitor the evolution over time of its value. Similar rules exist in other countries, but it is only France that does not allow the systematic depreciation of brands.

  Therefore the fact that this item has to be distinct, identifiable and defined by a method which allows its stock value to be measured is a reason given by certain companies for not isolating the heading 'brand', as they claim that brand valuation does not fulfil these criteria. They therefore prefer not to allocate the goodwill in order to depreciate it over a period covering its useful life, which in practice may vary from five to 40 years. By doing this the balance sheets contain substantial amounts of goodwill which is difficult to analyse.

- As for company accounts, a purchase of a brand leads to obligatory inclusion on the balance sheet: the transaction cost (whatever the valuation method used) is in line with the accounting principles for recording costs. In France the aim of the balance sheet is not to give the firm's economic value. In the case of an acquisition the cost and the economic value are the same. In the case of a partial exchange of assets during a restructuring, the brand can be noted as an asset which is separate from the business. The question which raises the most problems is whether or not brands created by the company should be included on the balance sheet. Accounting rules do not exclude the possibility of posting them to the balance sheet. The 4th European Directive allows it so long as national regulations permit their classification as an asset.

Generally speaking, international opinion, excluding Canadian and Australian, on the inclusion of created brands in the company's accounts is rather reserved. In France the work carried out in 1991 by the Commission des Investissements Immatériels of the CNC proposed the operational basis for the recording of created brands as asset. A whole section will be given over to this topic.

THE ACCOUNTING TREATMENT OF CREATED BRANDS

The Commission des Investissements Immatériels start from the assumption that the accounting of brands in consolidated accounts should logically be followed by a similar treatment in the individual accounts. The brand is an asset as defined by the International Accounting Standards Committee, which should be taken into account if:

- it is likely that the brand will bring about a future economic advantage which will have an influence over the whole company;
- the article has a cost or a value which can reliably be valued.

This definition makes no distinction between inclusion in the consolidated accounts and in the company accounts. Moreover, the fact that only those brands which are the object of a separate acquisition are included as an asset is slightly unusual: the way that a brand is obtained has an influence over the way that it is treated by accountants. These disparities are not justified. Why, in the same company, is it possible to acknowledge the value of purchased brands and impossible to acknowledge that of created brands?

If the value of created brands is not brought to the public's attention (by whatever means) there is a practical distortion of information which could have serious consequences for companies which have chosen a strategy of internal growth (Gelle, 1990). But those who oppose the inclusion of created brands have their own reasons for doing so:

- Acquired brands are accounted for at their purchased price which is determined by expected profits. In an effort to create homogeneity, brands which are created and developed internally should also be valued as a function of their expected profits. Respecting the principle of homogeneity of the treatment of the two types of brands creates therefore a heterogeneous balance sheet: the tangible assets are valued according to historical costs. In order to overcome this difference brands would have to be valued according to their past and cumulative costs.
- Not only do we not know when the accounting of such costs should start but also the accounting of internal brands would give rise to a high degree of uncertainty in the information. This would lead to the relaxing of the healthy principle of prudence and reasonable certainty. The valuation methods are all, as we have seen, extremely subjective and can lead to dispute: taking into account the enormous values attributed to some well known brands, the impact of this uncertainty on the reliability of financial information would be very serious.

When are you sure that the costs associated with launching a brand are going to result in a successful and lasting economic advantage, that is to say, to actually create an asset? This said, it is remarkable that we rarely ask this type of question when we are talking about buying a machine or constructing a factory. However, again there is no guarantee that the products that are going to be produced will be a success. Why then do intangible investments have to undergo different criteria to fixed assets?

- If the inclusion of brand assets which are created internally were allowed, it would be inconsistent to forbid the accounting of other intangible items such as know-how and human capital. However, then we would be faced with the problem of separability because very often it is impossible to disassociate these elements from the success of the brand. Nussenbaum (1990) replied to this argument by saying that it is natural that intangible assets interact between themselves and with tangible assets. Therefore to value brands is to give up valuing other types of intangible assets. According to German law the brand cannot be sold without the underlying tangible and intangible assets.

- For all of these reasons it would be difficult to allow the inclusion of created brands on the balance sheet. If the main objective is provide shareholders and analysts with information then there are other means. The accounting law of 30th April 1983 anticipates that when the application of an accounting direction is not sufficient to give a reliable image (...), then complementary information must be provided in the appendices. The appendices are part of the annual report because they are supposed to supplement the balance sheet and the income statement. However, it must be remembered that these amounts are only estimations. Some people fear that double accounting standards are developing: one will be controlled and objective but not reflecting reality, the other more valid but subjective and free. As we can see, the movement to an economy where capital no longer consists of just the land, the buildings or the machinery but also the intangible assets presents crucial choices to the information system of the company which was first created when these invisible items were not taken into account.

In June 1991, the Commission des Investissements Immatériels gave its recommendations concerning the inclusion of created brands as assets on the balance sheet. This report is interesting because it defines an accounting method to identify the commercial expenses which were used to create the assets. The method used is not *ad hoc* but is based on the principles of recording R&D expenses which also create intangible assets. In order to avoid any superficial controversies, it is important to define its viewpoint. Its objective is to be inserted into the existing accounting framework which governs French companies. This framework requires companies to respect the principal of historical costs and does not allow the revaluation of intangible items. The commission, which was chaired by I. de Kerviler, also tackled exclusively the question of new brands, that is those which would be created in the future, but not the question of brands which were created five, 10 or 20 years ago because this would be equivalent to revaluing them, which is forbidden under present accounting principles. The Commission des Investissements Immatériels looked at the principle of historical costs which in France is at the basis of all accounting entries, whereas in Anglo-Saxon countries the aim is to describe the financial value at a particular time. Respecting the rule of historical costs coincides with entering on the balance sheet the value of the acquired brands, with historical cost and purchase price being identical in this case.

Once these principles are respected, two questions needed to be answered:

- What expenses should be considered as assets?
- When should we start?

In fact, due to the uncertainty associated with launching new brands, the expenses incurred during such a process could not be considered as fixed assets. It was necessary to prove that they would contribute with some degree of certainty to the making of an asset which would be of future economical value to the company. As this is foreseeable, the further we progress, in time and in the project, the higher the probability that an economic advantage will be created. The costs at the outset associated with the creation of the project will be considered as expenses because the results of the project are too uncertain, too risky. There is no question of entering expenses on the balance sheet which would not have any future. As soon as we can prove that specific costs (for example, the costs associated with getting a brand listed by distributors and with advertising) associated with a distinct individual project (the launching of a new brand) are capable of generating a future economic value for the company with a reasonable probability, these costs have to be treated as current assets. Later, the maintenance costs, like advertising campaigns which maintain market share, will be considered as expenses unless it can be proved that a part of them has contributed to the sustained increase in market share in this same year, and should therefore be viewed as assets and increase the value of the brand included on the balance sheet.

An interesting element of the report of the Commission des Investissements Immatériels is that it opens a debate which is centred upon tax and competitive issues:

- There is no tax incentive for companies to consider advertising costs as assets rather than expenses. Therefore, it is necessary to solve in advance the tax problem linked to the non-deductibility of their depreciation. The uncertainty concerning the length of the depreciation period is no worse for brands than it is for buildings, for example, where their life is often longer than the depreciation period.
- The success of a brand needs time to be considered as such. It is only after a number of years that the success or failure of the creation of a brand is announced. Will the new luxury Lacroix brand still be around in ten years? Some brands need continuous and intensive advertising support years after their launch in order to become permanently established. How can you therefore speak about reasonable certainty when making the distinction between an expense and an asset, unless, of course, shareholders are subjected to a let-down by allocating an important provision for depreciation, thus attesting that the brand is costly but of little value? Besides the risk of erratic changes in the balance sheet that this may create, do we not risk overvaluing newly created brands – because the costs of launching new brands increase year after year?

- Finally it would be a pity if a national decision resulted in a handicap for local companies over their competitors in other countries, for example Germany, where such a practice does not exist. In any case it would be better to remain sensible by granting companies the freedom to include on the balance sheet, if they so wish, newly created brands.

COST-BASED BRAND VALUATION METHODS

When determining the value of a brand, difficulties arise from the concept of value. Not just one value but several values exist, depending on the point of view of the person carrying out the valuation; this is known as the premise of value. Value is a subjective notion in that it is determined by the subject that is evaluated and the way that it changes over time. The process is therefore contrary to the principles governing accounting and financial information: to be verifiable, objective and fair. From this point of view, the only acceptable methods are those based on historical or replacement costs. While not totally objective, they have the advantage of at least being only semi-subjective in the sense that independent valuations would arrive at roughly the same figures. Therefore in accounting terms the contribution to future profits is a necessary condition for the existence of an asset but is not a valuation method.

Valuation by historical costs

The brand is an asset whose value comes from investments over a period of time (even though accountants do not strictly regard this as a true form of investment). The logical approach would therefore be to add together all the costs associated with a particular period: development costs, marketing costs, advertising and communication costs, etc. These costs can be determined objectively, and will have been in past income statements.

As we can see, this approach allows us to overcome the tricky problem of separability, by isolating the direct costs associated with the brand and also by attributing to it the indirect costs such as the sales force and general expenses. Even though this method is simple and logical, it nevertheless raises the following practical difficulties which reintroduce a certain subjectivity:

- Over what period should costs be accounted for? Numerous brands are very old as we have seen: Coca-Cola dates back to 1887, Danone to 1919, Bull to 1933, Yves Saint Laurent to 1958, Dim to 1965. Should we include costs right from their beginnings? Everyone knows of old brands which no longer exist. Companies must go back in time and ask themselves if past advertising still has an effect today.

- Which costs should be taken into account? Investment in advertising has a dual marketing role: one part generates extra sales which can be measured immediately, while the other part builds brand awareness and image which facilitates future sales. The practical difficulty is in estimating year by year the weight that should be attributed to each part. Also, how far ahead are we looking when talking about future sales? On top of this we have to look at the advertising wear-out curves over a given time period. If, as has been shown in studies on the persistence of attitude changes, such effects decrease in a linear manner over, for example, five years, it may be that expenses arising over this period, including only 20 per cent of those for year $n-5$, can be posted.
- It is not simply a question of adding up the costs, you also have to take into account an appropriate discount rate which has to be calculated.

On top of the subjective nature of the answers to the above questions, valuation by costs causes several basic problems which are linked directly to a partial understanding of the brand:

- When creating a brand, a large part of the long-term investment does not involve a cash outlay, and therefore cannot be posted to the accounts. These include stringent quality controls, accumulated know-how, specific expertise, involvement of personnel, etc. All of these are essential for encouraging repurchase, for the brand's long-term reputation and for word-of-mouth. There would be no trace in the accounts of brands like Rolls Royce because there were no advertisements for it.
- One of the major strategies to create a strong brand consists of choosing a competitive launch price, which may be the same as that of competitors even though the product is upgraded. Swatch is an ideal example of this. They could have opted for a slight price differential, or a price premium, to cover the costs of innovation and of upgrading the product. They decided, however, to set an aggressive price which was equal to that of their competitors, thus maximising the brand's price/quality ratio and enhancing its attractiveness. This is one of its key success factors. Unfortunately, this non-cash investment would not appear in a system where only cash expenditures are registered.
- The method therefore favours brands whose value only comes from advertising and marketing and which have a significant price premium. It would not apply to brands such as Rolls-Royce or St Michael (Marks & Spencer's brand)

which advertise very little. It could also be said that past expenditure is not a guarantee of present value. There are several brands which are heavily advertised but which are of little value and are coming to the end of their life.

- This method is favourable to recent brands and *a fortiori* to internal brands which are in the process of being created, as we have already seen.

Valuation by replacement costs

To overcome the difficulties arising from the historical costs approach, it might be better to place oneself in the present and to confront the problem by resorting to the classic alternative – as we cannot buy this brand, how much would it cost to recreate it? By taking its various characteristics into account (awareness, percentage of trial purchases and repurchases, absolute and relative market share, distribution network, image, leadership, quality of the legal deposition and presence in how many countries), how much would we have to spend, and over what period, in order to create an equivalent brand?

Is it possible to remake Coca-Cola, Schweppes, Mars, Buitoni or Martell? Probably not. How about Benetton, Bang & Olufsen, Saab or Epson? More than likely. For a certain number of brands, the question no longer arises since it is impossible to recreate them. The context has changed too much:

- They were created in an era when advertising expenditure was negligible and the brand was nurtured over time by word-of-mouth. Today, it costs so much for a 1 per cent share of voice that it has become impossible to create a leading brand through unaided awareness. In any case unaided awareness is a restricted area and to gain access a competing brand must leave. This is because of memory blocks. There is no reason why today's well-known brands should allow themselves to be thrown out (see page 139).
- It is difficult to imitate the performance level of brand leaders. Backed by research and development and an intangible but very real know-how, they enjoy a long-lasting competitive advantage and a resulting image of stability. Any challenger is taking a risk. Unless they have access to the necessary technology, their chances of encouraging repurchasing and loyalty are virtually zero.
- Major retailers have now become exacting gate-keepers. They give pride of place to their own brands, only selling one or two national brands which tomorrow will be international.
- Finally, considering the high failure rate of new product launches, it is easy to understand the uncertainty of the return on the large amount of money that has to be invested in the long term. If you are going to pay a lot you might as

well buy certainty. Hence the clutter of takeover bids, raids, mergers and acquisitions of firms with strong brands that are already market leaders.

On the other hand, when these factors which hinder market entry are no longer present, the market is more accessible. The possibility of creating tomorrow's brand leaders from scratch ceases to be theoretical, even though uncertainty and the necessary time element may still exist. Therefore future Benettons will probably be created. Franchising allows wider market penetration without admitting defeat at the hands of major retailers. What is more, the fashion industry is open to new ideas. In this domain, style is more important than technology. Computer services and the hightech world in general are also open to innovation. Generally speaking, the future will see the emergence of new international brands, each positioned in its own particular niche. They will thus no longer seek global awareness but will aspire to be leaders in particular market segments.

Brand valuation by replacement costs nevertheless remains very subjective. It requires the combined opinions of experts and ambiguous procedures. On top of this it should be remembered that the aim of the valuation process is not, in itself, to arrive at a value but to get an idea of the economic value of the asset in question – in this case the brand. Cost methods focus on the inputs, whereas the economic value is based on the outputs – what the brand produces and not what it consumes. Profit is not generated through investments but through market domination and leadership.

VALUATION BY MARKET PRICE

When valuing a brand why not start with the value of similar brands on the market? This is how property or secondhand cars are valued. Each apartment or car is inspected and given a price that is above, equal to or below the average market price of similar goods.

Even though this method is very appealing, it raises two major problems when applied to brands. First, the market doesn't exist. Although such transactions are often cited in the financial pages, acquisitions and brand sales are relatively few. Brands are not bought to be sold again. In spite of this, we can get an idea of the multiples applicable to each sector of activity (from 25 to 30) thanks to the number of transactions that have taken place since 1983. Thus such an approach could tempt some wishing to value a brand.

However, there is a major difference between the real estate market and the market for brands which is relatively small. On the real estate market the buyer is a price-taker, that is, the price is fixed by the market. Irrespective of the use that he will make of the property, the price remains the same. For brands, the buyer is a price-setter, that is, he sets the price of the brand. Each buyer bases his valuation on his own views, on potential synergies and on his future strategy. Why did Unilever pay 700 million francs for Boursin, the well-known brand of cheese? It can be explained by the pressing need of this group to acquire shelf space in major supermarkets in which it had previously been absent. Having at its disposal a compulsory brand, they saw a way of opening the door to other speciality products. In April 1990 Jean-Louis Sherrer was bought for three times less than the price that Mr Chevalier paid for Balmain two months earlier. For Mr Chevalier, Balmain was a means of entry – or rather re-entry – into the luxury market. Hermès, which was already present on this market, didn't need to pay this price (Melin, 1990).

In abstract terms the purchase price is not the price paid for the brand but is the interaction between brand and purchaser. To use the price paid for a similar brand as a reference, without knowing the specific reasons behind that brand's purchase, ignores the fact that an essential part of the price probably included the synergies and the specific objectives of the buyer in question. Each buyer has his own intentions and ideas. The value cannot be determined by proxy.

This is what distinguishes fundamentally the market for brands from that for real estate, or for example for advertising agencies. In the case of the latter, norms and standards exist which are not dependent on the buyers' intentions (50 to 70 per cent of the gross margin on top of the net assets). Despite this, valuations in the luxury market frequently take into account recent transactions and use a multiple of the sales (1.5 for Yves Saint Laurent, 2 for Lanvin and for Balmain, 2.9 for Martell, 2 for Bénédictine).

Considering the difficulties which are inherent in the cost-based methods or in the referential methods on a hypothetical market, prospective buyers tend rather to look at the expected profits from brand ownership. Since the third type of approach relies on two major philosophies, we are devoting a special section to it.

VALUATION BY POTENTIAL EARNINGS

Since the brand aspires to become an asset, it is best to begin by a reminder of what an asset is. It is an element which will generate future profits with reasonable certainty. Valuation methods have been developed on the basis of expected returns of brand ownership. Naturally, these tie in fully with the purchaser's intentions. If he wishes to internationalise the brand, it will be of more value to him than to a buyer wishing to keep it as a local brand. The value measured by expected profits cannot be separated from the characteristics of the future buyer and from his strategies for the brand. This explains why the stock market value compared to a predator's value of a branded company will always be structurally lower. The former valuation is related to the existing business, taking into account current facts and figures provided by the firm. The latter comes from the over-valuation created by the prospect of synergies, complementary marketing processes and the attainment of strategic market positions.

The process of valuing the expected profits of the brand can be divided into three independent stages (see Figure 13.1):

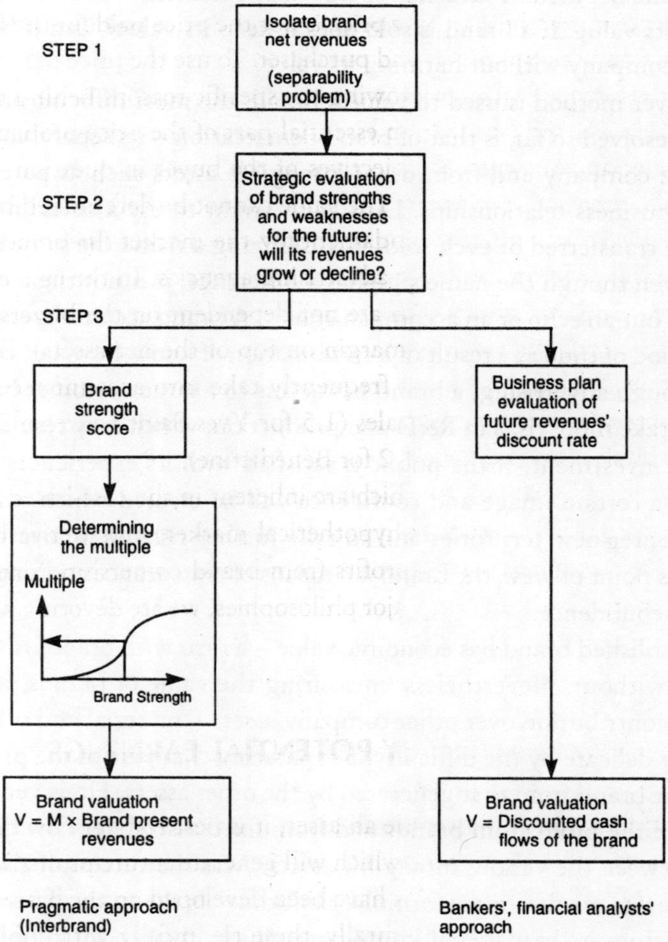

Figure 13.1 A multi-step approach to brand valuation

1 The first step involves separating and isolating the net income associated with the brand (and not with the company for example).
2 The second step is to estimate the future cash flows. This requires a strategic analysis of the brand in its market or markets.
3 The third step involves choosing, by using a classic financial method, a discount rate and period, and for the multiple method to determine precisely this multiple.

We will tackle these stages one by one.

The problem of brand separability

How can the net income attached to a brand be isolated? In fact, to buy a name is to buy its value. If a brand is sold does it keep its value? Can it be separated from the company without harming its value?

Whatever method is used to value a brand, the most difficult problem, and the least resolved so far, is that of brand demarcation – its separability from the rest of the company and from other intangible assets such as patents, know-how and business relationships. Legally, the right to use a brand name can, of course, be transferred or even sold. But is buying a name the same as buying a brand? Even though the name signifies a difference, it is not the creator of this difference but an echo or an accompanist of it. A brand accumulates its strength over a period of time as a result of a combination of know-how and communication. Through advertising, a brand has access to a large customer base and can therefore take more risks in R&D and production, which may result in a higher return on investment. If the public is satisfied with its experiences of branded products, a certain image and confidence will be created which will allow the brand to enter new territories and to take further risks in innovation. From a company's point of view, the brand is a means of reassurance and a source of stability and confidence.

An established brand has economic value – a firm with brands is worth more than one without. Nevertheless, measuring the value of brands, and of their marginal contribution over other company assets – material and otherwise – is made very delicate by the difficulty of separating that part of the profits generated by the brand from that generated by the other assets. However, it is simple to separate the profit from brands and from fixed assets. Yet how do we assign profits between the various intangible assets? Was the success of Zantac due to its brand or its revolutionary formula, ranitidine? Is the value of a service brand separable from its managerial know-how, which, though intangible, is real in the sense that it is created by management? If, for example, you buy an advertising agency which has a famous name but is without its top managers, is it still the same brand?

In fact, intangible assets interact between themselves so brand evaluation means that we do not value other assets. The brand includes their value. It would be a mistake to want to add them.

As we can guess, for accounting purposes it is almost impossible to isolate, in the strictest sense of the word, the specific economic value of the brand. The value of a brand derives largely from the expected synergies. The problem does not arise in the case of mergers and acquisitions, since more often than not the entire company is bought, including all of its intangible assets. All of these intangible assets are included in the financial valuation of the company which is only really different from the material assets whose intrinsic value and opportunity cost can be calculated without too much trouble. After the acquisition, the problem of separability arises as it is necessary to determine that part of the goodwill to be allocated to the brand. This figure will be influenced by accounting and tax considerations. Although it is virtually impossible to separate the brand from the other intangible assets, this does not impede valuation for internal purposes, since in this case the brand's value is considered as the sum total of all its synergies.

Separability ceases to be an accounting or theoretical problem when the brand is sold separately from the firm. This happened when the Buitoni brand was bought in 1989 by Nestlé. The remaining Buitoni company assets, such as factories and warehouses, were sold separately. It is important to examine whether those assets which were not sold with the brand were key success factors. A brand can only be separated if, despite its alienation from the rest of the company, it remains unchanged. This is not always the case.

The Smirnoff vodka brand can be separated in this way, whereas Pernod pastis less so, and IBM not at all. The reason for this is that there is little specific know-how required in producing vodka. If only the exclusive ownership rights of the brand (name, label and bottle) were bought and not the production facilities, it would still be possible to benefit from the brand's attraction with consumer and distributors. Smirnoff's reputation does not come from any specific characteristic of the liquid itself. However, its diffusion is due to the strength of the company that sells it. As vodka is practically a generic product, the only form of differentiation comes from brand image. Therefore it is only necessary to acquire the rights of ownership to the brand image (bottle, logo, label, name). Counterfeits and counter-brands reinforce this point by the way that they try to closely reproduce these images.

Would Pernod sell as well if it wasn't owned by Pernod-Ricard? The brand undoubtedly enjoys a high degree of awareness and is likely to be the first name that comes to mind when you think of pastis. But is the strength of the brand not over-estimated? Part of its sales are possibly due to the influence of Pernod-Ricard in commercial negotiations with distributors which results in the presence and prominence of the brand on shop shelves. Would Mars still be Mars if the brand were sold separately from its factories? No, because loyal Mars consumers have become used to a very specific taste, texture and smoothness which are part of the company know-how. Mars is a unique generic product, a brand-product, a 'branduct' (Swiners, 1979). The know-how is part of the brand and cannot be disassociated if the brand is to retain its value. On top of this it is only Mars who know how to produce a bar at this price!

Colgate-Palmolive wanted to get out of the nappies market so it sold its Caline brand in France for two or three million francs. The buyer, Celatose, went bankrupt a few years later. Caline's market share was not entirely due to its brand image and name; it had previously been created and nurtured by a permanent and costly emphasis on R&D and by the corporate power of Colgate-Palmolive over distributors. By acquiring only the Caline brand, Celatose had bought a homonym but not really the same brand. This is true in any sector where technology plays an important role, or where the brand makes a real and noticeable difference. The promise of security implied in the IBM name cannot be disassociated from the company, its logistics, its power, etc.

An asset is something which generates likely future profit as a result of the previous transactions or undertakings of the firm. Thus, according to this definition, a brand is an asset, whether it is acquired or created by the firm. As the above examples show, in many companies the brand is not a separable asset. Sometimes it is only a receptacle of values created by other intangible assets such as patents, know-how and customer relations which by themselves would not necessarily be sold. One step in resolving this difficulty lies in an understanding of the brand system and its interrelationship with other sources of product growth and its relationship with market share and profit (see Figure 13.2).

Figure 13.2 indicates the three essential sources of brand value or brand leverage. Profits attributable to the brand come either from a price premium resulting from higher quality and the risk premium, or from increased demand compared to a generic product, or from reduced production and distribution costs due to economies of scale and improved productivity thanks to the experience curve. This improved productivity can be used to finance the distribution demands which determine the presence and the prominence of the brand on shop shelves. It can also result in a reduction in the selling price, thus increasing the brand's competitive advantage and its quality/price ratio. This creates customer loyalty since each repurchase offers the same satisfaction – resulting from

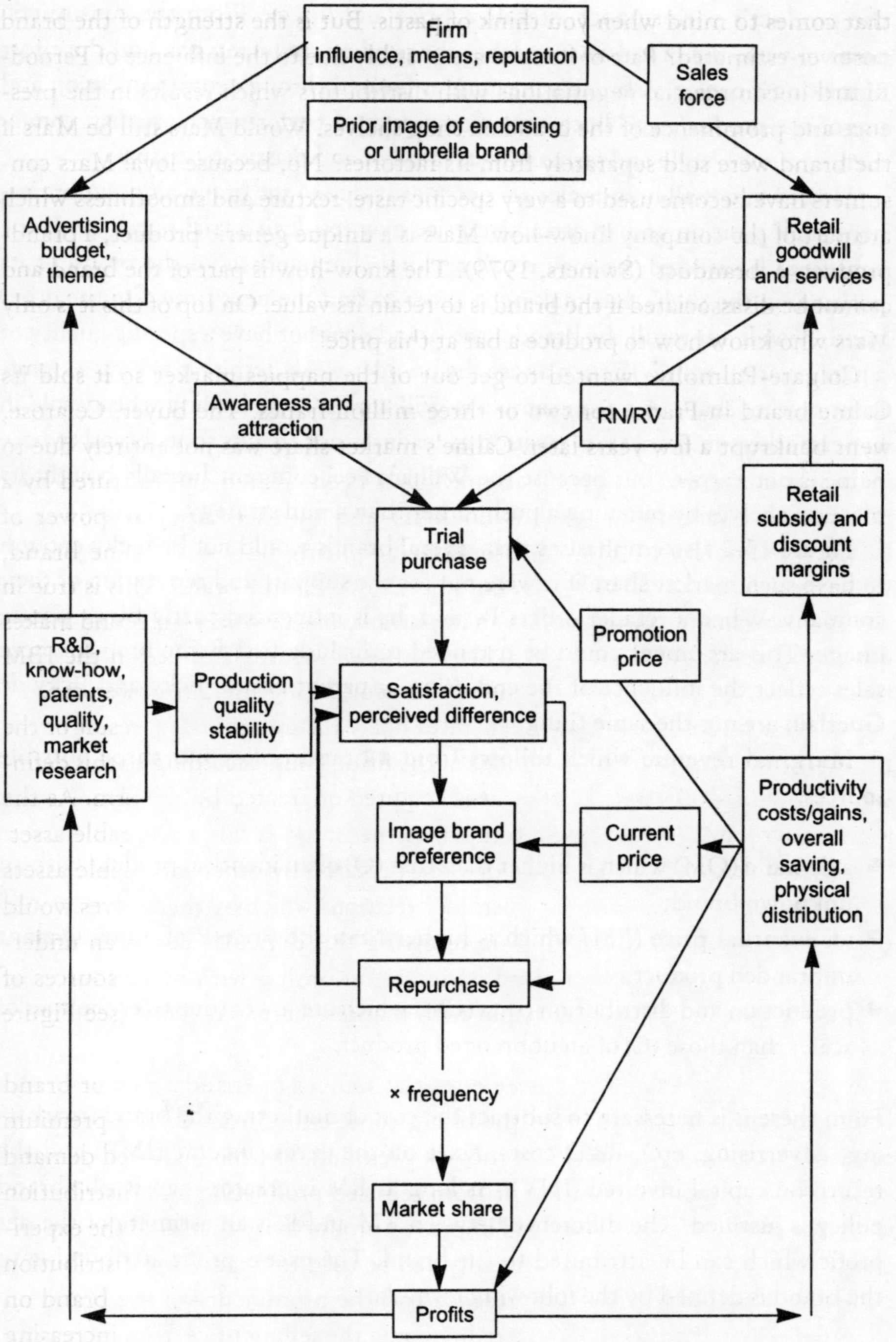

Figure 13.2 The brand system and the problem of separability

the product's performance, stability, price and image. From the consumers' point of view, the brand distinguishes the product, reducing risk and the effort of making a choice. A brand's meaning is created through communication and use of the product, and becomes an assurance of performance, quality, convenience, service, style and fashion by its familiar and reassuring nature.

However, not all brand sales are necessarily due to the brand alone. A prominent shelf position and an attractive price may result in a trial purchase. If the consumer is satisfied, he may recall a visual characteristic of the brand or its position on the shelf, thus making it easier to find the next time. On the other hand, he will not recall the brand if the brand does not have a specific quality or a particular meaning. In such a case the brand is weak despite it having a significant market share. A good example is William Peel, the leading whisky sold in hypermarkets in France: its position as leader is not thanks to its brand (whose name is not known) but because the William Peel company literally bought its place on shelves by pursuing a push rather than a pull strategy.

Figure 13.2 also emphasises that several brands would not be lucky enough to have such market share if it were not for the support and reputation of their company. When a retailer orders Pernod, he is influenced partly by corporate image. This argument could be extended to include first-name brands whose sales reflect the influence of the endorsing or parent brand. Jicky and Jicky de Guerlain are not the same thing.

Marginal revenue which follows from a brand policy has three possible sources:

- a demand (QM) which is higher than that (Q) of an identical product with an unknown brand;
- an eventual price (PM) which is higher than the price P of an equivalent unbranded product;
- production and distribution costs (CM) which are lower (due to economies of scale) than those (C) of an unbranded product.

From these it is necessary to subtract the cost of marketing the brand (marketing, advertising, etc), R&D costs, taxes on the excess income (IMP) and the return on capital invested (INV). As long as RM is greater than R, the brand policy is justified. The difference between RM and R is an estimate of the net profit which can be attributed to the brand. The excess profit attributable to the brand is defined by the following formula:

$$\mathrm{RM} - \mathrm{R} = \mathrm{QM}(\mathrm{PM} - \mathrm{CM}) - \mathrm{Q}(\mathrm{P} - \mathrm{C}) - \mathrm{MKTG} - \mathrm{R\&D} - \mathrm{IMP} - \mathrm{INV}$$

Empirically, what are the methods used to estimate this profit?

The price premium method This consists of taking the difference between the brand price and that of a generic product and multiplying it by the sales volume of the brand to obtain the turnover which is generated by the brand. Compared to the above equation, this frequent approach assumes that costs are identical (CM = C) and that there is an equal volume of sales from an unbranded product (QM = Q). Sometimes these hypotheses are well-founded, as in the valuation of champagne brands. The price premium method is used since, with champagne, the difference between the top and bottom of the range for one particular brand depends on the quality of grapes, the year and the ripening period. As a consequence, the cost price is virtually identical (C = CM). If demand outstrips supply, all bottles will be sold, with unknown brands selling just as well as a bottle of Veuve Clicquot (Q = QM) but of course not at the same price (PM = 2P). Thus it is easy to calculate the excess annual profit attributable to the brand, particularly since marketing budgets are lower in this sector and there is no R&D. Rémy-Martin was valued using this method. The difference between the starting sale price of a production company and the average price of a cognac brand which is not very well known was discounted over 15 years on the basis of average annual sales.

The problem with this method lies in its hypothetical nature, as a comparative generic product does not always exist. The appearance of generic colas is a recent market phenomenon. What is the generic equivalent of unique products such as Schweppes, Chanel or Mars? The idea of taking notional generic products is hardly realistic. A more serious problem is the fact that this valuation method implicitly assumes that all brands pursue a price premium strategy. This method over-values expensive small brands and under-values major brands such as Swatch, KitKat, Bic, etc that pursue an aggressive pricing strategy and derive their profit largely from consumer appeal, economies of scale and productivity.

The royalties method What annual royalties could the company hope to receive if it licensed the rights to use the brand? The answer to this question would form a means of directly measuring the brand's financial contribution and would also solve the problem of separability. The figure obtained could subsequently be used to calculate the discounted cash flows over several years. The difficulty is that this is not a very common practice in most markets. They are found in the luxury and textile markets.

From a conceptual point of view, it is not certain that this method properly separates just the value of the brand (Barwise, 1989). In fact companies often use licences to reach countries where their brand is not present. However, the royalty fee does not include solely the use of the brand. The brand owner also undertakes to supply a package of basic materials, know-how and services which allow the licensee to maintain the brand's appropriate quality level.

The brand sensitivity method In this case, the brand strength is not measured by the number of buyers, but by the number of people who recognise the brand (Kapferer and Laurent, 1992). This line of reasoning stems from the following accepted fact: a certain proportion of the buyers of brand X do not buy it just because it is X. They would just as soon buy Y or Z, or even an unknown brand. Their behaviour is determined mainly by the price but also by the fact that it may be the only product of its type in the store, or in this particular format, or is the most easily accessible due to its large shelf space. For low involvement products, the customer's behaviour is greatly influenced by such situational factors and very little by brand attachment. This is how major retailers decide where to place their own labels and copycat brands. Even though the buyer may be disappointed not to find his brands, he will not leave the store.

In any market a certain percentage of buyers are sensitive to certain brands. This brand sensitivity, which shows indirectly the influence that the brand has on the buying decision, can be measured. Among these consumers who are brand sensitive, there are only a few who know the brand and can therefore be truly influenced by it.

The formula for estimating this excess profit is defined by the following formula:

$$\text{SPM} = [\text{RM} - (t \times \text{ATM})] \times \text{Sensitivity} \times \text{Awareness}$$

where RM is the income generated by the brand, AT the tangible assets used for the brand's activities, t the average return on capital. Brand sensitivity is calculated by asking consumers a series of questions on the importance of the brand on their decision-making. Awareness captures the percentage of consumers who know the brand in question, even if only its name.

A variant of this approach which is founded on an indicator of brand sensitivity consists of defining explicitly the mechanisms which influence the brand. This approach measures the buying intentions of consumers who have a good or average image of the brand and of those who say they hardly, or don't, know the brand. The net contribution of a good or average brand image can be measured from the difference in buying intentions of the two groups. An analysis of a representative sample of buyers of brand A allows the separation of the real contribution of the brand. The sample is divided according to heavy, average or light consumers. The percentage of heavy consumers having a good or average image allows the theoretical buying intentions to be reconstructed, which, when weighed by the average buying volume of these heavy consumers, determines the volume due to the brand. An identical calculation may be carried out for average and light consumers. In this way the global volume attributable to the brand can be separated (Frey, 1989).

Separating supply effects from demand effects In today's consumer goods markets, brand sales sometimes depend more on the attitude of retailers than on that of consumers. Very few customers will change store if for a low involvement product their brand is not present. This explains why many retailers got rid of national brands from their shelves. They are protected by the inertia in the behaviour of weekly shoppers, who have no say in the matter.

How do we separate that part of a brand's gross sales which is due to its availability in the store and its prominence on the shelves from that due to the brand? The brand sensitivity approach relies on verbal answers to a questionnaire which normally comes from brand studies. When data from panels are available, a behavioural response to these questions is possible.

The principle is simple. Suppose we take four brands, each having a 25 per cent share of total sales and selling at the same price. The mathematical probability is that sales of each brand will be equal to 25 per cent of the total sales of the shelf. Any sales above or below this expected figure will result from the brand.

However, thanks to databases, panels can measure the effect of the percentage of shelf space given to a brand on its sales, and the effect of price on demand which again depends on the type of store (hypermarket or supermarket). It is this difference between gross sales (observed) and predicted sales – taking into account the brand's price, shelf space, etc – which is the real measure of a brand's strength:

$$\text{Brand strength} = \frac{\text{Actual sales}}{\text{Sales due to the supply}}$$

The separation methods examined above allow us to come up with a figure specifically attributable to the brand – either in the form of excess profit or of net cash flow. All that remains is to transfer them to the future activities of the brand as expected by the company, which justifies its acquisition or in any case its interest. A brand has much more value for its owner when it offers a strategic potential and possible extensions to areas beyond its original product (brand extension) and/or beyond its borders (globalisation).

A brand's value depends on how the acquiring company intends to exploit it, on the product categories that it will be extended to and on the markets that it should enter. But what are these forecasts worth? What is the uncertainty? The evaluation of their probability assumes that the brand undergoes a strategic analysis which enables an appreciation of its strengths, weaknesses, potential and capacity to maintain its position. Any price is a bet on the future: is the brand strong enough to resist the future?

Multi-criteria valuation of a brand's potential

A company acquiring a brand naturally seeks to profit from it. The brand is often assigned to products, markets or activities from which it was previously excluded. Such ambitions for the brand must be realistic and must take account of its intrinsic potential and the structural evolution of the market. What guarantee is there of the demand from which cash flows come? In practice, this requires auditing the brand according to a certain number of criteria which predict its future potential, either within its own market or beyond it. These criteria define the brand's strength and thus its strategic value. In turn, this brand strength is essential to determine either the multiple or the discount rate to be used in the assessment of the brand's financial value.

Several criteria lists have been suggested. The Interbrand Company ranks the brand according to seven different factors and adds all seven marks together which are weighted according to the importance of each factor. The resulting total gives an estimation of the brand's strength. Sorgem suggests a different analysis distinguishing the market value, the brand assets, the growth factors and the capacity of the company. A synthesis of these approaches leads to an evaluation of the brand according to the following criteria:

Market leadership Is the brand the leader in its markets? Can it remain so? We are now well aware of the relationship between market share and profitability, as well as the strategic advantage of having a dominant relative market share (Buzzell *et al*, 1975; Porter, 1980; Jacobson and Aaker, 1985). This criterion becomes even more important in the market for fast moving consumer goods, where large retailers are inclined only to stock market leaders. To be number three or four used to have value, but not really any more.

Although market share seems to be a simple, objective measure, a subjective judgement has to be given in order to define what is meant by 'market'. Depending on whether you have a narrow or broad notion of a market, the brand can be considered as either dominant or dominated. We know only too well the dangers of a short-sighted attempt to equate product and market. The weightings allotted to first, second and third place (60 per cent compared to 50 per cent and 40 per cent) which determine the value of the relative market share are very subjective.

The analysis is not limited to an examination of current market share but also extends to the potential for expansion. If we compare two brands, A and B (see Table 13.1), we see that A clearly has a current market share greater than that of B, but loyalty to B (repurchase rate) is double that of A. Brand B has a strong growth generator, which should be exploited by investing in increasing awareness and availability, in order to increase the brand's penetration. Certain markets are more fluid – leadership can be contested or new segments permanently appear (eg high-tech or fashion). Therefore if a company has the necessary resources, B is a more promising brand than A.

Table 13.1 Comparative brand profiles

	Brand A	Brand B
Awareness (% of people who know the brand) ×	50	40
Trial (proportion of those people who know the brand who have already bought or used it) ×	40	35
Repurchase (proportion of initial users who continue to use it) ×	20	40
Consumption rate (compared to the market average) ×	110	100
Availability (per cent of people who can easily find the brand) =	70	20
Use share (equivalent to the market share)	3.1	1.1
Potential (with 100 per cent awareness and 100 per cent RN/RV retail presence)	8.8	14

The established status of the brand If a brand has loyal clients, it can then act to reduce uncertainty. This factor defines the stability of the brand. Older brands, which over time have amassed a loyal, satisfied clientele, are now an integral part of the market, almost its very substance. In the United States, General Electric is practically a national emblem, an institution in the family home; the same goes for Renault in France, Hoover or St Michael in the UK, Bayer in Germany. This characteristic is known as brand franchise, a term which describes well the long and ever-renewed process by which a brand succeeds in creating a high degree of loyalty. In order to do this the company analyses customer needs, invests in R&D and develops a communication mix in order to give full meaning to the brand.

Prospects for the current market When a brand is valued, it is already available in certain markets. What are the intrinsic prospects for these markets? Are they stable, declining or growing? Are newcomers to be expected? Do entry barriers exist to protect the market (superior technology, economies of scale, distribution, advertising)? Could the market become a market for distributors' own brands? Is brand sensitivity strong?

The quality of the image and of brand awareness There are several ways to measure brand awareness: top of the mind, unaided and aided. We place more emphasis on unaided brand awareness because this is a sign that the consumer spontaneously considers the brand as a reference and a key player on the market. When measuring brand image, we analyse three factors:

- **reputation for quality**. This is the key to long-term survival, to the justification of a price which is higher than that of distributors' own-brands and to consumer loyalty.
- **differentiation**. How many brands are liked and perceived as attractive but are no longer considered to be different? Who doesn't like Andrex? Fighting against private labels, this brand was unable to maintain its perceived difference which is the key factor in consumer brand preference.
- **consumer involvement in the brand**. If the consumer can say that 'this is a brand for me', the brand shows its relevance and its ability to adapt with time, and that it knows how to evolve with its consumers, both as a product and in its way of communicating.

Product strength A brand cannot be valued independently of the quality of its physical support. Is this support unique? Can it be copied? It is certain that the brand, its image and awareness play a role in influencing consumer preferences but it is also important to be lucid and far-sighted. How capable is the product of provoking a preference in blind tests? In these post economic crisis years, after a decade where our failing was to place too much confidence on intangible assets, buyers have again begun to appreciate a products's real value, thus the following question: Is it possible to uphold and maintain over time the know-how which is the main advantage of many products? For example, this is the strong point of all Ferrero's brands (Kinder, Nutella, Mon Chéri, etc). The same goes for Kellogg's, who still control more than 50 per cent of the breakfast cereal market.

The potential for brand extension This criterion relates to the brand's ability to diversify by entering markets other than its present ones. There are several different ways of measuring this potential, for example the brand's existing awareness in markets where it is not present, and the ability of certain features of its identity to support products that the company wishes to diversify into. Seiko, for instance, is known everywhere. Seiko has over time become synonymous with precision, attention to detail, aesthetic quality and modern appeal through its watches. The basic concept of the brand lies in its intimate link with time. The brand is legitimate in the optical lens market, since glasses are also intimately linked with time and ageing. They are also objects of precision with aesthetic qualities – good looks conceal age. Thanks to its established awareness and image, it is ready for such a brand extension.

The potential to internationalise Italian cooking is appreciated everywhere. This explains why Buitoni has a lot of potential in every European country. It was not simply internationalisation which created this potential, but rather Buitoni's global, pan-European marketing strategy. This was the determining factor which attracted Nestlé's interest in Buitoni and in Rowntree. Legal factors must also be taken into account when evaluating international potential. Bearing in mind the legal disparities that exist between countries, it is important to evaluate the power and the extent of brand protection in the countries that the company is considering.

Investments in the brand Those brands which have enjoyed continuous support are more valuable than those that have received intermittent, periodic investments without any long-term consistency. This support is illustrated by the advertising budget. Its effects can be witnessed by the richness and depth of the brand image, its clarity of identity, its level of awareness, how much it is liked, and the recognition of its associated signs (eg colours, symbols, logos, personality, slogans). These criteria define the quality of the memory of those brands which are in the consumers' mind.

The legal protection of brands Brands have an economic value. Thus, they are not only of interest to raiders but also to counterfeiters. The latter are eager to profit from part of the cash flow which is generated by the brand (and its distinctive signs) due to the confidence that it has acquired over time. The legal protection of brands seeks to limit this form of embezzlement. Major risk areas where counterfeiting is common demand extra protection. Where legally possible, the name and any distinguishing features of the brand (eg design, packaging, logo, codes, etc) should be registered. For example, Coca-Cola have registered throughout the world their two names (Coca-Cola and Coke) and their distinct logo. The company is also trying to register the distinctive shape of its bottles. In cases where the brand name itself is difficult to protect, the creation of a distinguishing graphic identity may give further protection to the brand since it too can be registered.

The capabilities of the company The capabilities of the company must be measured when valuing the brand. The latter is a potential which demands constant investing in R&D, marketing and advertising. The value of the brand depends on the means that the company has to invest.

Calculating the brand's value

In practical terms, what can we do with a brand profile which is based on the above criteria? There exist two opposing schools of thought (see Figure 13.1). The first school, that of the financial analysts, uses the brand profile to evaluate the business plan and the expected net future cash flows, using the current market for the brand or new anticipated markets as the starting point. The brand profile is compared with profiles of other brands in similar or closely related sectors. Financial analysts use the brand profile as a means of analysing and estimating how realistic the predicted cash flows and the discounting rate (which is a measure of risk) are. The second school is more empirical and it calculates a weighted sum of the grades on each criterion total and this is an estimate of the brand's strength. This combined figure allows the calculation of a suitable multiple which is used in the financial valuation of the brand. The differences between these two approaches highlight two different philosophies to tackle the problem of valuation with both necessarily producing different results. We will first analyse the discounted cash flow method and then the multiple method.

Discounted cash flow This is the classic method of valuing all investments, whether tangible or intangible. The analyst calculates the anticipated annual income attributable to the brand over a five or 10 year period. The discount rate used is the weighted average cost of capital, which if necessary is increased to take account of the risks arising from a weak brand (that is to reduce the weight of future revenues in the calculation of the present value). Beyond this period, the residual value is calculated by assuming that the income is constant or growing at a constant rate for infinity (Nussenbaum, 1990). The following formula is used:

$$\text{Value of the brand} = \sum_{t=1}^{N} \frac{RB_t}{(1+r)^t} + \frac{\text{Residual value}}{(1+r)^N}$$

where:

RB_t = Anticipated revenue in year t, attributable to the brand

r = Discounting rate

$$\text{Residual value after year } N = \frac{RB_n}{r} \text{ or } \frac{RB_N}{r-g}$$

where:

g = rate of revenue growth

This is the classic model for valuation by the discounted cash flow method, even though analysts offer numerous variations of it (Mauguère, 1990; Melin, 1990). This method was used to value Cognac Hennessy at 6.9 billion francs, based on a capitalisation of its net revenue over 25 years at a rate of 6.5 per cent (Blanc and Hoffstetter, 1990).

This method was also used to value the Candia milk brand as part of a restructuring programme. The final figure, which was around 1.8 billion francs, was the result of a business plan within which two questions were discussed:

- Knowing that milk is a commodity, what percentage of Candia's future sales will be generated by products which are heavily marketed, differentiated and have a strong identity which justifies a price premium?
- At how much do we estimate the price premium that Candia can demand over more ordinary products? In such markets, even a tiny difference may amount to huge profits.

Sceptics of this method (Murphy, 1990; Ward, 1989) object to its three sources of uncertainty: the anticipation of cash flows, the choice of period and the discount rate:

- By definition any forecast is uncertain. This does not apply only to brands, but to any investment evaluation – tangible or intangible – which is calculated by the above method. For brands, cash flow forecasts could be ruined if a competitor launched a superior product which was not accounted for in the calculations. This argument overlooks the fact that these forecasts were made after an in-depth analysis of the brand's strengths and weaknesses (on the basis of the criteria presented earlier). It can be assumed that these were included when the anticipated cash flows were calculated. In any case the discounting rate takes into account the anticipated risk factor.
- A second criticism lies in the subjective nature of the choice of a discounting rate. However, on the one hand analysts test the sensitivity of their findings against variations in this rate, and on the other hand, this rate is fixed by taking into account stable company data, such as its average cost of capital. The only subjective factors are the risk premium and the future rate of inflation. Furthermore, very often the risk is zero from the purchaser's point of view as he feels that success is a certainty.
- Finally, there are those who criticise the choice of period for calculating cash flows. Why 10 years and not 15? What is the value of forecasts made so far ahead? On the one hand the brand may disappear after only a few years and on the other in certain volatile sectors three years is already a long time (eg laptop computers).

This is where the pragmatic and the realistic view of certain UK valuers comes from. They believe that brand value should be based only on that which is certain, ie the net income of the brand at the moment. This is the basis of the multiple method. Brand value is calculated by applying a multiple to the current profits of the brand, measured over three years ($t-2$, $t-1$, t).

The problem is then to estimate as precisely as possible this multiple. A lot of companies have their own norms. For example, Pernod-Ricard uses a multiple which is between seven and 10 when buying a national brand and between 10 and 13 for an international brand. LVMH valued Dior at 4 billion francs which was 27 times its profits and twice its turnover. FNAC was sold for 3 billion francs even though its gross income is only 150 million francs.

The multiple method In the financial valuation of companies, it is typical to examine what is known as the price/earnings ratio (P/E). This ratio links the market capitalisation of a firm to its net profits. A high ratio is a signal of high investor confidence and optimism in the growth of future profits. Even though the brand is not the company, the same reasoning can be applied:

$$\text{Firm: P/E} = \frac{\text{Market value of equity}}{\text{Known profits}}$$

$$\text{Brand: Multiple} = \frac{\text{Value to be calculated}}{\text{Net profits of brand}}$$

The only difference lies in the fact that for a brand there are no data on its market capitalisation because it doesn't exist, therefore it is this that we are trying to calculate. This notional market value of equity is the price to be paid for the brand (before the effect of overbidding). In order to calculate this, it is necessary to determine M, the multiple which is equivalent to the P/E ratio specific to the brand.

This method is widely used in the UK, particularly by the Interbrand company. There are four stages:

1 **Calculating the applicable net profit.** Interbrand uses the profits for the last three years (*t*–2, *t*–1, *t*), thus avoiding a possibly atypical evaluation based upon a single year. These profits are discounted to take account of inflation. A weighted average of these three figures is calculated in accordance with what we consider to be the most and least important years. This weighted average after-tax net profit which is attributable to the brand forms the basis of all calculations.

2 **Assessing the brand's strength.** This method uses a set of marketing and strategic criteria to give the brand an overall mark. Interbrand uses only seven of these factors and takes a weighted sum of the individual marks for each factor in order to calculate the overall mark, as can be seen in Table 13.2 (Penrose, 1990).

3 **Estimating the multiple.** A relationship necessarily exists between the multiple (an indicator of confidence about the future) and this score for brand strength. If this relationship was known precisely, the multiple would then be predicted by the brand strength score. For this, Interbrand developed a model known as the 'S-curve' which plots the multiple against brand strength.

The model is based on Interbrand's examination of the multiples involved in numerous brand negotiations over recent periods – in sectors close to the one being studied. The P/E of the companies with the closest comparable brands are used. Interbrand then reconstructed the company's profile and brand strength. Plotting the multiples (P/E) against the reconstructed scores results in an S-shaped curve (see Figure 13.3).

Table 13.2 A method of valuing brand strength

Factor of valuation	Maximum score	Brand A	Brand B	Brand C
Leadership	25	19	19	10
Stability	15	12	9	7
Market	10	7	6	8
Internationality	25	18	5	2
Trend	10	7	5	7
Support	10	8	7	8
Protection	5	5	3	4
Brand strength	100	76	54	46

Source: Penrose (1990)

4 **Calculating brand value.** This is calculated by multiplying the applicable net brand profit by the relevant multiple.

We can illustrate this method by an actual case. In 1988 Reckitt & Colman valued its brands in this way. They valued household and hygienic goods where they were market leaders, as well as food products (condiments) where they were also a leader, and finally pharmaceutical goods where they had an average position.

The specific situation enjoyed by those brands in the first group is as follows:

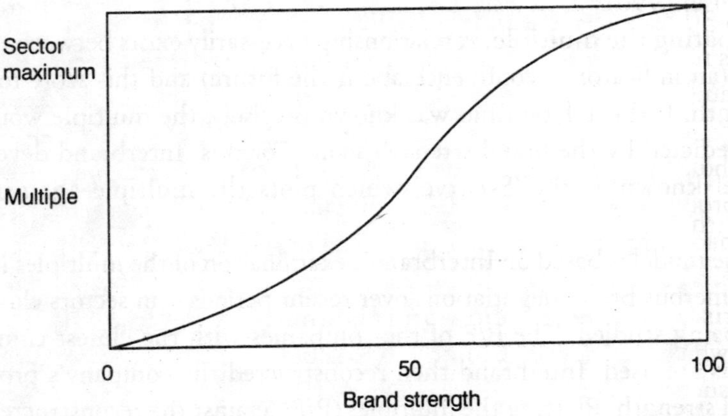

Figure 13.3 The Interbrand S-curve - relation between brand strength and multiple

- world leadership
- growing markets, with few new entrants except for distributors' own-brands;
- unaided brand awareness (eg Airwick) high in the UK and in Anglo-Saxon countries but less so in France;
- customers' brand loyalty;
- strong brand image and assurance of quality;
- for each of its brands, little possibility for diversification.

Reckitt & Colman estimated that 5 per cent of profits on these brands came from sales under distributors' own-brands. Interbrand considered that the remaining 95 per cent was the brand's gross profit. The income generated by the brand can be calculated by subtracting the expected return on investment from net assets. The net revenue was weighted according to the importance of each brand and discounted for the previous three years. The following results were obtained for each category:

- household and hygienic products: £53.8 million;
- food products: £24.7 million;
- pharmaceutical goods: £17.1 million.

What multiple should be applied? For the first group, the multiple used by Reckitt & Colman in 1985 when buying Airwick was applied. A multiple of 17 was used for food products and was based on recent transactions in the sector during the last few years, for example the BSN–Nabisco takeover bid. Finally, a multiple of 20 was used for the pharmaceutical group. In fact, recent transactions in the pharmaceutical industry had been using multiples which were closer to 30. A lower multiple was chosen in this case because of Reckitt & Colman's relatively weak position in the sector. By applying these figures to the net revenue in each category, the following brand values were estimated:

- household and hygienic products: 53.8 × 20 = £1076 million;
- food products: 24.7 × 17 = £420 million;
- pharmaceutical goods: 17.1 × 20 = £342 million.

Comparison of the cash flow and the multiple methods The multiple method which was developed in the UK is becoming a classic. It was, in fact, used by such companies as Rank Hovis McDougall and Grand Metropolitan whose decisions to post brand values to their balance sheets caused a controversy which is still not settled. It is also the method which communicates the most through books, articles and seminars. The simplicity of the method used is such that it is uncharacteristic of the stringent world of financial analysis. All this said, is it valid?

First, the multiple method is not all that different from the classic method of discounted cash flow. It is a particular example of it.

When a constant and infinite annual cashflow is expected, the present value of the brand is defined thus:

$$\text{Brand Value} = \frac{RB}{(1+r)} + \frac{RB}{(1+r)^2} + \frac{RB}{(1+r)^3} + \ldots + \frac{RB}{(1+r)^\infty} = \frac{RB}{r}$$

As we can see, the multiple is none other than the inverse of the cost of capital adjusted for risk ($1/r$). If a constant growth rate (g) of annual income is expected, the multiple is:

$$B = \frac{1}{r-g}$$

Equations aside, the point to remember is that we cannot reproach the method of discounted cash flows for making certain hypotheses, since the multiple approach is itself a particular hypothesis which is equally as questionable but not explicit. It draws its apparent validity from the fact that all its calculations are based upon:

- net profits attributable to the brand over the previous three years;
- marketing data and the subjective opinions of managers regarding brand strength;
- multiples based on recent transactions by similar companies;
- an S-curve, using information from a database to plot these multiples (or P/E ratios) against brand strength scores.

However, face validity (or appearance) does not mean validity *per se*. In its present form, Interbrand's method poses various problems:

1. Market multiples which were used as parameters for the S-curve are not valid indicators of the strength of the brands even though they were the mainstay of these transactions. In fact the final transaction price includes both the estimated value of the brand and a certain amount which is due to overbidding. For example, in the fight between Jacob Suchard and Nestlé, the initial bid was 630 pence and the final bid was 1075 pence! Market prices include the effect of this overbidding and thus overvalue the brand. It is therefore rather curious that we are trying to link market multiples to a value for brand strength as this value

ignores the effect of overbidding. For this reason a certain doubt arises about the applicability of this method to value and post to the balance sheet unacquired, internally created brands. The value attributed to the asset will be greater than the value of the brand as it will include an unspecified amount which is a result of overbidding! The fact that companies may nevertheless have used this method to represent their brands as assets in no way validates this approach.

2. Even in a market where there is no overbidding, the stated multiple measures the value of the brand from the point of view of the potential buyer. It expresses his vision, his strategies and any synergies that he may expect. The fact that in 1985 BSN did not buy Buitoni despite it being reasonably priced does not mean that Buitoni was worth less but means that it was worth less in the eyes of BSN. In 1988 Nestlé valued it at several billion Swiss francs. It again seems strange to try to relate market multiples, which are closely linked to the buyer, to the scores for brand strength, which are calculated by an outsider and do not include the synergistic benefits. This poses a problem when internally created brands are posted to the balance sheet. They are valued in the context of a 'going concern' according to their current benefit to the companies who own them. On the other hand, multiples supplied by the market are calculated with the idea of using them for a totally different reason.
3. For the moment, no illustrations of the S-curve showing the variance around the curve have been published. This variance is a measure of the quality of the empirical relationship between the two variables. As it is, the curve would have us believe that there is zero variance, which is impossible. A single brand strength score probably corresponds to several multiples or at least to a range of values (within which the S-curve is found). Such uncertainty causes problems as in reality the financial value of a brand is very sensitive to even a slight change in the multiple. Going back to the Reckitt & Colman's household and hygiene brands, we see that a one point variation in the multiple results in either a £53.8 million increase or decrease in the value of the brand. This is a far cry from the principles of prudence, reliability and rational certainty which govern accounting practice and information.
4. The very validity of the S-curve is questionable. Interbrand uses the following argument: a new brand grows slowly during its early stages. Then, once it moves from being a national brand to being an international one, its growth is exponential. Finally, as it moves from the international to the worldwide arena, its growth slows once more. For example, the difference between Buitoni's purchase and resale price signalled the transition of a national brand to a European wide one.

Experience shows that brands are susceptible to large threshold effects. Their strength with customers and retailers is developed in stages. Thus today a moderately known brand may be worth virtually the same as a little known one. However, beyond a certain threshold, it grows in value.

Research on brand awareness has shown that, in markets with intensive communication, it is only once a brand has reached a certain level of aided awareness that its unaided awareness will start to increase. This is due to a memory block. Likewise, major retailers are replacing middle of the range brands with their own products. These brands rely more on supply than on demand and they would cease to be sold if the retailers replaced them with their own brands. Thus their future is very unstable. This would lead us to believe that the relationship between brand strength and the multiple – provided that both are assessed by the same potential buyer – is better illustrated by a stepped graph (See Figure 13.4).

In conclusion, the widespread use of the multiple method is not proof of validity, as we have just seen, but testifies to its simplicity and handiness for non-specialists, and therefore its internal educational value. A small variation in the chosen multiple leads to important differences in the value of the brand. The present method of choosing the multiple is unsatisfactory from the point of view of reference multiples and of the brand strength scores. What can we make of a total score which is obtained after subjective weightings of factors which are sometimes redundant or in any case correlated? This wish for simplicity is to the detriment of the method's validity. Despite its claim to be accurate, the multiple method in its present form is just as subjective as that of discounted cash flows. To use a hundred or so criteria instead of seven would change nothing. By doing this, we introduce a certain amount of redundancy between the criteria, which results in more weight being given to some factors. As long as the method is subjective, it should

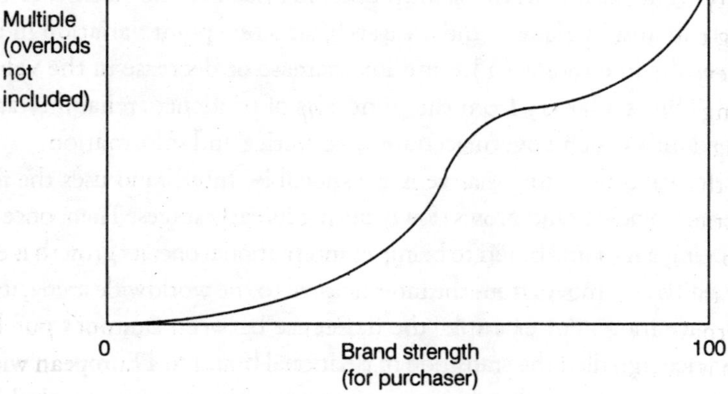

Figure 13.4 Stepped graph showing relationship between brand strength and multiple

remain transparent. The multi-criteria method gains nothing from being summarised in a single score since there are many implicit hypotheses in the weightings. The brand profile should be used instead to make a realistic, valid business plan, materialising in discounted cash flows. There is, therefore, a choice between a method which is precisely false and one which is vaguely true.

BRANDS, BALANCE SHEETS AND FINANCIAL INFORMATION

Having analysed the various methods of valuing a brand, we can now take a more realistic look at the question of including brands on the balance sheet. UK companies posed this question for two different reasons:

- The first relates to the specific rules in the UK, which deal with the treatment of goodwill after a merger or an acquisition. The normal procedure, which is by no means obligatory, is to deduct the goodwill directly from the owners' equity, thus removing from the balance sheet the acquired brand(s) and the goodwill (which is the difference between the purchase price of the target firm and its book value). This allowed UK firms to avoid the other accepted means of dealing with goodwill, which is depreciation. The problem with depreciation is that it reduces the distributable income of a firm. This is quite embarrassing after a merger or an acquisition. Time has shown that directly charging goodwill to reserves produces a perverse effect. It certainly leaves profits intact, which pleases shareholders, but it also results in an artificial deterioration of the firm's financial status. By reducing the reserves and thus in turn the firm's owners' equity, most of the financial ratios which were dependent on owners' equity were changed. For example, borrowing capacity is calculated by examining the debt to capital equity ratio. However, brands are bought in order to be developed, thus creating a need for more money in order to finance the marketing and communication budgets. The firm therefore runs the risk of not being able to borrow enough money to finance this development, due to the fact that its only capital has been drastically reduced as a result of accounting practices. To overcome this perverse effect, British companies have broken with tradition and opted for the method of depreciating goodwill. For example, in 1988, Ladbroke went so far as to re-enter the value of the Hilton International brand on its balance sheet even though the goodwill associated with its purchase in 1987 had been deducted from its reserves that year.
- Firms which had not acquired any brands, but which possessed strong self-created ones, considered that they were getting a raw deal. In fact, an acquired brand could be included on the balance sheet but not an internal brand. Thus it

seemed that the net assets of companies who created brands by their own efforts but who were not allowed to include them in their accounts were lower than those of their counterparts. This could result in shareholders receiving misleading information and could attract raiders. Nestlé's takeover bid for Rowntree and the difference between the value of the shares before the bid and the price paid by Nestlé are often given as an example of market inefficiency. Shareholders would have undervalued Rowntree because the value of its brands were not included on the balance sheet and would thus have quickly accepted Nestlé's bid. In order to avoid this risk and to be protected from raiders, Rank Hovis McDougall decided to include on its balance sheet a value for the brands that it had created and developed itself. Firms are allowed to do this according the Companies Act 1985. Moreover, in the UK, it is possible to revalue intangible assets (and thus brands) whenever a company wants, whereas in France the difference in the re-evaluation figure would immediately be taxable.

At this point, the debate becomes international. Since methods of dealing with goodwill differ from country to country, disparities may exist between the way that firms present company accounts following a merger or an acquisition. In France, for instance, companies have to depreciate the goodwill. However, the 7th European directive states that goodwill can be posted as 'identifiable assets'. Brands are the ideal assets because they are not depreciated. This is what BSN did. Since the 1989 financial year, the company has decided to value those brands which have arisen from recent transactions and which are included in goodwill and not to depreciate them. By doing this they increased their net income in 1989 by 99 million francs. The decision not to depreciate brands makes financial sense. Companies which have bought brands have to invest a lot in communication to support them. These budgets are posted as expenses and thus reduce net profit. It would be strange to lower profits further by depreciating brands whose advertising – among other things – is precisely aimed at maintaining their value. On the other hand, if the firm stopped investing in the brand, the fact that the brand is not depreciated would be invalid. Luckily, the law allows for the possibility of depreciating a brand as soon as any decrease in its value is anticipated.

Nevertheless, in France, Article 12 of the Business Code, which forbids the revaluing of intangible assets, opposes the inclusion of internally created brands on the balance sheet. A difference also exists between the accounting methods that UK firms use for internal brands. With time these differences should disappear. World standards are needed in a world where competition is global. The IASC (International Accounting Standard Committee) is about to forbid the direct deduction of goodwill from reserves. The problem of created brands is as yet unresolved.

Conclusion

Companies now realise that their brands are an essential asset, even though they do not appear on the balance sheet. To consider a brand as an asset has important implications for management. The main idea is to capitalise on a few brands. They have to be constantly nourished by new products in order to maintain their market share. To get the most from them means that it is necessary to concentrate all one's efforts over the long term on a few viable brands to increase their potential and value. Several brands which were part of our youth and still exist in our conscious awareness will soon disappear.

The emphasis that we placed on the financial value of brands throughout the 1980s has given us a wrong idea of what they actually are. We saw them as short-term speculative values. The famous goodwill is the result of continuous efforts. This is the price that has to be paid if a brand is to be able to reconquer a market.

The future lies in the hands of those companies which understand brands and are able to instil this understanding throughout their organisation. Even if a company's culture is internally focused, what the brand stands for reminds us of the competitive priorities and the need for continuous improvement in serving the market by the creation of new products.

To understand the brand requires, above all else, a true brand professional who knows everything about it, is able to integrate all of its facets, richness and dynamism, and has an intimate relationship with it. This is even more necessary when there is a high staff turnover and brand managers are constantly changing. It is good to have integrated the corporate culture, but it is better if the brand manager is immersed in the meaning of the brand of which he is in charge.

It is not just the marketing managers who have to understand what a brand stands for. Everybody, throughout the organisation, must consider the brand in a professional light, become an active supporter of it and play an essential part in its functioning. Thus, all those who are involved in the production process, in factories, in laboratories, and those who are responsible for the maintenance and growth of these brands, have a part to play. The people involved at the other end of the chain, both nationally and internationally, all the way to the shopfloor assistant and the after-sales service staff who have an influence on the brand's performance well after the goods are sold, must also be involved.

Finally, to believe in the brand's future value means placing one's faith exactly where it should be, at top management level which must guarantee over the long term the management and the continuous enrichment of the company's assets, be they human, financial or brands.

Bibliography

Aaker, D (1991) *Managing Brand Equity*, The Free Press, New York.

Aaker, D (1996) *Building Strong Brands*, The Free Press, New York.

Aaker, D and Biel, A (1993) *Brand Equity and Advertising*, Lawrence Erlbaum, Hillsdale, New Jersey.

Aaker, D and Keller, K L (1990) 'Consumer Evaluations of Brand Extensions' *Journal of Marketing*, January, vol. 54 (1), pp27–41.

Aaker, J (1995) 'Conceptualizing and Measuring Brand Personality' Working Paper No 255, Anderson Graduate School of Management, UCLA.

Advertising Research Foundation (1995) *Exploring Brand Equity*, Advertising Research Foundation, New York.

Agefi (1990) 'Le Goodwill, Objet de Controverse en Europe', 1 February.

Alba, J W and Chattopadhyay, A (1986) 'Salience Effects in Brand Recall' *Journal of Marketing Research*, vol. 23, p369.

Ambler, T and Styles, C (1996) 'Brand Development Versus New Product Development' *Marketing Intelligence and Planning*, vol. 14, no 7, pp10–19.

Arnold, T (1989) 'Accounting for the Value of Brands' *The Accountant's Magazine*, February, p12.

Baillot, J (1990) 'La marque et l'automobile' *Humanisme et Entreprise*, 181, June, pp5–8.

Baldinger, A (1992) 'What CEOs are Saying About Brand Equity', *Journal of Advertising Research*, July/August, 32(4), pp6–12.

Barwise, P (1989) *Accounting for Brands*, London Business School.

Barwise, P (1993) 'Brand Equity: Snark or Boojum' *International Journal of Research in Marketing*, vol. 10, no 2, pp93–104.

Berard, C (1990) 'La marque: élément du patrimoine de l'entreprise' *Revue de l'E.N.A.*, 202, May, pp24–5.

Berry, N C (1988) 'Revitalizing Brands' *Journal of Consumer Marketing*, 5 (summer), pp15–20.

Birkigt, K and Stadler, M M (1980) *Corporate Identity: Grundlagen, Funktionen, Fallbeispiele*, Verlag Moderne Industrie, Munich.

Birol, J and Kapferer, J N (1991) 'Les campagnes collectives' Internal document, Agence Sicquier-Courcelles/HEC.

Blackett, T (1985) 'The Role of Brand Valuation in Marketing Strategy' *Marketing and Research Today*, November, pp245–7.

Blackston, M (1992) 'Building Brand Equity by Managing the Brand's Relationships', *Journal of Advertising Research*, May/June, 32(3), pp79–83.

Blanc, C and Hoffstetter, P (1990) 'L'évaluation des marques' Research paper, under the direction of Kapferer, J N, June, Jouy-en-Josas.

Boddewyn, J, Soehl, R and Picard, J (1986) 'Standardization in International Marketing: Is Ted Levitt in Fact Right?' *Business Horizons*, pp69–75.

Bon, J, Michon, C and Ollivier, A (1981) 'Etude empirique de la démographie des marques: le rôle de la publicité' Fondation Jours de France pour la recherche en publicité, Paris.

Botton, M and Cegarra, J J (1990) *Le nom de marque* McGraw-Hill, Paris.

Boush, D (1993) 'Brands as Categories' in *Brand Equity and Advertising* (Aaker, D & Biel, A eds), Lawrence Erlbaum, New Jersey, pp299–312.

Brandenburger, A and Nalebuff, B (1996) *Coopetition*, Doubleday, New York.

Broadbent, S (1983) *Advertising Works 2*, Holt, Rinehart and Winston, London.

Brodbeck, D and Mongibeaux, J F (1990) *Chic et Toc: le vrai livre des contrefaçons* Balland, Paris.
Broniarczyk, S and Alba, J (1994) 'The Importance of the Brand in Brand Extension' *Journal of Marketing Research*, vol. XXXI, May, pp214–28.
Brown, T and Dacin, P (1997) 'The Company and the Product: Corporate Associations and Consumer Product Responses' *Journal of marketing*, vol. 61, no 1, January, pp68–84.
Buchan, E and Brown, A (1989) 'Mergers and Acquisitions' in *Brand Valuation*, ed. Murphy, J, Hutchinson Business Books, London, pp81–94.
Buck, S (1997) 'The Continuing Grocery Revolution' *Journal of Brand Management*, vol. 4(4), pp227–238.
Burgaud, D and Mourier, P (1989) 'Europe: développement d'une marque' *MOCI*, 889, pp125–8.
Buzzell, R D (1968) 'Can you Standardize Multinational Marketing?' *Harvard Business Review*, Nov-Dec.
Buzzell, R D and Gale, B T (1987) *The PIMS Principles*, Free Press, New York.
Buzzell, R D, Gale, B T and Sultan, R G (1975) 'Market Share – A Key to Profitability' *Harvard Business Review*, Jan-Feb, pp97–106.
Buzzell, R D and Quelch, J A (1988) *Multinational Marketing Management* Addison Wesley, New York.
Buzzell, R D and Quelch, J A (1990) *The Marketing Challenge of 1992* Addison Wesley, New York.
Cabat, O (1989) 'Archéologie de la marque moderne' in *La marque* (eds Kapferer, J N and Thoening, J C) McGraw-Hill, Paris.
Carpenter, G and Nakamoto, K (1990) 'Competitive Strategies for Late Entry Into Market With a Dominant Brand', *Management Science*.
Carratu, V (1987) 'Commercial Counterfeiting' in *Branding: A Key Marketing Tool* (ed Murphy, J) McGraw-Hill, London.
Carroll, J M (1985) *What's in a Name?* Freeman, New York.
Cauzard, D, Perret, J and Ronin, Y (1989) *Image de marque et marque d'image* Ramsay, Paris.
Channon, C (1987) *Advertising Works 4*, Cassell, London.
Chanterac, V (1989) 'La marque à travers le droit' in *La Marque* (eds Kapferer, J N and Thoenig, J C) McGraw-Hill, Paris.
Chateau, J (1972) *Les sources de l'imaginaire* Editions Universitaires, Paris.
Chinardet, C (1994) *Trade-Marketing*, Editions d'Organisation, Paris.
Clarke, D G (1976) 'Econometric Measurement of the Duration of Advertising Effect on Sales' *Journal of Marketing Research* vol. XIII, November, pp345–50.
Claycamp, H and Liddy, L (1969) 'Prediction of New Product Performance' *Journal of Marketing Research*, 6(3), November, pp414–20.
Cohen, M, Eliashberg, J and Ho, T (1997), 'An Anatomy of a Decision Support System for Developing and Launching Line Extensions' *Journal of Marketing Research*, vol. 34(1), February, pp117–129.
Conseil National de la Comptabilité (1989) 'La formation du capital commercial dans l'entreprise' 27.A.89.16, September.
Corstjens, J and Corstjens, M (1995) *Store Wars: The Battle for Mindspace and Shelfspace*, Wiley, London.
Cooper, M (1989) 'The Basis of Brand Evaluation' *Accountancy* March, p32.
Cooper, M (1989) 'Brand Valuation in the Balance' *Accountancy* July, p28.
Crimmins, J (1992) 'Better Measurement and Management of Brand Value', *Journal of Advertising Research*, July/August, 32(4), pp11–19.
Cross, R and Smith, J (1994) *Customer Bonding*, NTC Business Books.
Crozier, M (1989) *L'Entreprise à l'Ecoute: Apprendre le Management Post-Industriel*, InterEditions, Paris.
Dacin, P and Smith, D (1994) 'The Effect of Brand Portfolio Characteristics on Consumer Evaluations of Brand Extensions', *Journal of Marketing Research*, vol. XXXI, May, pp229–42.
Darby, M and Karni, E (1973) 'Free Competition and the Optimal Amount of Fraud' *Journal of Law and Economics*, 16(1), pp67–88.
Davidson, J H (1987) *Offensive Marketing*, Gower Press, London.
Dawar, N and Anderson, P (1992) 'Determining the Order and Direction of Multiple Brand Extensions' Working Paper no 92/36/MKT, INSEAD.

De Chernatony, L (1996) 'Integrated Brand Building Using Brand Taxonomies' *Marketing Intelligence and Planning*, vol. 14, no 7, pp40–45.

De Chernatony, L and McDonald, M (1994) *Creating Powerful Brands*, Butterworth – Heinemann, Oxford.

Defever, P (1989) 'L'utilisation de la communication électronique sur les lieux de vente' *Revue française du marketing*, vol. 123 (3), pp5–15.

Degon, R (1994) 'La Marque et le Prix' *Journée IREP La Marque*, September, pp28–38.

Dhalla, N K (1978) 'Assessing the Long Term Value of Advertising' *Business Review*, vol. 56, Jan-Feb, 1978, pp87–95.

Diefenbach, J (1987) 'The Corporate Identity as the Brand' in *Branding: a Key Marketing Tool* (ed Murphy, J), McGraw-Hill, London.

Dubois, B and Paternault, C (1995) 'Understanding the World of International Luxury Brands' *Journal of Advertising Research*, vol. 35 (4), Jul–Aug, pp69–76.

Durand, G (1964) *L'imagination symbolique* PUF, Paris.

Durand, G (1969) *Les Structures Anthropologiques de l'Imaginaire* Bordas, Paris.

Duvillier, J P (1987) 'L'absence d'enregistrement à l'actif du fonds de commerce' *Revue française de comptabilité* October, 183, p36.

Dyson, P, Farr, A and Hollis, N (1996) 'Understanding, Measuring and Using Brand Equity' *Journal of Advertising Research*, vol. 36 (6), Nov–Dec, pp9–21.

East, R and Hammond, K (1996) 'The Erosion of Repeat – Purchase Loyalty' *Marketing Letters*, 7 (2), pp163–171.

Eliade, M (1952) *Images et Symboles*, Gallimard, Paris.

Farquhar, P H (1989) 'Managing Brand Equity' *Marketing Research* September, vol. 1(3), pp24–33.

Farquhar, P H (1994) 'Strategic Challenges for Branding' *Marketing Management*, vol. 3 (2), pp9–15.

Feldwick, P and Bonnal, F (1995) 'Reports of the Death of Brands Have Been Greatly Exaggerated' *Marketing and Research Today*, vol. 23 (2), May, pp86–95.

Feral, F (1989) 'Les signes de qualité en France à la veille du grand marché communautaire et à la lumière d'autres systèmes' *CERVAC*, Université d'Aix Marseille 3, October.

Financial Times (1993) *Accounting for Brands*, London, FTBI Report.

Fourcade, A and Cabat, O (1981) *Anthropologie de la publicité* Fondation Jours de France pour la recherche en publicité.

Frey, J B (1989) 'Measuring Corporate Reputation and its Value', Marketing Science Conference, Duke University, 17 March.

Fry, J N (1967) 'Family Branding and Consumer Brand Choice' *Journal of Marketing Research* IV, August, pp237–47.

Fry, J N, Shaw, D, Haehling, C and Dipchand, C (1973) 'Customer Loyalty to Banks: A Longitudinal Study' *The Journal of Business* 46, pp517–25.

Gali, J (1993) 'Does Consumer Involvement Impact Evaluations of Brand Extensions?' unpublished doctoral dissertation, HEC Graduate School of Management.

Gamble, T (1967) 'Brand Extension', in *Plotting Marketing Strategy* (ed. Adler, L). Interpublic Press Book, New York.

Garbett, T (1981) *Corporate Advertising*, McGraw-Hill, New York.

Geary, M (1990) 'Fusions et acquisitions: le problème de Goodwill', in *Séminaire: Le traitement du Goodwill* 1 February, PF Publications Conférences, Paris.

Gelle, T (1990) 'La comptabilisation des marques' HEC research paper, under the direction of Collins, L, May, Jouy-en-Josas.

Glemer, F and Mira, R (1993) 'The Brand Leader's Dilemma' *McKinsey Quarterly*, no 2, pp34–44.

Greener, M (1989) 'The Bomb in the Balance Sheet' *Accountancy*, August, p30.

Greig, I and Poynter, R (1994) 'Brand transfer: Building the Whirlpool Brand in Europe' *Esomar Conference Proceedings*, 26–29 October, Building Successful Brands, pp65–78.

Guest, L (1964) 'Brand Loyalty Revisited: A Twenty Years Report' *Journal of Applied Psychology*, vol. 48 (2), pp93–7.

Hague, P and Jackson, P (1994) *The Power of Industrial Brands*, McGraw-Hill, London.

Hallberg, G (1995) *All Consumers Are Not Created Equal*, Wiley, New York.

Hamel, G and Prahalad, C K (1994) *Competing for the Future*, Harvard Business School Press, Boston, MA.

Hamel, G and Prahalad, C (1985) 'Do You Really Have a Global Strategy?' *Harvard Business Review*, Jul-Aug.

Heather, E (1958) 'What's in a Brand Name' *Management Review*, June, pp33–5.

Heller, R (1986) 'On the Awareness Effects of Mere Distribution' *Marketing Science*, vol. 5, summer, p273.

Hite, R and Fraser, C (1988) 'International Advertising Strategies of Multinational Corporations' *Journal of Advertising Research*, August/September, vol. 28(4), pp9–17.

Hoch, S (1996) 'How should National Brands Think about Private Labels?' *Sloan Management Review*, 37 (Winter), pp89–102.

Hoch, S and Banerji, S (1993) 'When Do Private Labels Succeed?' *Sloan Management Review*, Summer, pp57–67.

Hout, T, Porter, M and Rudder, E (1982) 'How Global Companies Win Out' *Harvard Business Review*, Sept-Oct.

Hussey, R and Ong, A (1997) 'Accounting for Goodwill and Intangible Assets' *Journal of Brand Management*, vol. 4(4), pp239–247.

IREP (1994) *La Marque*, Seminar on Branding, September, Institut de Recherches et d'Etudes Publicitaires, Paris.

Jacobson, R and Aaker, D (1985) 'Is Market Share All that It's Cracked Up to Be?' *Journal of Marketing*, vol. 45, 4, Fall, pp11–22.

Jacoby, J and Chestnut, R (1978) *Brand Loyalty and Measurement* John Wiley, New York.

Jaubert, M J (1985) *Slogan, mon Amour* Bernard Barrault Editeur, Paris.

Joachimsthaler, E and Aaker, D (1997) 'Building Brands Without Mass Media' *Harvard Business Review*, vol. 75(1), Jan-Feb, pp39–52

Jones, J P (1986) *What's in a Name: Advertising and the Concept of Brands* Lexington Books, Lexington.

Kapferer, J N (1983) 'Le Nom de L'Entreprise, Premier Véhicule de son Influence' 3e journée d'Etudes du CRCS, November, Paris, pp105–18.

Kapferer, J N (1984) *Les chemins de la persuasion* Dunod Entreprise, Paris.

Kapferer, J N (1985) 'Réfléchissez au Nom de votre Société' *Harvard – l'Expansion*, Autumn, pp104–18.

Kapferer, J N (1986) 'Beyond Positioning, Retailer's Identity' *Esomar Seminar Proceedings*, Brussels, 4–6 June, pp167–76.

Kapferer, J N (1988) 'Maîitriser l'Image de l'Entreprise: le Prisme d'Identité' *Revue Française de Gestion*, Nov-Dec, pp76–82.

Kapferer, J N (1989) 'Consommateurs: l'Etonnant Silence' *Le Nouvel Economiste*, 22 December.

Kapferer, J N (1990) 'La Marque est-elle encore à la portée des PME?' in *Le Défi de la Moyenne et Petite Entreprise*, Paris, pp193–6.

Kapferer, J N (1990) 'Marque de Fabrication ou Marque de Distributeur?' *Le Monde*, 8 March.

Kapferer, J N (1990) 'Une opposition Idéologique: le Produit ou la Marque' *Revue Vinicole Internationale*, March, pp84–5.

Kapferer, J N (1990) 'La Marque Malade de la Publicité' *Fortune*, April, 25, p23.

Kapferer, J N (1990) 'Le Grand Commerce est-il Consumériste' *Revue Française de Gestion*, May.

Kapferer, J N (1990) 'Vraies Marques ou Fausses Marques' *Humanisme et Entreprise*, 181, June, pp17–26.

Kapferer, J N (1990) 'Marque, Consommation, Consumérisme' *Revue de l'E.N.A.*, Sept-Oct.

Kapferer J N (1995) 'Stealing Brand Equity: Measuring Perceptual Confusion Between National Brands and Copycat Own-label Products' *Marketing and Research Today*, vol. 23(2), May, pp96–103.

Kapferer J N (1995) 'Brand Confusion: Empirical Study of a Legal Concept' *Psychology and Marketing*, vol. 12(6), pp551–568.

Kapferer, J N and Laurent, G (1983) *Comment Mesurer le Degré d'Implication des Consommateurs* Institut de Recherches et d'Etudes Publicitaires, Paris.

Kapferer, J N and Laurent, G (1983) *La Sensibilité aux Marques*, Fondation Jours de France pour la Recherche en Publicité, Paris.

Kapferer, J N and Laurent, G (1988) 'Consumers' Brand Sensitivity: A New Concept for Brand Management' in *Defining, Measuring and Managing Brand Equity*, Marketing Science Institute: A Conference Summary, Report pp88–104, MSI, Cambridge, MA.

Kapferer, J N and Laurent, G (1992) *La Sensibilité aux Marques*, Editions d'Organisation, Paris.

Kapferer, J N and Laurent, G (1996) 'How Consumers Build their Perception of Mega-Brands' unpublished working paper, HEC Graduate School of Management.

Kapferer, J N and Thoenig, J C (1989) *La Marque* McGraw-Hill, Paris.

Kapferer, J N and Thoenig, J C *et al.* (1991) 'Une analyse empirique des effets de l'imitation des marques par les contremarques: mesure des taux de confusion au tachystoscope' *Revue Francaise du Marketing*, January, 136, pp53–68.

Kapferer, J N and Variot, J F (1984) 'Le prisme d'identité: nouvel outil de diagnostic et de maîitrise de l'image', Fourth CRCS study paper, November, pp17–36.

Kapferer, J N and Variot, J F (1985) 'Les six facettes de l'image du distributeur' *Points de vente*, 15 October, 288, pp44–7.

Keller, K L and Aaker, D (1992) 'The Effects of Sequential Introduction of Brand Extensions', *Journal of Marketing Research*, 29(1), February, pp35–50.

King, S (1973) *Developing New Brands* John Wiley and Sons, New York.

Kleiber, G (1990) *La Sémantique du Prototype*, Presses Universitaires de France, Paris.

Knox, S (1996) 'The Death of Brand Deference' *Marketing Intelligence and Planning*, vol. 14, no 7, pp35–39.

Kotler, P and Dubois, B (1991) *Marketing management* Publi-Union, Paris.

Krief, Y (1986) 'L'Entreprise, l'institution, la marque' *Revue française du marketing*, 109, pp77–96.

Krief, Y and Barjansky, M (1981) 'La marque: nature et fonction' *Strategies*, 261 and 262, pp37–41, 32–6.

Kripke, S (1980) *Naming and Necessity*, Harvard University Press, Cambridge, MA.

Laforet, S and Saunders, J (1994) 'Managing Brand Portfolios: How the Leaders Do It' *Journal of Advertising Research*, vol. 34, no 5, pp64–7.

Lakoff, G (1987) *Women, Fire and Dangerous Things*, University of Chicago Press, Ill.

Lane, V and Jacobson, R (1995) 'Stock Market Reactions to Brand Extension Announcements' *Journal of Marketing*, vol. 59(1), pp63–77.

Laurent, G and Kapferer, J N (1985) 'Measuring Consumer Involvement Profiles' *Journal of Marketing Research*, vol. XXII, pp41–53.

Laurent, G, Kapferer, J N and Roussel, F (1987) 'Thresholds in Brand Awareness' 40th ESOMAR Marketing Research Congress Proceedings, Montreux, September 13–17, pp677–99.

Laurent, G, Kapferer, J N and Roussel, F (1995) 'The Underlying Structure of Brand Awareness Scores' *Marketing Science*, vol. 14(3), pp170–179.

Leclerc, F, Schmitt, B H and Dube-Rioux, L (1989) 'Brand name à la française? Oui, but for the right product!' *Advances in Consumer Research*, vol. 16, pp253–7.

Levitt, T (1967) 'Market Stretching' in *Plotting Marketing Strategy*, (ed. Adler, L) Interpublic Press Book, New York.

Levitt, T (1969) 'The Augmented Product Concept', in *The Marketing Mode: Pathways to Corporate Growth*, McGraw-Hill, New York.

Levitt, T (1981) 'Marketing Intangible Products and Product Intangibles' *Harvard Business Review* vol. 59 (3) May/June, pp94–102.

Levitt, T (1983) 'The Globalization of Markets' *Harvard Business Review* May/June.

Lewi, C and Kapferer, J N (1996) 'Consumers' Preference for Retailer's Brands', Esomar Conference Proceedings – The Big Brand Challenge, October 9–11, pp229–41.

Lindsay, M (1990) 'Establish Brand Equity Through Advertising' *Marketing News* January 22, pp16–17.

Loden, D J (1992) *Mega Brands*, Irwin, Illinois, USA.

Loken, B and Roedder John, D (1993) 'Diluting Brand Beliefs: When Do Brand Extensions Have a Negative Impact?' *Journal of Marketing*, vol. 57, July, pp71–84.

Mac Innis, D J and Nakamoto P K (1990) 'Examining Factors that Influence the Perceived Goodness of Brand Extensions' Working Paper No 54, University of Arizona.

Macrae, C (1991) *World Class Brands*, Addison-Wesley, England.
Macrae, C (1996) *The Brand Chartering Handbook*, Addison-Wesley, Harlow, UK.
McKenna, R (1991) *Relationship Marketing*, Addison-Wesley, Reading, MA.
McKinsey Corp (1990) *The Luxury Industry*, McKinsey, Paris.
McWilliam G (1989) 'Managing the Brand Manager' in *Brand Valuation,* (ed. Murphy, J) Hutchinson Business Books, London, pp154–65.
Magrath, A J (1990) 'Brands Can Either Grow Old Gracefully or Become Dinosaurs' *Marketing News*, January 22, pp16–17.
Marconi, J (1994) *Beyond Branding*, Probus Publishing Co, Chicago.
Margolis, S E (1989) 'Monopolistic Competition and Multiproduct Brand Names' *Journal of Business* vol. 62 (2), pp199–210.
Marketing Mix (1987) 'Monter une gamme: un problème majeur', 17, November, pp40–6.
Marion, G (1989) *Les images de l'entreprise* Les Editions d'Organisation.
Martin, D N (1989) *Romancing the Brand* American Management Association, New York.
Mauguère, H (1990) *L'évaluation des entreprises non cotées* Dunod Entreprise, Paris.
Maurice, A (1989) 'Enquête sur les contremarques: Les apprentis sorciers' *Références*, May, pp16–20.
Mazanec, J A and Schweiger, G C (1981) 'Improved Marketing Efficiency Through Multiproduct Brand Names?' *European Research* January, pp32–44.
Meffert, H and Bruhn, M (1984) *Marken Strategien in Wettbewerb* Gabler, Wiesbaden.
Melin, B (1990) 'Comment Evaluer les Marques' Research paper, under the direction of Kapferer, J N, HEC, June, Jouy-en-Josas.
Meyers-Levy, J (1989) 'Investigating Dimensions of Brand Names that Influence the Perceived Familiarity of Brands' *Advances in Consumer Research*, vol. 16, Association for Consumer Research, pp258–63.
Mongibeaux, J F (1990) 'Contrefaçons et contremarques' *Revue de l'E.N.A*, Sept-Oct.
Moorhouse, M (1989) 'Brand Accounting' in *Brand Valuation*, (ed. Murphy, J) Hutchinson Business Books, London, pp143–53.
Muller, M and Mainz, A (1989) 'Brands, Bids and Balance Sheets: Putting a Price on Protected Products' *Acquisitions Monthly* April, 24, pp26–7
Murphy, J (1989) *Brand Valuation* Hutchinson Business Books, London.
Murphy, J (1990) *Brand Strategy*, Director Books, London.
Nedungadi, P and Hutchinson, J W (1985) 'The Prototypicality of Brands' in *Advances in Consumer Research*, vol. 12 (eds Hirschman, E and Holbrook, M), Association for Consumer Research, pp498–503.
Nelson, P (1970) 'Information and Consumer Behavior' *Journal of Political Economy*, 78 (2), pp311–329.
Neuhaus, C F and Taylor, J R (1972) 'Variables Affecting Sales of Family-Branded Products' *Journal of Marketing Research* 14 (November), pp419–22.
Nussenbaum, M (1990) 'Comment évaluer les marques' *Option Finance* 7 May, 113, pp20–2.
Olins, W (1978) *The Corporate Personality* Mayflower Books, New York.
Olins, W (1989) *Corporate Identity* Thames and Hudson, London.
Oliver, T (1987) 'The Wide World of Branding' in *Branding: a Key Marketing Tool* (ed. Murphy, J) McGraw-Hill, London.
Pariente, S (1989) *La concurrence dans les relations industrie-commerce* Institut du commerce et de la consommation, Paris.
Park, C W, Javorskey, B J and Mac Innis, D J (1986) 'Strategic Brand Concept-Image Management' *Journal of Marketing*, 50 (October) pp135–45.
Park, C W, Milberg, S and Lawson, R (1991) 'Evaluation of Brand Extensions', *Journal of Consumer Research*, vol 18, September, pp185–193.
Pearson, S (1996) *Building Brands Directly*, MacMillan, London.
Peckham, J O (1981) *The Wheel of Marketing*, The Nielsen Company, Chicago.
Pendergrast, M (1993) *For God, Country and Coca-Cola*, Maxwell MacMillan, New York.
Penrose, N (1989) 'Valuation of Brand Names and Trade Marks' in *Brand Valuation* (ed Murphy, J) Hutchinson Business Books, London, pp32–45.

Perrier, R (1989) 'Valuation and Licensing' in *Brand Valuation* (ed Murphy, J) Hutchinson Business Books, London, pp104–12.
Pettis, C (1995) *Technobrands*, Amacom, New York.
Porter, M (1980) *Choix stratégiques et concurrence*, Economica, Paris.
Pourquery, D (1987) 'Mais ou est donc passé Béatrice Foods?' *Le monde affaires*, 7 November, pp10–12.
Publicis (1988) 'Advertising in Europe' September, 1.
Quelch, J and Harding, D (1996) 'Brands Versus Private Labels, Fighting To Win' *Harvard Business Review*, Jan–Feb, vol. 74 (1), pp99–111.
Quelch, J and Hoff, E (1986) 'Customizing Global Marketing' *Harvard Business Review* May/June.
Quelch, J and Kenny, D (1994) 'Extend Profits, not Product Lines' *Harvard Business Review* Sept–Oct, vol. 72 (4), pp153–164.
Ramsay, W (1992) 'The Decline and Fall of Manufacturer Branding' Esomar Conference Proceedings – The Challenge of Branding, 28–30 October, pp233–252.
Rangaswamy, A, Burke, R and Oliva, T (1993) 'Brand Equity and The Extendibility of Brand Names' *International Journal of Research in Marketing*, vol. 10, no 1, pp61–75.
Rao, V R, Mahajan, V and Varaiya, N (1990) 'A Balance Model for Evaluating Firms for Acquisition', Working Paper, Graduate School of Management, Cornell University, January.
Rapp, S and Collins, L (1994) *Beyond Maxi-Marketing*, McGraw-Hill.
Rastoin, N (1981) 'Sortez vos griffes' *Coopération – distribution – consommation* 5, pp26–35.
Reddy, S, Holak, S and Bhat, S (1994) 'To Extend or Not to Extend' *Journal of Marketing Research*, May vol. 31, pp243–262.
Rege, P (1989) *A vos marques*, Favre, Lausanne.
Regouby, C (1988) *La Communication globale*, Les Editions d'Organisation, Paris.
Reichheld, F (1996) *The Loyalty Effect*, Harvard Business School Press, Boston, MA.
Resnik, A, Turney, P and Mason, J (1979) 'Marketers Turn To Counter Segmentation' *Harvard Business Review*, vol. 57 (3), pp115–129.
Revue Française de Comptabilité (1989) 'Le Débat sur les Marques en Grande-Bretagne' October, 205, p19.
Revue Française de Comptabilité (1990) 'Incorporels identifiables: le projet australien' January, 208, p11.
Ries, A and Trout, J (1987) *Le Positionnement* McGraw-Hill, Paris.
Riezebos, H (1994) *Brand-Added Value*, Eburon, Delft, Holland.
Riezebos, H and Snellen, M (1993) 'Brand Names Changes', Erasmus, Management Report Series, no 149.
RISC (1991) 'Brand Value and Management in the Luxury Industry', September, International Research Institute on Social Charge, Paris.
Rosch, E (1978) 'Principles of Categorization' in *Cognition and Categorization* (Rosch and Lloyd eds), Lawrence Erlbaum, New Jersey, pp27–48.
Rosch, E and Lloyd, B (1978) *Cognition and Categorization*, Erlbaum, Hillsdale, NJ.
Rubinson, J (1992) 'Marketers Need New Research Tools to Manage the Complex Brand Portfolios of the 90s' *Marketing Research*, vol. 5 (3), pp7–11.
Rutteman, P (1989) 'Mergers, Acquisitions, Brand and Goodwill' *Accountancy* September, p27.
Rutteman, P (1990) 'Boosting the Profits of the Brands Industry' *Accountancy* January, pp26–7.
Samways, A and Whittome, K (1994) 'UK Brand Strategies: Facing the Competitive Challenge', A Financial Times Management Report, Financial Times, London
Santi, M (1996) 'The Determinants of Profitability among Suppliers of Distributors' own Brands', unpublished working paper, HEC Graduate School of Management.
Saporito, B (1986) 'Has Been Brands Go Back to Work' *Fortune*, 28 April, pp123–4.
Sattler, H (1994) '*Der Wert von Marken*', Research Paper no 341, Institut für Betriebswirtschaftslehre, Kiel University.
Saunders, J and Guoqun, F (1996) 'Dual Branding: How Corporate Names Add Value' *Marketing Intelligence and Planning*, vol. 14, no 7, pp29–34.
Saunders, J and Watters, R (1993) 'Branding Financial Services' *International Journal of Bank Marketing*, 11 (6), pp32–38.

Schechter, A (1993) 'Names Changes Increase' *Marketing News*, American Marketing Association, 1 March 1, p1.
Schlossberg, H (1990) 'Brand Value can be Worth more than Physical Assets' *Marketing News* 5 March, p6.
Schnaars, D (1995) *Imitation Strategies*, Free Press, New York.
Schwebig, P (1988) *Les communications de l'entreprise* McGraw-Hill, Paris.
Seguela, J (1982) *Hollywood Lave Plus Blanc* Flammarion, Paris.
Selame, E and Selame, J (1988) *The Company Image* John Wiley and Sons, New York.
Simon, C J and Sullivan, M W (1989) 'The Measurement and Determinants of Brand Equity: A Financial Approach' Working Paper, October, University of Chicago.
Smith, D and Park, C W (1992) 'The Effects of Brand Extensions on Market Share and Advertising Efficiency', *Journal of Marketing Research*, 29, August, pp296–313.
Stobart, P (1989) 'Brand Valuation: A True and Fair View' *Accountancy* October, p27.
Stobart, P (1994) *Brand Power*, MacMillan, Basingstoke.
Sudovar, B (1987) 'Branding in the Pharmaceutical Industry', in *Branding: a Key Marketing Tool* (ed Murphy, J) McGraw-Hill, London.
Sullivan, M (1988) 'Measuring Image Spillovers in Umbrella Branded Products', Working Paper, The Graduate School of Business, University of Chicago.
Sullivan, M (1991) *Brand Extension and Order of Entry*, Marketing Science Institute, Report no 91–105, Cambridge, MA.
Sullivan, M (1992) 'Brand Extensions: When to Use Them' *Management Science*, vol. 38, June, pp793–806.
Swiners, J L (1979) 'Bilan critique du rôle de la copy-stratégie dans la pratique publicitaire actuelle' *IREP*, June, 19.
Tauber, E (1988) 'Brand Leverage: Strategy for Growth in a Cost-Control World', *Journal of Advertising Research* Aug-Sept, vol. 28 (4), pp26–30.
Taylor, R (1987) 'The Branding of Services' in *Branding: a Key Marketing Tool* (ed. Murphy, J) McGraw-Hill, London.
Tchakhotine, S (1952) *La Propagande Politique*, Gallimard, Paris.
Thil, E and Baroux, C (1983) *Un Pavé dans la Marque* Flammarion, Paris.
Thiolon, B (1990) 'La Marque et la Banque' *Humanisme et Entreprise*, 181, June, pp29–32.
Thoenig, J C (1990) *Les performances économiques de l'industrie de produits de marque et de la distribution*, ILEC, Paris.
Touche Ross Europe (1989) *Accounting for Europe Success by A.D. 2000*. Internal Report, London.
Tuvee, L (1987) L'Histoire du Marketing Global: Bibliographie Commentée' *Revue Française du Marketing*, vol. 114 (4), pp19–48.
Sapolsky, H M (1986) *Consuming Fears: The Politics of Product Risks*, Basic Books, New York.
Sappington, D and Wernerfelt, B (1985) 'To Brand or Not to Brand?' *Journal of Business*, 58 (July), pp279–93.
University of Minnesota Consumer Behavior Seminar (1987) 'Affect Generalization to Similar and Dissimilar Brand Extensions' *Psychology and Marketing*, 4 (Fall), pp225–37.
Upshaw, L (1995) *Building Brand Identity*, Wiley, New York.
Veblen, T (1889) *The Theory of The Leisure Class*, Macmillan, New York.
Viale, F (1994) *'Faut-il Inscrire les Marques au Bilan?' Les Echos*, November 11.
Viale, F and Lafay, F (1990) *'Les Marques: Un Nouvel Enjeu pour les Entreprises' Revue Française de Comptabilité*, no 216, October, pp92–99.
Ville, G (1986) 'Maîtriser et optimiser l'avenir d'une marque' Esomar Congress Proceedings, pp527–41.
Villemus, P (1996) *La Déroute des Marques*, Editions d'Organisation, Paris.
Ward, K (1989) 'Can the Cash Flows of Brands Really be Capitalized?' in *Brand Valuation*, (ed Murphy, J) Hutchinson Business Books, London pp70–80.
Watkins T (1986) *The Economics of the Brands: A Marketing Analysis* McGraw-Hill, Maidenhead.
Wentz, L (1989) 'How Experts Value Brands' *Advertising Age* 16 January, p24.
Wernerfelt, B (1988) 'Umbrella Branding as a Signal of New Product Quality' *Rand Journal of Economics*, 19, (Autumn), pp458–66.

Wernerfelt B (1990) 'Advertising Content When Brand Choice is a Signal' *Journal of Business*, vol. 63 (1), pp91–8.

Winram, S (1987) 'The Opportunity for World Brands' in *Branding: a Key Marketing Tool* (ed Murphy, J) McGraw-Hill, London.

Yentis, A and Bond, J (1995) 'Andres Comes out of the Closet' *Marketing and Research Today*, vol. 23 (2), May, pp104–112.

Yoshimori, M (1989) 'Concepts et stratégies de marque au Japon' in *La marque* (eds Kapferer, J N and Thoenig, J C) McGraw-Hill, Paris.

Young, R (1967) 'Multibrand Entries' in *Plotting Marketing Strategy* (ed Adler, L) Interpublic Press Book, New York.

Young & Rubicam (1994) *Brand Asset Valuator*, Young & Rubicam, London.

Yovovich, B G (1988) 'What is Your Brand Really Worth?' *Adweek's Marketing Week* August 8, pp18–24.

Yovovich, B G (1995) *New Marketing Imperatives*, Prentice Hall, Englewood Cliffs, NJ.

Zaichkowsky, J and Simpson, R (1996) 'The Effect of Experience with a Brand Imitator on the Original Brand' *Marketing Letters*, vol. 7 (1), pp31–39.

Zareer, P (1987) 'De la valeur des marques de commerce' *C A Magazine* February, p72.

Index

Page references in **bold** indicate figures or tables